A BRIEF GUIDE TO

WILLIAM SHAKESPEARE

Highlights from the series

A BRIEF GUIDE TO

WILLIAM SHAKESPEARE

With an Introduction by
PETER ACKROYD

ROBINSON

RUNNING PRESS
PHILADELPHIA · LONDON

Constable & Robinson Ltd
3 The Lanchesters
162 Fulham Palace Road
London W6 9ER
www.constablerobinson.com

First published in the UK by Robinson,
an imprint of Constable & Robinson, 2010

A copy of the British Library Cataloguing in Publication
Data is available from the British Library

UK ISBN 978-1-84901-048-1

1 3 5 7 9 10 8 6 4 2

First published in the United States in 2010
by Running Press Book Publishers

9 8 7 6 5 4 3 2 1

Digit on the right indicates the number of this printing

US Library of Congress Control Number: 2009935111
US ISBN 978-0-7624-3854-9

Running Press Book Publishers
2300 Chestnut Street
Philadelphia, PA 19103–4371

Visit us on the web!

www.runningpress.com

Printed and bound in the EU

CONTENTS

INTRODUCTION
by Peter Ackroyd

Every day, somewhere in the world, a book is published on the work and life of William Shakespeare. His influence is ubiquitous and pervasive. The phrases and aphorisms of his plays and poems have now entered the general fabric of the English language. That is why, in 2000, he was named as the most significant human being in the previous thousand years of British history. Those who have never read a line of his work consider him to be a token of the national consciousness, an image of the culture that has transcended time. He is quoted endlessly. His plays remain the single largest contribution to contemporary London theatre; they are also filmed and televised at frequent intervals.

Yet he still remains largely unknown and unknowable. The recorded events of his life are not in themselves notable. His features are not known. His religion is unclear. His opinions were never reported. The details of his conversation have not survived. The descriptions of him by his contemporaries are few and impressionistic. So in large part he is a historical enigma. The measure of his 'invisibility' is found in the fact that many other candidates have been put forward as the writer of his plays.

His early life in Stratford, his marriage, and his descent upon London suggest that he was a quick, intelligent and ambitious young man. It has been said that Shakespeare was in some sense uneducated, and that a few years in the local grammar school could not have adequately prepared him for the work ascribed to him. But this kind of snobbery misunderstands the nature of genius; Charles Dickens had far less of a formal education than Shakespeare, but no one has ever doubted the authorship of his novels. Shakespeare had learned enough, and more than enough, to become a lord of language.

He came to London in 1586 or 1587; on his arrival he was twenty-two or twenty-three years old. His first years in the capital are lost in a mist, but the fact that he soon became both an actor and a writer of plays suggests that he had found his true vocation at a very early age. It is likely, in fact, that he came to London in the first place as an aspiring performer. His earliest dramas have no doubt become the victim of time and chance, discarded as soon as they were no longer serviceable; he may have revised some of them at a later date, where they took the form by which we now know them. There may have been very early versions of *Hamlet* and of *King Lear*. It is also likely that in these early years he wrote the first drafts of the history plays that became his single most distinctive contribution to the theatre of the 1580s and 1590s. These were plays of battle and of dynastic struggle, composed in a high style of ornate rhetoric.

In the first two years of his residence in London he seems to have composed some six or seven plays. It is important to note that he also acted in them. In the beginning he would have been taught how to sing, to dance and to tumble like an acrobat. He also learned how to fence. He was a young man of the theatre in every sense: energetic and nimble, hard-working almost to the point of exhaustion, and willing to take on any theatrical task he was assigned. He would 'doctor' plays, and write the odd scene or two for other playwrights. An indication of his success is that he was already being attacked by his rivals; the principal charge was that of plagiarism, to which he was undoubtedly prone. His rustic origins were also quoted against him by those who had benefited from education at one of the two universities.

Such was his early fame, however, that with the death of Christopher Marlowe in 1593 he was recognized to be the pre-eminent playwright in London. This is also the time when we can first begin securely to date and identify his plays. *The Two Gentlemen of Verona* and *The Comedy of Errors* are among the earliest of what has become known as the canon. These were hard-edged and Italianate comedies, based firmly on classical originals. But his writing was not confined to drama; his genius was too volatile and too spirited to be restricted to one medium. Throughout 1593 the theatres were closed by the invasive presence of the plague, known at the time as 'the sickness'. So he turned his attention to poetry, and in the summer of that year *Venus and Adonis* emerged on the stalls of the booksellers.

Only a short while later, upon the reopening of the theatres, Shakespeare joined the Lord Chamberlain's Men – a band of brothers who represented the most significant force in the English theatre of the time. He was part of this company for the rest of his life. He remained in the acting profession for another twenty years, a longevity that required energy and vitality as well as endurance. He did not perhaps take the major roles; these were generally reserved for his contemporary, Richard Burbage. Theatrical legend over the centuries has claimed that he played the Ghost in *Hamlet*. It is not unlikely. From various hints and asides it has also been concluded that he liked to play 'kingly' roles, and that he was adept at portraying age or dignity. He did not take the main parts because his role was also one of 'director' as well as player. He would have instructed his fellows at rehearsal, and therefore needed space and time to watch them.

He began writing plays for his new company almost at once, and in 1595 emerged *Romeo and Juliet* as well as *A Midsummer Night's Dream*. These romantic dramas were a world away from the history plays and comedies that he had previously written; the range and variety of his gift must have been as obvious to his contemporaries as it is to posterity. He was a worker of wonders. He also had a great facility in composition, to judge by Ben Jonson's remark that 'in his writing (whatsoever he penned) he never blotted out [a] line'. He was in a direct and literal sense inspired. He did not know where the words came from. He just knew that they came. He did not understand what he was writing until he had written it. He discovered his meaning only after he had conceived it in words. His words are indeed remarkable, with a fluency and grace that are lifted by the music of his verse. He rarely originated a plot, but he brought together all his sources in an alchemical act of transformation.

And how did he seem to his contemporaries? Many people remarked upon his sweetness and his courtesy. He was variously called 'civil', 'generous' and, most often, 'gentle'. This did not mean tender or mild. It implied that he possessed the attributes of a gentleman, combining courtesy and modesty with a proper respect for his superiors. Ben Jonson stated that 'he was indeed honest, and of an open, and free nature', while John Aubrey passed on the information that he 'was very good company'. So we might expect to find an affable and good-humoured man, not given to eccentric or violent behaviour.

This is one of the reasons why Shakespeare has been acclaimed as the writer who in his own life fully represents the tendentious quality of Englishness. The playwright lived in mixed company, high and low, and was not overwhelmed by a sense of his own importance. He was not self-obsessed or pretentious, but seemed to those who met him to be the epitome of what we might call ordinariness. He did not draw attention to himself. His life as a playwright and as an actor emphasizes that he was an eminently practical man. If his plays were too long, he would cut them. He would write to order, exploiting the most recent fashion or the most sensational news. It has been remarked by generations of actors that his lines, once remembered, remain in the memory; they are what the great nineteenth-century actor Edmund Kean described as 'stickable'.

Yet Shakespeare was not cut off from the deep sources of his art. He reclaimed the English language at the same time as he restored the essential themes of English literature from the days of the Anglo-Saxons. He wrote of dreams and visions; he invoked ghosts and witches; he was in love with English history, and he revived the spectacle and pageantry of the medieval religious plays. Most importantly, like Chaucer and Dickens, he was eager to marry the 'high' and 'low' elements of his world. His dukes are followed on stage by clowns. Lear has his fool and Hamlet his gravedigger. Comedy and tragedy, pathos and farce, piety and vulgarity are effortlessly placed within an inclusive and accommodating medium that is no less than the human imagination itself.

So, to paraphrase Coleridge, he was like a meteor kindling its own material as it moves through the darkness. The farcical servants of the early comedies become Iago or Malvolio; the clown becomes the gravedigger of *Hamlet*; the sexual jealousies within the early *The Merry Wives of Windsor* turn murderous in *Othello*. In *Macbeth* the words and themes anticipate *Antony and Cleopatra*; the language of *Henry V* anticipates that of *Julius Caesar*. He moves onward, revolving all these worlds in his head.

By the time he wrote the later plays he had become a wealthy man, regularly sending back money to his family in Stratford. He was instrumental in gaining the title of 'gentleman' for his father, John Shakespeare, and he knew that the honour would in time be bequeathed to him. It was important to him to become a man of standing in his native Stratford, and in the spring of 1597 he purchased a large house in that town. As a boy he had passed New Place every day on his way to school, and it must have occurred to him that it would be a fine place in which to live. And so it proved.

In London itself he had transcended the often opprobrious connotations of the acting profession; an actor was, in many circles, considered to be little more than a vagrant. Shakespeare, however, was already wealthy and respectable; by the end of the century his work was being compared in the public prints with that of the classical dramatists. He had made the profession of dramatist a reputable one. When the Lord Chamberlain's Men moved to the newly built Globe in 1599, it was his plays that the public came to see. This was the arena in which *Julius Caesar*, *King Lear*, *Macbeth* and *Othello* were first performed.

On the accession of James I in 1603, the Lord Chamberlain's Men took on the new title of the King's Men. There was a change in venue also, when the company leased the Blackfriars Theatre for a period of twenty-one years. This was an indoor theatre, holding no more than 700, whereas the Globe was open to the sky and to thousands of spectators. Always an astute and adept professional, Shakespeare adjusted to the intimacy of the new theatre by writing plays that make far more use of music and of songs; he also devised a system of acts and intervals that had not been possible in the uninterrupted spectacles performed at the Globe.

It has been said that at the end of his career Shakespeare had grown tired of the theatre, but there is very little evidence of that. He rented the 'gatehouse' at Blackfriars, for example, so that he might be closer to the plays and to the players. He was, however, returning more frequently to his family in Stratford, where eventually he retired to die in 1616. It is possible that he died of typhoid fever, but his death is as little known as his life.

In his will he left the 'second best bed' to his wife, Anne, but this is no evidence of disagreement or disharmony. This was the bed in which they had slept together. The other terms of his will suggest what is only to be expected – that he was always practical and businesslike in his dealings with the world. His death did not excite much attention at the time, and the first biographical notices did not appear until fifty years later. The Folio or complete edition of his plays had been published in 1623, but by the end of the seventeenth century there were three further editions of the collected works. From that time forward the enthusiasm and admiration gathered momentum. The Shakespeare Jubilee was held in the summer of 1769, with much triumph and celebration. It was only the beginning of a fervour that has lasted for almost 250 years, and shows no signs of abating. William Shakespeare will live as long as the English language itself.

Peter Ackroyd
London, 2009

A BRIEF BIOGRAPHY

Early Life

Shakespeare was born in Stratford-upon-Avon on 22 or 23 April 1564 and died exactly fifty-two years later on 23 April 1616. Very little is known for certain about his life, though there are a lot of stories; what facts there are have been studied so carefully by scholars that we can get a fairly good picture.

Shakespeare's father, John, was a glove-maker with a sideline dealing in farm products. He had once been fined for going out with his friends and building a dunghill in the middle of the street. He had married his wife, Mary, seven years prior to Shakespeare's birth, and done rather well out of it: her father had given him some money, a house and fifty acres of land. The couple had already had two daughters, but infant mortality was high in those days and neither sister had lived to see the birth of William, the eldest son. Just after William's birth the plague hit Stratford, killing one in seven of the population, but the baby survived.

John and Mary went on to have five more children and John started doing very well for himself. In 1568 he became bailiff of the town and so it is reasonable to assume that he was able to send William to the local grammar school, where he would have been taught Latin. Life at the school was rigorous. William would have gone there aged seven, and from then on school would have lasted from 6 a.m. to 6 p.m., six days a week, every week of the year. There were no holidays except holy days, such as Christmas and Easter.

During the 1570s, John Shakespeare's business dealings began to go wrong. It got to the point that he was afraid to go to church in case debt collectors caught up with him. This must have had an effect on the eldest son, as his family's position in the small town (not to mention his hopes of an inheritance) slumped. William may well have had to leave school early and there is a story that he was bound apprentice to a butcher. (There is also a story that before killing pigs he would make grand execution speeches, which were so good that people would come and watch, but it is probably apocryphal.) Whatever happened, it didn't stop him from doing what teenage boys have always done, and in 1582 he got a girl pregnant.

The girl was called Anne Hathaway and she was eight years older than William. His family didn't want him to marry her; their signatures are not on the marriage licence, which would have been odd even if he wasn't still legally a minor. But he did marry her and six months later she gave birth to a daughter, whom they called Susanna. A year later Shakespeare was to write in *Twelfth Night*: 'Let still the woman take/An elder than herself, so wears she to him,/So sways she level in her husband's heart'. Shakespeare was eighteen, 'a handsome, well-shaped man, very good company, and of a very ready and pleasant smooth wit'. Anne Hathaway was twenty-six.

How the boy ended up having to marry the woman is perhaps best left to the imagination. We do know that two years later they had more children, twins, whom they named Hamnet and Judith. Then there is a blank.

The Missing Five Years
We know that in 1585 Shakespeare was in Stratford making babies. We're pretty sure that by 1590 he was in London

making plays. We don't know what happened in between, but given the amount of time that has been expended on studying Shakespeare, it is unsurprising that there are a lot of theories.

One of the more plausible theories is that he went off to be tutor to a rich man's son. This would have given him access to books, helping to explain how a boy from Stratford ended up writing plays that were far better than those written by his more academic peers. However, although Shakespeare's works show that their author read widely, they never show that he devoted time or scholarship to any particular book.

Other theories are based on the language Shakespeare used in his writing later on. He knew a lot of nautical terms and so it has been suggested that he was a sailor. He might therefore have been to Italy, where so many of his plays are set. He certainly didn't go to Egypt, as he didn't know what pyramids looked like – he thought you could be hanged from them. In *Antony and Cleopatra* the Egyptian queen thinks it possible to 'make/My country's high pyramides my gibbet/And hang me up in chains'.

A thousand other ideas have been put forward. It is unlikely that we will ever know the truth. It is possible that Shakespeare went straight to London in 1585; we can be pretty sure that he was there by 1590.

London

The city that Shakespeare arrived in was very different to the modern capital. Technically London was what is now known as 'the City', the financial district: just one square mile on the north bank of the Thames, surrounded by medieval city walls. However, the population was growing fast and built-up areas had begun to spread out into the surrounding fields. This was important because anything outside the city walls was outside the legal jurisdiction of the City of London.

It wasn't only criminals who chose to keep beyond the walls. The puritan city fathers objected to other immoral activities: bear-baiting, ape-baiting, cock-fighting, prostitution and theatres. Acting was seen as a kind of lying, while commoners dressed up as lords was a threat to social hierarchy; moreover, the big crowds bunched together helped to spread the plague, which regularly swept through the city.

By modern standards, London was a strange mixture of the civilized and the barbaric. Singers sang madrigals to the accompaniment of a lute and the heads of criminals were displayed on spikes over London Bridge, where birds of prey would eat out their brains and eyeballs. Noblemen in fine clothes could compose sonnets with ease and then pay to watch the spectacle of bear-baiting or an ape being torn apart by dogs. The city was violent: of Shakespeare's two great literary contemporaries, Marlowe and Jonson, one was stabbed to death in a pub brawl and the other killed a man in a duel. Yet these same men were poets of astonishing ability.

Unlike Jonson, John Marston or Thomas Dekker, Shakespeare never set any of his plays in contemporary London, so it is hard to know how the city affected him. However, the cruelty in his comedies and the merriment in his tragedies would have appeared far more natural in his surroundings than they would now.

1590–94

It is said that Shakespeare started out looking after the horses of visitors to the theatre. The first evidence we have of him in London is a pamphlet written by the poet and playwright Robert Greene.

> There is an upstart crow, beautified with our feathers, that with his *tiger's heart wrapped in a player's hide*, supposes he is as well able to bombast out a blank verse as the best of you; and being an absolute Johannes Factotum, is in his own conceit the only Shake-scene in a country.

Already Shakespeare was successful enough to be making

other writers jealous. And already Shakespeare had written *Henry VI Part 3*, because Greene's line, 'tiger's heart wrapped in a player's hide', is making fun of Shakespeare's line, 'Oh, tiger's heart wrapped in a woman's hide.' We can therefore assume that he had written *Henry VI Parts 1 and 2*. Furthermore, Shakespeare was not only a playwright, but an actor or 'player'.

There is a postscript: Greene died of plague before his pamphlet was published and it was his friend Henry Chettle who prepared it for the press. In his preface to a later edition, Chettle said that he regretted not having struck out certain passages that have been:

> offensively by one or two taken ... I am as sorry as if the original fault had been my fault, because myself have seen his demeanour no less civil than he excellent in the quality he professes [i.e. his profession]. Besides, diverse of worship have reported his uprightness of dealing, which argues his honesty, and facetious grace in writing, that approves his art.

This fits very well with other descriptions of Shakespeare's character – quiet, polite and amiable – and it may have been these same qualities that soon secured Shakespeare a rich patron. In April 1593 *Venus and Adonis* was published with a dedication to Henry Wriothesley, Earl of Southampton.

Having a patron was important not only in terms of prestige, but because of money and the plague. Whenever the plague struck London all the theatres were closed, as the crowds were the perfect place for infection to spread. The players would be forced to go touring in the countryside, where they would earn very little money. A worse fate awaited those who stayed in London, where the cramped, crowded, unhygienic conditions would have killed Shakespeare as easily as they did Greene. Shakespeare would have been able to go and stay at the Earl of

Southampton's country estate, away from the plague, and there earn good money composing poetry for him.

In 1594, a year after *Venus and Adonis*, *The Rape of Lucrece* was published. Between them, the two poems notched up twelve editions in Shakespeare's lifetime. Moreover, they started to make Shakespeare's name famous. Playwrights had roughly the same status as screenwriters do today. Though we know the names of film stars, we are very unlikely to know the writers of even the most famous movies. We remember Humphrey Bogart in *Casablanca*, but not the Epstein brothers who wrote the script. With these two published poems, one of the world's most famous names first made it into print.

1594–1601
Up to now Shakespeare's writings had been good and profitable, but not great. If he had died in 1594 we would hardly remember him now on the basis of plays such as *The Two Gentlemen of Verona*, *King John* or *Titus Andronicus*. Indeed, *Richard III* is the only play from 1593 or before that is still regularly performed. All that was to change.

The plays he now began to write are still in performance all over the world. Between 1594 and 1601 he completed his historical cycle with *Richard II*, both parts *of Henry IV* and *Henry V*. Queen Elizabeth herself saw *Henry IV* and liked the character of Falstaff so much that she asked Shakespeare to write a play about Falstaff in love. He fulfilled the request with *The Merry Wives of Windsor*, a comedy to go alongside *A Midsummer Night's Dream*, *Much Ado About Nothing* and *Twelfth Night*, among others. Moreover, *Romeo and Juliet* and *Julius Caesar* were considerable improvements on *Titus Andronicus*.

There are many ways of explaining his improvement. For one thing, he became a member of the Lord Chamberlain's Men, a respectable new theatre company that gave Shakespeare financial and professional stability. His plays would be performed by the best actors in the country, so he could make his characters more complex. His comedies became darker:

The Merchant of Venice and *Much Ado About Nothing* both involve serious threats of death. At the same time, his tragedies became sweeter – *Romeo and Juliet* has none of the rape and cannibalism of *Titus Andronicus* – and his history plays were less likely to divide the world neatly into heroes and villains (with the exception of *Henry V*). Also Shakespeare became less formal: he started to switch easily between prose and verse, used enjambments, gave feminine endings to his iambic pentameters and practically abandoned rhyme. The truth behind all these points is that Shakespeare was growing older and wiser and becoming more confident.

On 11 August 1596, Shakespeare's only son, Hamnet, was buried in Stratford; he had lived only eleven years. Such early deaths were common. We cannot tell what effect this had on Shakespeare, who was, after all, living apart from his family. His pace of writing seemed to slow that year to only one play, so it is tempting to think of him returning home to tend to his dying son, but that is only speculation. We know that Shakespeare returned home quite often; he broke his journeys at the Golden Cross Inn in Oxford, where he stayed often enough to become godfather to William D'Avenant, the landlord's son.

Shakespeare was now going up in the world. People often like to think of him as a genius who was above any concern for such vulgar matters as cash, but all the evidence points the other way. Shakespeare had seen, during childhood, what lack of money had done to his father, and as soon as he started to earn real money himself he began to save and invest.

In 1597 Shakespeare bought New Place, the largest house in Stratford. We can imagine the reaction in a small town to the return of a local boy made good. Shakespeare was only thirty-three, and it was just fifteen years earlier that he had been a debtor's son in a forced marriage. Now he was a man of substance. Nor was this Shakespeare's last investment in property. As his career progressed, he bought another cottage in Stratford, inherited two houses from his father and acquired more than 100 acres of farmland. On the basis of some ancestors and his maternal grandfather's position as a gentleman, he managed to obtain a coat of arms that would have improved his social standing. Shakespeare was a man who wanted not only money but also position and property in his home town.

A couple of years later, in 1599, Shakespeare made his most famous and most profitable investment. He was part of a consortium that combined to build the Globe Theatre on the south bank of the Thames. Now Shakespeare not only took money for writing and acting, he also received a share of the total ticket receipts.

Shakespeare had become a rich man. A Stratford man wrote to a relative in London in 1597 advising him that if he needed to borrow money, William Shakespeare was the man to go to. How this position affected the writing of *The Merchant of Venice* we can only guess.

Shakespeare's plays were now popular enough to be pirated under his name. Authors had very few rights and publishers were in the habit of bribing bit-part actors to get them scripts for publication. This was not as simple as it sounds, as each actor would be given only his own lines to learn. The results were the 'bad quartos', versions of his plays that were nothing more than what a poor actor could remember of the performance. For example, the bad quarto of *Hamlet* was pirated by an actor who played either Rosencrantz or Guildenstern: their lines are perfect, but the sections of the play in which they do not appear are filled with errors.

In 1598 Shakespeare appeared as an actor in *Every Man in His Humour*, a comedy by a young playwright called Ben Jonson. He and Jonson were to become the best of friends. Shakespeare may even have been godfather to Jonson's son. There are numerous stories of them drinking together in the Mermaid Tavern on Fleet Street. A later account has this to say of Shakespeare:

> Though his genius generally was jocular and inclining him to festivity, yet he could, when so

disposed, be solemn and serious ... Many were the
wit-combats betwixt him and Ben Jonson; which
two I behold like a Spanish great galleon and an
English man-of-war; master Jonson (like the
former) was built far higher in learning; solid, but
slow, in his performances. Shakespeare with the
English man-of-war, lesser in bulk, but lighter in
sailing, could turn with all tides, tack about, and
take advantage of all winds, by quickness of his wit
and invention.

The Sonnets and Shakespeare's Sexuality

In 1598 Francis Meres published his *Paladis Tamia* in which he
refers to the 'mellifluous and honey-tongued Shakespeare' and
also to the circulation of 'his sugared sonnets among his private
friends'. So although the sonnets were not published until
1609, this seems to be the best place to discuss them and the
light they may throw on Shakespeare's private life.

First of all, it should be pointed out that people often wrote
love sonnets when they weren't in love at all, making up a
romance as an excuse to write poetry. A modern equivalent
would be pop music: if one were to listen to every Beatles
album back-to-back and take them literally, one would be
forced to conclude that the band members fell in love, split up
and got the blues on an almost weekly basis. In fact, Paul
McCartney had only three girlfriends over the whole period. If
we read Shakespeare's sonnets biographically, we *may* be
making exactly the same mistake.

There are 154 sonnets. The first 126 are written to an aristocratic young man, the rest to an unnamed 'dark lady'.
Neither has ever been identified, although it is often assumed
that the young man was Henry Wriothesley, Shakespeare's
patron. The first sonnets encourage the young man to marry
– we can imagine an impatient father hiring Shakespeare to
talk his son into getting a wife. However, the tone soon
changes: Shakespeare writes that he loves the young man and

later becomes upset when he starts an affair with the dark lady.

This has led many people to assume that Shakespeare was bisexual, but this is not necessarily the case. Writing of the young man, Shakespeare says that he is as beautiful as a woman:

> And for a woman wert thou first created;
> Till Nature, as she wrought thee, fell a-doting,
> And by addition me of thee defeated,
> By adding one thing to my purpose nothing.
> But since she pricked thee out for women's pleasure,
> Mine be thy love, and thy love's use their treasure.
> (Sonnet 20)

An explanation of these lines may be required. The female personification of nature made a woman so beautiful that she fell in love with it. Nature, being a woman, therefore decided to add 'one thing' to her beautiful creation, namely a penis, 'she *pricked* thee out'. Shakespeare, being a man, has no use for such things that are 'to [his] purpose nothing'. Since the young man has a penis to give women pleasure, the young man should love Shakespeare, but have sex – 'love's use' – with women.

Shakespeare explicitly states that he doesn't have sex with other men. He also explicitly states that he does have sex with the dark lady and, moreover, the young man seems to be having his way with her as well every time Shakespeare turns his back.

Shakespeare seems to have thought sex was dirty and hated himself for liking it: 'Enjoyed no sooner but despised straight'. The whole of Sonnet 129 harps on this one theme. And it stretches through his plays: 'The rank sweat of an enseamed bed' is how Hamlet describes it; Iago sees people being as 'prime as goats'; Antony's lust loses him an empire. It is difficult to find a pleasant reference to sex anywhere in Shakespeare – certainly never the sweet embraces of Milton.

It is possible that Shakespeare disliked his relationships with women precisely because they involved sex, and liked his relationships with men because they didn't. Sonnet 144 would seem to confirm this opinion. This may be more understandable when we consider that it was sex that had trapped Shakespeare in a marriage to a much older woman with whom his relations seem to have been strained. It could also be the result of repressed homosexual feelings, but that is for psychiatrists to argue about. From a historical point of view, we know that Shakespeare had sex with more than one woman, and he explicitly stated that he did not have sex with men.

1601–16

So we have a picture of a quiet, polite, funny man of the world. He had money in his pocket, several houses, a rich patron, he liked a drink and was a little hung up about sex. Yet now his comedies became rather odd. *Troilus and Cressida*, *All's Well That Ends Well* and *Measure for Measure*, which were written between 1601 and 1604, are commonly grouped together and called the 'problem plays'. They are comedies in which nothing works out right: justice is confounded, love thwarted and morality thrown out of the window.

There is a story dating from this period: a lawyer called Manningham heard a piece of gossip on 13 March 1602 and noted it down in his diary. Richard Burbage, Shakespeare's lead actor, had been performing in a revival of *Richard III*. A lady in the audience had been so impressed with him that she had sent a note backstage inviting him to come to her house later that night. He was to announce himself to the servants as Richard III and would be directed up to her bedroom.

Shakespeare found out about the note and went to the address himself, said his name was Richard III and was shown upstairs. By the time poor Burbage arrived, Shakespeare was already engrossed, and when a confused servant knocked on the bedroom door to announce that *another* Richard III had arrived, Shakespeare simply said to tell him that William the Conqueror came first.

It was probably just after this event that Shakespeare wrote *Hamlet*, as the play is thought to have appeared first in 1603. Burbage would have played the lead and it has been reported that Shakespeare played the part of the Ghost. If this is true – and it seems likely – then Burbage would have been forced to describe Shakespeare like this:

> See what grace was seated on this brow
> Hyperion's curls, the front of Jove himself,
> An eye like Mars to threaten and command,
> A station like the herald Mercury
> New lighted on a heaven-kissing hill,
> A combination and a form indeed
> Where every good did seem to set his seal
> To give the world assurance of a man.

We can read this as Shakespeare having a laugh by forcing his colleague Burbage, who played Hamlet, to say how good-looking he was. Yet it must be remembered that this is a serious scene and Shakespeare must have been able to carry off the description (albeit with make-up, costume, and perhaps a wig). Despite the joke, Shakespeare must still have been a handsome man.

In 1603, Queen Elizabeth died childless. She was succeeded by James VI of Scotland who now became James I of England. James liked the theatre, and he enjoyed Shakespeare's plays in particular. He took the Lord Chamberlain's Men, the company to which Shakespeare belonged, and made it the King's Men. Shakespeare was now technically part of the royal household. Although this does not mean that he lived in the palace, it did mean that his plays were almost certain to be performed at court, thus providing him with more money.

Over the next five years, he produced *Hamlet*, *Othello*, *King Lear*, *Macbeth* and *Antony and Cleopatra*. It is tempting to draw biographical conclusions from these plays, to see in this period Shakespeare's 'solemn and serious moods'. In *Hamlet*, he played the part of a cuckold; in *Othello* he wrote about a man who wrongly believes his wife is cheating on him. *King Lear* is about a man whose daughters turn against him; in the same year, Shakespeare's daughter Susanna married. Macbeth is consumed by guilt and Antony leaves his hated wife far away while he is led to ruin by a dark lady, as in the sonnets.

It is tempting to construct a torrid life story from all this. Yet it can only be speculation. By that rationale, we could as easily deduce from *Antony and Cleopatra* that Shakespeare was in charge of a large empire, or from *A Midsummer Night's Dream* that he had had a bad experience involving fairies.

By 1607, Shakespeare had written the greatest tragedies and comedies that would ever be achieved in English and he seems to have known it. Shakespeare understood how good he was. When he wrote in Sonnet 18 that 'So long as men can breathe or eyes can see,/So long lives this, and this gives life to thee', he wasn't being arrogant: he was right. This may explain his subsequent career. When you have written your masterpiece, what is there left to do but experiment?

Timon of Athens and *Coriolanus* are both very stylized tragedies that seem to be aiming for some sort of aesthetic simplicity rather than the raw, sprawling power of *King Lear* or *Hamlet*. And then, between 1608 and 1611, come the four romances, or reconciliation plays as they are sometimes known: *Pericles*, *Cymbeline*, *The Winter's Tale* and *The Tempest*.

It is here, more than anywhere else, that we may be justified in trying to deduce Shakespeare's life from his writings. All these plays have similar themes and settings; it may even be that they were composed as a cycle to be seen together. All of them involve sea voyages to or around the Mediterranean, three of them shipwrecks. Two involve a husband who is insanely and unjustifiably jealous of his wife with whom he is then reconciled. Three involve a lost child being found, and all involve forgiveness. When one character, or one play, tells us something, it may only be an imagined character or a necessary story. When themes linger from one work to another, we are entitled to see a writer musing or brooding over a few fixed ideas.

Many people have tried to see Prospero, especially his last lines, as being an embodiment of Shakespeare, yet where there is a reconciliation, there must first have been a sundering. If we see other plays as perhaps describing turmoil in Shakespeare's family life, then these later works must have been seen as evidence of forgiveness, reconciliation and calm. Maybe this is why, in 1611, he moved back to Stratford and retired.

1611–16
Shakespeare's retirement is perhaps the most extraordinary aspect of his career. No other writer or artist of comparable ability has ever decided to simply go home, put his feet up and enjoy his money. It is, above all, evidence that Shakespeare viewed writing as a job – one he did very well, but nonetheless a means to an end.

Shakespeare had cash and property to spare. For years he had been raking in money from his poems, his plays, his acting, a share of the receipts at the theatre, interest on loans and rent from his properties. In 1613 he was able to buy a house in London, presumably for occasional trips down to the capital. He even collaborated with John Fletcher, a younger writer, with a couple of plays – *Henry VIII* and *The Two Noble Kinsmen* – though it is clear that he didn't devote the full scope of his genius to them. He was happy to return to the town of his birth, to the place where he had once been bound apprentice to a butcher, and to the wife he had married thirty years earlier. His daughters were grown up. In 1613, during a performance of *Henry VIII*, the Globe Theatre burnt down; it must have seemed like a final parting.

All was not sweetness and light in Shakespeare's family life. Early in 1615, his daughter had to sue a man for slander after he called her an adulterer and accused her of having venereal disease. The following year, his other daughter Judith, twin sister of the deceased Hamnet, married in haste, presumably because, like her mother, she was pregnant.

At this time Shakespeare's health must have been failing. On 25 March 1616, he made his will, leaving, among other things, his second best bed to his wife. According to a later account by a Stratford vicar who knew Shakespeare's daughter and son-in-law, Shakespeare's fellow playwrights Jonson and Michael Drayton came up from London to visit him, 'they had a merry meeting, and it seems drank too hard, for Shakespeare died of a fever there contracted'.

His death came on 23 April 1616, fifty-two years after his birth. He was buried in the chancel of Stratford Church; on his tombstone there is an inscription that can still be read today:

> Good friend, for Jesus' sake forbeare
> To dig the dust enclosed heare;
> Bleste be the man that spares these stones,
> And curst be he that moves my bones.

Presumably he was afraid of suffering the same fate as Yorick in *Hamlet* – having his bones dug up and thrown into the charnel house to make way for new bodies. When Anne Shakespeare died in 1623 she had wanted to be buried beside him, but the sexton was too impressed by the epitaph and wouldn't open the grave.

SHAKESPEARE'S STAGE

Influences

When the travelling players come to Elsinore, Hamlet orders them not to overact. 'It out-Herods Herod', he tells them, words that probably refer to Shakespeare's earliest experience of theatre: the miracle plays.

Miracle plays were dramatic depictions of parts of the Bible, usually of Jesus' life. The role that everyone remembered from these was Herod, who was portrayed as a madman who screamed and raved his way through the performance. In Chaucer's *The Miller's Tale*, written 200 years previously, Absalom 'pleyeth Herodes upon a scaffold hye' in order to try and get a girl's attention. This was a long tradition, but it was still active in Shakespeare's day.

Sometimes these plays were acted by professional travelling players, sometimes (as in Chaucer's description) by local amateurs. The acting and the standard of the writing was, with a few exceptions, very low, yet these plays were performed everywhere, and for most of the population of sixteenth-century England it would have been the only drama they had ever seen. This meant that miracle plays defined the expectations of the majority of theatre-goers.

These plays had two very important effects. First, they were acted without any scenery, often on top of carts. Second, the action shifted from place to place and from time to time. Partly because there was no set, it was possible to have one scene in Jerusalem, the next in Egypt and the next in Bethlehem. You could go from Jesus' birth to death in the space of an hour or so.

There was one further aspect of the miracle plays that was to be carried over into Shakespeare's drama: toilet humour. Many later readers and critics of Shakespeare have found it odd that in a serious play like *Othello* or *Macbeth* the tragic subject matter can be interspersed with jokes about farting or impotence. However, there was a precedent for this. In the miracle plays the Devil was often presented for comic effect as being helplessly incontinent and flatulent. If toilet humour can fit into a play about the son of God, then it certainly wouldn't seem improper in a human tragedy.

Shakespeare may also have seen travelling players performing secular plays, although this is less certain. Sometimes, as in *A Midsummer Night's Dream*, these were performed by local amateurs, but more usually they would be performed by professionals. Actors preferred to stay in the city, where there was more money, but often necessity drove them, like the actors in *Hamlet*, to become strolling players, touring the country and performing to anyone who would pay them.

Often they would set up in the courtyard of an inn. The Golden Cross in Oxford, where Shakespeare often stayed later in his life, is a good surviving example of what conditions would have been like. The common people would have been sat around the courtyard drinking and getting drunk, while those who could afford it could hire a private room on the first floor and watch from there. This division – poor people standing on the ground, while the rich sat above – would be replicated in Shakespeare's theatre.

The third influence from Shakespeare's childhood would have been school. Shakespeare almost certainly attended the local grammar school, where he would have had to learn Latin. This would have involved reading works by the Roman playwright Plautus, and we know that often pupils would have to put on performances of his plays. Plautus would have differed considerably from the miracle plays and strolling players. For one thing, Plautus obeyed the classical unities: his plays take place over one day and are set in one location. Moreover, the plot was a single, logical whole, rather than the episodic collection of tales in the miracle plays.

Shakespeare ignored the unities of time and place, but he does seem to have taken on board the unity of action (though not always). The other main difference between Shakespeare's experience of Plautus and other dramatists was that Plautus was actually very good. Most miracle plays were just trying to present Jesus' life; their writers, on the whole, were not trying to produce poetry or great literature, whereas Plautus was.

Classical drama was also being revived far away from Shakespeare's home town. This was the time of the English Renaissance and in universities people were rediscovering the great dramatists of antiquity. Their favourite was Seneca, the playwright and moralist whose tragedies are filled with high-flown rhetoric, terrible sins and revenge. Yet the Renaissance was not simply a period of reading. Elizabethan writers were intent on imitating and even surpassing the classics.

The result was the emergence of the university and inns-of-court writers, men like John Lyly, who wrote plays in imitation of their classical forebears. These plays were not populist; they were written by educated, sophisticated playwrights for an educated, sophisticated audience. What they did produce was the idea that modem drama could be as clever, as witty and as beautiful as classical drama.

The Stage as Shakespeare Found It
When Shakespeare arrived in London in about 1590, all these ingredients had been rolled together in contemporary drama. The two most popular playwrights were Marlowe, who wrote

Doctor Faustus, Tamburlaine and *Edward II*, and Thomas Kyd who wrote *The Spanish Tragedy*, probably the most popular play of the Elizabethan age.

Marlowe was a graduate of Cambridge University. He was well educated and had translated works by Ovid and Lucan. It would have been natural for him to write refined university drama, but he didn't; he went to the popular playhouses of London. For one thing, London was where the money was, but more importantly it suited his style. Marlowe liked power, violence, big speeches and grand passions. Faustus wants to know and enjoy everything; Tamburlaine wants to take over the world.

Marlowe's plays, like the miracle plays, sped across space and time with scenes set hundreds of miles apart and spanning many years. He also telescoped time so that in *Doctor Faustus* the final scene is meant to encompass a whole hour, when in fact it only lasts a few minutes. Shakespeare was to use this same effect in *Hamlet*, where a few minutes of action are meant to fill the time between midnight and dawn

Also in *Doctor Faustus*, Marlowe could switch easily from the fight between good and evil for a man's soul, to jokes about drinking and sex, just as the miracle plays could introduce toilet humour into the life of Christ.

Kyd was very similar, if a little less extreme than Marlowe. He too was educated; he had translated a play by Seneca. Yet he, too, chose to write for the people.

Neither of these writers were particularly subtle; if they weren't trying to out-Herod Herod, they were coming close. They wrote grand set-piece speeches for the leading actor of the day, Edward Alleyn. Hamlet may be referring to Alleyn's style of acting when he says:

> Speak the speech I pray you as I pronounced it to you,
> trippingly on the tongue; but if you mouth it as many
> of your players do, I had as lief the town-crier spoke
> my lines. Nor do not saw the air too much with your

hand, thus, but use all gently; for in the very torrent, tempest, and, as I may say, whirlwind of your passion, you must acquire and beget a temperance that may give it smoothness. Oh, it offends me to the soul to hear a robustious periwig-pated fellow tear a passion to tatters, to very rags, to split the ears of the ground-lings, who for the most part are capable of nothing but inexplicable dumb shows and noise. I would have such a fellow whipped for o'erdoing Termagant — it out-Herods Herod. Pray you avoid it.

The Stage Itself

Now that Shakespeare's Globe has been reconstructed on London's South Bank, visitors to London can see for them-selves what an Elizabethan theatre was like. The original Globe was not built until 1598, but there were two main playhouses – The Theatre and The Rose – already built along roughly the same lines.

The theatre was built to resemble the inn courtyards in which secular Elizabethan drama had its roots. The cheapest tickets were for the 'groundlings', who stood in the middle with the open sky above them. If it rained, they got wet. Around them were two levels of seats that were roofed over to protect their occupants from the weather. As in the inn courtyards, the most expensive were the ones on the first floor. The whole audience would drink, eat nuts and heckle. Indeed there are reports of people not being able to hear the play being performed above the cracking of nuts. So much for the audience.

The stage was a platform on one side of the central open space, raised about 5 feet (1.5 metres) above the ground. This allowed an actor to creep underneath to a trapdoor in the middle, out of which he could climb to play, for example, Mephistopheles in *Faustus*. In *Hamlet*, the actor playing the Ghost would have called his parting words from under the stage, which is why Hamlet refers to 'this fellow in the cellerage'.

At the far side of the stage there was a small curtain that could be drawn back to reveal an inner room large enough to contain a bed or a throne. This would, therefore, have been opened for the final scenes of *Hamlet* or *Othello*, or in *A Midsummer Night's Dream* Titania and Bottom could remain there for most of the play with the curtain occasionally being drawn aside to reveal the progress of their affair.

There were two doors, one on either side of the stage, through which almost all the exits and entrances would have been made. Hence in Kyd's *The Spanish Tragedy* there is the stage direction: 'He goeth in at one door and comes out at another.' This means that when two characters meet we can assume that they came in by different doors, and similarly when they part that one leaves via one side of the stage and one via the other.

Above the stage, supported on two pillars, was a balcony. This was used most famously in *Romeo and Juliet.* The balcony could also double as castle battlements or city walls, as in *Henry VI Part 1* where 'The French leap o'er the walls in their shirts', or in *Antony and Cleopatra* as the 'monument' of Act IV.

Above the balcony was a small window called the 'top'. It was rarely used, but one example is *Henry VI Part 1*, where Joan la Pucelle is to give a signal 'by thrusting out a torch from yonder tower'.

These were the details. Two important points of principle remain. First, there was no scenery; the lines spoken by the actors had to conjure up the location, whether it was a city street or a blasted heath. This is particularly important in scenes like *King Lear*, Act IV, Scene 5, where Edgar uses words to fool his father into thinking that they are on the edge of a cliff so high that: 'The fishermen that walk upon the beach/Appear like mice'. Not only would this have fooled Gloucester, it would have confused the audience, who were used to believing an actor's description of his surroundings.

The other important point is that the stage jutted out into the crowd, which is why Hamlet refers to his world as a 'promontory'. The conventional modern equivalent in a play like Oscar Wilde's *The Importance of Being Earnest* is the room with one wall missing, where the audience are separated from the actors by a clear line and a proscenium arch.

Shakespeare's stage had three levels and no scenery. It was far more versatile than most modern theatres because it left far more to the audience's imagination.

The Acting Companies

In 1572 the Act for the Punishment of Vagabonds made it law that an acting company had to be licensed and backed by a nobleman. Strolling players would commonly go from town to town and, when they couldn't find acting work, would supplement their incomes with begging, con artistry and odd jobs. From now on, this was illegal. The result was that most actors had to give up the theatre and get steady jobs, while the best players were forced to organize themselves into companies and obtain endorsement and protection from a nobleman. Hence the aristocratic titles attached to theatrical companies like Leicester's Men, the Queen's Men or Oxford's Men.

This was not to say that the company membership was fixed. Players moved between the companies freely and often. Good actors were poached for their skills and bad actors could be forced to leave one company and find work elsewhere. Also, companies would merge or fold. Lord Strange's Men joined forces with the Admiral's Men; the Queen's Men disappeared.

A patron did not guarantee either work or money; it was purely nominal. Most towns were run by their own middle classes, the city fathers or bailiffs, who were often puritans and therefore disapproved of the theatre. Only the clout of a letter of licence from an important aristocrat could overrule and override their censure.

The reason that the companies were always someone's 'men' was that they were always all male. There were no women on stage and female parts had to be taken by adolescent boys whose voices had not yet broken. In *A Midsummer Night's*

Dream, Act I, Scene 2, they give the part of Thisbe to Francis Flute, who protests 'let not me play a woman, I have a beard coming'. Similarly, Cleopatra is afraid that someday she will 'see/Some squeaking Cleopatra boy my greatness/I'th' posture of a whore' (IV, 2). This is one of the reasons that, in plays of the time, female characters often dress up as boys. It meant simply that the boy actor could stop pretending to be a woman and go back to being, as in *Twelfth Night*, someone 'not yet old enough for a man, nor young enough for a boy'.

Most acting companies would also have to employ jobbing actors for minor roles. These players would receive less money than the actual company members, their parts would be less significant and they could be laid off when the play they were employed for had finished its run, which was often a matter of days.

Some acting companies bought plays from writers who were nothing to do with them; others stole plays from writers who had no recourse to the law. Others had actors in the company who could write plays themselves. This was the case with Shakespeare and Ben Jonson.

In London, where the money was, were theatres that were often run by impresarios who might hire them out from the theatre owners. Impresarios would employ an acting company to appear at their theatre and then pay them out of the money they received from ticket sales. The impresario would loan the acting companies money to buy costumes and new plays to perform, or sometimes he would buy the play himself. More often than not it was the impresario who made the real money.

When the plague hit London, as it often did, or when times were hard, the players would be forced out of the city. They would take their aristocratic licence and tour the countryside and provincial towns. During these tours they would make far less money and would often be forced to sell their costumes or playscripts in order to pay their debts.

It is uncertain in which company Shakespeare began working. In 1594 there was a big shake-up in the acting world, which left only two major companies in London: the Admiral's Men and the Lord Chamberlain's Men. The Admiral's Men had as their lead actor Edward Alleyn and tended to perform the old plays of Marlowe and Kyd. The Lord Chamberlain's Men had as their star Richard Burbage, as well as the best new playwright, William Shakespeare.

The most significant aspect of the company structure was that a play would be provided to fit the actors, rather than vice versa. In most modern productions, a play is written and then auditions are held to select the cast. In Shakespeare's day the reverse was true, and he was forced to produce his plays accordingly. For example, every acting company contained a clown – in Shakespeare's company his name was Will Kempe – and this clown would be something of a star. Therefore, every play had to include a part for the clown. Lear has his fool, Hamlet meets a comical gravedigger and *A Midsummer Night's Dream* has its Bottom.

One of Shakespeare's great abilities was to treat these necessities not as restrictions, but as catalysts for his imagination. In Marlowe's *Faustus*, the comic scenes seem irrelevant and could easily be cut out without damaging the play (they usually are in modern productions). Whereas, *King Lear* without the Fool would be almost as bad as *Hamlet* without the Prince.

It is therefore possible to work out from Shakespeare's plays the range of actors he had in his company. For example, there must have been a tall, thin, pale actor who played Sir Andrew Aguecheek and Cassius, with a 'lean and hungry look'. There were, during the mid-1590s, two boy actors, one of whom was short and dark and the other tall and blond. For them Shakespeare wrote the parts of Hermia and Helena in *A Midsummer Night's Dream*, and Olivia and Viola in *Twelfth Night*. Thus Hermia believes that the boys don't love her because she is 'tawny' and 'dwarfish'.

Another detail that we can pick out is that between around 1606 and 1608 Shakespeare had a superb boy actor for whom to write. We don't know the boy's name, but we can be sure that Shakespeare would not have created the parts of Cleopatra and Lady Macbeth unless he had someone who could take on such demanding roles. Boy actors could only work for a few years before their voices broke and puberty took hold; when Hamlet greets the players, he notices that one's 'face is valanced [with a beard] since I saw thee last'. (When envisaging an original production, it is also worth remembering that *all* men had beards and usually wore hats.)

It was the skill of the actors that allowed Shakespeare to write good parts, and the most skilled was Richard Burbage, the star of the Lord Chamberlain's Men. Shakespeare would have been a great writer anyway, but it is no exaggeration to say that without Burbage there would have been no *Hamlet*, no *Macbeth* and no *Lear*. It was his superb talents, his subtle, understated style of acting (as opposed to Edward Alleyn's bombast) that allowed Shakespeare to create such complicated characters.

Development

In 1599 Shakespeare, along with Burbage and others, became a sharer in the receipts of the new Globe Theatre, thus cutting out the role of the impresario and theatre owner. In 1603, when James I came to the throne of England, the Lord Chamberlain's Men became the King's Men. They were now summoned to perform in court far more often.

Plays could be political, especially when performed in front of the monarch, but many critics with their own political agenda have exaggerated this. The most famous example was Essex's rebellion. In 1601 the Earl of Essex, the Queen's former favourite, tried to lead a coup and his supporters paid the Lord Chamberlain's Men to put on a performance of *Richard II*. Shakespeare certainly didn't write the play for this purpose; the work was old and 'long out of use', and the performance doesn't seem to have achieved its purpose, as the rebellion failed. Famously, Queen Elizabeth heard of what had happened and commented: 'I am Richard II, no ye not that?'

Elizabeth had seen that a play about one monarch being

deposed could be read as a topical reference to her. This can be taken in conjunction with Hamlet's use of the players to upset Claudius as evidence that theatre could be topical even if it did not refer to topical events. The result is that any play can be taken to refer to almost anything.

This interpretation falls down in two places. First of all, Shakespeare did not write *Richard II* for Essex's rebellion and very few people turned up to the rebels' performance. Second, in *Hamlet*, the play refers very precisely to a particular and rather odd form of murder whereby the attacker pours poison in his victim's ear. Shakespeare was not really a political writer. For example, whatever we draw out of *Julius Caesar* in favour of a republic can be dashed by *Coriolanus* or *Henry V*.

Some critics see literature as important only in so far as it contains political messages, and treat Shakespeare's plays accordingly. This seems to be a mistake. Shakespeare depicted the world as he saw it without trying to change it. The Elizabethan stage was descriptive rather than prescriptive; the one time that it was used to try to bring about a change of government, it failed both politically and, more importantly, at the box office.

Hamlet and the Eyrie of Children

One of the most famous references in Shakespeare's work to contemporary acting conditions is in *Hamlet*. The players that the Prince knew in Wittenberg have left the city and been forced to go out touring. In fact, Shakespeare knew several actors who had gone on tour to Elsinore in Denmark, including the clown Will Kempe, who would have been able to give him a first-hand account of what it was like to perform there. However, the players in *Hamlet* have been forced to go on the road because there is no work left for them in the city. This is not because of plague or legal conditions, but because the public prefers to go and see child actors, 'an eyrie of children'.

Two companies of child actors had recently been formed in London, one in 1599, the other in 1600. *Hamlet* was probably first performed in 1603. However, these lines have been taken far too seriously by some commentators. The child actors seem to have enjoyed a very brief period of success, probably until the death of Queen Elizabeth in 1603, and then dwindled. By 1608 both companies were defunct.

That same year Shakespeare's company took on the lease of the Blackfriars Theatre. This was very different to the Globe: it was indoors, rectangular in shape, relatively small and lit by candles. It resembled the conventional theatre of today and would have been far better suited to quiet, sentimental works like Shakespeare's late romances than to the grand passions of plays like *King Lear* or *Tamburlaine*. It is uncertain whether Shakespeare now started writing primarily for this new venue; we know, for example, that *Henry VIII* was performed at the Globe, but the change of setting would fit with the change in style and tone that characterizes his late romances.

More importantly, it reflects a new tendency in the history of theatre. The masque had now truly come into fashion at court. Masques were delicate plays designed to please aristocratic tastes. They have none of the exuberance or bawdiness that characterized the plays performed at the Globe. From now on a split emerged between the works seen by the lower classes on Bankside and plays aimed at the courtiers and aristocrats who could afford to pay significantly more for the refined surroundings of an indoor theatre.

This split should not be overstated: it was only just beginning and would not reach its height until after Shakespeare's death. Yet the change was under way; the proscenium arch, which split the audience from the actors, had arrived and would be a standard feature of theatres for the next 300 years.

In 1611 Shakespeare returned to Stratford-upon-Avon, leaving London and its theatres behind. He had witnessed and played a part in a huge change in drama. In the space of twenty years it had been transformed from a cheap form of entertainment unworthy of the name of literature to an entertainment of kings and commoners alike and then to a refined and restricted art form. The stage had moved from the wagons of the strolling players, to the profitable bustle of the Globe and then to the indoor comfort of Blackfriars. Through all this Shakespeare had managed to adapt himself to the changing fashions and requirements of the stage for which he wrote.

The story of Shakespeare's stage has a sad and abrupt epilogue. After his retirement Shakespeare collaborated on a play called *Henry VIII*, or *All Is True*. Sir Henry Wotton, writing to his nephew, gives this account of a performance by Burbage and the King's Men in June 1613:

> Now to let matters of state sleep, I will entertain you at the present with what happened this week at the Bankside. The King's Players had a new play, called *All Is True*, representing some principal pieces of the reign of Henry VIII, which was set forth with many extraordinary circumstances of pomp and majesty, even to the matting of the stage; the Knights of the Order, with their Georges and Garter, the Guards with their embroidered coats, and the like: sufficient in true within a while to greatness very familiar if not ridiculous. Now King Henry making a masque at the Cardinal Wolsey's house, and certain cannons being shot off at his entry, some of the paper, or other stuff wherewith one of them was stopped, did light on the thatch, where being thought at first but an idle smoke, and their eyes more attentive to the show, it kindled inwardly and ran round like a train, consuming within less than an hour the whole house to the very ground.
>
> This was the fatal period of that virtuous fabric; wherein yet nothing did perish, but wood and straw, and a few forsaken cloaks; only one man had his breeches set on fire, that would perhaps have broiled him, if he had not by the benefit of a provident wit put it out with bottle-ale.

PUBLISHING SHAKESPEARE'S PLAYS

During Shakespeare's lifetime, playwrights cared little about seeing their work in print. Only a rare drama was actually intended to be read as well as performed. Writers would usually sell their plays to the theatrical company that staged the performances, and if the company committed a particular play to paper, it would create only one copy – the official copy – in the form of a promptbook.

A promptbook was a transcript of the play used during performances, cluttered with stage directions, instructions for sound effects and the names of the actors. If a play was printed for a reading audience, it was often without the author's consent. Unprincipled publishers would steal the promptbook and sell copies for about fivepence apiece. In March 1599, the theatrical manager Philip Henslowe endeavoured to induce a publisher who had secured a playhouse copy of the comedy *Patient Grissell*, by Dekker, Chettle and Haughton, to abandon the publication of it by offering him a bribe. The publication was suspended until 1603.

In subsequent years, the Lord Chamberlain, on behalf of the acting companies, many times warned the Stationers' Company against 'procuring publishing and printing plays by means

whereof not only they [the actors] themselves had much prej-
udice, but the books much corruption, to the injury and
disgrace of the authors'. In 1604, in fear that his work would be
pirated, John Marston hesitantly published his comedy *The
Malcontent*; his comment on the process aptly summarizes the
Elizabethan attitude towards publication: 'Only one thing
afflicts me, to think that scenes, invented merely to be spoken,
should be enforcively published to read.'

The Quartos

Before the publication of the First Folio in 1623, twenty-two
of the thirty-eight plays in Shakespeare's canon had appeared
in quarto format (see box, page 40): *The Troublesome Raigne
of John King of England* (1591), *Richard II*, *Richard III*,
Romeo and Juliet, *Henry IV Parts 1 and 2*, *Henry VI Parts 2
and 3*, *Henry V*, *The Taming of the Shrew*, *Love's Labour's
Lost*, *The Merchant of Venice*, *A Midsummer Night's Dream*,
Much Ado About Nothing, *Titus Andronicus*, *The Merry Wives
of Windsor*, *King Lear*, *Hamlet*, *Pericles*, *Othello*, *Troilus and
Cressida* and *The Two Noble Kinsmen*. All but *Othello* (1622)
and *The Two Noble Kinsmen* (1634) were published prior to
the date of Shakespeare's retirement from the theatre in about
1611. It is unlikely that Shakespeare was involved directly with
the printing of any of his plays, although it should be noted
that two of his poems, *Venus and Adonis* and *The Rape of
Lucrece* were almost certainly printed under his direct super-
vision.

The plays printed originally in quarto format were branded
fraudulent by the editors of the First Folio, Heminge and
Condell, who wrote in the preface to their collection that fans
of Shakespeare's works had been cheated by 'diverse stolen
and surreptitious copies, maimed and deformed by the frauds
of injurious impostors that expos'd them'. They believed that
most of the quartos in circulation had been either stolen
outright by unscrupulous printers who plagiarized the official
promptbooks belonging to Shakespeare and his company, or

horribly reconstructed from the memory of people who had seen the plays performed.

Heminge and Condell were right to be concerned about the integrity of Shakespeare's great works. The flaws in some of the quartos are wretched. Take for example the opening of Hamlet's famous soliloquy: 'To be, or not to be, that is the question:/Whether 'tis nobler in the mind to suffer/The slings and arrows of outrageous fortune' (III.1.58–60). In the quarto version of 1603 we have: 'To be or not to be. Aye, there's the point/To die to sleep, is that all? Aye all.'

Heminge and Condell's accusations were taken very seriously, and early scholars believed without question that the First Folio was the only authoritative Shakespearean manuscript, and that 'all of the quartos were poor texts, dishonestly obtained without the consent of the company for which Shakespeare was writing'. Thus, the twenty-two quartos were relegated to the heap of pirated material.

However, in the late nineteenth century the academic community began to challenge the claims made by the editors of the First Folio and to reassess the validity of the quartos. Led by the late A.W. Pollard, whose *Shakespeare Folios and Quartos* (1909) and *Shakespeare's Fight with the Pirates and the Problems of Transmission of His Text* (1917, revised 1920) are fundamental studies, scholars began an investigation of publishing contradictions in Shakespeare's day and a more thorough examination of the quartos and folios themselves.

As a result, the modern belief is that, far from being the ruling practice in the Elizabethan book market, piracy was exceptional, and that Elizabethan printers, taken as a whole, were neither exceptionally stupid nor exceptionally dishonest. It is now believed that only ten of the quartos are corrupt or unauthorized: *The Troublesome Raigne of John King of England*, *The Taming of the Shrew*, *Henry VI Parts 2 and 3*, *Romeo and Juliet* (the 1597 quarto), *The Merry Wives of Windsor*, *Henry V*, *Hamlet*, *King Lear* and *Pericles*. The remaining plays are classified as 'good' or authentic quartos.

Hamlet and *Romeo and Juliet* are unique in that they were published twice each in quarto format and the earlier quartos of the two are considered 'bad', while the latter two are now considered 'good' quartos.

The First Folio

By the time John Heminge and Henry Condell were ready to collect Shakespeare's works into a single volume, the Elizabethan disdain for plays as reading material was waning. The general population was beginning to consume published plays with increasing voracity, and some notable authors were taking great pains to polish their plays for a reading audience. In 1616 Ben Jonson issued a folio volume of nine of his works, called *The Workes of Benjamin Jonson*. Although some of Jonson's fellow playwrights ridiculed his decision to publish his writings, Jonson's collection granted a new status of respectability to drama in print, and became an inspirational archetype for Heminge and Condell's 1623 folio volume of Shakespeare's collected plays.

Heminge and Condell had been Shakespeare's fellow actors in the Chamberlain's Men (later the King's Men). They intended, as outlined in the preface to the First Folio, to compile Shakespeare's work 'without ambition either of self-profit or fame, only to keep the memory of so worthy a friend and fellow alive as was our Shakespeare'. They included thirty-six plays in the First Folio, under the headings 'Comedies', 'Histories', and 'Tragedies', and, in addition to preparing and correcting the bad quartos by comparing them to the authoritative promptbooks, they introduced to Elizabethan readers plays that were previously unpublished in quarto form, including *All's Well That Ends Well*, *As You Like It*, *Antony and Cleopatra*, *The Comedy of Errors*, *Cymbeline*, *Coriolanus*, *Henry VIII*, *Timon of Athens*, *Julius Caesar*, *Macbeth*, *Measure for Measure*, *The Tempest*, *Twelfth Night*, *The Winter's Tale* and *The Two Gentlemen of Verona*.

Heminge and Condell wished to make the First Folio as handsome as possible, so they added special touches throughout the collection. They decided upon the Droeshout portrait for the title page, and on the page opposite they printed ten lines by Ben Jonson, praising the lifelike exactness of the portrait. They also took pains to include a list of twenty-six 'Names of the Principal Actors in all these plays', and a table of contents. They dedicated the Folio to the Earls of Pembroke and Montgomery, and inserted four sets of verses on Shakespeare by Jonson, Hugh Holland, Leonard Digges and an enigmatic figure who went by the initials 'I.M.', possibly the English writer and translator James Mabbe.

Three additional folios appeared after the first, in 1632, 1663 and 1685. These later folios were copied from the first edition and contain omissions and mistakes. With the exception of the Third Folio – because of its inclusion of *Pericles* (omitted in the First Folio), in addition to six apocryphal plays – the later folios are not as important, academically speaking, as the first.

Publishing Formats

Quarto
A quarto is a book in which eight pages are printed on a single sheet which is folded twice to form four leaves. The average quarto contains about 100 pages and is about 6¾ x 8½ inches (17 x 21.5 centimetres) in size.

Folio
A folio is a book in which each sheet is folded over only once through the middle, forming two leaves (or four pages). The First Folio has 454 leaves and is approximately 8½ × 13⅜ inches (21.5 x 34 centimetres) in size.

Apocrypha
The term apocrypha is given to the collection of twelve plays that some scholars believe to be Shakespeare's, but are not officially part of the current canon of works because no real proof of authenticity has ever been brought forth. They include: *Locrine, The London*

Prodigal, The Puritan, Thomas Lord Cromwell, Sir John Oldcastle, Arden of Feversham, A Yorkshire Tragedy, The Birth of Merlin, Edward III, Fair Em, Mucedorus and *The Merry Devil of Edmonton*

The Plays

Shakespeare's 'history plays' represent a unique contribution to English literary history. He devoted ten dramas to the history of England, and can be said to have created a new medium. The history plays are in themselves a secular re-enactment of the mystery plays that had once satisfied the English public with their ritual.

Shakespeare also changed the understanding of English history. The plays were so powerful and so memorable that their versions of the past became accepted by subsequent historians. The accounts of Wars of the Roses, for example, have until recent years been determined by Shakespeare's analysis of the events of the time. Henry V and Henry VI are essentially Shakespearian creations, and every biography of Richard II mentions the play of that name.

THE HISTORY PLAYS

Shakespeare tells the story of the Wars of the Roses through the eyes of the Tudors. King Richard II (who reigned 1377–99) is a weak and ineffective king, but as king he is God's representative on earth. Bolingbroke, Richard's cousin, usurps the crown and becomes Henry IV (1399–1413). Whatever his virtues, he can never be forgiven for the crime of sacrilege, flouting God's commands and thereby upsetting the natural order.

Henry IV's reign is one long series of revolts, against which Henry can only set brute force. He cannot appeal to God or legal authority because of the way he has come by the throne. However, Henry IV passes on the crown to his son, Henry, believing that he has paid the price for his crime and that his son will reign without constant challenge. Henry V (1413–22) is indeed successful and distracts potential revolt by uniting the nobles in a war to 'regain' France, the throne of which he has a dubious claim through his mother. At Agincourt he defeats the French and epitomizes chivalry and patriotism.

Then the worst happens. Henry dies young, leaving a child crowned as Henry VI (1422–71). The nobles take sides – the House of Lancaster supporting Henry VI and the House of York supporting the claims of the Duke of York. The so-called Wars of the Roses – Lancaster's red rose against York's white – tear the kingdom apart.

Finally, the Yorkists prevail and Edward IV (1461–83) becomes king. When he dies, his son is still a child. Edward

IV's brother, Richard Crookback, shuts his nephew, the rightful king, Edward V (1483), in the Tower of London, where he and his younger brother are murdered on Richard's orders. Richard III is now king but his wickedness brings speedy punishment and, with God's help, an obscure Welsh noble overcomes Richard on Bosworth Field and is crowned Henry VII (1485–1509).

Shakespeare makes it clear that the Tudor dynasty, which Henry founds, is specially blessed for righting the original wrong done to Richard II. By marrying Elizabeth of York (the queen depicted on playing cards) he unites the warring factions and brings to an end the Wars of the Roses.

The wars have severely depleted the power of England's nobility, while the authority of the sovereign has been strengthened. Any attack on a Tudor monarch, Shakespeare implies, would not only be unpatriotic but sacrilegious.

Richard II

The Tragedy of King Richard II was probably written in 1594 or 1595, the fifth play in the sequence of Shakespeare's history of the English kings but the first in historical time. From the deposition of King Richard II arise all the troubles that were to plague the Houses of Lancaster and York. The play was entered for publication in the Stationers' Register in August 1597 and published in the same year under the title *The tragedie of King Richard the second. As it hath beene publikely acted by the Right Honourable the Lorde Chamberlaine his servants.*

Sources

The story of the reign is taken from Raphael Holinshed's *Chronicles of England, Scotland and Ireland* (1587) [first published in 1577], but the play covers only the last three years of King Richard's life. Some important events are simplified or invented, such as the scene where Richard publicly renounces the throne; no such ceremony took place. It is also possible Shakespeare had read Samuel Daniel's poem 'The Civil Wars between the Two Houses of Lancaster and York', published at about the same time Shakespeare was writing his play.

Main Characters
King Richard II
Born on 6 January 1367, he reigned from 1377 to 1399. He became king aged ten on the death of his grandfather, the warlike Edward III. Richard's father Edward the Black Prince, the hero of the Battle of Poitiers (1356), predeceased his father and, at least according to Shakespeare, Richard grew sick of being unfavourably compared to his father and grandfather. He angered his uncles and other great lords, the crown's traditional advisers, by preferring to rule through upstarts, men from a lower class entirely dependent on the king.

Queen Isabel
King Richard's second wife, the daughter of King Charles VI of France. Born in 1389, she flees to France when King Richard is deposed and dies there aged twenty in 1409.

John of Gaunt, Duke of Lancaster
One of the most important of the late king's advisers, John of Gaunt is King Richard's uncle. Very near death at the play's opening, he personifies patriotism and the virtues of the old England. In his famous deathbed speech, he upbraids his nephew for his reliance on disreputable men and curses him.

Henry Bolingbroke, Duke of Hereford (later King Henry IV)
King Richard's cousin, the son of Richard's uncle, John of Gaunt, Duke of Lancaster, Henry is exiled by Richard, but after his father's death he returns to England to recover his title and lands, and ends by deposing the king and taking the throne for himself.

Edmund of Langley, Duke of York
Richard's uncle and brother of John of Gaunt, he is made Lord Governor of England while Richard is in Ireland attempting to

subdue the rebels. When Bolingbroke returns to claim his inheritance, York dithers between his loyalty to King Richard and his belief that Bolingbroke has right on his side. Without the power to withstand Bolingbroke, he reluctantly joins with him but is racked with guilt for having betrayed his trust.

The Duke of Aumerle and Earl of Rutland
The son of Edmund, Duke of York, Aumerle is a cousin of both King Richard and Bolingbroke. He remains loyal to Richard but after his deposition swears fealty to the new king, Bolingbroke, now Henry IV. In a scene of pure farce, his father discovers he is involved in a plot to kill King Henry and he, his father and his mother (the Duchess of York) rush to see the King, his father to accuse his son of treason and his mother to beg for her son's life.

Thomas Mowbray, Duke of Norfolk
In Act I, Mowbray is accused by Bolingbroke of treason and of complicity in the death (before the play opens) of King Richard's uncle, the Duke of Gloucester. Mowbray appeals to the King, hinting that he was only obeying his orders, but the King sends him into permanent exile while, at the same time, banishing Bolingbroke for six years.

The Duchess of Gloucester
The aged widow of the murdered duke and sister-in-law to John of Gaunt and the Duke of York. In a powerful speech (I.2), she urges York to avenge his brother's death.

The Bishop of Carlisle
Loyal to King Richard, the bishop bravely speaks out against Bolingbroke ascending the throne. In Act IV, Scene 2, he accuses Bolingbroke of sacrilege in taking it upon himself to remove from the throne God's anointed representative and calls Bolingbroke a traitor and as a result is promptly arrested.

Bushy, Bagot and Green
Servants of King Richard, despised by the great lords of England. Bushy and Green are executed by Bolingbroke but Bagot escapes.

Henry Percy
The son of the Earl of Northumberland, nicknamed 'Hotspur'. Father and son ally themselves to Bolingbroke but will prove themselves thorns in the side of the new king.

The Earl of Northumberland
Bolingbroke's strongest ally – powerful, greedy and unscrupulous. King Richard forecasts that he will betray his new king as he has betrayed him.

Sir Piers Exton
Exton assassinates Richard in Pomfret Castle, believing he is acting under King Henry's orders but Henry disavows him and weeps over Richard's coffin.

The Plot
In a highly stylized scene of formal ritual couched in high-flown verse, King Richard II arbitrates in a dispute between his cousin, Henry Bolingbroke, and Thomas Mowbray, Duke of Norfolk. Each accuses the other of treason and Bolingbroke accuses Mowbray of murdering his uncle, the Duke of Gloucester, among other crimes. Mowbray half admits being involved in the murder and of attempting to murder John of Gaunt, the Duke of Lancaster, but says he has confessed this and has been absolved by Gaunt.

The natural end of these claims and counterclaims would be trial by arms, death deciding who was the guilty party, but ill-advisedly King Richard intervenes and banishes the two men – Mowbray for life and Bolingbroke for six years. In so doing, the King has given Bolingbroke and his father, John of Gaunt, a grudge that will fester over the years of Bolingbroke's exile.

John of Gaunt has meanwhile been urged by the widowed
Duchess of Gloucester to avenge the murder of her husband,
but Gaunt refuses. He says it is God's duty to take revenge –
the unspoken reason being that it was God's representative,
King Richard himself, who ordered his uncle's murder.

Relieved to be rid of his enemies, King Richard with his
cronies decides he can now turn to subduing Ireland, but he
cannot afford to pay for a war. He hears his uncle, the Duke of
Lancaster, is dying and decides to seize all the Duke's lands and
wealth. He arrives at the Duke's deathbed hoping to find his
uncle already dead, but he is not quite dead and rails at his
nephew for his crimes against England. Just before the King
arrives, Gaunt has been speaking to his brother, the Duke of
York, about England – 'this sceptred isle' – and in a famous
speech describes the country as a 'precious stone set in a silver
sea'.

As soon as King Richard departs for Ireland, Bolingbroke
returns illegally to England – his banishment is still in force –
to claim his inheritance. He argues, speciously, 'As I was
banished, I was banished Hereford, But as I come, I come for
Lancaster.'

He is supported by the Duke of Northumberland, and many
other lords rally to his cause. The Duke of York, the king's
representative while the King is in Ireland, half-heartedly
upbraids his nephew but acknowledges he has no power to
prevent him marching on London.

Meanwhile, King Richard returns, but the Welsh army he
had been expecting has dissolved. Only the day before, Richard
is told, the army disbanded, hearing he was dead. The King –
not a man of action – sits upon the ground and bewails his fate,
cursing Bolingbroke. In a memorable speech he despairs,
telling his followers 'to sit upon the ground and tell sad stories
of the death of kings'.

At Flint Castle in Wales, Bolingbroke and King Richard
meet. Bolingbroke denies that he has come to seize the crown,
but Richard, becoming more royal in stature as his physical

power disintegrates, openly calls him a liar. He teases Bolingbroke, one moment agreeing to everything he demands and the next moment reminding him that it is he who has the right to demand obedience. In a highly theatrical but moving speech, Richard debases himself: 'What must the King do now? Must he submit? The King shall do it. Must he be deposed? The King shall be contented. Must he lose the name of King? A God's name, let it go.'

Queen Isabel, meanwhile, as she walks in the garden of the Duke of York's house near London, is filled with foreboding. She and her ladies-in-waiting overhear an aged gardener and his assistant discuss affairs of state. In a vivid metaphor, the gardener likens England to the garden. 'Go thou,' he tells his assistant, 'and like an executioner, Cut off the heads of too fast-growing sprays that look too lofty in our commonwealth.' He hints that the king will soon be deposed, and the Queen, unable to remain silent, comes out from her hiding place and berates him. She curses him: 'Gardener, for telling me these news of woe, Pray God the plants thou graft'st may never grow.'

Bolingbroke summons King Richard to abdicate the throne in public view, despite the Bishop of Carlisle forbidding him in God's name. King Richard, in Westminster Hall, dispossesses himself of his crown in an outpouring of powerful and moving poetry and makes Bolingbroke an unwilling partner in his game of self-betrayal. The Duke of Northumberland attempts to end the charade and is reprimanded by Richard.

In Act V Richard, on his way to 'Julius Caesar's ill-erected tower', the Tower of London, is waylaid by the Queen and they say farewell. Richard urges her to leave immediately for France.

The Duke of York vividly describes Bolingbroke's triumphant entry into London as King Henry IV. There follows the farcical scene of the Duke accusing his son Aumerle of treason. The whole family goes to the King, Aumerle and his mother to ask clemency and the Duke to ask for his son's punishment.

The new king forgives Aumerle, but he knows that his entire reign will be spent fighting insurrection since his claim to the throne is ill-founded. He also complains of his son, the future Henry V, who spends his time with low company in London's brothels and taverns and never comes to court.

In prison, Richard tries to come to terms with the disasters that have befallen him and, in a touching scene, compares his prison cell to his former kingdom. He is visited by a groom who tells Richard, to his chagrin, how proudly his horse Barbary carried the new king.

The groom makes way for Exton, the king's murderer. Exton brings the dead king before the new king and Henry is, or pretends to be, horrified at the crime. Henry vows to make a pilgrimage to the Holy Land 'to wash this blood off from my guilty hand'.

Henry IV Part 1
Sources
The first part of *Henry IV* is the sequel to *Richard II*. It was probably written in the autumn of 1597. *Richard II* had been published that summer and was selling well. This new play, however, had less history and more comedy. As mentioned above, in *Richard II*, King Henry's eldest son and heir, familiarly known as Prince Hal, was happy to spend his time in London's taverns rather than take his rightful place at court. This gave Shakespeare the freedom to paint a vivid portrait of the life led by ordinary people and to contrast it with the war and conspiracy-obsessed life of the king and his advisers, England's great lords and magnates.

For historical facts, Shakespeare once again went to Holinshed's *Chronicles*, from which he took ten episodes. Setting the drama during 1402–03, Shakespeare takes liberties with historical facts and figures. For example, the real Hotspur was not the same age as Prince Hal, and Shakespeare's Mortimer is a conflation of two people.

Falstaff and his cronies are fictional. In the first version of *Henry IV*, Falstaff is called Oldcastle; there was a real Sir John Oldcastle, but he was a valiant knight, not a fat ruffian. The historical Oldcastle was, however, tried and convicted of heresy, so it is possible Shakespeare changed the name of his character to Falstaff to make it clear there was no connection between the two. Shakespeare also draws on the figure of the 'arrogant soldier', a stock figure in classical Roman comedies, and on the Lord of Misrule from folk-festival tradition.

There were many stories of Henry, Prince of Wales' wild youth and there was a play already in existence called *The Famous Victories of Henry V*, which featured a robbery by the Prince on Gad's Hill. It was Shakespeare's genius to transform whatever lay to hand into a living, breathing picture of England two centuries before his own time.

Main Characters
King Henry IV (1399–1413)
Born in 1366, Henry has usurped his cousin's throne and is now worn down by guilt and anxiety – guilt at being responsible for the death of King Richard II, God's anointed representative, and anxiety as to whether or not he can pass on the throne to his eldest son, who shows no interest in, or aptitude for, kingship. 'So shaken are we, so wan with care …' he says. Paradoxically, the rebellions against him are easily put down, but still this does not bring him peace.

Prince Hal
Henry, Prince of Wales, the future Henry V, was born in September 1387 (he is also referred to as Prince Harry or Harry Monmouth). His father, the King, believes him to be a wastrel, but in fact he is merely observing his future subjects and learning what it means to be a king. His 'regal' qualities emerge as the play unfolds, but he can appear deceitful and cold-eyed, using Falstaff and his friends while, at the same time, they think they are using him.

Henry Percy, also known as Hotspur

Hotspur, or Harry Hotspur as he is sometimes called, is, as his nickname indicates, proud, fiery, honourable and brave – a true hero. He is the son and heir of the Earl of Northumberland, who helped Henry to his throne but whom, as King Richard foretold, now feels he has not been adequately rewarded. King Henry envies Northumberland for having such a son, but Hotspur's weakness is that his short temper and rash pursuit of honour and glory lead him to revolt against the king without first assuring himself of the full support of the nobility.

Thomas Percy, Earl of Worcester

Hotspur's shrewd, manipulative uncle and the mastermind behind his rebellion. King Henry has him executed after its failure.

Henry Percy, Earl of Northumberland

Hotspur's father, who did so much to gain Henry his crown, is now the king's enemy, but he falls 'crafty sick' before the Battle of Shrewsbury and denies his son the army that might have turned the tide in the rebel's favour.

Owen Glendower

Leader of the Welsh and a major figure in Welsh history. He joins with the Percys in their revolt against the king. He marries his daughter to Edmund Mortimer, Earl of March, who has a strong claim to the throne of England.

Sir John Falstaff

An old, fat man, between the age of fifty and sixty-five, he more or less lives in the taverns and brothels of Eastcheap, one of the poorest areas of London. He is Prince Hal's guide, mentor and father figure. His wit and cunning make him a match for the Prince.

Ned Poins, Peto and Bardolfph
Vagabonds and drinking friends of Falstaff. Poins is the ring-leader, a swaggering highwayman.

Mistress Quickly
The good-hearted hostess of the Boar's Head tavern, a seedy drinking house where Falstaff has his headquarters.

Lord John of Lancaster
Prince Hal's younger brother and a dutiful son of the King.

Sir Walter Blunt
A loyal and trusted ally of the king and a great soldier. He is killed at the Battle of Shrewsbury by the Earl of Douglas while acting as decoy for the king.

The Earl of Westmoreland
One of the king's most trusted military leaders and political advisers.

The Plot

King Henry IV, still racked with guilt for King Richard's death and his usurpation of the throne, longs to go on a pilgrimage or crusade to expiate his sins but rebellion at home prevents him from leaving. Both the Scots and the Welsh are in arms. Edmund Mortimer has been taken prisoner by the Welsh prince, Owen Glendower. Young Henry Percy (Hotspur) has been victorious against the Scottish rebel, Archibald, Earl of Douglas. The King contrasts his son's idle and dissolute life with the chivalrous and noble behaviour of Hotspur and is saddened, fearing for the future of the Royal House of Lancaster. Hotspur has taken many valuable prisoners but, to the King's fury, refuses to hand them over to him. He sends for Hotspur to explain himself.

Prince Hal, the King's wayward son and heir, is to be found not at court, where he ought to be, but drinking and making mischief with Sir John Falstaff and his friends in the taverns of London. They plan a robbery on a band of pilgrims on Gad's Hill. At first Prince Hal refuses to take part, but Poins persuades him to play a practical joke on Falstaff. When Falstaff and his ruffians have carried out the robbery, he and the Prince will come upon them in disguise and relieve them of their loot. The fun will come from hearing Falstaff brag about his courage after the event. The Prince makes it plain to the audience that he will return the pilgrims' possessions to them. It would be beneath him to take part in a real robbery. He makes it clear to us that he is only 'friends' with ruffians like Falstaff and Poins so that he can amaze his subjects when he becomes king. Then he will throw off his former life and reveal himself to be a true king.

Hotspur has come to court, where he quarrels with the King about the Scottish prisoners and the King's refusal to ransom Lord Mortimer, Hotspur's brother-in-law, who is a captive of the Welsh. The King refuses to yield and calls Mortimer a traitor because he has learnt that Mortimer has married Owen Glendower's daughter. Later, the King explains that his real reason for refusing to ransom Mortimer is that he has a better claim to the throne of England than his own and was proclaimed by King Richard to be his heir. Hotspur and his uncle, the Earl of Worcester, plot a rebellion against the King, who seems so ungrateful for the help they gave him to unseat Richard and become king.

Falstaff's robbery at Gad's Hill takes place and the Prince and Poins relieve them of their spoils. Later, at the Boar's Head, Falstaff tells his tale of being overwhelmed by a strong band of ruffians, his story getting ever more outrageous. When Prince Hal reveals that it was he and Poins who stripped him of his ill-gotten treasure, Falstaff pretends he knew who they were all the time and was just stringing them along.

The Sheriff comes to the Boar's Head and summons the Prince to attend his father to prepare for war against the rebels, which he does. The King berates his son for the dissolute life he is living and fears it means the Prince must hate him. The Prince swears his allegiance and tells his father he will kill Hotspur. The Prince gives Falstaff a commission in the army and they all go off to war.

The rebels are in disarray – Glendower's army is not ready to march and even Hotspur's father, the Earl of Northumberland, claims he is too sick to march with the rebels. Hotspur is undeterred. On the battlefield of Shrewsbury the rebels are defeated and Prince Hal kills Hotspur.

Falstaff, who has made money from recruiting men on the way to the battle and then letting them buy their release from the army, avoids danger on the battlefield by pretending to be dead. Prince Hal kills Hotspur and then sees Falstaff lying on the ground, apparently dead. He speaks well of him over his 'dead' body, but as soon as the Prince goes, Falstaff gets up, stabs the dead Hotspur in the leg and claims that he, not the Prince, killed him.

Henry IV Part 2
Sources
Written soon after publication of *Henry IV Part 1* in the spring of 1598, the play was published on 23 August 1600. The historical events in the last years of the reign of Henry IV after the Battle of Shrewsbury, which concludes *Henry IV Part 1*, are not very dramatic, so Shakespeare concentrated on the purely fictitious adventures of Sir John Falstaff and his friends.

It would be pleasant to think that Shakespeare's Justice Shallow and Silence are based on people he knew, but there is no evidence of it. *Henry IV Part 2* completes the education of Prince Hal and prepares the way for the apotheosis of Shakespeare's historical plays, *Henry V*.

Main Characters
King Henry IV
Henry has achieved his ambition, the throne of England, but it hasn't brought him happiness. He knows he will always be seen

as a usurper who has deposed the rightful king and God's anointed representative on earth. This gives licence for any of his subjects to rebel, and although he has beaten all-comers, 'uneasy lies the head that wears the crown'. His eldest son is a disappointment to him and his health is declining.

Prince Hal, later to become Henry V
Prince Hal roisters with his low friends in the taverns of London, but he is preparing to throw them off and rise in glory to true kingship. His relationship with his father is strained, but behind the misunderstanding we perceive a mutual loyalty and regard.

Prince John, Duke of Lancaster; Humphrey, Duke of Gloucester; and Thomas, Duke of Clarence
Sons of King Henry IV and younger brothers of Prince Hal. They share their father's suspicions of their elder brother and are pleasantly surprised when he proves to them he is worthy of ascending the throne.

Mowbray and Hastings
Lords who plot with the Archbishop of York to overthrow the king.

The Earl of Northumberland
The King's old friend and now his greatest enemy. He is partly responsible for the death of his son, Hotspur, because he failed to bring his army to the Battle of Shrewsbury in which Hotspur was killed.

The Lord Chief Justice
The most powerful representative of the law in England. Upright and just, he does not hesitate to reprimand Prince Hal and his cronies, even though he knows that he may suffer for it when Prince Hal becomes king. However, when the time

comes, the Prince rewards him for his courage in upholding the law without fear or favour.

Sir John Falstaff

Falstaff plays the clown, patronizes Prince Hal and brags to his friends that when the old King dies he will be among the greatest in the realm. When he rushes back to London on hearing of Henry IV's death, Prince Hal, now King Henry V, rejects him brutally.

Page

A small boy Prince Hal has assigned to serve the bloated Falstaff and make him look ridiculous.

Poins, Peto, Bardolph and Ancient Pistol

Falstaff's henchmen. Bardolph has a nose swollen and red from excessive drinking and Poins is a swaggering cutpurse (pick-pocket). Ancient (or Ensign) Pistol is a noisy, bellicose ex-soldier always looking for a fight.

Justice Shallow, Justice Silence and their servant Davy

Shakespeare parodies the ignorant and foolish Justices of the Peace, the king's representatives in towns and villages throughout England. The servant Davy is the only competent member of Shallow's household. Falstaff, who has known Shallow when they were both young men in London, despises the old man, plays on Shallow's snobbery to borrow money off him and otherwise tricks and cheats him. Shallow and Silence, as their names indicate, are comic characters whom the 'groundlings', the poorer members of the audience, would have enjoyed seeing guyed.

Mistress Quickly

The good-hearted proprietor of the Boar's Head tavern. She is half in love with Falstaff and allows him to borrow money from her with little hope of having it repaid.

Doll Tearsheet
Falstaff's favourite prostitute and a good friend of Mistress Quickly. Streetwise and not as easily bamboozled as Mistress Quickly she, too, is half in love with Falstaff.

Fang and Snare
Humorously incompetent officers of the law called upon by Mistress Quickly to arrest Falstaff (reminiscent of Dogberry and his constables in *Much Ado About Nothing*).

The Plot

A prologue to the play meditates on the way rumour brings false intelligence of great events before the truth is known. The Earl of Northumberland, skulking in his castle instead of supporting his son Harry Hotspur in his rebellion against the king, first hears the rebels have been victorious but eventually he learns the truth: the rebels have been defeated and his son killed by Prince Hal. Northumberland swears he will have his revenge.

Falstaff and his page, a small boy designed to make the fat old man look ridiculous, receives a summons from the Lord Chief Justice to answer a charge of highway robbery. Falstaff is forgiven by the Justice because of his supposed good behaviour at the Battle of Shrewsbury – in fact all lies. Falstaff has been called to join Prince John's army, which is to fight the Earl of Northumberland and other rebels. Mistress Quickly, proprietor of Falstaff's favourite tavern, the Boar's Head in Eastcheap, is demanding of two constables that they arrest Falstaff for the debt he owes her. The Lord Chief Justice appears unexpectedly and commands Falstaff to make reparation to Mistress Quickly. Falstaff manages to persuade her not to pursue her claim. He plans a farewell dinner with the prostitute Doll Tearsheet before he goes off to the wars.

Prince Hal receives an absurd letter from Falstaff (the fat knight) and decides to play a practical joke on him. He and Poins will dress up as tavern serving-men, and spy on Falstaff.

Falstaff has his dinner with Doll Tearsheet and insults the Prince, not realizing who he is addressing. The Prince reveals himself. Falstaff is once again summoned to join the king's army, and Doll and Mistress Quickly bid him a tearful farewell.

The Earl of Northumberland is insisting on joining battle with the King, though both his son's widow and his wife tell him it is too late; he ought to have supported Hotspur when there was a chance of victory.

King Henry, meanwhile, in a soliloquy, meditates on why a great king cannot sleep while the meanest of his subjects can.

In rural Gloucestershire, Falstaff comes upon his old friend Justice Shallow and his fellow Justice of the Peace, Silence. Shallow recalls the good old days when he and Falstaff had been students together at the Inns of Court in London, how they had drunk together and visited prostitutes.

Falstaff arrives and begins to recruit soldiers for the wars. He chooses men rich enough to buy themselves out of the army and ends up taking the worst sort of ragamuffin.

Prince John tricks the rebels into disbanding their army, then arrests and executes the rebel leaders. Meanwhile, Falstaff, still with an undeserved reputation as a brave soldier, manages to get Sir John Coleville, a rebel lord, to surrender himself to him.

In London, the King rejoices to hear that the rebels have been defeated, but then falls sick. Prince Hal is sent for, but when he reaches his father's bedside, he thinks he is dead. He removes the crown that the King has beside him and takes it into another room. The King awakes and finds himself alone and the crown gone. His younger sons tell him they left their brother, the Prince of Wales, alone with him. The Prince returns and is upbraided by his father but the Prince explains he thought he was dead and meant no disrespect. Urgently, the King lectures his son that when he ascends the throne he must trust no one. He hopes that though his reign has been plagued by rebellions, he will pass on to his son a more united kingdom and advises he makes war against the French in order to distract potentially dangerous lords. The King is taken into a chapel called Jerusalem and he remembers how he had always wanted to die in the Holy Land on a Crusade, expiating his sins. Ironically, he will die in Jerusalem despite never having reached the Holy Land.

Falstaff hears of the King's death, visits Justice Shallow to borrow money, and returns to fling himself at the feet of the new king. Prince Hal, now King Henry V, rejects Falstaff and the life he has led. The Lord Chief Justice, whom the new king has commended for chastising him when he was the Prince of Wales, returns to banish Falstaff from the court, though he will receive a small pension.

Henry V
Sources
References in the Chorus before Act V to the Earl of Essex's triumphal departure for Ireland on 29 March 1599 date the play precisely. It was entered at the Stationers' Register on 4 August 1600. Again, it is based very closely on Holinshed's *Chronicles* (cited in full on p.46; then to be referred to as *Chronicles*), though Shakespeare also drew on Edward Hall's The *Union of the Two Noble and Illustre Families of Lancaster and York*, commonly called Hall's *Chronicle* [cited later as Hall's *Chronicle*] (1542) and the anonymous *The Famous Victories of Henry V.*

Main Characters
Henry V
The son of Henry IV, who, on returning to England from exile to claim the title Duke of Lancaster, had deposed King Richard II. Henry's guilt at this sacrilegious act had haunted him all his reign. As he lies on his deathbed, he tells his son: 'To thee it shall descend with better quiet, better opinion, better confirmation' (*Henry IV Part 2*, IV.3).

Shakespeare sets out to make Henry V the epitome of kingship. He has all the virtues a king needs. He is brave, chivalrous, cunning, a great orator and even saintly. He believes in the idea of England and has the ability to touch the hearts of ordinary soldiers and make them believe in him. In the scene where he woos Katharine, the King of France's daughter, he shows himself to be witty, self-deprecating and sexy.

He can, however, be ruthless and revengeful. To the modern audience, there is a troubling scene where he orders the killing of the French prisoners after the Battle of Agincourt.

The Archbishop of Canterbury
A powerful cleric who urges Henry to pursue his claim to the French crown.

The Duke of Exeter
Thomas Beaufort, Duke of Exeter, a loyal henchman to Henry V and a great soldier.

The Duke of York
One of only four titled Englishmen killed at the Battle of Agincourt.

The Earl of Salisbury
A devoted friend of the King, he fought at Agincourt and was killed during the reign of Henry VI at the Siege of Orléans (1428).

Lord Scroop
Henry, Lord Scroop, third baron of Masham, is treasurer to Henry IV. Henry V sends him on an embassy to France. Henry V has him executed when he finds he is plotting with the French to kill him. His betrayal is particularly painful to Henry as he 'didst bear the key to all my counsels' and knew 'the very bottom of my soul'.

Sir Thomas Grey
Son-in-law of the Earl of Westmoreland, he is another conspirator executed by the King.

The Earl of Cambridge
Second son of the Duke of York, he is the third conspirator executed by the King.

Charles VI, King of France
Shakespeare paints him as a great king and a worthy opponent of Henry V.

The Dauphin
The French king's son and heir, he is arrogant and rash, insulting Henry with his gift of tennis balls.

The Dukes of Orléans, Bourbon, Berri, Bretagne, Beaumont and Rambures
Overconfident French lords who believe it will be easy to beat the raggle-taggle English army on the field of Agincourt.

Katharine
The charming daughter of the French king, whose English lesson is one of the light-hearted moments that provide a welcome break from war and politics.

Pistol
A comic character from *Henry IV Part 2*, a friend of Falstaff's – dishonest, bawdy and quarrelsome, he is a likeable rogue. He is devoted to the King and helps to show how the King inspired loyalty in even the lowliest of his subjects.

Bardolph
Another of Falstaff's companions, he is executed for robbing a church when in France with the army.

Corporal Nym
An underworld character; aggressive but cowardly, he is also greedy and predatory.

The Boy
He accompanies Pistol and Bardolph to the wars but quickly learns to despise them. He dies at Agincourt guarding the English camp with other boys; his killing by the French angers the King as it goes against the rules of war.

Captain Fluellen
A Welsh captain and an officer in Henry's army, he is honourable, quick-tempered and sincerely attached to the King whom he is proud to call Welsh.

Captains Gower and Macmillan
Welsh and Scottish respectively, they are two officers in the king's army; their presence helps to show how the King unites Wales, Scotland and England.

Mistress Quickly
Proprietor of the Boar's Head tavern in Eastcheap, her description of the death of Falstaff is one of the play's most poignant moments.

The Plot
The year is 1415 and the Chorus opens the play by telling the audience they must use their imagination to 'piece out' the limitations of the theatre to picture kings, wars, court and taverns – in France and England.

Henry V is contemplating war with France. For his sake and that of the audience, the Archbishop of Canterbury makes the case for Henry being the rightful king of France. It is very complicated however, and depends on inheritance on the female side, which, under Salic law, the French do not accept.

The French ambassador arrives and delivers the Dauphin's insulting challenge – a box of tennis balls. The Chorus then informs us 'the youth of England are on fire' with patriotism. However, as always, there is a threat from disaffected lords and the King deals with conspiracy harshly, executing the traitors, to emphasize that while he is away in France there must be no rebellion at home.

In a London tavern, Mistress Quickly is saying farewell to Nym, Bardolph, Pistol and the Boy, who are off to France with the king's army. She speaks movingly of Falstaff's death.

Outside the gates of Harfleur, the English army prepares for one final charge to take the town. King Henry rouses his men with a famous speech beginning: 'Once more unto the breach dear friends', once again making it clear that while in the past only the great lords would be expected to show loyalty and patriotism, Henry required even the ordinary soldier to fight for him and for England. Harfleur is taken.

Writing mostly in French, Shakespeare, now shows Katharine, the daughter of the French king, learning English from her maid.

The King hears that Bardolph has been arrested for robbing a church and, despite once having caroused with him in the Boar's Head, decides he must die as an example to the army of what happens to looters.

Near Agincourt, the French nobles are boasting of their horses and longing for battle with the English, whom they despise. In the English camp, Henry V puts on a disguise and walks through his men to discover how ready they are to fight against seemingly overwhelming odds. The disguised King exchanges gloves with a soldier who fears the King will sue for ransom. The day of battle dawns and Henry rouses his army with a great speech of pride and patriotism.

The French are routed and even Pistol captures a French soldier but, to the Boy's disgust, instead of killing him takes money from him. The King is told that the defeated French, against the law of arms, have murdered the boys guarding the English camp. He orders French prisoners to be killed.

The King returns the glove he has taken off the soldier while in disguise. The King receives news that only a handful of English are dead, while 10,000 French have been killed.

Pistol has a quarrel with Fluellen, the Welsh captain, then confesses he has heard that back in England his wife has died of despair and that he has decided to return home and live a life of thievery.

King Henry makes a treaty with the French king and takes his daughter Katharine as part of the agreement. He courts her in a scene of wit and charm, signalling peace after war.

The Chorus ends the play by looking forward to the disastrous reign of Henry VI, in which all that Henry V has gained will be lost.

Henry VI Parts 1, 2 and 3
Sources
Philip Henslowe, the owner of several London playhouses including the Rose, notes in his diary for 3 March 1592 the performance of a new play called *Henry VI*, for which his share of the takings was £3.16s.8d. – a record sum – and the play was performed fifteen times in six months, well above the average. We know the second and third parts of *Henry VI* were in existence by the summer of 1592 because the playwright Robert Greene, who died in September 1592, quotes from *Henry VI Part 3* in his diatribe *The Groatsworth of Wit*.

Shakespeare used as his sources for the events of Henry VI's reign Holinshed's *Chronicles* and Edward Hall's *Chronicle*. In *Henry VI Part 1* Shakespeare is free with historical facts, for instance having Henry referred to as an 'effeminate boy' when, in reality, Henry was less than a year old. *Parts 2* and *3*, however, keep much closer to historical fact.

Main Characters
King Henry VI (1422–61)
Henry VI became king when he was less than a year old. He grew up meek, pious and unsuited to his role as ruler of an England in constant turmoil, and was unable to follow the example of his father, the warrior King Henry V, and complete the conquest of France. He was to lose almost all the lands his

father had won in France. He suffered periods of mental illness and his weakness led to the so-called Wars of the Roses, the long battle for power between the great Houses of Lancaster and York.

Charles, Dauphin of France
Born 10 November 1433, Charles spends his reign trying to recapture his lands from the English. He is aided by La Pucelle (Joan of Arc) and dies in battle on 5 January 1477.

Joan La Pucelle (Joan of Arc)
Shakespeare describes her from the English point of view: not as a saintly warrior but as a harridan and a whore. She is captured by the Duke of York and, at her trial, first claims to be a virgin and then to be pregnant. The English burn her at the stake as a witch.

Humphrey, Duke of Gloucester
Fourth son of King Henry IV and the King's loyal friend, he is made Lord Protector but is dragged down by his enemies when his wife is found guilty of witchcraft.

Henry Beaufort, Bishop of Winchester
The Duke of Gloucester's great rival, Beaufort is the illegitimate son of John of Gaunt. He makes peace with Gloucester and dies in April 1447.

Richard Plantaganet, Duke of York
Although his father once had claims to the throne, young Richard Plantaganet lost all his titles when his father was put to death. He has a difference of opinion with the Duke of Somerset and each chooses a rose as a symbol of their cause. Plantaganet chooses a white rose and Somerset a red rose. King Henry VI makes him Duke of York and gives him control of the English troops in France. Captured at the Battle of Wakefield, he is stabbed to death by Queen Margaret.

Edward, Duke of York, later King Edward IV
Brave but 'wanton', he becomes king owing to his brother's ruthlessness in murdering King Henry in the Tower of London.

Richard, Duke of Gloucester (the future Richard III)
Brave and unscrupulous, he revenges his father's death, Richard Plantaganet, and makes himself king.

George, Duke of Clarence
Edward IV's second brother, who betrays him but is later reconciled.

Lord Clifford
He kills the Duke of York's young son, Rutland, in revenge for his father's murder. He dies at the Battle of Towton.

Lord Talbot
General of the English troops in France and much feared by the French, he dies with his son at Bordeaux on 17 July 1453.

The Duke of Somerset
The Duke's quarrel with Plantaganet costs Talbot his life when he delays sending Plantaganet reinforcements.

The Earl of Suffolk
He captures Margaret, daughter of the King of Naples, a princess of no fortune. He then falls in love with her, but, because he is already married, woos her on behalf of King Henry.

The Earl of Warwick
Warwick (Queen Margaret calls him a kingmaker) first supports the Yorkist faction but transfers his allegiance to Queen Margaret when Edward, Duke of York, marries Lady Grey instead of the French king's daughter.

Queen Margaret
The formidable wife of Henry VI. She fights for King Henry, while he would rather be allowed to pray in peace.

Jack Cade of Ashford
A Kentish rebel whose rebellion is put down by Lord Clifford.

The Plot
Henry VI Part 1
King Henry V is hardly in his coffin before the great lords of the realm are quarrelling over who is to rule the kingdom until King Henry VI comes of age. Gloucester is named Lord Protector and he accuses the Bishop of Winchester of not having prayed hard enough for the late king. Bedford tells them to stop their quarrelling and asks the ghost of Henry V to help England prosper.

News comes that the French have recaptured eight towns. Bedford, the Regent of the French lands under English control, says he will return to France. More news comes: the French are in revolt and brave Talbot has been captured.

Despite Talbot's capture, the English continue to besiege Orléans. King Charles is told of a 'holy maid' called Joan who claims she has God's power with her. To prove it, she beats the King in single combat. Joan refuses to be the King's lover and says she must remain a virgin for her sacred task, to save France.

Back in London, the Bishop of Winchester prevents the Lord Protector from gaining access to King Henry. The two men curse each other and they begin to fight until the Mayor of London orders them to stop.

In France, Orléans has been ransomed and returns to his army. Salisbury is killed by a well-aimed French gun and the French, inspired by Joan La Pucelle, attack. Joan and Talbot engage in single combat but she decides to spare him. The French rejoice at their victory but then the English counter-attack and the French quarrel among themselves. Talbot is almost captured by the Countess of Auvergne.

In London, in the Temple Garden near the law courts, Plantaganet and Somerset quarrel over precedence. Plantaganet picks a white rose and Somerset a red rose and their allies follow suit. Warwick foretells that these two roses will make many men bleed in battle. The dying Mortimer, with his claim to the throne, names Plantaganet as his heir. Winchester and Gloucester continue their quarrel, but in the end they agree to a truce.

In France, Joan finds out the weak points of Rouen, held by the English, and prepares an attack on the city. Still, the battle is nearly lost when Joan convinces the Duke of Burgundy to transfer his allegiance from the English to the French. In Paris, Henry is crowned King of France and tries to make peace between his quarrelling lords.

Talbot besieges the town of Bordeaux but is killed with his son because Somerset has delayed sending him reinforcements. King Henry, with the backing of the Pope, wants to make peace with France. Suffolk woos the beautiful Margaret, daughter of the King of Naples, on behalf of King Henry, as Suffolk himself is already married.

Joan is now a captive of the English and shows her 'wickedness' by refusing to acknowledge her father, the simple shepherd, and by first claiming to be a virgin and then to be pregnant.

Henry VI Part 2

Henry's marriage to Margaret does not please many of his lords. Duke Humphrey, who sees himself as heir to the throne by descent from Edward II, has a foolish wife who tries to make her husband king by sorcery and makes an enemy of Queen Margaret. Duke Humphrey resigns his office as Lord Protector when his wife is declared guilty of witchcraft. Despite being innocent of any wrongdoing, Duke Humphrey is also arrested.

York goes to Ireland with an army to suppress an Irish rebellion and gives covert support to Jack Cade's revolt, hoping to benefit from civil war. Suffolk has Duke Humphrey strangled in his bed; he tries to pretend the death is natural, but Warwick accuses him of murder. Suffolk flees to France but is captured by pirates and beheaded. Jack Cade leads his march on London, but Lord Clifford persuades his followers to lay down their arms and Jack Cade is killed. With this rebellion over, the Duke of York plans to start a new one. He quarrels with Henry and Queen Margaret and calls on his sons, Edward and hunchbacked Richard, to support him. Civil war breaks out and the King flees to London. The white rose has had its first victory.

Henry VI Part 3

The Duke of York has defeated King Henry at the Battle of St Albans. King Henry is aware that his own claim to the throne is weak because Henry IV deposed the rightful king, Richard II. He therefore agrees to make the Duke of York his heir, but his followers accuse him of cowardice. York's followers are also displeased because they don't want York to have to wait until Henry is dead to be king. The Duke of York is finally persuaded by his sons to raise an army and depose the king.

Queen Margaret, too, has raised an army on the king's behalf; they defeat the Yorkists and the Duke of York is killed. Lord Clifford, seeking vengeance for the death of his father at York's hands, kills Rutland, York's youngest son and still a child. To the dismay of the King who wishes to put an end to the bloodshed, there is another battle between the Yorkists and Queen Margaret. The Yorkists win.

The Earl of Warwick, a prominent Yorkist, wants Edward to marry the daughter of the King of France, but Edward is infatuated with a beautiful young widow, Elizabeth, Lady Grey. King Henry is captured and sent to London.

In France, Queen Margaret is pleading for help from the French king. Warwick arrives to woo the king's daughter for Edward, not knowing Edward intends to marry Lady Grey. When he hears the news of the marriage, he throws in his lot with Queen Margaret.

In England, Edward's brothers also disapprove of their brother's marriage. The Duke of Clarence, Edward's younger brother, decides to follow Warwick and marry his daughter. Hunchback Richard remains loyal to Edward, not because he loves him but because he hopes to gain the throne through him. Edward is captured by Warwick but his brother Richard rescues him and sends him to Flanders for safety.

King Henry, released from prison, hands over his realm to Warwick and Queen Margaret to rule between them as he retires to live out his life in meditation. However, Edward returns from exile with an army and captures King Henry, locking him in the Tower of London. Edward besieges Warwick at Coventry; and the Duke of Clarence finds he cannot fight his brother and deserts the Earl of Warwick. In the battle that follows, Warwick is killed. The Lancastrians are defeated, but Queen Margaret and her son refuse to give in. At Tewkesbury, the Queen is captured and the Prince, her son, stabbed to death in revenge for Rutland's murder. Richard has one more murder to commit. He goes to the Tower and stabs King Henry to death.

Edward, now King Edward IV, forecasts peace and prosperity. He has the throne and a son to succeed him. Queen Margaret is in exile; he believes his brothers love him. He does not understand that his brother Richard will do anything necessary to seize his crown.

Richard III
Sources
The culmination of Shakespeare's great historical cycle, *Richard III* was probably written in 1592 or 1593. Some scholars believe Christopher Marlowe may have written some scenes. The main source, as for the other plays in the series, was Holinshed's *Chronicles*. Holinshed based his account of the reign of Richard III on Edward Hall's *Chronicle*, and he in turn had used Sir Thomas More's *The History of King Richard III* and Polydore Virgil's *Historia Angliae*.

Shakespeare invented and embellished the facts as he knew them, as his object was to show how the wicked king was the inevitable result of King Henry IV's act of sacrilege, usurping the rightful king, God's representative on earth. The Tudors did not wish to encourage rebellion; they wanted to show how important it was that the monarch should free himself or herself from England's great feudal lords, who had brought terrible civil strife to the country. Only God's intervention, in the shape of Henry Tudor, could set things to rights and bring peace.

Main Characters
Richard III
Formerly the Duke of Gloucester, he was brother to Edward IV. He was born in 1452 at Fotheringay Castle in North-amptonshire. Whatever the historical reality, Shakespeare paints him as a villain: unscrupulous, totally self-interested, cynical, ambitious and manipulative. His physical deformity (which may not be a historical reality), compounds the picture. For all this, it is Shakespeare's genius that he manages to make the character complicated, interesting and attractive so that we regret his downfall, however well deserved. He is killed at the Battle of Bosworth Field on 22 August 1485.

The Duke of Buckingham
Richard's right-hand man, who helps him to power and is then discarded. He is as ambitious and unscrupulous as Richard himself but without Richard's perverse attractiveness.

King Edward IV
Richard's elder brother, he dies on 9 April 1483 leaving his widow, Elizabeth, to Richard's not-so-tender mercies.

George, Duke of Clarence
Richard's elder brother, whom he persuades King Edward to imprison and then have put to death.

Queen Elizabeth
Edward IV's wife and then widow. She rightly fears Richard, who destroys her and her family, the Woodvilles. She has ten children including the two young Princes, who Richard, their uncle, will murder in the Tower.

Dorset, Rivers and Grey
Earl Rivers is Queen Elizabeth's brother; the Marquis of Dorset and Lord Grey are her sons from her first marriage. They are all enemies of Richard; as soon as King Edward is dead, Richard has Rivers and Grey killed, but Dorset manages to flee and survives.

Lord Hastings
He makes the mistake of trusting King Richard and dies.

Lady Anne
Anne is the young widow of Edward, Prince of Wales, son of Henry VI. Lady Anne hates Richard for killing her husband, but, despite this, he has the gall to woo and win her for his wife.

The Duchess of York
Richard's widowed mother, she tries to protect her grand-children from him and ends by cursing him.

Queen Margaret
Widow of King Henry VI, she lingers on into the new reign, angry but impotent, cursing Richard and the Yorkists.

King Edward V and Richard, Duke of York
These are 'the Princes in the Tower', King Edward's children done to death by their wicked uncle. (Some writers have tried to prove that though imprisoned by Richard, they were actually murdered in the next reign by Henry VII; but the evidence now seems to support Shakespeare's belief that

Richard had them killed. He could hardly allow Edward V, the legitimate king, to live while he reigned.)

Tyrrell
The Princes' murderer.

Lord Stanley, Earl of Derby
Richmond's stepfather, who helps Richmond to the throne.

Richmond, later King Henry VII
A *deus ex machina*, Henry arrives at Bosworth to kill the wicked King, bring peace and prosperity to England and end the Wars of the Roses by uniting red rose and white. Shakespeare glorifies the Tudor dynasty as the culmination of his great cycle of history plays.

The Plot

Richard, Duke of Gloucester, takes the audience into his confidence. His brother is now King Edward IV, and England is at peace. Richard, however, is not suited to peaceful pastimes such as dancing. He is deformed, ugly and accustomed to war. He will endeavour to make himself king.

He begins by making his brother Edward – who is ill and easily swayed – suspicious of George, Duke of Clarence, Richard's elder brother. Richard takes the trouble to persuade Clarence that he is his friend and that he is in prison because of the machinations of the Queen and her family. Richard brags that Clarence will soon be dead. It is important he dies before the King, as Clarence might be considered his heir.

Richard comes across Lady Anne weeping over the bier of her husband, Henry VI's eldest son whom Richard killed. He decides to woo and marry her, partly to give his claim to the throne more weight and partly for the pure pleasure of being so perverse. He is successful.

The Queen is justifiably fearful that, if the King dies, she and her sons will be in danger from Richard. Edward, the eldest, is still a child and too young to rule, so the likelihood is that his uncle Richard will be made Lord Protector. Richard pretends to be innocent and blames the Queen and her relations for the bad feeling at court. King Edward makes them all promise not to quarrel. King Henry's widow, Queen Margaret, curses the lot of them.

In the Tower, Clarence tells of the dream he has had, in which he is visited by his murderers who drown him in a butt of malmsey (sweet Madeira wine).

Richard makes Edward feel guilty about allowing his brother Clarence to be killed, though of course it was actually his doing. Shortly afterwards, King Edward dies. Richard and his henchman the Duke of Buckingham take his nephew, the child Prince, now Edward V, and his brother Richard away from their mother and house them in the Tower. Queen Elizabeth takes her younger children and seeks refuge with the Church. Richard orders the execution of the Queen's kinsmen Rivers and Grey.

Richard and Buckingham send Catesby to sound out whether Lord Hastings will agree to Richard becoming king in place of Edward V. Hastings refuses and is arrested and executed. Richard and Buckingham shamelessly woo the Lord Mayor of London and he is persuaded to call on Richard to take the throne. Richard pretends to be reluctant and Buckingham has to 'plead' with him. Buckingham tries to stir up feelings against the dead King Edward and hints that his son, Edward V, now in the Tower, is illegitimate. Buckingham reports back that the common people do not accept this slander.

Richard, now king, asks Buckingham to kill the Princes in the Tower, but this is one step too far even for Buckingham and he declines. Richard has to hire a villain called Tyrrell to do the job for him, with Catesby's assistance.

Richard decides he must murder Buckingham and also his own wife, Anne, as he wants to marry King Edward IV's daughter, Elizabeth of York. Just when Richard feels he has gained everything he desires, he hears that many of the nobility are flocking to join Henry, Earl of Richmond, who has landed in Wales with a large army.

Two queens – old enemies – Margaret and Elizabeth join to curse Richard. Richard tells Elizabeth he wants to marry her daughter; she is horrified and suggests bitterly that he should just kill her without bothering to marry her first. Richard is pleased to hear that Buckingham, once his friend and now his enemy, has been captured and his army defeated. Richard prepares to do battle with Richmond.

Richard is suspicious of Stanley, Earl of Derby, a powerful nobleman with a large army at his back; so he takes the Earl's son as hostage until the battle is done and his father has proved himself loyal. Buckingham is executed without being allowed to see Richard – the man he made king.

The night before the battle, Richard is plagued by bad dreams and sees the ghosts of those he has murdered. In contrast, Richmond has sweet dreams. After a fierce battle the following day, Richard is killed and Earl Stanley crowns Richmond to be King Henry VII. England is at last at peace.

Henry VIII
Sources
The Famous History of the Life of King Henry VIII was performed as a new play at the Globe Theatre on 16 June 1613. It was a memorable performance, not least because the Globe caught fire and burnt to the ground.

Usually considered to be Shakespeare's last play, it is a series of set-pieces rather than a coherent play. Some scholars believe John Fletcher wrote parts of it. However, there is no evidence, beyond a study of the language of the play, to indicate that anyone other than Shakespeare is the author.

Main Characters
King Henry VIII
Born 28 June 1491, Henry, when the play opens, is reliant on his chief minister, Cardinal Wolsey. The King needs a male

heir and Wolsey is required to have the King's marriage to Katharine of Aragon annulled so that he can remarry.

Cardinal Wolsey

The King's chief minister, Wolsey effectively runs the country with little interference from the King. He hopes to prove to the Pope that the King's marriage is incestuous because Katharine was betrothed first to the King's elder brother, Arthur, who died young. Wolsey wants to engineer an alliance with France; as part of the treaty, Henry would marry the French king's daughter. Unfortunately, Henry has other ideas. He has become besotted with Anne Bullen (Anne Boleyn).

In the end, Wolsey is rejected by the King he has served so loyally and wishes he had served God with the same devotion as he has served Henry.

Queen Katharine

The Queen rails against Wolsey for persuading the King to divorce her. She refuses to let him judge her. She speaks with dignity of her twenty years as a queen and she cannot forgive Wolsey for allowing her to be cast off for not producing a male heir. Before she dies, she forgives Wolsey when she hears her attendants speak well of him.

The Duke of Buckingham

Buckingham is Wolsey's great enemy. The Cardinal accuses him of plotting to take the throne and he is executed.

Anne Bullen (Anne Boleyn)

Anne Bullen first meets Henry VIII at one of Wolsey's dinner parties. The King decides to marry her after his divorce from Queen Katharine; but when they do marry, she gives birth to a girl, Elizabeth, not the longed-for boy.

Thomas Cranmer
As Archbishop of Canterbury, Cranmer tries to marshal legal opinion on the King's side when he decides to have his marriage annulled. His chief rival is Gardiner, Bishop of Winchester. Gardiner plots to have him tried for treason, but the King protects him and he lives to baptize Princess Elizabeth and forgive Gardiner.

Cardinal Campeius
Campeius is the pope's representative over the royal divorce; he plays an equivocal role in the proceedings.

The Duke of Norfolk
One of the great lords who resent Wolsey's power over the King, particularly as he comes from a lower class than the King's traditional advisers. Norfolk eventually brings about Wolsey's fall from power.

Thomas Cromwell
A friend of Wolsey, he is distraught when his mentor is brought down, but Wolsey tells him to continue to serve the king.

The Plot
The Prologue tells the audience that this is to be a serious play, not a bawdy romp. Norfolk and Buckingham discuss King Henry's meeting with the King of France (an event now known to historians as the Field of the Cloth of Gold), when each king tried to outdo the other in magnificence. Norfolk says it was organized by Cardinal Wolsey, and Buckingham complains at his arrogance and ambition. Buckingham declares that he thinks Wolsey is plotting against him. Enter the Sergeant-at-Arms to arrest Buckingham.

Queen Katharine kneels before the King and begs him on behalf of his subjects to lower their taxes. The King blames Wolsey and agrees to release anyone in prison for not paying their taxes. The King hears the case against Buckingham.

King Henry, disguised as a shepherd, arrives at Wolsey's great dinner, but Wolsey, of course, sees through his disguise. The King flirts with Anne Bullen, one of Wolsey's guests.

Buckingham is executed and Wolsey is generally thought to have plotted his downfall. The nobles grumble that the upstart Wolsey is bankrupting the nobility of England. The King has decided to divorce his queen, and Campeius, the Pope's envoy, brings the Pope's judgement on the affair.

Anne Bullen feels sorry for the Queen but is pleased at being admired by the King. Queen Katharine pleads with the King and asks how she has offended him. She blames Wolsey, but he says he has nothing against her and the King supports the Cardinal. Wolsey and Campeius visit the Queen and Katharine upbraids them.

The lords gather to plot against Wolsey. They have intercepted letters from the Cardinal to the Pope asking the Pope not to grant the King his divorce until he gets over his infatuation with Anne Bullen. The King is upset and complains about Wolsey's huge wealth. Wolsey declares his loyalty to the King but recognizes his career is over. The lords turn on the Cardinal and Cranmer weeps to see him so harried. The Cardinal tells Cranmer to stay loyal to the King and serve him well.

Cranmer, the Archbishop of Canterbury, marries the King to the beautiful Anne Bullen. Queen Katharine hears Wolsey has died and forgives him his sins. Katharine, too, is near death. Cranmer is under attack from Gardiner, Bishop of Winchester, his great rival, but the King protects him.

Cranmer baptizes Princess Elizabeth and foretells her greatness.

King John
Sources
The first printed text we have of *The Life and Death of King John* is from the First Folio (1623), but it is one of twelve of Shakespeare's plays listed by Francis Meres in his *Palladis Tamia* (1598). There is no mention of the play by any other of

Shakespeare's contemporaries, so we can only guess it was written between 1595 and 1597. If so, the topic of foreign invasion would have been of considerable interest to the play's audience, who were hearing of a new armada being prepared in Spain, while England's relations with France were deteriorating. The play appeals for patriotism and unity in the face of danger from abroad.

Shakespeare's main source was the two-part anti-Catholic play, printed in 1591, *The Troublesome Raigne of John King of England*. There had also been a morality play by Bishop John Bale called *Kyng Johan*, thought to have been written in the 1530s. As usual, Shakespeare had Holinshed's *Chronicles* to consult, but he mainly relied on *The Troublesome Raigne*.

Main Characters
King John (1199–1216)
Born in December 1167, the third son of King Henry II. His elder brother, Richard the Lionheart (1157–99), was king before him. Legally, his dead brother Geoffrey's son, Arthur, should have become king, but John takes the throne because Richard appointed him. The legitimacy of his rule is, therefore, in doubt, though primogeniture was less important at that period of England's history than having on the throne a man capable of ruling and waging war. A child king was feared as it could lead to weakness at the top, usually ending in civil war.

John's indifference to papal decrees and his willingness to steal from the monasteries also make him vulnerable to attacks on his legitimacy. His murder of Arthur (18 October 1216 at Newark Castle) makes him an outcast.

Queen Eleanor (or Elinor)
King John's mother, Eleanor, encourages John to keep a strong hold on his throne and fight off all challenges. Eleanor's death in France is a blow to John and it means he is not kept informed about the threat of French invasion.

Philip
The King of France, Philip is Arthur's champion. However, he is not to be relied upon and lets his son, Louis, marry John's niece Blanche.

Arthur
The rightful heir to the throne. His mother Constance and King Philip of France are his champions, but he would prefer to live the life of a simple shepherd.

Philip the Bastard (the Bastard)
The illegitimate son of Richard the Lionheart. A mischievous rogue but a valiant soldier, he becomes John's main supporter. He has bad luck and loses half his army, but his honourable behaviour makes him respected.

Louis and Blanche
Louis is the King of France's son, who marries Blanche, John's niece.

Pandolf
The pope's envoy. He excommunicates John for his anti-church activities and encourages Philip to depose him. John eventually promises the Pope obedience. Pandolf accepts his repentance and makes peace between England and France.

Hubert de Burgh
Hubert is assigned to look after Arthur, but King John asks him to kill the boy. He is touched by Arthur's innocence and cannot hurt him, but falsely reports to the King that he has carried out the killing. When John repents of having ordered Arthur's murder, he is relieved to be told by Hubert that the boy is not in fact dead. Unfortunately, Arthur has fallen to his death from the castle walls and Hubert is accused of having killed him.

Constance
Arthur's mother and champion.

Faulconbridge
Philip the Bastard's younger but legitimate brother,
Faulconbridge loses his lands to his brother but regains them
when the Bastard forfeits them.

The Plot
The setting is England and France, about 1200. King John
receives a messenger from the King of France claiming the
throne of England, Ireland and those parts of France in English
hands on behalf of Prince Arthur, King John's nephew.

Faulconbridge and his half-brother, Philip the Bastard,
come before the King, each claiming to be their father's heir.
Philip the Bastard is the elder, but Faulconbridge claims Philip
is the son of Richard the Lionheart and so has no legal right to
inherit. Queen Eleanor, impressed with the Bastard, asks
whether he would not rather be Lionheart's bastard and hand
over his estates to his brother. The Bastard agrees and is
knighted by the king and renamed Sir Richard Plantaganet.

Outside the French town of Angers, held by the English, the
French (with Arthur and his mother) prepare to meet a new
English army. The English and French lords exchange insults
and the sweet-tempered Arthur wishes he was not the cause of
this strife. The citizens of Angers say they will yield up their
town to whoever wins the battle and proves they are king of
England – John or Arthur. The wily King John suggests Louis,
King Philip of France's son, might like to marry his niece
Blanche, meaning that Arthur and his mother Constance are
thrown over.

The Pope's envoy, Cardinal Pandolf, arrives and demands of
King John why he has barred the Pope's nominee from
becoming Archbishop of Canterbury. John refuses to be
dictated to by an Italian priest, so Pandolf allies himself with
Arthur. To Blanche's horror, her wedding day is ruined when

battle breaks out. King John captures Arthur. John gives Arthur into the care of Hubert de Burgh and hints that he would like him to murder Arthur.

King John has a second coronation in order to make his lords swear allegiance to him again. They ask him to show clemency towards Arthur. The King agrees but news comes that Arthur is dead and the lords go off to attend his funeral. Hubert, accused by the King of murdering Arthur at his request, says that Arthur is not dead after all, as he felt too much pity for the boy. However, in a rash escape attempt Arthur has jumped to his death from the castle walls.

There is much confusion as to how Arthur dies, many believing King John had him killed. King John submits to Pandolf and is reconciled to the Pope. In the ensuing battle between the French and the English, the English win but King John is poisoned and dies. The English lords swear allegiance to the new King Henry III.

Note on *Edward III*

On 1 December 1595, the publisher Cuthbert Burby entered on the Stationers' Register a book entitled *Edward III and the Black Prince their wars with the King John of France*. It was not until 1760 that there was any mention of Shakespeare being the author, when Edward Capell included it in his edition of the complete works. He argued that the quality of the play was such that it simply had to be by Shakespeare. The play deals with only part of Edward III's reign (1327–77): the conquest of France (1340–56) and the King's passion for the Countess of Salisbury. The play's author uses material from William Painter's *Palace of Pleasure* (1575) Holinshed's *Chronicles* (1587) and Jean Froissart's *Chronicle* (translated into English in 1523).

One of the main reasons for thinking the play may be by Shakespeare is that it shares a line with Sonnet 94: 'Lilies that fester smell far worse than weeds.' The play is also reminiscent of *Measure for Measure* (c. 1603) as it deals with a virtuous woman being bullied by a powerful man. The 2002 production by the Royal Shakespeare Company at Stratford-upon-Avon used a text edited by Richard Proudfoot and Nicola Bennett, who make a strong case for *Edward III* being Shakespeare's lost history play.

THE GREEK AND ROMAN PLAYS

The Roman historians had become indispensable reading for the educated class of Elizabethan England. Shakespeare himself, in the grammar school at Stratford-upon-Avon, had studied Sallust and Caesar. He had also read Plutarch's *Parallel Lives*. Through these sources he became acquainted with the known facts of classical history, but his imagination was more important than his learning. The Roman historians were adept at giving character sketches of their protagonists. They were also able to convey moral lessons on the nature of politics in their own time. In his Roman plays, Shakespeare followed their example by creating memorable portraits of generals and commanders, while at the same time obliquely commenting on the politics of his own period through his description of their actions. In *Julius Caesar*, for example, he opens a disquisition on the merits of political assassination. Any debate on such a theme in the sixteenth century would have led him to the prison or the noose.

The history of ancient Rome fascinated the Tudors because it seemed to provide a template for modern kingship. So many lessons could be learned and so many parallels drawn from the story of how the republic had given way to empire and declined into chaos.

In particular, *Julius Caesar* tells how a great general becomes arrogant and tyrannical. He is torn down by noble Brutus and the other conspirators. Brutus has high ideals and wishes to preserve the republic, which Caesar has threatened. Unfortunately Brutus is not ruthless enough and Caesar's friends, notably Mark Antony, take up their swords against him and civil war breaks out.

When the war is over, Antony is triumphant. He is to rule the eastern half of the empire, while Caesar's adopted son, Octavius, is to rule the western half, with the help of Lepidus, a rich patrician who is soon disposed of.

In *Antony and Cleopatra*, Shakespeare tells of Antony's obsessive love for Cleopatra, Egypt's queen. Debilitated by a life of luxury and idleness, the once great soldier refuses to do his duty as a Roman. He makes the fatal mistake of marrying Octavius' sister and then abandoning her for Cleopatra. Octavius makes war against his former friend and defeats him. Antony dies and Octavius becomes the great emperor Augustus. Unbridled authority has replaced a corrupt republic.

Coriolanus tells a similar story from an earlier period in Roman history. The great soldier Coriolanus chafes against the restrictions of democracy. He joins with his old enemy, and Rome is soon at his mercy. Coriolanus' mother pleads with him to spare Rome. After much anguish, he betrays his ally and does as she wishes, signing his own death warrant as he does so.

All these plays deal with the subject of authority: how it can be restrained and made acceptable without reducing the state to anarchy. Shakespeare and his contemporaries believed that there was a natural order in the universe. Everyone had their place, their duty and their rights. When anything disturbed this natural order, disaster followed.

Timon of Athens
Sources
The play was first published in 1623 in the First Folio, among the tragedies between *Romeo and Juliet* and *Julius Caesar*. It is not the most fluent of Shakespeare's plays and scholars have speculated whether the version we have was cut or edited by some other hand, or if part of it was written by another playwright; but it is most likely that this is a first version of a play Shakespeare never got round to revising or rewriting. The style is that of Shakespeare's later period when he wrote *King Lear* and *Coriolanus*. The source of the play is an anecdote in Plutarch's *Parallel Lives*, in the 1579 English version by Sir Tomas North (who was translating from a French version by Jacques Amyot). In his 'Life of Marcus Antonius', which Shakespeare also used in *Julius Caesar* and *Antony and Cleopatra*, he tells the story of Timon's ungrateful friends. The story also appears in one of the *Dialogues* of Lucian, a second-century Greek writer.

Main Characters
Timon
A wealthy Athenian who enjoys giving presents to his friends and expects nothing in return. Timon finally discovers his absurd generosity has bankrupted him. His erstwhile friends refuse to help him and he takes off into the forest to become a hermit. He discovers a stash of gold, but his bitterness against mankind prevents him returning to his former position in society.

Apemantus
A little like Lear's Fool, Apemantus scorns Timon for relying on his wealth to buy friends. When Timon loses everything, Apemantus accompanies him into the forest and they enjoy insulting one another.

Alcibiades
Alcibiades is a soldier. When one of his friends is sentenced to

death, Alcibiades protests and is banished. He meets Timon in the woods and they discuss what a pleasure it would be to sack Athens. Timon funds the army with which Alcibiades will destroy Athens.

Flavius
One of Timon's servants, who tries to warn him that he will soon be bankrupt. When Timon leaves Athens, Flavius and his other servants mourn his fall. He tries to help Timon, and Timon says he is the only honourable man in Athens and rewards him with gold.

Lucullus, Lucius, Sempronius, Ventidius
Timon's ungrateful friends.

The Plot
Meeting in Timon's house in Athens are several 'friends' each with something to sell – a jeweller, a painter and a poet. Timon pays the debt of a friend of his, Ventidius, and has him released from prison. He helps an old man get his daughter married off and then does business with his guests. Apemantus arrives and rails at Timon for allowing himself to be flattered and fawned over. There is a feast and Apemantus is banished to a table on his own so that his sour humour does not infect the rest of the party.

Timon's servant, Flavius, tries to warn Timon that his money is running out. Servants arrive whose masters are owed money by Timon. He tries to borrow money and cannot believe it when he is refused. All his so-called friends abandon him.

Meanwhile, Alcibiades is pleading with the senators for the life of a friend who has acted foolishly. The senators refuse to listen to Alcibiades and his friend is condemned to death.

Timon holds a new feast but his guests are presented with dishes of steaming water and stones instead of food. They think Timon has gone mad. He stands outside the city wall and curses mankind. Flavius and the other servants are sad; they ask who would want to be rich if it leads to so much unhappiness.

Timon is now a hermit living in a cave in the forest. He finds a cache of gold and calls it a 'yellow slave' and reburies it. Alcibiades arrives with a prostitute but does not recognize Timon, who calls himself Misanthropos. Alcibiades says he would like to help Timon but has little money, yet he gives him a little gold. Alcibiades announces he is going to sack Athens and Timon is so pleased with the idea he hands over the gold he has discovered so Alcibiades can raise an army.

Apemantus comes to chide Timon and they rail at one another. Timon gives gold to some robbers so they can do their worst. Flavius, Timon's good servant, arrives and offers Timon his money, and Timon is forced to admit there is one honest man in the world. He sends Flavius away with some gold. The poet and the painter have heard about Timon's gold and come to try and ingratiate themselves with him. Senators arrive and beg Timon to return to Athens as they realize they have been unfair to him. Alcibiades is placated and his and Timon's enemies are surrendered to him. Timon's epitaph is found; it says: 'Here lie I, Timon; who, alive, all living men did hate'.

Troilus and Cressida
Sources
One of Shakespeare's late plays, written shortly after *Hamlet*. The earliest record of the play is an entry in the Stationers' Register dated 7 February 1603, so it was probably written in 1601 or 1602.

The play falls into two parts: the first tells how Troilus obtained the love of Cressida with the help of Pandarus, her uncle; and how she was taken to the Greek camp, where she misbehaved. There is no ancient source for this tale, but by Shakespeare's time it was a popular story and 'Cressida' and 'Pandar' were words already used to mean 'whore' and 'pimp'. Chaucer's is the best-known version.

The second part of the play tells the story of how the Greeks, upset by Achilles' withdrawal from the fight, arrange for Ajax to challenge Hector to single combat. Hector then kills Achilles' friend Patroclus and is in turn treacherously slain by Achilles. This story is to be found in Homer, and Shakespeare would have used George Chapman's translation of *The Iliad*.

Main Characters
Troilus
A prince of Troy, Troilus is the son of King Priam and the younger brother of Hector and Paris.

Cressida
A beautiful young Trojan woman, the daughter of Calchas, a Trojan priest who defected to the Greeks. She becomes Troilus' lover.

Diomedes
The Greek warrior who seduces Cressida.

Antenor
A Trojan commander who is exchanged for Cressida after his capture by the Greeks.

Calchas
Cressida's father, a Trojan priest who has defected to the Greeks.

Pandarus
Cressida's uncle, who runs between his niece and her lover like a cheerful good-hearted pimp.

Priam
King of Troy and father of Hector, Paris and Troilus.

Hector
A true hero, the greatest warrior on the Trojan side, Hector is

respected even by his enemies. Hector is married to Andromache.

Ulysses
The wily Ulysses is one of the Greek commanders.

Achilles
The son of Peleus and Thetis, Achilles is the greatest of the Greek warriors but he is also an arrogant and vicious thug who sulks in his tent whenever he feels he has been slighted. This is not Homer's Achilles but Shakespeare's creation.

Patroclus
Achilles' young friend and (probably) lover, with a gift for mimicry.

Ajax
A brave warrior but stupid and easily outmatched by more cunning warriors.

Agamemnon
The Greek general and elder brother of Menelaus.

Menelaus
The King of Sparta, Menelaus is Agamemnon's brother and is married to Helen.

Helen
The most beautiful woman in the world, her seduction by Paris leads to the Trojan War.

Paris
The Prince of Troy who steals Helen from her husband, Menelaus.

Nestor
Greek commander; Nestor is too old to be a warrior but he is wise.

Thersites
A familiar 'clown' figure – found in several of Shakespeare's plays, for example Apemantus in *Timon of Athens* – he rails at the world and abuses all mankind.

The Plot
The Prologue announces that the play takes place when the Trojan War has been going on for seven years.

Prince Troilus tells Pandarus he cannot fight because he is desperately in love with Cressida, Pandarus' niece. But the Trojan commander, Aeneas, brings word that Paris has been wounded in combat with Menelaus, and Troilus is spurred to rejoin his Trojan comrades on the battlefield.

In another part of the city, Cressida is talking about how Ajax has managed to overcome the Trojan prince Hector, which has made Hector furious. Cressida's uncle, Pandarus, arrives and praises Troilus to the skies. Cressida enjoys being pursued by Troilus and deliberately plays hard to get.

In the Greek camp, the generals are arguing and discussing Achilles, who is refusing to fight and stays sulking in his tent. There comes a challenge from Hector to fight any Greek warrior. Wily Ulysses suggests putting up Ajax to fight him. If Ajax wins, it will annoy Achilles and spur him on to fight. If he fails, it will not be as disheartening for the army as if Achilles had been defeated.

Ajax summons his slave, the acerbic Thersites, and orders him to find out more about Hector's challenge. Thersites abuses his master and is beaten for his pains. Achilles passes by and claims to be the obvious warrior to challenge Hector; this evokes a sneer from Ajax.

In Troy, the generals consider handing over Helen to the Greeks and ending the war. Cassandra, who is doomed never to have her prophecies believed, says that if Helen remains in Troy the city will be burned. Troilus and Paris argue that Helen is well worth fighting a war over.

Agamemnon goes to see Achilles but Patroclus refuses him entry to the tent, saying Achilles is ill. The generals praise Ajax to annoy Achilles and announce that he will be the warrior to fight Hector. Pandarus unites Troilus and Cressida and urges them to embrace. The young lovers promise to be faithful to one another.

Meanwhile, Cressida's father, the priest Calchas, who has betrayed Troy to join the Greeks, asks Agamemnon if he will, as a favour, exchange his daughter for the Trojan commander Antenor. Agamemnon agrees and orders Diomedes to supervise the exchange.

On Ulysses' advice, the Greek warriors scorn Achilles in the hope of shaming him into rejoining the fight. Patroclus also advises his friend to rejoin the war in case people start calling him a coward.

Diomedes comes to Troy to take Cressida back to the Greek side to be with her father. The lovers say a sad farewell to each other. In the Greek camp, Ulysses insults Cressida, calling her a loose woman and a whore.

Ajax and Hector fight and then call a truce. Hector, unarmed, goes to meet the Greek commanders and Achilles says he will kill him the next day in battle. Thersites brings Achilles a letter from the Trojan princess he loves, asking him not to fight the next day.

Diomedes decides to have Cressida for himself. He woos her and her resistance is soon overcome. Troilus witnesses this scene and pledges to kill Diomedes. The next day Hector is getting ready for battle but his wife, Andromache, and his sister, Cassandra, beg him not to go as they have both had bad dreams. Even his old father, Priam, begs him not to fight. Hector takes no notice and determines to fight. Troilus, too, is determined to fight and tears up an unread letter from Cressida.

In the ensuing battle, Patroclus is killed. When Achilles sees his friend's body, he goes back to the battlefield to get his revenge. Achilles and his men find Hector, with his helmet off, and kill him. The Trojans are much dismayed and Troilus, entering the city to bring the bad news, meets Pandarus and curses him.

Titus Andronicus
Sources
The first mention of *Titus Andronicus* occurs in Henslowe's diary in December 1593. It was played at the London Playhouse, The Rose, by the Earl of Sussex's Men. There is a reference in the diary to a play called *Titus and Vespasian*, acted by Lord Strange's Men on 11 April 1592; some scholars believe this may be *Titus Andronicus* under an earlier name, but this is unlikely as Vespasian and his son Titus would suggest a very different story in a different period of Rome's history.

Though now regarded as crude and excessively violent, it was a popular play for at least twenty years after it was written. Shakespeare was probably trying to rival Thomas Kyd's highly successful revenge tragedy, *The Spanish Tragedy* (1592), which in turn was inspired by Seneca's gruesome tragedies such as *Thyestes*, which Shakespeare knew. He would also have known the popular legend of unhappy Philomela, which Ovid recounts in his *Metamorphoses*, though there were other versions of the tale.

In this story, Tereus King of Thrace ravishes his wife's sister Philomela and tears out her tongue to prevent her telling anyone what he has done. Dumb she may be, but Philomela tells her story anyway by means of embroidery on a garment. Her sister takes revenge by killing (and cooking) the son she had by Tereus, and tricking him into eating his child. Philomela is turned into a nightingale and her sister into a swallow.

Main Characters
Titus Andronicus
A Roman general and the father of Lavinia and Lucius.

Titus has spent the last ten years fighting Rome's enemies and winning honour for himself and his country. He is so exhausted by war that he rejects the chance of becoming emperor and is at first respected for his self-restraint. However, like Lear, he leaves a vacuum of power that leads to bloody civil strife.

Saturninus
The eldest son of the last emperor, Saturninus is recommended by Titus to be emperor instead of himself. He shows no gratitude and would rather have Titus dead than be a living example to the people of how an emperor should behave.

Lavinia
She spurns Saturninus' offer to become empress as she is in love with Bassianus. She is raped and mutilated by Chiron and Demetrius. Mute, she haunts the stage and witnesses her father's revenge.

Lucius
Titus' son, he defends his sister when her father is furious that she has run away with Bassianus.

Bassianus
Saturninus' younger brother. He is betrothed to Lavinia and runs off with her when Saturninus tries to take her from him. He is murdered by Chiron and Demetrius.

Tamora
Queen of the Goths, mother of Chiron and Demetrius, she shows herself to be a caring mother who comprehends what it means to be merciful, but chooses to be savage and lascivious. She encourages her sons to rape Lavinia and says she does not know the meaning of pity.

Aaron
Tamora's Moorish lover, Aaron, like Iago, is the epitome of villainy. He is evil personified except in his love for his child.

Chiron and Demetrius
Sons of the Goth queen Tamora, they lust after Lavinia and personify depravity. They are killed by Titus, who feeds their corpses to their mother.

Marcus Andronicus
A Roman tribune, Titus' brother represents sanity and offers an alternative to madness and depravity.

The Plot
When the Roman Emperor dies, the people elect the victorious general, Titus Andronicus, to succeed him, to the dismay of the former Emperor's sons, Saturninus and Bassianus. Titus enters with four living sons and two in coffins. He also brings with him his captives: Tamora, queen of the Goths, her three sons and Aaron the Moor. Despite Tamora's pleas, Titus demands the ritual killing of Tamora's eldest son in exchange for his dead offspring.

Titus refuses to become emperor and says Saturninus should take the throne. Saturninus returns the compliment by claiming Lavinia, Titus' daughter for his empress. But Lavinia is in love with Bassianus, who spirits her away with the aid of Lavinia's brothers.

Publicly humiliated, Saturninus decides to make Tamora his empress. Her sons, Chiron and Demetrius lust after Lavinia and Aaron incites them to rape her. Bassianus and Lavinia find Tamora in the forest with her lover Aaron and insult her. Chiron and Demetrius kill Bassianus and rape and mutilate Lavinia. Aaron frames Titus' sons Quintus and Martius for Bassianus' murder and Saturninus executes them despite Titus' pleas.

Lavinia's uncle, Marcus, discovers her and laments over her

mutilation and brings her to her father. Aaron tricks Titus into cutting off one of his hands. Lucius, his son, leaves to raise an army among the Goths. Lavinia writes in the sand, using a staff held in her mouth, the names of Chiron and Demetrius.

Lucius, at the head of a Goth army, finds Aaron the Moor. He also captures Aaron and Queen Tamora's child, intending to hang the child and then the father. Aaron takes delight in confessing all his evil deeds and Lucius says hanging is too good for him. Meanwhile, Titus murders Tamora's sons Chiron and Demetrius and bakes them in a pie, which he will serve at a banquet for Tamora. Titus kills Lavinia to put her out of her misery. Titus kills the empress, Saturninus kills Titus and Lucius kills Saturninus.

Julius Caesar
Sources
Written in 1599, *The Tragedy of Julius Caesar* was first printed in the First Folio (1623). The story of Julius Caesar and his assassination was well known in Shakespeare's time, but his main source would have been Sir Thomas North's translation of Plutarch's *Lives of the Noble Grecians and Romans*. Plutarch was a Greek philosopher (born AD 46) whose *Lives* were psychological studies of great men written for readers who would already have known the basic history. These moral studies inspired Shakespeare to dramatize events through the personalities and indirectly comment on contemporary politics. (Many people feared that when Queen Elizabeth died, there would be civil war.)

Main Characters
Julius Caesar
Born in 100 BC. The play opens in 44 BC and Julius Caesar is all but emperor of Rome. A victorious general, he is arrogant enough to ignore ill omens and is tempted to accept the mob's offer of a crown. His only flaw seems to be that he is an epileptic.

Calpurnia
Caesar's wife, Calpurnia warns Caesar that she has dreamed his life is in danger, but he ignores her.

Marcus Brutus
Brutus admires Caesar as a man but fears he will become a dictator and betray the republic. His sense of honour makes him easy to manipulate and Caesar's enemies are able to make him the respectable figurehead of their conspiracy.

Portia
Brutus' wife, the daughter of a noble Roman, Portia demands to be taken into her husband's confidence and wounds herself to prove her worthiness. She eventually kills herself when it looks as though her husband will be defeated by Antony and Octavius.

Cassius
A talented general and friend of Caesar, Cassius is the true leader of the conspiracy. Wily and courageous, he lacks integrity and is defeated by Antony.

Casca
Another leading conspirator, Casca hates Caesar for his arrogance.

Antony (Marcus Antonius)
Caesar's much-loved friend, who, to save his own life, pretends not to blame Brutus and Cassius when they kill Caesar but cleverly sways the crowd against the conspirators.

Octavius
Caesar's adopted son, Octavius returns to Rome shortly after Caesar's assassination and joins with Antony against the conspirators. Cold, authoritative and efficient, he will become emperor.

Lepidus
After the civil war has been won, Antony, Octavius and Lepidus rule as a triumvirate, but Antony does not rate the latter worthy of the honour and he is soon dispensed with.

Cicero
Cassius would have liked to have recruited Cicero, a Roman senator famous for his oratorical skills, but Brutus forbids it, perhaps fearing for his own position as head of the conspiracy.

The Plot
After a pun-filled opening scene in which the instability of the Roman mob is established, Caesar enters. There is to be a ceremonial race through the city in which Antony is to take part, and Caesar asks him to touch his wife Calpurnia as he runs because legend suggests it will make her fertile. A soothsayer in the crowd shouts a warning to Caesar to beware the Ides of March (the 15th of March). Caesar talks to the soothsayer but dismisses his warning.

Cassius persuades Brutus to lead a conspiracy against Caesar, who they fear will become a tyrant. Cassius recalls that even Caesar is not perfect; he is subject to epileptic fits. Caesar returns and comments, when he catches sight of Cassius, that he distrusts thin men.

Brutus and Cassius ask Casca what happened when the crowd urged Caesar to take the crown. Casca says Caesar rejected the crown but reluctantly and then had some sort of fit. He adds that Cicero spoke but he could not understand what he said: 'it was Greek to me'.

The weather is stormy, presaging political unrest, and Cassius arranges for letters to be thrown into Brutus' windows urging him to rebel against tyranny. In the middle of the night the conspirators come to Brutus' house and discuss what must be done. Brutus refuses to let them kill Antony (which proves to be a mistake) and tells them not to try to recruit Cicero.

Brutus' wife Portia challenges her husband to tell her what is planned but he refuses, even when she shows she is brave enough to wound herself and not betray her pain. The next morning, Caesar's wife Calpurnia tries to persuade her husband not to go to the Senate as she has had a bad dream about it – involving fountains of blood. One of the conspirators, Decius, arrives to make sure Caesar does go to the Senate. Decius says Calpurnia's dream is not to be feared but portends great things – and says Caesar is again to be offered a crown.

In the street, the soothsayer once again tries to warn Caesar, but Caesar refuses to read his letter listing the conspirators. In the Senate, another of the conspirators, Metellus Cimber, asks that Caesar will pardon his brother who has been exiled, but Caesar refuses. The conspirators stab Caesar, who is most hurt by Brutus' dagger. 'Et tu, Brute?' he asks reproachfully.

The conspirators try to explain to the crowd that they have liberated Rome from tyranny. Foolishly Brutus gives Antony leave to speak over Caesar's coffin and he rouses the people against the conspirators who have to flee the city.

Antony joins with Octavius, Caesar's adopted son, and the wealthy Lepidus to fight the conspirators. There is to be civil war.

In his tent before battle, Brutus upbraids Cassius for taking bribes and the two men quarrel. But Brutus lets slip that he has heard his wife has committed suicide; Cassius immediately forgives his friends for insulting him and the two proud men make peace. Brutus, as usual making the wrong decision, over-rides Cassius' forebodings and says the armies should march to Philippi. Brutus dreams of meeting Caesar's ghost, who tells him they will meet again at Philippi.

Owing to a misunderstanding during the battle, Cassius believes they are defeated and kills himself. Brutus mourns his friend's death and then kills himself. The victorious Antony and Octavius arrive and Antony calls Brutus 'the noblest Roman of them all'.

Antony and Cleopatra
Sources
The Tragedy of Antony and Cleopatra was written in 1607 or 1608. It was printed first in 1623. As usual Shakespeare used North's translation of Plutarch's *Lives* as his source. Plutarch's 'Life of Marcus Antonius' gave him all the facts and the basis for many of the speeches, including the famous description of Antony's first sight of Cleopatra on her barge.

The play begins four years after the demise of Julius Caesar and covers a ten-year period. The Roman Empire is now ruled by Antony in the East and Octavius in the West. Written after *Macbeth* and *King Lear*, the play's many brief scenes demand a fluid production; this shows Shakespeare's mastery of his art. As he had warned his audience at the beginning of *Henry V*, they had to use their imagination and not be circumscribed by the physical stage on which world events were being portrayed.

Main Characters
Antony
The once feared soldier, friend of the great Julius Caesar, is now in thrall to Queen Cleopatra, in whose scented, silken bonds he seems entrapped. He knows his duty but prefers to ignore it.

Enobarbus
Antony's most loyal supporter until his final betrayal, he recognizes his master's weakness but forgives him as he, too, is in thrall to Cleopatra (he describes her beauty in ecstatic terms).

Cleopatra
The Queen of Egypt and Antony's lover, as she had once been Julius Caesar's. She is Greek, not Egyptian, and she is volatile, seductive and theatrical. She kills herself on 29 August in 30 BC.

Charmian and Iras
Cleopatra's attendants, who die alongside her.

Octavia
Octavius Caesar's sister, given by Octavius to Antony as wife
to seal their treaty, she is quickly abandoned in favour of
Cleopatra. In her meekness and purity, she returns to Octavius
humiliated. She dies in 11 BC.

Octavius Caesar
The nephew and adopted son of Caesar, Octavius rules the
empire with Lepidus and Antony. Coldly efficient, his relations with Antony are always strained as he feels Antony is
neglecting his duty by staying with Cleopatra. Destined to be
the first, and perhaps greatest, Roman Emperor, he symbolizes
Western values against the lures of the exotic East.

Marcus Aemilius Lepidus
The third and weakest member of the triumvirate, he tries to
keep the peace between Antony and Octavius.

Pompey
Born in 106 BC, Pompey is the son of a great general and is
popular with the Roman people, posing a threat to Antony and
Octavius. He has the opportunity to murder both of them
when they feast on his ship but is too honourable to do so. He
dies in 48 BC.

The Plot
Cleopatra is imploring Antony to tell her again how much he
loves her. A messenger from Rome arrives, but Antony is
reluctant to hear him. Cleopatra tells him he should, but he
ignores the advice and his soldiers are shocked by his disrespect for Rome.

Cleopatra and her handmaids ask a fortune-teller to predict
their future. Charmian and Iras are told they will outlive the

queen they serve. Cleopatra sends for Antony but then runs away, playing hard to get. Antony is chided by Rome's messenger for lying abed in Egypt while Octavius has to defeat a rebel army on his own. Another messenger arrives and gives Antony news that his wife Fulvia is dead. Antony feels guilty. He has long wanted her dead but now regrets her death. Enobarbus tries to comfort him. Antony decides he must break with Cleopatra and go back to Rome. Cleopatra tries every trick – such as pretending to be ill – to keep Antony with her.

In Rome, Octavius is complaining to Lepidus about Antony and Lepidus tries to defend him. Cleopatra is missing Antony, but he sends her a pearl by messenger as a token of his love. Cleopatra asks the messenger whether he left Antony happy or sad – either would be wrong.

Pompey discusses the military situation with his lieutenants. He is amazed to hear that Antony has escaped Cleopatra and gone to Rome. Pompey will now have to face Antony and Octavius.

In Rome, Antony and Octavius quarrel over old insults and misunderstandings. They make peace and Antony agrees to marry Octavius' sister, the pure Octavia. When they are gone, Enobarbus describes Cleopatra to Octavius' officers: 'Age cannot wither her …'

Antony promises Octavia that he will behave now he has married her, but his protestations do not ring true.

A messenger arrives and tells Cleopatra that Antony is married to Octavia. Cleopatra is predictably upset and asks the messenger for a full description of her rival. Antony, Lepidus and Octavius make peace with Pompey and feast on his boat. Pompey is tempted to have his enemies murdered but resists as it would be dishonourable to kill his guests.

Cleopatra hears from her messenger that Octavia is old and not beautiful and therefore unlikely to keep Antony faithful.

Antony complains to Octavia that since he has left Octavius, he has made war on Pompey and killed him. He has also got rid of Lepidus. Octavia does not know whom she should support: her brother or her husband. He uses this as an excuse to send her to Rome to make peace with Octavius – and to be rid of her.

Octavius takes it as an insult when his sister arrives in Rome without a proper escort and prepares for war with Antony. Cleopatra persuades Antony to fight a battle with Octavius on the sea, which all his generals think is a thoroughly bad idea. Antony is winning the sea battle but then Cleopatra and her ships abandon the battle and Antony is defeated. Antony is ashamed of himself, but despite being betrayed by Cleopatra, he still loves her.

Antony sues for peace but Octavius will have none of it. Cleopatra is tempted to betray Antony and accept an offer of mercy from Octavius. Enobarbus decides the time has come to leave Antony; he is shamed when Antony, far from blaming him, sends his belongings after him.

Unexpectedly, Antony wins a land battle against Octavius and celebrates well into the night. Antony then loses another sea fight when Cleopatra's navy defects to Caesar. Antony is furious with Cleopatra and the Queen locks herself in her monument and sends word she is dead. Antony is heartbroken and ceases to think of fighting. He falls on his sword but fails to kill himself. Antony hears Cleopatra is, in fact, alive and he is taken to her monument. There he is lifted up to join her, and dies.

Cleopatra wants to know how the victorious Octavius will treat her. She fears she will be taken to Rome and paraded as Octavius' captive. Cleopatra tries to do a deal with Octavius but does not believe he will treat her with dignity. Dressed in her fine royal garments, she presses a poisonous asp to her bosom and dies. Her handmaidens follow suit.

Coriolanus
Sources
First published in 1623, *Coriolanus* may have been written

between 1607 and 1609 – there are a few possibly topical references to events in these years – but there is no real evidence to
indicate precisely when the play was written. There are no
contemporary references to it in diaries of the period.

Coriolanus is set not in Rome of the first century AD, as was
Julius Caesar and *Antony and Cleopatra*, but more than two
centuries earlier, when Rome was just one Italian city state
among many fighting for survival. The story is set after the fall
of Tarquin, the last king of Rome, and records the struggle
between plebeians and patricians during Rome's transition
from monarchy to republic.

Once again Shakespeare found the story in Plutarch's *Lives*
– that of Caius Martius Coriolanus, written in the first decade
AD and translated by Sir Thomas North in 1579. Plutarch
describes Coriolanus as proud, choleric and impatient, and
Shakespeare was happy to elaborate on this. Many speeches in
the play are close to Plutarch (as translated by North); for
instance, where the ladies of Rome make their final and
successful appeal to Coriolanus to spare Rome.

The play has often been performed at moments of political
tension when a 'strong man' threatens to take over the state.

Main Characters
Caius Martius
Roman general Caius Martius is given the name 'Coriolanus'
after he leads the Roman armies to victory against the Volscian
city of Corioli. Brave, honourable and a successful leader of
men in time of war, in peacetime he is too impatient, arrogant
and inflexible to be popular. He is stubbornly aristocratic and
despises the plebeians. He is exiled and returns with a Volscian
army to revenge himself on ungrateful Rome.

Volumnia
Caius Martius' mother, Volumnia, is devoted to her son and
attempts to make him bow his knee to the plebeians in order to
gain political power. She is proud of his wounds won in battle

and, in turn, is the only person whom Caius Martius respects.

Virgilia
Virgilia is Caius Martius' loyal wife, but he rather despises her for being afraid he will be killed in battle and leave her a widow. Volumnia also despises her 'weakness', but Virgilia has no interest in Caius Martius' political career, only in his role as a man and the father of her son Martius.

Menenius
A Roman nobleman and Caius Martius' old friend and loyal supporter, Menenius is a wise and shrewd politician but even he cannot make Martius behave politely to the mob.

Brutus
Brutus is elected – along with Sicinius – as one of the people's tribunes to serve as their representative in government. He sees Martius as the enemy of the people, but when the Volscians threaten, he recognizes Martius' worth as a soldier.

Tullus Aufidius
Aufidius is the Volscian general – Martius' great rival in war but his friend when Martius is exiled from Rome. He hopes Martius will help him destroy Rome, but in the end Martius betrays him and, at his mother's pleading, spares the city.

The Plot
In Rome, the common people – the plebeians – are rioting against their rulers, accusing the Senate of hoarding grain while they starve. In particular, they blame Caius Martius, a general and a nobleman who they see as an enemy of the people. The mob meet Menenius, a patrician and a friend of Caius Martius, who tells them the Senate has their best interests at heart. He compares the Senate to the stomach, which stores food and dispenses it to the rest of the body as it is needed.

Caius Martius himself appears and curses the mob. He

mentions that the Senate is permitting the plebs to elect five tribunes to act as their representatives and look after their interests. News comes that a Volscian army is preparing to attack Rome and it is led by the Volscian general Tullus Aufidius. Caius Martius hopes this threat will drum some sense into the plebeians.

Aufidius is about to leave the Volscian city of Corioli to march on Rome. The Volscian senators say Aufidius can always return to Corioli if the Romans threaten it.

In Rome, Volumnia, Caius Martius' mother, is saying she would rather her son be a great warrior and get honourable wounds than be embraced by her husband. Valeria, a noble friend of Volumnia's, brings news that while one army is going out from Rome to meet the Volscian army, Caius Martius is leading another to attack the city of Corioli.

At Corioli, the Romans are driven back by the city's defenders, but Caius Martius leads another attack in which he is cut off from his troops by the enemy. Trapped within Corioli, he manages to reach the city gates and open them so that the Roman army can enter and take the city.

Still bleeding from his battle wounds, Martius takes part of his army to aid Cominius, who is retreating before Aufidius and the Volscian army. Martius briefly engages Aufidius in single combat. The Volscians are defeated. Martius refuses to take any of the spoil of the city and is hailed 'Coriolanus' for his part in winning the war.

In Rome, Volumnia speaks proudly of her son's victory and prepares to welcome him – now called Coriolanus – with the Senate at the Capitol.

The tribunes of the people fear Coriolanus will now be made consul, but before that can happen he has to go through the ritual of showing his wounds to the people and begging their support; the tribunes know he is too proud to do this.

Later, in the marketplace, Coriolanus shows his wounds to the people and, though they think him arrogant, they believe he deserves to be made consul. Brutus and Sicinius, the tribunes, demand to know why the plebeians voted to make Coriolanus consul; they urge them to go to the Senate and say they have changed their mind. Coriolanus is furious and refuses to return to the market place and beg the people's pardon for his arrogance. He draws his sword against the people.

His mother pleads with him to be less openly contemptuous of the people, but he cannot do it and he is banished from Rome. Outside the city gates he says goodbye to his wife and mother and swears to have his revenge. He takes refuge with his old enemy the Volscians and they welcome him, hoping that he will help them destroy Rome. Coriolanus and his Volscian army march on Rome; the people beg his wife and mother to ask him to spare the city.

Aufidius is getting jealous that Coriolanus is stealing his thunder. He taunts Coriolanus that he will betray them and submit to the pleas of his Roman friends not to attack Rome. Coriolanus says he will see no more Roman embassies, but when his family arrive he cannot resist their prayers. Aufidius, furious at this betrayal, encourages the Roman people to turn on Coriolanus and he is stabbed to death. The Senate orders a hero's funeral, and a remorseful Aufidius helps to carry Coriolanus' body through the city.

THE COMEDIES

Comedy is the leading principle of Shakespeare's art and the natural expression of his imagination. Every one of his plays has a comic scene, even the most tragic or romantic of them; consider the musings of the porter in *Macbeth* and the exploits of Trinculo in *The Tempest*. Tragic matters, in particular, can evoke low and farcical conclusions. His comedy is as various as his genius, from the linguistic allusiveness of *Love's Labour's Lost* to the broad comedy of a transvestite Falstaff in *The Merry Wives of Windsor*.

Any of Shakespeare's plays with a happy ending is, strictly speaking, a comedy. They range from light-hearted farces such as *The Comedy of Errors* through subtle celebrations of love and lust such as *A Midsummer Night's Dream* to painful and enigmatic investigations into the meaning of virtue, love and faithfulness such as *Measure for Measure*.

Shakespeare would have seen his women played by boys and he particularly delighted in ambiguous sexuality. His girls, played by boys, disguise themselves as boys to woo their men before revealing themselves to be women. Often he draws his characters out of the real world into forests or woods, where

they can confront their true, animal selves and explore their
sexuality. Most dramatically, in *A Midsummer Night's Dream*,
the young lovers lose themselves in the woods, mingle with
fairies and are bewitched. A plain, honest citizen is transformed
into an animal and is made love to by the queen of the fairies.
Confusion reigns and the world is turned upside down before
wrongs are righted and order restored.

In *Twelfth Night*, Shakespeare makes fun of a steward who
presumes to love above his station: his own mistress – something
quite out of place in an ordered universe. In *Measure for Measure*,
a girl refuses to give up her virginity to save the life of her brother.
Love and lust are what make us human, but deciding which is
which is a struggle and there may not be a right answer.

As in the history plays, Shakespeare insists that there is a
natural order in which everything has its place, but sometimes
order has to descend into anarchy before it becomes apparent
who should be paired with whom.

The Comedy of Errors
Sources
The play is first mentioned in an account of revels held by the
law students at Gray's Inn during the Christmas holidays of
1594-95. This account, known as *Gesta Grayorum*, was not
published until 1688. The play's existence is also mentioned by
Francis Meres in his *Palladis Tamia* in 1598.

It is thought to have been written in 1592 or 1593 because
there are references in the play to events of those years, for
example the capture of a rich Spanish galleon sailing back from
South America laden with silver and a huge amount of pepper
(see Act III, Scene 2).

The Comedy of Errors is a version of a Roman comedy by
Plautus called *The Menechmus Twins*. Shakespeare took the
idea of the twins from Plautus, as well as the shrill-voiced wife,
the doctor, the courtesan and much else. However, equally as
important as Plautus is the influence of the Italian romances,
with which Shakespeare was very familiar. There is evidence of

the Italian influence in names like Angelo, and in Ephesus having an abbess sound more Italian than Greek, while twins being mistaken for each other was a device often used on the Italian stage.

Main Characters
The Brothers Antipholus
Identical twins, separated in a shipwreck – one lives with his father in Syracuse, the other in Ephesus.

The Brothers Dromio
Identical twins, servants of the Antipholus twins.

Aegeon
Father of the Antipholus twins.

Adriana
Wife to Antipholus of Ephesus.

Luciana
Adriana's sister, with whom the Syracuse Antipholus falls in love.

Abbess Aemelia
The abbess at Ephesus who shelters Antipholus.

Pinch
The doctor or magician who declares Antipholus mad.

The Plot
A merchant from Syracuse arrives at Ephesus. Since the two cities are at war with one another, the merchant, Aegeon, is condemned to death unless he can come up with a large sum of money by dusk.

Aegeon is the father of identical twins who themselves had twin servants. There is a shipwreck and the twins are parted.

Aegeon now has only one of the twins, Antipholus, and when he grows up Antipholus goes in search of his twin. He never returns to his father and so eventually Aegeon goes in search of Antipholus. He has had no luck and is now exhausted and despairing.

Antipholus is sightseeing in the marketplace in Ephesus. He sends his servant Dromio back to the inn with a bag of gold. Dromio returns momentarily – except that it is not Dromio but his twin, the servant of Antipholus' 'lost' brother who happens also to be called Antipholus. This 'lost' twin has been living in Ephesus for many years and is married to Adriana, who has a sister called Luciana. Their servant is calling his master home for dinner and, inevitably, thinks he has found his master and Antipholus thinks this is his servant. They have a confused conversation about gold and coming home to dinner.

Antipholus discovers his gold is safe and his servant is denying ever having had that conversation about going home to dinner. Adriana and Luciana find them, and Adriana believes they have found her errant husband. Confused, Antipholus decides he might as well accept this strange invitation to dinner with people he does not know and he and his servant Dromio go 'home' with the ladies. When Adriana's real husband, accompanied by a friend, returns for his dinner he is refused entrance. This Antipholus thinks he will have his revenge by having dinner with a courtesan and he will give her the gold chain he was going to give his wife.

In the house, Antipholus is falling in love with Luciana, but she is shocked to be made love to by – so she thinks – her brother-in-law. Dromio is having a similar sort of problem in the kitchen with the maid.

Totally confused, Antipholus decides to leave this strange city where people ask him to dinner and act as if he is married to them. He tells Dromio to find him a boat so that they can leave Ephesus. He is given a gold chain by a goldsmith and assumes it is just another strange thing in this mad city. When the goldsmith tries to get paid for the chain, he goes to the other Antipholus who says he has never had the chain. The goldsmith has him arrested. Antipholus sends his servant to get money from his house, which he does but brings it to the 'wrong' Antipholus.

Antipholus is visited in jail by his wife and sister, the courtesan – who has not had the gold chain she has been promised – and a magician called Pinch. They agree Antipholus and his servant are mad and Pinch takes them off to the asylum.

The other Antipholus – trying to escape Ephesus – gets into a fight and has to take refuge with an abbess. The Duke, who is passing the abbey, hears all about it and soon the 'mad' Antipholus arrives, having escaped from Pinch, and makes his complaint to the Duke. Then the abbess brings out her Antipholus and the two brothers have a joyful reunion.

The Taming of the Shrew
Sources
A play called *The Taming of a Shrew* was entered in the Stationers' Register on 2 May 1594 and performed by the Lord Admiral's Men and the Lord Chamberlain's Men, briefly amalgamated, in June 1594. This may not have been Shakespeare's play – the names of the characters are different – but the plot is very similar. It could be a pirated edition of Shakespeare's play, though usually pirated editions of the plays have the same character names as the originals.

The Taming of the Shrew was published in the First Folio of 1623 and the style is that of Shakespeare's earlier work. Shakespeare's play includes references to villages in Warwickshire, while the alternative 'pirated' version is set in Athens.

There are no obvious sources for *The Taming of the Shrew* though certain scenes are reminiscent of other works. There is, for example, an Italian play called *Il Suppositi* translated by George Gascoigne as *The Supposes* and performed in 1566. This features a man changing places with his servant and wooing a girl, as Bianca is wooed in *The Taming of the Shrew*, but it is not so uncommon a device that Shakespeare might not have found it elsewhere. There are many references to strong-willed women in Elizabethan writing – for instance *A Merry Jeste of a Shrewde and Curste Wyfe* (1550) – and the device of having a play within a play was not uncommon (Kyd's *The Spanish Tragedy* is introduced in this way). It is a way of making clear that this is not a 'realistic' play but a male fantasy.

Main Characters
Katharina
Katharina or Kate, the shrew of the title. She is the elder daughter of Baptista Minola and lives with him in Padua. She is too sharp-tongued and quick-tempered to find a husband – until she meets Petruchio.

Petruchio
A rich man from Verona, Petruchio is loud, boisterous, quick-witted and frequently drunk. He wants to find a rich wife and does not care if that means putting up with a shrew.

Bianca
Kate's younger sister and her opposite in character, being sweet and good-tempered. Several men woo her but her father refuses to let her marry until her sister is married.

Baptista
One of the wealthiest men in Pisa, Baptista is good-natured but determined to get his daughter Kate off his hands.

Lucentio
A young student from Pisa who falls in love with Bianca. He disguises himself as a teacher to get near her, but this gives him problems when his father, Vincentio, visits Padua.

Tranio
Lucentio's servant, who takes his master's place when Lucentio assumes his disguise.

Gremio and Hortensio
Two gentlemen of Padua, suitors for Bianca's hand in marriage. Hortensio pretends to be a music teacher in order to woo Bianca.

Grumio
Petruchio's servant, the 'fool' of the play who provides comic relief.

The Plot

Christopher Sly, a drunken beggar, is having a row with the hostess of an alehouse. When she leaves him, he falls into a drunken stupor. He is found by a nobleman returning from the hunt who decides to have some fun with him. He wants to discover if circumstances make the man. Sly will be treated as a lord. Served fine wine and rich food by the nobleman's servants, will Sly behave like a lord?

When Sly wakes he cannot understand what has happened to him: a poor tinker being treated as if he were important. The servants tell him he has lost his memory but is now recovered. They show him his 'wife' – a page dressed in woman's clothes – and Sly is convinced he really is a lord. A group of players act out a play for him and this is where *The Taming of the Shrew* really begins.

Lucentio arrives in Padua with his servant Tranio. A crowd gathers: it is Bianca and her father, Baptista, with Bianca's two suitors, Hortensio and Gremio, and Bianca's noisy sister, Katharina. Baptista says he will not allow Bianca to marry until his elder daughter Katharina is married, but everyone says she is such a shrew that no one will ever be as rash as to marry her, not even for her father's wealth. When Kate and Bianca and their father have left, Bianca's suitors discuss how they can find Kate a husband.

Lucentio, who has been listening to all this, decides he is in love with Bianca, but to get close to her he will have to disguise himself as a schoolmaster – Baptista has mentioned he is looking for one to teach Bianca.

Petruchio has just arrived in Padua with his servant, and Gremio and Hortensio learn that he has come to look for a wife. Petruchio does not seem to mind when Hortensio calls Katharina a shrew. As long as she is rich, that is all that matters.

Tranio arrives dressed in his master's clothes, while Lucentio is accepted by Baptista to be his daughter's schoolmaster.

Next morning, Katharina is bullying Bianca. She has tied up her sister and is beating her, and she is annoyed with her father when he comes to break up the fight. Petruchio arrives and, blunt as always, asks Baptista for Katharina's hand in marriage. The two 'schoolmasters' start to ingratiate themselves with Bianca – Hortensio, disguised as a music master called Litio, and Lucentio, disguised as Cambio, an expert in classical languages.

Petruchio and Katharina engage in a lengthy verbal duel. When Baptista returns, Petruchio, to Katharina's amazement, says that they have already agreed to be married the next Sunday, but strangely she does not contradict him.

Tranio, dressed as his master, Lucentio now makes an offer for Bianca's hand and he outbids Gremio with fantasies of wealth. Baptista says he can marry Bianca if his father will guarantee his wealth.

Lucentio and Hortensio in their schoolmaster disguises are pretending to teach Bianca but are actually wooing her. Lucentio has the best of it. Later, Tranio informs his master that he needs to find a father for him and perhaps it would be better if he simply eloped with Bianca.

The next day is the wedding but the groom, Petruchio, is late and Baptista and Kate are worried. At last Petruchio turns up, not in his wedding finery but in old clothes, riding a diseased old horse. The wedding is a farce. Petruchio swears at the altar and knocks down the priest, but somehow the marriage is completed and Petruchio announces he is not waiting for any celebrations but will take his wife off straightaway. Kate has a terrible journey to Petruchio's house and then is not fed or allowed to rest. Hungry and exhausted, Kate is taken by Petruchio to the tailor to be fitted out with fine clothes, but predictably Petruchio finds fault with everything and will not let her have what she wants. Petruchio says they will go back to her father's house, she still in her old clothes.

Meanwhile, Lucentio is progressing well with Bianca and they have found a man who will pretend to be Lucentio's father.

On their way back to Padua, Petruchio makes absurd remarks and makes his wife agree with him that the moon is really the sun and so forth.

Just as Lucentio is about to marry Bianca, his real father, Vincentio, turns up and there is a misunderstanding with the man Lucentio has hired to pretend to be his father. Vincentio is arrested. He is saved when Lucentio and Bianca return from the church where they have been married. Lucentio has to admit his little deception but is forgiven by his father and by Baptista, his father-in-law.

Petruchio, to prove Katharina is really tamed, makes her kiss him in the middle of the street.

There is a rowdy feast. The men still believe Petruchio has been landed with a shrew, so Petruchio suggests a test. Each man sends for his wife and each man finds his wife unbiddable. Only Kate comes at Petruchio's bidding and she is sent to bring back the other wives. In front of them, Kate makes a speech of subservience, saying a wife owes her husband the duty a subject owes his prince.

The Two Gentlemen of Verona
Sources
The Two Gentlemen of Verona was first printed in the First Folio of 1623. It is one of the twelve plays listed by Francis Meres in his Palladis Tamia in 1598. It is thought Marlowe alludes to the play in his poem 'Hero and Leander', which was unfinished at his death in May 1593; the language and style of the play suggests it may have been written in that year. Shakespeare was influenced by the work of John Lyly. In

Euphues, Lyly makes his hero fall in love with Lucilla, his friend's betrothed, but, unlike Silvia in Shakespeare's play, Lucilla returns his love.

Shakespeare also owed a debt to the Portuguese writer Jorge de Montemayor, whose *La Diana Enamorada* is similar in plot to *The Two Gentlemen of Verona* but ends less happily. The Portuguese play was translated into English and performed at court in 1585. Debates on romantic love had long been the subject of literary works by Geoffrey Chaucer and Francis Bacon, among others.

Main Characters
Proteus
One of the two gentlemen of Verona and supposedly Valentine's best friend. He is Julia's sweetheart at the beginning of the play, but when he joins Valentine at the Duke's palace, he falls in love with Silvia and attempts to steal her from Valentine.

Valentine
The second of the two gentlemen, Valentine is Proteus' best friend and Silvia's lover. Banished to the forest after Proteus betrays to the Duke his plan to elope with Silvia, Valentine becomes king of the outlaws.

Julia
Proteus' beloved and mistress to the servant Lucetta. Desiring to travel to Milan to visit Proteus, Julia disguises herself as a boy in order to avoid lecherous advances along the way. Calling herself Sebastian, she does Proteus' bidding, delivering the ring she had earlier been given by him to his new beloved, Silvia.

Duke of Milan
Silvia's father, who wants her to marry the boorish but wealthy Sir Thurio. The Duke banishes Valentine when he hears of his plan to elope with Silvia.

Lucetta
Julia's servant, who considers love from a practical point of view.

Launce
Proteus' comic servant, with a poorly trained dog called Crab. He falls in love with an ugly but wealthy maid.

Speed
Valentine's page, Speed is a friend of Launce.

Thurio
Thurio is Valentine's foolish rival, rich but unpleasant.

Sir Eglamour
The gentleman upon whom Silvia calls to help her escape from the Duke's court.

The Plot

Valentine bids an emotional farewell to his dear friend Proteus, explaining that he must leave Verona for Milan to broaden his horizons and educate himself. Proteus responds that his passion for Julia keeps him in Verona. Valentine leaves, upbraiding him for being a fool for love. Speed, Valentine's clownish servant, enters and Proteus asks him if he delivered his letter to Julia and what was her reaction. Speed says she made no reaction and did not even give him a tip.

Julia is discussing love with her servant Lucetta. She lists all her suitors and asks Lucetta to choose who she thinks would be the best lover. She chooses Proteus and confesses to pretending to be Julia and accepting a love letter from him – the one delivered by Speed. They quarrel and Lucetta tears up the letter. Julia is reduced to reading words of love on the scraps of paper she has left behind.

Proteus' father, Antonio, decides to send his son to the emperor's court in Milan. He wants to give the good news to his son and finds him reading a letter from Julia saying she returns his love. Foolishly, instead of showing his father Julia's letter, he lies and says it is from Valentine and Antonio gives him the good news he is going to join him in Milan. Proteus is upset and wishes he had showed his father Julia's letter.

In Milan, Speed shocks his master, Valentine, by revealing that he knows he is in love with Silvia. Silvia and Valentine have a misunderstanding about a love letter.

Proteus and Julia part after exchanging rings. Launce, Proteus' servant, and his dog Crab have a comic scene together.

Silvia enjoys seeing two of her suitors – Valentine and the boorish Thurio – squabble over her. Proteus arrives and Valentine introduces him to Silvia, later admitting he has fallen in love with her and they plan to elope. Proteus, too, has fallen in love with the beautiful Silvia and forgotten his sweetheart Julia. He decides to betray both Julia and his friend by informing the Duke – Silvia's father – of their intended elopement.

Back in Verona, Julia plans to follow Proteus to Milan, disguised as a boy and calling herself Sebastian.

The Duke discovers Valentine with a rope ladder on his way to elope with Silvia and, in a rage, banishes him. The Duke asks the treacherous Proteus to help get his daughter married to Thurio.

Valentine, banished from Milan, meets a band of outlaws and tells them the tale of his lost love. They beg him to become their leader and he agrees.

In Milan, Proteus tricks Thurio and woos Silvia for himself, but she is not impressed and calls him false and disloyal. Julia overhears all this and is distressed. Silvia calls on Sir Eglamour to help her escape from Thurio and Proteus. Proteus meets Julia, now dressed like a boy and calling herself Sebastian; he does not recognize her but likes her. Proteus asks 'Sebastian' to deliver Julia's ring to his new love, Silvia, which she does. Silvia dislikes Proteus and is intrigued to hear from 'Sebastian' how he has wronged Julia.

The Duke announces that Silvia has disappeared and they all go off to search for her. Silvia is captured by the brigands and Sir Eglamour deserts her.

Proteus rescues Silvia from the outlaws; Valentine, hidden in the forest, overhears Proteus beg Silvia to return his love. She refuses. When Proteus tries to rape her, Valentine reveals himself and curses him. Proteus begs for forgiveness. Valentine pardons him and generously offers him Silvia. Julia, still dressed as Sebastian, hears this and faints. Julia reveals her identity and Proteus is once again in love with her.

Thurio, the Duke and the outlaws arrive and Thurio admits he does not really love Silvia. Valentine marries Silvia, Proteus marries Julia and the outlaws are pardoned.

Love's Labour's Lost
Sources
A witty and erudite discourse on the nature of love. It is not known exactly when it was written, but it was certainly before 1598; scholars have come up with various dates between 1588 and 1596. The best guess seems to be that it was written for performance at Christmas 1593 when Shakespeare was twenty-nine, possibly for the entertainment of the Earl of Southampton and his guests. Southampton refused to marry, showing a disdain for hetero-sexual love, to the annoyance of his guardian, Lord Burghley.

Shakespeare took some of his characters' names, such as the Duc de Longueville, from those noblemen who had served in France with Henry of Navarre in 1591. The play also contains references to the School of Night, a group of intellectuals, including Sir Walter Raleigh and the playwrights Christopher Marlowe and George Chapman, who met in the early 1590s.

Main Characters
Ferdinand, King of Navarre
Referred to in the play simply as 'The King', he is a scholar who has sworn to sacrifice earthly pleasures – including women – in his pursuit of wisdom.

Berowne, Longueville, Dumaine
Three lords, friends of the King, who join with him in abjuring worldly delights but still manage to fall in love with Rosaline, Maria and Katharine.

The Princess of France
The Princess is not given a name. She pays a visit to the King and outwits him.

Rosaline, Maria, Katharine
Three attendants to the Princess of France.

Don Armado
'A fantastical Spaniard', Don Armado is a proud, swaggering, clownish figure with a strong sense of honour. He has a page called Moth and falls in love with a country wench called Jaquenetta.

Costard
A clown or fool, he causes chaos and utters the occasional snippet of wisdom.

Jaquenetta
A country wench.

Holofernes
A schoolmaster who Shakespeare uses to mock a certain kind of academic pedantry.

Sir Nathaniel
A curate.

Dull
A 'simple' constable.

Boyet
A honey-tongued diplomatist.

Mercade
The messenger of death – a figure in black.

The Plot
The King and his friends discuss setting up an academy, and they all swear that for three years they will turn their backs on worldly pleasures and devote themselves to learning. Berowne, one of the King's friends, is sceptical that they will be able to keep their oath – particularly in regard to giving up female company – but signs up anyway.

Costard, the clown, is condemned by the King to a week on bran and water for consorting with a country girl called Jaquenetta. Don Armado is Costard's accuser; he too is in love with Jaquenetta.

The Princess of France arrives at the King's court unexpectedly and the King tells her he has to lodge her and her attendants in a field so as not to break his oath. The King meets the Princess; and the King's friends fall in love with the Princess' attendants. Armado frees Costard and gives him a letter to take to Jaquenetta. Berowne also asks Costard to deliver a love letter – to Rosaline, the Princess' lady-in-waiting. Costard naturally delivers the letters to the wrong woman.

Jaquenetta asks Nathaniel and the schoolmaster, Holofernes, to read her letter aloud. They realize the letter is not for her.

Berowne has written a poem to Rosaline but he hides it when he hears the King coming; the King has also written a love poem but his is to the Princess. The King hears Longueville coming and he hides. Longueville, too, has a love poem and he, too, hides when Dumaine enters proclaiming his love for Katherine.

All reveal themselves and chide each other for breaking their oaths. Only Berowne, who was not overheard in his declaration of love, is able to pretend to have kept his oath. However,

Berowne is able to justify their falling in love by arguing that to look at a woman is to understand the meaning of beauty.

Holofernes and Nathaniel speak disparagingly of Don Armado's intellect. Armado enters and tells them he has been charged by the King to arrange some masque or pageant and asks for their help.

The Princess examines a jewel the King has given her; and her ladies confess to having had love tokens from the King's friends.

Boyet tells the Princess that the King and his companions, dressed as Muscovites, are coming to woo them. The Princess tells her ladies to veil themselves to confuse the men. They succeed in fooling the men and then mock the King and his friends for their disguises, which they have seen through.

The masque or play takes place. Costard, Don Armado, Holofernes and Nathaniel are mocked by the nobles and Holofernes reprimands them for being unkind. The merry-making is abruptly ended when Mercade enters to inform the Princess that her father, the King, is dead. The King and his friends are persuaded by the Princess to become hermits for a year and then seek their loves once more if they still feel the same way.

Don Armado asks the King's permission to sing a final song, which they do.

A Midsummer Night's Dream
Sources
The play was written in late 1594 or early 1595; there are references to the very bad summer of 1594. There is no record of early performances, but *A Midsummer Night's Dream* was entered in the Stationers' Register on 8 October 1600. However, there are so many references to wedding preparations in the play that it is likely it was written for a particular wedding, perhaps that of William Stanley, Earl of Derby, who married Lady Elizabeth Vere, Lord Burghley's granddaughter, on 26 January 1595.

The plot was Shakespeare's own, though he had Plutarch's

Life of Theseus to hand and perhaps Chaucer's 'The Knight's Tale' from *The Canterbury Tales*, the opening lines of which are reflected in the opening scene of *A Midsummer Night's Dream*, where Theseus is to marry the Amazon queen Hippolyta.

The play-within-a-play of Pyramus and Thisbe, two characters from Greek mythology, was well known. It is to be found in Ovid's *Metamorphoses*, Book IV, which had been translated by Arthur Golding in 1567. There are, of course, also echoes of Shakespeare's own comedies, *Love's Labour's Lost* and *The Two Gentlemen of Verona*.

Main Characters
Theseus
The heroic Duke of Athens who is to wed the Amazon queen Hippolyta. Appearing only at the beginning and end of the play, he represents order and good sense. The actor who plays Theseus often plays Oberon as well.

Hippolyta
The Amazon queen who submits herself to the authority of her lord and master, Theseus.

Philostrate
Theseus' appointed Master of the Revels, in charge of the wedding celebrations.

Titania
The queen of the fairies. She resists her husband, Oberon, when he wants to steal from her a 'lovely boy stolen from an Indian king' whom she has among her attendants. Oberon puts a spell on her and makes her fall in love with 'an ass'.

Oberon
The king of the fairies. In his war with Titania, he makes his servant Puck obtain a love potion that creates havoc among the mortals.

Puck
Oberon's fairy servant – a mischievous, quick-witted sprite, well-known to country people. He loves to play tricks on mortals and he confuses the love affairs of the young people who get lost in the forest. Also called Hobgoblin, Puck is similar to Pan, the ancient god of confusion, and it is he who is the play's catalyst.

Egeus
Hermia's father, who brings a complaint against Lysander, the man his daughter wants to marry.

Hermia
Egeus' daughter, who is in love with Lysander, but her father orders her to marry Demetrius. She elopes with her lover but gets lost in the forest.

Demetrius
A young man of Athens, Demetrius loves Hermia at the beginning of the play and has her father's permission to marry her. Unfortunately, Hermia's affections lie elsewhere.

Helena
She is desperately in love with Demetrius, but he loves her school friend Hermia. Only after Puck has opened Demetrius' eyes when they are wandering about in the forest does he return her love.

Lysander
A young man of Athens in love with Hermia, Lysander only gains Hermia's father's permission to marry her after Demetrius and Helena get together.

Nick Bottom
Bottom, the weaver, has amused the 'groundlings' ever since Shakespeare created him: a simple working man with ideas

above his station. He is ebullient, boastful, convinced of his talent to amuse, inventive, lovable and irrepressible. Above all, he is a dreamer and he dreams of making love to the queen of the fairies. He is the star of the play 'Pyramus and Thisbe', put on to amuse the Duke and his friends, and during rehearsals in the forest he is turned into an ass by Oberon. Ridiculous and self-important, he is one of Shakespeare's best-loved characters.

Peter Quince
A carpenter who can read and counts himself as an intellectual. He is in nominal control of the play that the labourers are to put on before the Duke but, like other directors after him, he finds he is constantly being upstaged by his lead player, Bottom.

Francis Flute
The bellows mender, who is chosen to play Thisbe in 'Pyramus and Thisbe'; he is disconcerted to find it is a woman's part and decides to use a high, squeaky voice.

Robin Starveling
A tailor who plays the part of Moonshine in 'Pyramus and Thisbe'.

Tom Snout
A tinker who plays the wall that separates the lovers, Pyramus and Thisbe.

Snug the Joiner
He is 'slow of learning' but, as he plays the lion, (in 'Pyramus and Thisbe') he does not have to learn any lines. He can roar as he thinks fit, but he has to be careful not to scare the ladies.

The Plot
Theseus, the Duke of Athens, is to marry Hippolyta, the Queen of the Amazons. Egeus complains to the Duke that his

daughter's affections have been stolen by Lysander, whom she now intends to marry against his wishes. He wants her to marry Demetrius. Theseus warns her that if she disobeys her father, she risks being sentenced to death or to a celibate life in a convent. Lysander does not help matters by being impertinent to Egeus.

Later, Lysander persuades Hermia to elope with him and take refuge with an aunt of his. Foolishly, they take Helena into their confidence, but she is not happy because she loves Demetrius, who will not look at her as he is in love with Hermia. Hermia says that when she and Lysander are gone perhaps then Demetrius will love her, but Helena is not convinced.

A group of common labourers decide to put forward a play to entertain the Duke on his wedding night. If their play is chosen they will be well rewarded. Quince, the most learned of them, suggests they rehearse 'The Most Lamentable Comedy and Most Cruel Death of Pyramus and Thisbe', which tells the story of lovers separated by their parents' feud, and who speak to each other through a hole in a wall. Quince assigns each of them a part in the play; Bottom, the weaver, thinks he can play all the parts, but has to make do with playing Pyramus, the hero. Each man considers his part; Flute takes some persuading to play the female role of Thisbe, while Snug, who is to play the lion, wonders if he will remember his lines and is relieved to find he has none – all he has to do is roar.

In the forest, Oberon and Titania, the king and queen of the fairies, are bickering about a 'lovely boy', a favourite of the queen's, whom Oberon wants for himself. Titania is obdurate and Oberon decides to take his revenge by putting a spell on her so that she falls in love with the first person she sees when she wakes up, however horrible he might be. He sends his servant Puck to seek a white-and-purple flower called love-in-idleness, whose juice is a powerful love potion.

Helena has brought Demetrius into the forest to waylay Hermia and Lysander, hoping that the favour she is doing him will make him love her, but of course it does not. Lysander has to confess that he has lost the way and they will have to sleep out in the open. Hermia tells him not to sleep too close to her in case he is tempted to do what he should not. Puck views the scene and decides to take a hand in these mortal tussles of love by spreading around a little of his potion.

To rehearse their play and avoid being seen by their neighbours, the labourers meet in the forest. All goes well until Bottom is 'translated' into an ass by mischievous Puck. Bottom does not understand why all his friends run away in fear.

Titania wakes and the first thing she sees is Bottom, now with the head of a donkey, and she falls madly in love with him. When the mortal lovers awake, they too have been confused by Puck. Demetrius falls in love with Helena, and so does Lysander. Hermia thinks the men are playing a trick on her. Demetrius and Lysander have a wild fight with each other, but Puck so misleads them that there is no chance of them hurting one another.

Bottom and Titania dally with one another until Oberon takes pity on her and takes the spell off her eyes. She is horrified by what she has loved. Oberon also orders Puck to take off Bottom's head and he returns to Athens believing he has had a most wonderful dream.

The young lovers awake and all is put to right. Lysander and Hermia are in love and now Demetrius loves Helena. Egeus has to accept the inevitable. The Duke decrees they will share his wedding day.

The play chosen to amuse the Duke and his friends is 'Pyramus and Thisbe'. The audience laughs at the labourers for all the wrong reasons and mock their honest efforts, but they have their reward and are not too insulted.

They all join in a dance and then Puck prepares the house for the lovers and makes apology for the play.

The Merchant of Venice
Sources
Probably written in 1595 or 1596, the first recorded performance was in February 1605 before King James I. He

enjoyed it so much he saw a second performance that same month.

The idea for the story of the strange wooing of Portia, in which the suitor had to 'choose the right box', was traditional. One version is given in a medieval collection of stories known as *Gesta Romanorum*.

The story of the pound of flesh was also well known and one version very similar to that in *The Merchant of Venice* can be found in *II Pecorone* (The Dunce) written by Ser Giovanni Fiorentino in 1378 but not printed until 1558. It was not translated into English in Shakespeare's time. It tells the story of Ansaldo, a Venetian merchant who borrows money from a Jew for his godson, Giannetto. Giannetto is wooing a lady of Belmonte and she disguises herself as a lawyer to tell the Jew he must take exactly a pound of flesh in settlement of the debt.

Another important influence on Shakespeare was Marlowe's very successful *The Jew of Malta*, but Marlowe's Jew was a monster of wickedness quite unlike Shakespeare's Shylock. It should be remembered that Shakespeare perhaps would not have met a Jew, as at that time Jews had been banished from England.

The Merchant of Venice was entered in the Stationers' Register on 22 July 1598. The play is arguably Shakespeare's first mature play.

Main Characters
Antonio
Antonio is the rich merchant of the title. He lends money freely without interest, which angers the Jewish moneylenders. He borrows money from Shylock to lend to his friend Bassanio and foolishly signs his name to a bond that permits Shylock a pound of his flesh if he is unable to repay the money by the due day. (To modern readers, Antonio is seen as an anti-Semite, though in Shakespeare's day his contempt for the Jews would have been considered unremarkable.)

Shylock

Shylock, the Jewish moneylender, is not the stock villain of Elizabethan theatre but a living, breathing human being. He gains the sympathy of a modern audience for the way he is treated by the Christians, who take delight in stealing away his daughter and robbing him. His desire for revenge is understandable, and when Portia defeats his plan to take his pound of flesh, the audience is left feeling uneasy, as in *Twelfth Night* when Malvolio's suffering seems out of proportion to his 'crime'.

Portia

An heiress whose father has insisted she choose her husband in a strange way. The man she must marry will be invited to choose a casket, and he has to choose not the gold or silver but the lead casket, thereby showing true modesty. She is glad when a black Prince from Morocco fails to guess the right casket and makes an unpleasant – but no doubt unexceptionable to Shakespeare's audience – remark about the colour of his skin. Later, when she learns Bassanio's friend is in trouble, she shows her cleverness and determination by dressing up as lawyer, saving Antonio and taking vengeance on Shylock. She also takes delight – her disguise being so effective – in teasing Bassanio by demanding from him the ring that she had given him, making him swear never to part with it.

Bassanio

Antonio's best friend, he borrows money from him in order to woo the wealthy Portia. No one, not even the lady herself, seems to think there is anything wrong about this rather unromantic gesture/pretence for making love to a woman. There is a suggestion that Bassanio and Antonio might have been lovers and Bassanio certainly comes across as superficial and something of a spendthrift. However, he is clever enough to choose the right casket and gain a wife.

Jessica

Shylock's disloyal and empty-headed daughter betrays her father by eloping with a Christian and stealing her father's gold. It is likely Shakespeare's audience found the trick she played on her father uproariously funny, but a modern audience may find her behaviour less attractive.

Launcelot Gobbo

The clown, who begins as Shylock's servant but switches his allegiance to Bassanio. He enjoys teasing his blind father, Old Gobbo.

The Plot

The wealthy Venetian merchant Antonio habitually lends money to his friends without interest, but when Bassanio asks him for a loan so he can woo Portia, an heiress living some way off in Belmont, he has to confess he has no money to lend. All his wealth is tied up at sea in several trading ships. However, he is happy for Bassanio to raise money using his name as guarantor. Bassanio has borrowed money from him before, but he explains to Antonio that if he can marry Portia all his money troubles will be over.

Bassanio goes to the Jew Shylock, Antonio's great enemy. Shylock hates Antonio as one who lends money without interest, thereby spoiling his business, and as a Christian who despises him for his race.

In Belmont, Portia is considering her suitors. By her father's will, she has to marry the man who chooses the right casket. There are three: one of gold, one of silver and one of lead. There are three serious suitors: the black Prince of Morocco, the Prince of Aragon and Bassanio, whom she confesses she favours above the others.

Back in Venice, Shylock learns that Antonio is in danger of losing all his wealth because his ships are on perilous voyages. He nevertheless agrees to lend Bassanio the money he needs, with the help of his friend Tubal. He taunts Antonio and reminds him how badly Antonio has treated him in the past. Antonio calls him a devil and tells him to lend his money knowing him to be an enemy – he does not pretend to be anything else. The deal is done. Seeming to relent, Shylock asks only that if the money is not repaid by the due date, he will claim from the merchant a pound of his flesh. Antonio and Bassanio treat the bond as a joke, as a pound of his flesh can be of no value to Shylock. Launcelot Gobbo decides to leave Shylock's service and is taken on by Bassanio. Shylock's daughter, Jessica, has also decided to leave. She has fallen in love with a Christian, Lorenzo, and will convert to Christianity for his sake.

In Belmont, the Prince of Morocco chooses the gold casket and finds he has made the wrong choice. It contains only a skull and a scroll that points out to him that 'all that glistens is not gold'. Portia heaves a sigh of relief, saying she could never bring herself to marry a black man. The Prince of Aragon fares no better. He chooses silver and discovers a portrait of a 'blinking idiot'.

Back in Venice, Shylock discovers that his daughter has run away, taking with her a considerable amount of treasure. Shylock swears revenge. He says he is not made of stone; he has eyes, hands, affections and passions as anyone else: 'If you prick us do we not bleed?'

In Belmont, Bassanio chooses the lead casket and wins his Portia. She does not mind that he is poor and gives him a ring that he swears never to take off his finger. His friend Gratiano is meanwhile falling for Portia's servant Nerissa and she, too, gives her lover a ring.

Their happiness is shattered when Bassanio receives a letter from Antonio telling him that he needs money as his ships have all foundered and Shylock is claiming his pound of flesh. Bassanio hurries off with money from Portia to pay off Shylock. Unfortunately, Shylock says it is too late – he does not want money; he wants his pound of flesh and appeals to the Duke to let him have what is owed him.

Portia arrives in Venice disguised as a man. She calls herself 'Balthasar' and comes with a recommendation from a famous lawyer. As Shylock sharpens his knife, Balthasar calls on him to relent, but he will not. However, just as he is about to cut into Antonio's chest, she tells him that he may have his pound of flesh but not a drop of blood. Furthermore, as a Jew seeking to take the life of a Christian, his life is forfeit.

Shylock realizes he has been bested and tries to salvage something by at least getting his money back. Balthasar says it is too late for that and all his money will be seized by the state. He is fortunate that the Duke decides to spare his life. He is told he must convert to Christianity, and then he might get some of his money back.

'Balthasar' and his clerk – Portia and Nerissa in disguise – ask as a fee only the rings on the fingers of Bassanio and Gratiano. Reluctantly, they part with their rings. When they return to Belmont, the girls, who got there ahead of them, ask why they have not got their rings. The men try to explain but Portia and Nerissa pretend not to believe them. Then they confess the trick they have played and the lovers are happy again. Their happiness is complete when they receive letters to say that Antonio's ships have not been lost but have returned safely and the merchant of Venice is once again rich.

Much Ado About Nothing
Sources
Probably written in 1598, it was entered in the Stationers' Register in August 1600.

The story of how Claudio, having fallen in love with Hero, renounces her when he is persuaded to believe she talked with her lover on the night before her wedding, is to be found in many works. Spenser uses one version in *The Faerie Queene*, book II, canto iv, and there is another version by Matteo Bandello in Italian, published in 1554. Shakespeare must have read this later version as he uses some names in *Much Ado* that occur in Bandello's story.

There may be another play, now lost, which Shakespeare used when he was writing *Much Ado*; certainly the Hero-Claudio story is different in style to the Beatrice-Benedick story, and there are signs of various layers or strands in the play not always in harmony. However, the play performs well and the stylistic differences that are noticeable when *Much Ado* is read aloud are not so apparent when the play is staged.

Main Characters
Leonato
A well-to-do elderly noble, Leonato lives in Messina with his daughter Hero and his niece Beatrice.

Hero
Leonato's beautiful young daughter, innocent, gentle and forgiving. She falls in love with Claudio and, when he believes Don John's slander, she almost dies of grief.

Beatrice
Leonato's niece, she is high-spirited and witty. She likes jokes and puns and delights in carrying out a war of words with Benedick. She believes she will never marry, as does Benedick, and they have to be tricked by their friends into confessing their feelings for one another. When Hero is spoken badly of, she complains that were she a man she could avenge her injury, but as a woman she has to find a man to act for her. She calls on Benedick to kill Claudio.

Benedick
An aristocrat and a close friend of Don Pedro. He has returned from war determined to have a good time. He is captivated by Beatrice but considers her too sharp-tongued to fall in love with. His friends persuade him that beneath Beatrice's wit there is real feeling for him, but their love is interrupted when Beatrice tells him to kill Claudio and avenge her wronged cousin Hero.

Claudio

A Florentine lord, he has no character to speak of until he shows himself stupid and suspicious. He so mistakes the gentle Hero as to think her false on the word of a man – Don John – known to be treacherous.

Don Pedro

Don Pedro is the Prince of Aragon, who brings a party of soldiers back from the wars to Messina.

Don John

Known as the Bastard, he is Don Pedro's brother. Melancholy and sullen, he becomes the villain of the play when he ruins Hero's happiness.

Margaret

Hero's maid, who is tricked into helping Borachio and Don John deceive Claudio.

Borachio

Don John's man, he makes love to Margaret so he can ensnare Hero. *Borachio* means 'drunkard' in Italian.

Conrad

One of Don John's men – possibly even his 'minion'.

Dogberry

The comic policeman, who, along with his deputy, Verges, brings Don John and the other conspirators to justice, but the villains have to spell out their villainy since Dogberry makes very little sense. He uses words he half understands and is one of Shakespeare's funniest clowns.

The Plot

Leonato, who lives in the Italian town of Messina, is preparing to welcome home from the wars Don Pedro of Aragon and several of his friends. Among them is Claudio, who, as soon as he arrives, confesses to Don Pedro his love for Leonato's daughter Hero. He had met her before the war but could not declare his love until the fighting was over. When Claudio says he is shy, Don Pedro offers to woo Hero for him.

A friend of Claudio's, Benedick, is also of the party. He is known to Beatrice, Leonato's niece, who lives with him, a high-spirited, bold girl, quite different from the gentle Hero. Beatrice is eager to continue her war of words with 'Signor Benedick', as she calls him. Benedick appears and he and Beatrice begin to spar with one another.

Leonato believes Don Pedro, not Claudio, woos his daughter and warns her to be careful.

The villainous 'bastard' brother of Don Pedro, Don John, is talking with his henchmen. Borachio has overheard Don Pedro and knows he is going to woo Hero for Claudio. He suggests to his master that they can make trouble.

At the masked ball that evening, Don Pedro flirts with Hero but she repels him. Don John informs Claudio that, contrary to what his brother had promised, he intends to woo Hero for himself. The jealous Claudio immediately believes he is betrayed, but soon Don Pedro brings Hero to him and he realizes the Prince has been true to him. Beatrice says she will never marry, and when, half-jokingly, Don Pedro offers to marry her she gently refuses, saying he is too grand for her.

Claudio and Hero's wedding is to take place in a week and they decide, at Don Pedro's suggestion, to employ the intervening days in getting Beatrice and Benedick to confess their love to one another.

Meanwhile, Don John and his men plan to trick Claudio into believing Hero is unchaste. Borachio has seduced Hero's maid, Margaret, and he will make love to her in the window of her mistress' bedroom: Claudio will see and think it is Hero meeting her lover.

There follows a comic scene in which, quite separately, Beatrice and Benedick overhear their friends talking about how Beatrice loves Benedick and vice versa. The plan works: they recognize their love for each other and Benedick is mocked for saying he will now get married, having for so long set his face against marrying.

Don John sets his plan in motion by offering to prove to Claudio that Hero is a whore. The 'watch' – Dogberry and Verges and their fellows – overhear the villains discussing their plan to blacken Hero's name, but they cannot get Leonato to listen when they come to see him because he is busy with preparations for Hero's wedding.

At the wedding, Claudio publicly disgraces Hero by calling her a whore and refuses to marry her. Hero faints. Leonato, the priest who was to marry her, Beatrice and Benedick decide to pretend to Claudio and the Prince that she is dead. While she is in hiding they will have time to clear her name. Beatrice calls on Benedick to prove his love for her by challenging Claudio to a duel and killing him.

Dogberry and his friends question Don John's men and learn how Claudio has been tricked. They tell Leonato and then Claudio, who repents for having treated Hero so shamefully. Leonato tells him he has another daughter and Claudio, if he truly repents, must marry her without ever seeing her face. He promises to do this and, of course, the 'hidden' daughter turns out to be Hero. The evil Don John is captured and all ends happily.

As You Like It
Sources
First published in 1623 in the First Folio, it is the only play in the First Folio that is divided into acts and scenes. It was probably written after June 1599, when the Privy Council ordered that some notorious books of satires should be burned. This is alluded to in Act I, Scene 2, when Celia says: 'the little wit that fools have was silenced ...'

The new Globe, which opened for business in the summer of 1599, had as its motto *'Totus mundus agit histrionem'* (The whole world acts the actor) and this is referred to by Jaques when he begins his famous speech: 'All the world's a stage/And all the men and women merely players' (II.7).

Shakespeare based *As You Like It* on a story by Thomas Lodge called *Rosalynde, or Euphus's Golden Legacy*, published in 1590 and a bestseller at the time. In the introduction to *Rosalynde* Lodge uses the expression: 'If you like it, so.' Lodge's source was the medieval English poem *The Tale of Gamelyn*.

The play was both a 'pastoral romance' and a satire of pastoral ideals comparable to Ben Jonson's *Every Man and His Humour*, but *As You Like It* is above all a play of character. Jaques has no essential part in the plot but has all the best speeches and is the most interesting character in the play. This is Shakespeare creating a new kind of theatre that was to culminate in *Hamlet*.

Main Characters
Rosalind
The daughter of the banished Duke, Rosalind is determined, high-spirited and something of a tomboy. She falls in love with Orlando and woos him with warmth and wit.

Orlando de Boys
The youngest son of the late Sir Rowland de Boys, Orlando is treated as a slave by his elder brother. Intelligent, though 'never schooled' he is brave but otherwise rather colourless.

Adam
Orlando's aged servant, who is just and loyal, offering his master his life savings. He accompanies him into the forest and almost dies of hunger and exposure.

The Banished Duke
Rosalind's father has been banished by his evil younger brother, Frederick, who has usurped his dukedom. He lives in the Forest of Arden with his merry men and is melancholy at times but not bitter.

Duke Frederick
The banished Duke's unfeeling brother, whose conversion at the end of the play is unexplained and unconvincing.

Celia
The evil Duke Frederick's daughter, who sees her cousin Rosalind as a sister and takes her part against her father.

Touchstone
A professional jester at Duke Frederick's court, Touchstone accompanies Rosalind and Celia into the forest. Like Feste in *Twelfth Night*, he is a wise and learned 'fool'. He mocks himself and the idea of love by going through a form of marriage with Audrey, a simple and unattractive country wench.

Jaques
A melancholy courtier who has accompanied the banished Duke into exile. He meditates on human folly and philosophizes on life.

Charles
Charles the wrestler is kind-hearted but stupid. He wrestles with Orlando in front of Duke Frederick and is defeated.

Phebe and Silvius
Phebe is a shepherdess who falls in love with Rosalind when she is dressed as a boy but has to make do with her shepherd lover, Silvius.

Corin
An aged shepherd, simple but wise, who satirizes the artificiality of court life.

The Plot
The Duke has been exiled by his evil younger brother,

Frederick, who has usurped his dukedom. The banished Duke now resides in the Forest of Arden with several of his friends. The banished Duke's daughter, Rosalind, has been allowed to stay at court because of her friendship with Duke Frederick's daughter Celia.

Orlando, the youngest son of the late Sir Rowland de Boys, is being treated badly by his elder brother Oliver. He is not fed or housed properly and he has not been schooled as his rank warrants. He complains of this to Adam, his father's old servant. Oliver refuses to give Orlando the money his father left him, and Orlando is so enraged that he attacks his brother. Oliver still refuses to give his brother his inheritance, so Orlando decides to go to court to try his luck. Oliver persuades the wrestler Charles to kill Orlando when they wrestle in front of the Duke.

Rosalind and Celia watch with the rest of the court the wrestling match between Orlando and Charles. They beg Orlando not to fight as they believe he will be badly hurt, but Orlando persists. Duke Frederick asks Orlando what his name is and is not happy when he learns he is the son of his old enemy, Rowland de Boys, but Rosalind remembers Orlando's father as her father's friend and gives him a chain she has been wearing. Orlando defeats Charles but is warned to leave court as the Duke will try to harm him. The Duke decides he can no longer tolerate having his niece at court and orders Rosalind to follow her father into exile. Celia defies her father and says if Rosalind is banished then she will go with her. To go into the dangerous forest, Celia puts on old clothes and Rosalind dresses like a man.

Orlando also goes into the forest, accompanied by Adam who gives him his life savings. In the forest, Rosalind, now calling herself Ganymede, and Celia, who calls herself Aliena, chance upon two shepherds: Corin, an old man, and Silvius, a boy. Silvius talks of his love for the disdainful Phebe. Orlando and Adam are exhausted and hungry when they come across the exiled Duke, who treats them kindly. Jaques makes his famous speech about the seven ages of man. The banished Duke is pleased to discover Orlando is the son of his old friend. Orlando writes poems for Rosalind and hangs them on the trees. Rosalind decides to tease Orlando by teaching him how to woo, knowing he will not recognize her in boys' clothes.

Touchstone makes love to the country wench Audrey, despite her being ugly and stupid. He pretends to marry her. Silvius is getting nowhere with Phebe and when Rosalind tries to help him, Phebe falls in love with her, thinking, of course, that she is a boy. She tricks Silvius into taking a love letter from her to 'Ganymede'.

When Orlando is late for her lesson in wooing, Rosalind is annoyed and berates him. She takes the joke to extremes by making Celia play the part of a priest who 'marries' her to Orlando. Rosalind is now deeply in love with Orlando. She receives Phebe's letter and pretends to Silvius that it is an angry letter when in fact it is a love letter. She reads poor Silvius the letter and he sees he has been tricked. Rosalind says Silvius is a fool to waste his love on such a girl as Phebe and advises him to tell her she – or rather Ganymede – will never marry her.

Oliver, Orlando's wicked brother, arrives in search of him and he explains to Rosalind that he has seen the error of his ways. Orlando's goodness has converted him. In conversation with Orlando, Oliver reveals that has fallen in love with Celia. He says he will live the life of a shepherd and give Orlando all his wealth.

All is now ready for the pairing-off. Rosalind and Celia shed their disguises. Only Phebe is unhappy: when she discovers Ganymede is in fact a woman, she has to marry Silvius. Duke Frederick has also had a change of heart and decides to change places with his brother. Jaques says he will stay with Frederick and not go back to court with the restored Duke.

Twelfth Night, or What You Will
Sources
Twelfth Night was probably written in 1600 or 1601 and

printed in the First Folio of 1623. The play makes reference to a new map of the Indies, which appeared in 1600. (Maria says of Malvolio in Act III, Scene 2: 'He does smile his face into more lines than is in the new map with the augmentation of the Indies').

The earliest reference to *Twelfth Night* is to be found in the diary of John Manningham, a barrister of the Middle Temple. On 2 February 1602 he records seeing a performance of *Twelfth Night*, which he compares to *The Comedy of Errors*.

Shakespeare had many different sources to draw upon for *Twelfth Night*, but the plot is closest to a story called *Apolonius and Silla* by one Barnabe Riche in a collection entitled *Riche His Farewell to Militarie Profession*. Another source was an Italian play about confused identities called *Inganni* (The Deceived).

The play's title has nothing to do with the story but may have been planned for the feast of Epiphany, 6 January 1601. Queen Elizabeth I paid the Lord Chamberlain's Men to entertain a visiting Italian nobleman by the name of Orsino, but this may only be a coincidence.

Main Characters
Orsino
The Duke of Illyria, Orsino is in love with Olivia, a wealthy widow. She is in mourning for her brother and does not return his love, which makes him melancholy. He finds himself falling in love with Viola, which is embarrassing since he thinks she is a boy called Cesario.

Viola
A lady of Messaline and twin sister of Sebastian, Viola has survived a shipwreck but believes her brother was drowned. For safety's sake, she disguises herself as a boy and calls herself Cesario. She seeks protection at Orsino's court and falls in love with him, but is unable to declare her love because he thinks she is a boy – and that he is in love with Olivia.

Olivia

Olivia is a noblewoman and the object of Orsino's affection. She uses the death of her brother as an excuse for rejecting Orsino's overtures of love. She falls for Orsino's messenger, Cesario, not realizing the boy is, in fact, a girl. Fortunately, she is happy to take Sebastian, Viola's twin, in exchange for Viola.

Sebastian

Viola's twin brother, he has not, as Viola feared, been drowned. He is handsome and brave, if rather impetuous, and falls in love with Olivia.

Sir Toby Belch

Uncle to Olivia, Sir Toby is a rogue, lovable or not depending on how he is played. He takes advantage of his relationship to Olivia to put down the steward Malvolio, who torments him for his drunken behaviour and has ideas above his social station. He marries Olivia's maid, Maria, whom he admires for her wit and love of practical jokes. He makes money out of the foolish knight Andrew Aguecheek. He likes good food and wine, is often uproarious, to the irritation of his niece, and is sometimes cruel.

Malvolio

Olivia's steward, so consumed with self-love he is easily persuaded that Olivia loves him and will honour him by marrying him. Maria plays a practical joke on him, forging a letter he thinks is from his mistress. He is almost driven to madness by her rejection of his efforts to please her – wearing yellow 'cross-gartered' stockings and smiling all the time. He is consigned by Sir Toby to a dungeon; when he is eventually released, instead of forgiving his enemies, he swears he will get his revenge.

Maria

Olivia's maid or lady-in-waiting. Maria is intelligent, witty and loves a good joke. She thinks up the scheme to trap Malvolio, but in the end regrets her cruelty to him and confesses the plot to her mistress. She marries Sir Toby.

Feste
One of Shakespeare's most entertaining clowns. He is melancholy, witty and wise. He amuses Olivia and makes her laugh even when she wants to be sad and mourn her brother. He takes delight in tormenting Malvolio because he dislikes his pomposity and contempt for clowning. He sings wonderfully sad songs and helps set the mood of the play.

Antonio
A brave sea captain who follows Sebastian even though he is in danger in Orsino's dukedom. He lends Sebastian money and is confused when Viola, indistinguishable from her brother when dressed in men's clothes, refuses to acknowledge the debt.

The Plot
Duke Orsino is lovesick for Olivia, but she will have nothing to do with him. She is in mourning for her brother and not in the mood for love, despite Feste proving to her that she is wrong to be sad because her brother is now in heaven.

Viola has survived a shipwreck, but she believes her brother Sebastian has drowned. She decides to ask for refuge from Orsino, but to protect herself she goes disguised as a boy called Cesario. Orsino takes to Cesario at once and employs him/her to go to Olivia and plead his love for her.

Olivia is having trouble with her uncle, Sir Toby Belch. She does not approve of his excessive drinking and carousing. Sir Toby wants her to marry his friend, the rich but foolish Sir Andrew Aguecheek, to whom he is in debt. Viola, disguised as Cesario, arrives at Olivia's house but is refused entrance by her steward, Malvolio. Viola refuses to go away and in the end is permitted to see Olivia – or rather she allows 'Cesario' into her presence. She is veiled and Viola has to ask her to reveal herself so she can recite her prepared speech praising Olivia's beautiful face. Olivia still declines to accept Orsino's love but finds herself falling for his messenger and asks Viola ('Cesario') to come again. She sends Malvolio after Viola with a ring that she tells Malvolio to say she cannot accept. Viola knows she has given Olivia no ring and it dawns on her that Olivia has fallen in love with her, thinking her to be a man.

Sir Toby Belch, Sir Andrew and the clown Feste arrive home drunk, and dance and sing noisily. Maria comes to tell them to behave themselves but is soon joining in the fun. Malvolio arrives and threatens them all with being turned out of the house. Sir Toby is furious to be reprimanded by a mere steward and promises to be revenged. Maria says she has a plan. She will forge a letter for Malvolio to find, which will seem to have come from her mistress and will appear to show that she is in love with her steward. It will urge him to appear before her smiling, dressed in yellow, cross-gartered stockings. Maria knows this will infuriate Olivia because she is feeling sad and the smiles of her steward will seem out of place, particularly as he is normally so solemn. And yellow is a colour she hates.

Sir Andrew Aguecheek begins to give up hope of marrying Olivia when he sees her being charming to Cesario. He decides, encouraged by Sir Toby, to challenge the boy to a duel. Sir Toby believes there will be much amusement in seeing the cowardly Sir Andrew fighting Cesario, whom he rightly guesses not to be physically valiant. Olivia sends for Malvolio, wanting someone serious to talk to, but when she finds he is smiling and dressed in yellow stockings she thinks he has gone mad and asks Sir Toby to deal with him. Sir Toby takes this as permission to incarcerate the luckless steward in a dungeon.

The farcical duel takes place between Sir Andrew and Viola. Antonio interrupts the duel to protect Viola, believing her to be her twin, Sebastian. Antonio has befriended Sebastian, who has not been drowned but is at this very moment sightseeing in the city. Antonio has many enemies in the town and has decided to lie low, but he has lent Sebastian money in case he finds something he wants to buy. Now Orsino's men arrive on the scene and arrest Antonio. He begs Viola, still believing him to be Sebastian, to help him and at least return to him the money he has borrowed. Of course Viola does not know what he is talking about, but she begins to guess that her twin may, after all, be alive.

Sir Andrew decides that Viola is as cowardly as him and tries to renew the duel, but unfortunately he has come upon Sebastian – not Viola – and Sir Andrew is badly knocked about by the young man. Olivia arrives and comforts Sebastian – thinking she is comforting Cesario. Sebastian is delighted to have this beautiful woman fuss over him, and when Olivia suggests they marry he agrees.

Malvolio is being tormented by Feste, who pretends he is a priest, Sir Topas. But Malvolio is at last provided with paper and pen so he can appeal to his mistress. Orsino arrives at Olivia's house with Cesario in tow and Olivia greets Cesario as 'husband'. The confusion increases when Sir Andrew and Sir Toby arrive and accuse Cesario of beating them up.

Finally, Sebastian turns up and the twins greet each other with joy. All is explained and Olivia and Sebastian seem happy in their marriage. Viola, revealed as a woman, promises to marry Orsino, and Sir Toby is to marry Maria.

The Merry Wives of Windsor
Sources
The play was entered in the Stationers' Register on 18 January 1602 by a printer called John Busby and it was included in the First Folio in 1623. It was probably written in 1597 or 1598. The first performance may have been on 23 April 1597 at a feast for the Order of the Garter, attended by Queen Elizabeth. There are references to this in Act V, where the fairies are bidden to Windsor Castle to anoint the chairs of the Order of the Garter.

There is a tradition that Shakespeare wrote a new play about Sir John Falstaff at Queen Elizabeth's request, she having so much enjoyed the character in *Henry IV*. This story dates from

1702, when a playwright called John Dennis rewrote *The Merry Wives* as *The Comical Gallant*.

Another tradition is that Shakespeare was mocking Sir Thomas Lucy, a local squire, in the first scene of the play. Nicholas Rowe in his account of the life of Shakespeare (1709) told a story of the young Shakespeare getting into trouble with Sir Thomas for poaching deer from his estate.

Shakespeare was probably rewriting an old play, now lost, as some of the rather stiff verse would seem to be by someone other than Shakespeare. There are similarities with Henry Porter's play *Two Angry Women of Abingdon* (1599) and *II Pecorone*, a 1588 play by Ser Giovanni Fiorentino.

There are some links between *The Merry Wives* and Ben Jonson's *Every Man in His Humour*, first played in September 1598. The jealous husband, Ford, and the silly young man, Slender, resemble Jonson's Thorello and Stephano. It is likely that the actor who played Slender would also have played Sir Andrew Aguecheek in *Twelfth Night*, Osric in *Hamlet* and Roderigo in *Othello* – all silly young gentlemen.

The Falstaff of *The Merry Wives* has little in common with the Falstaff of *Henry IV* except his size. Shakespeare seems most interested in satirizing middle-class life in Stratford.

Main Characters
Master Ford
A jealous husband who, when he learns Falstaff is aiming to seduce his wife, disguises himself as 'Brooke' and goes to the Garter Inn to find out Falstaff's plans. He eventually learns to control his jealousy.

Mistress Ford
She lives in Windsor with her jealous husband. She and her friend Mistress Page both receive love letters from Sir John Falstaff. They decide to tease him by making him believe he is in with a chance of seducing them. She hopes she will be able to prove to her husband that she is a faithful wife.

Master Page

A citizen of Windsor who trusts his wife and does not believe
Falstaff will be able to seduce her. However, he must learn to
listen to his daughter and let her choose who she will marry.

Mistress Page

Page's wife, she joins with her friend Mistress Ford to trick
Falstaff. She is in dispute with her husband as to which of two
men should marry their daughter. She favours Doctor Caius,
while her husband favours Slender.

Anne Page

She likes neither of the two men her parents want her to marry.
She elopes with her lover, Fenton, and returns to chide her
parents for not listening to her.

Master Fenton

Anne Page's chosen lover, he is high-born but poor.
Anne's father believes Fenton is after his daughter's money,
which to begin with he is, but he ends up sincerely in love with
her.

Doctor Caius

Caius, the local doctor, is Mistress Quickly's master. He is
French and is mocked for his accent. He wants to marry Anne.

Master Slender

Anne's other suitor, Slender is reduced to talking nonsense
when he is in Anne's presence. He loses Anne to Fenton.

Sir Hugh Evans

Sir Hugh is the local clergyman and is mocked for his Welsh
accent. He joins with Doctor Caius to have his revenge on the
mockers.

Mistress Quickly
A housekeeper who works for Doctor Caius. She is everyone's messenger and backs Fenton to marry Anne Page.

Justice Shallow
Shallow is a figure of fun – a representative of the law without the necessary wisdom to have his authority respected.

Bardolph, Nym and Pistol
These are Falstaff's men, but they betray his plans to the husbands of the women he is planning to seduce.

The Plot
Sir Hugh Evans is discussing with Justice Shallow and Master Slender how the latter can marry Anne Page. Falstaff arrives with his followers – Bardolph, Nym and Pistol. Shallow accuses Falstaff of having beaten his men and killed his deer and Falstaff admits it. Slender says he was beaten and robbed by Falstaff's men, but they say he was too drunk to know what happened.

They are invited into Master Page's house, though Slender remains reading love poems outside. Sir Hugh comes out to him and asks him if he is prepared to marry Anne Page. Slender says he could and that, in time, love would grow between them. Slender is alone with Anne but is unable to say anything sensible to her.

Falstaff arranges to live in the Garter Inn and it is here he makes plans to seduce Mistress Ford. He likes her but, more importantly, thinks she has control over her husband's wealth. For the same reasons he decides to try to seduce Mistress Page. Pistol and Nym refuse to have anything to do with such a low scheme and they decide to tell the two husbands what Falstaff is planning.

Mistress Quickly, Doctor Caius' servant, thinks that Slender would be a good husband for Anne Page but knows her master also wants to marry the girl. Quickly tries to assure her master that Anne will marry him but really she believes Anne will marry neither Caius nor Slender. Perhaps she loves Master Fenton?

Mistress Page and Mistress Ford laugh at Falstaff's letters to them. They are indignant that he should think either of them would be attracted to the fat old man. They decide to lead him on so he will spend money he cannot afford on them, but Mistress Ford says they must keep the whole project secret from her husband, who is very jealous. However, Pistol and Nym tell both husbands what Falstaff is planning and they are furious. Page does not think his wife would be untrue to him, but Ford is not so sure.

At the Star and Garter, the innkeeper agrees to introduce Ford to Falstaff under the name of Brooke so he can learn more of his plans. Falstaff receives a message from Mistress Ford that he may visit her the next day when her husband is out. Mistress Page, too, leaves word she will see him. Ford, disguised as Brooke, asks Falstaff for help as he wishes to seduce Mistress Ford. Falstaff agrees. Ford is furious and cannot wait to catch Falstaff with his wife the next day and prove to Page that his jealousy is justified.

Caius and Evans are persuaded by their friends to fight a duel, but they suspect they are being fooled and plot their revenge.

The next day, Falstaff goes to woo Mistress Ford, unaware that he is being spied on. He says he wished her husband dead so he can marry her. A servant announces the arrival of Mistress Page and Falstaff hides in a laundry basket. Mistress Page rushes in saying that their husbands are on the way to search the house. Falstaff appears from out of the laundry basket and Mistress Page pretends to be surprised. Falstaff just has time to whisper that really he loves her when he has once again to hide in the basket of dirty clothes. Servants carry out the basket and the jealous husbands arrive but, of course, find no sign of Falstaff. The men decide to go hunting the next day.

Fenton declares his love to Anne Page. He admits he first

loved her for her money because, though he is high-born, he is poor, but that he now loves her for herself. Anne tells him to try to get her father's consent to the marriage. Page arrives and tells Fenton to leave his daughter alone.

Falstaff arrives back at the Star and Garter soaking wet, having been thrown in the Thames with the dirty laundry. Mistress Quickly arrives and says Mistress Ford wants Falstaff to visit her again and that it was all a mistake his being thrown in the Thames. Ford arrives disguised as Brooke and Falstaff infuriates him by bragging that he has been invited to visit Mistress Ford again.

Once again Falstaff has only just begun his wooing of Mistress Ford when he has to hide as Mistress Page arrives. Once again Falstaff learns that the jealous Ford is on his way to search his house for the intruder, but this time Falstaff refuses to hide in the laundry basket. Instead he dresses in women's clothes. Ford arrives and believes he has found Falstaff in the laundry basket and is irate when he finds only dirty laundry. Ford mistakes Falstaff – dressed in women's clothes – for an old aunt he particularly dislikes and chases him/her out of the house.

The wives believe they must by now have taught Falstaff a lesson but decide on one last trick so that Falstaff is shamed in public. The wives tell their husbands about their teasing of Falstaff and Ford asks forgiveness of his wife for his unfounded jealousy. Mistress Ford says she will persuade Falstaff to go into the forest dressed as the legendary Herne the hunter. All the children of their neighbours will dress up as fairies and torment him with pinches and Falstaff can be made to admit his dishonourable scheme to seduce respectable women.

All goes to plan and Falstaff is publicly mocked. Anne frustrates her parents' plans to marry her off to a man she does not care for and elopes with Fenton. Anne rebukes her parents for not trusting to true love and all ends in feasting and merriment.

All's Well That Ends Well
Sources
First printed in the First Folio of 1623, seven years after Shakespeare's death, *All's Well That Ends Well* was never popular; there is no mention of it in contemporary records or quotations from it in plays by other playwrights. It was written sometime between 1601 and 1604 and is often paired with *Measure for Measure* since both feature a wife tricking her husband into paying her her rightful dues.

The source of *All's Well* is a story in Boccacio's *The Decameron*, which Shakespeare followed closely. He would have read it in a translation by William Painter, published in 1566. Shakespeare's main addition – and one of his most appealing characters – is that of the Countess of Rousillon, the Count's mother.

Main Characters
Helena
The play's heroine, the orphan daughter of a great doctor, she is the ward of the Countess of Rousillon and is hopelessly in love with Bertram, the Countess' son. She is resourceful, determined and courageous.

Bertram
The Count of Rousillon, he is handsome and well liked, but he treats Helena badly by marrying her unwillingly and then abandoning her.

The Countess of Rousillon
Bertram's mother and Helena's guardian, a wise discerning woman who appreciates Helena's worth and condemns her son for his ill treatment of her.

The King of France
Bertram's liege lord, the King is miraculously cured by Helena when he is close to death. Like the Countess, he loves and admires Helena.

Lafew
An old French nobleman and a friend of the Countess who offers the King advice.

Parolles
Bertram's friend, Parolles is a coward and a braggart who is eventually exposed and disgraced.

Diana
A young virgin whom Bertram attempts to seduce, Diana helps trick him into sleeping with his lawful wife.

The Plot

Since her father's death Helena has been the ward of the Countess of Rousillon, a wise and kindly elderly noblewoman. The Countess' husband has recently died and the new count is her son Bertram. A brave, handsome but callow young man, Bertram is sent to serve his liege lord, the King of France. Helena loves Bertram but she is a commoner and Bertram is a nobleman so she knows it can come to nothing. As he leaves, Parolles, a disreputable friend of Bertram's, jokingly urges Helena to find a husband and lose her virginity.

Bertram arrives at the court of the King of France. The king laments the loss of Bertram's father and also the death of Helena's father, a great doctor whom the king believes would have been the only man who could have cured him from the disease that is killing him.

Helena is forced to admit to the Countess that she loves her son. She says she is going to the French court to offer the king her services as a doctor. The Countess reluctantly gives her permission. Helena is brought before the king and tells him that her father has left her with a powerful medicine with which she can save his life. The king is doubtful but agrees to Helena's offer. If she cannot cure him in two days, her life will be forfeit; but if she does effect a cure then the king will allow her to marry whom she chooses.

The king is cured and Helena chooses Bertram, but Bertram does not want to marry her. He thinks she is beneath him, but the king compels him to marry Helena. Bertram tells Parolles he will never consummate the marriage but will send Helena back to his mother.

The Countess receives a letter from her son telling her he will stay abroad rather than consummate his marriage with Helena. Helena, too, has a message from Bertram: only when she bears his son, he declares, will he call her his wife. Since he refuses to sleep with her, it is not likely to happen.

Helena leaves a message for the Countess to say she is going on a pilgrimage. In fact Helena has gone to Florence, where Bertram is residing. She learns he is much taken with a girl called Diana.

Two lords, meanwhile, suspect that Bertram's friend Parolles is a coward and they decide to make him believe he has been captured by the enemy. They are sure he will quickly be persuaded to turn traitor. Bertram is sceptical, still believing Parolles to be the brave soldier he claims to be.

Helena confides in Diana and her mother, and together they plan to trick Bertram into believing he has seduced Diana when in fact he will have bedded his own wife.

The trick on Parolles works and he is revealed to be a coward. The trick on Bertram also works and he sleeps with his wife, thinking she is Diana.

Thinking Helena is dead, the Countess offers to marry Bertram to the daughter of Lafew, a noble friend. Bertram is agreeable, but the King of France notices he is wearing Helena's ring. She has tricked Bertram into exchanging rings when they slept together. Bertram says he does not know how he came by it. Diana and her mother arrive and Diana tells how Bertram seduced her and that is how he came by the ring. Then Helena appears and the true story is told. Bertram has to admit the conditions he has made have been met: Helena is now his true wife and he repents his past behaviour to her.

Measure for Measure

Sources

The play was performed for King James I on 26 December 1604 and was probably written earlier that year. There is a reference to peace negotiations, which are thought to be those between England and Spain in August 1604. *Measure for Measure* was first printed in 1623 in the First Folio.

Shakespeare may have used a play called *Promos and Cassandra* by George Whetstone, published in 1587, as his source, but he may also have drawn on another play, now lost, for some of the incidents in *Measure for Measure*.

The theme of the play is 'judge not that ye be not judged' but it is not an easy play for modern readers, who may have little sympathy for Isabella when she refuses to sleep with Angelo to save her brother's life.

Main Characters

Angelo

While the Duke is away, Angelo rules Vienna and is intolerant of all bad behaviour, even though he himself is far from perfect, having deserted his pregnant girlfriend.

Isabella

A virtuous and noble girl who is about to enter a convent. She goes to Angelo to plead for her brother's life and is horrified when he says he will spare him if she sleeps with him.

Claudio

Isabella's brother who expects his sister to sacrifice herself for him.

Vincentio

Duke Vincentio is the ruler of Vienna who temporarily abdicates, leaving Angelo in his place. Instead of going abroad, he disguises himself and stays near at hand to watch how Angelo behaves.

Escalus
A wise lord who urges Angelo to be merciful.

Lucio
A comic friend of Claudio's who tries to help him.

Mistress Overdone
The local brothel-keeper whose establishment Angelo means to shut down.

Pompey
Mistress Overdone's servant, a clown.

Mariana
Angelo's pregnant betrothed, whom he has deserted.

The Plot
The Duke of Vienna is taking leave of absence and has decided to put Angelo in his place. Angelo is honoured to assume the post of deputy but modestly urges he be tested to see if he is fit for the position. His concerns are brushed aside by the Duke.

The brothel-keeper, Mistress Overdone, tells how Claudio is in prison and is sentenced to be beheaded for having got Julietta pregnant. She hears that all the brothels are to be closed.

Claudio has promised to marry Julietta but they are still awaiting her dowry; he blames his arrest on Vienna's new ruler. He sends word to his sister Isabella to ask her to plead with Angelo to spare him.

Isabella is about to enter a convent and is glad that her liberty will be restricted. She hears of what has happened to her brother and agrees to go to Angelo.

Angelo at first refuses to relent but begins to weaken, seeing how beautiful and virtuous Isabella is. He tells her to come back later and when she does he says if she will sleep with him then he will spare her brother's life. It takes Isabella some time before she understands what a horrible choice is being put before her. She says her brother would not want her to sacrifice her virtue for him and threatens to tell the world what a hypocrite Angelo is. Angelo retorts that no one will believe her and she will feel guilty for letting her brother die.

She goes to visit her brother in prison and, to her amazement, he urges her to sacrifice her virtue for him. Isabella calls him a beast and a faithless coward. She storms off and Claudio is visited by the Duke, who warns him that even if his sister agrees to sleep with Angelo he will still be executed. Claudio now feels ashamed of his cowardice. The Duke suggests that Isabella agrees to sleep with Angelo but at the last moment swaps places with Mariana, Angelo's deserted mistress. The Duke says it will be no sin as Mariana is virtually Angelo's wife, even though he will not acknowledge it.

The Duke expects to hear that Claudio is reprieved, but instead Angelo sends word to the prison that he must be executed. The Duke suggests the provost executes the convicted murderer Barnadine instead and sends his head to Angelo. He will not notice that it is not Claudio's head. Or, better still, they may not need to execute anyone because the pirate Ragozine has died in the night and they can use his head.

When Isabella arrives at the prison the Duke decides not to tell her the truth and instead informs her that her brother is dead.

The Duke sends word to Angelo that he is returning to take up the reins of power and Angelo is worried.

The Duke enters the city and Isabella loudly accuses Angelo of his crimes. Mariana also accuses him of being a faithless husband. Angelo says he is the victim of a conspiracy, but the Duke reveals that he has been in the city all the time disguised as a friar and knows that Angelo is indeed a villain. Angelo begs that rather than being put to death he marry Mariana.

The Duke sends for the murderer and pardons him and then Claudio is brought in veiled. The Duke reveals that Claudio is alive after all and then, rather surprisingly, asks or rather commands Isabella to marry him. She does not reply.

THE TRAGEDIES

Shakespeare's tragedies represent the finest body of writing in the English language. They contain a world of woe but they furnish glimpses of mercy and holiness; the agony of Lear and of Othello, the doubt of Hamlet and the ambition of Macbeth, are purged in what can be seen as an act of spiritual renovation. The spirit of the audience is moved and lifted in a kind of communal celebration. Humankind must suffer and endure. There is no other course. But in the acceptance of that condition, there is the possibility of transcendence. And of course, in the work of Shakespeare, there is always the further palliative of broad comedy. The role of Iago in *Othello*, for example, was first played by Robert Armin; he was the resident 'fool' of the Lord Chamberlain's Men. Mercy, pity, and folly, go hand in hand.

These four tragedies can be considered the summit of Shakespeare's achievement: *Hamlet*, *Othello*, *King Lear* and *Macbeth*. They repay repeated reading and watching, always revealing fresh moments of insight into the human condition. There can be no definitive reading of any of these plays, no definitive performance and no definitive answers to the questions they raise.

Hamlet is the most ambiguous and enigmatic of plays. It tells how the young prince encounters the ghost of his murdered father and swears to avenge him. He must kill his uncle, his father's brother, who committed the murder to steal the throne and make the queen his own.

For Freud this was a seminal text, seeming to reveal the basic, if unacknowledged, truth that all sons wish to kill their fathers and sleep with their mothers. It is idle to speculate on what Shakespeare himself thought *Hamlet* was about. All we can say is that each generation has interpreted the play in a different way – none more valid than any other but always helping us understand who we are and how we are motivated. Almost every line of the play is rich with imagery and littered with similes and metaphors that have become part of common usage/well-known in the English language. The play can seem one long 'quotation', so familiar is its sublime poetry, but such is its sinuosity it remains forever fresh.

King Lear, too, is a pinnacle in Shakespeare's oeuvre. It is the story of a king who strips himself of authority, persuades himself that he knows who loves him and who does not, and in the end descends into a hell of madness before finding peace and reconciliation. It has inspired every great actor and a host of modern playwrights from Harold Pinter to Samuel Beckett. The exploration of the nature of madness, the need to strip oneself of all one's illusions and face the world naked to discover who we really are, has made this play eternally important; but above all, it captures our imagination as a tale of a real man in agony.

Macbeth seems simpler – a play about overweening ambition – but it is much more than this. Like *King Lear*, it is a play about discovering who we are and what our place is in the scheme of things.

Othello is the archetypal tragic hero: a noble man seduced by pure evil to kill the thing he loves most. The power of the poetry carries the play into another realm in which human desire is shown to be weak and foolish. What is natural and what is unnatural? What is the nature of jealousy? What is evil and how do we recognize it? What does it mean to love? These are just some of the questions raised in this great tragedy.

Romeo and Juliet is Shakespeare's tragedy of love. It moves us with its depiction of young love frustrated by the enmities of parents. It has inspired many writers and composers; the theme of communities at war, reconciled only by the death of children, is always going to be important. The play's ecstatic poetry captures the intensity of teenage desire, which young people will always find expresses their own emotions in language they could not hope to emulate.

Hamlet

Sources

One of Shakespeare's best-known and probably most popular plays, *Hamlet* is, according to his recent biographer, Anthony Holden, 'the most ambitious revenge tragedy of them all'. It is Shakespeare's longest play.

There are three versions of *Hamlet*. Shakespeare wrote the play around 1600–01 and it was entered into the Stationers' Register on 26 July 1602. The first edition was printed in about 1603 but is regarded as a 'bad quarto' – i.e. not printed from authoritative texts. Another very different edition was published in 1604, which according to the printer was 'the true and perfect copy'; and, finally, the supposedly authoritative version appeared in the First Folio in 1623. The compilers claimed these texts were 'cured, and perfect of their limbs ... absolute in their numbers, as he conceived them'. The numerous impressions of the play have long caused consternation among literary scholars, not to mention actors never quite sure which to use. Today, the version most in use is a collation of the 1604 and 1623 editions, with the interesting bits from the 1603 edition thrown in for good measure. Some scholars still dispute that the 1604 edition is a separate work and should not be added to the First Folio.

Shakespeare used as his basis the now lost play known as *ur-Hamlet*, which he may even have helped to write. That work used Danish historian Saxo Grammaticus' story of the deranged Prince Amleth of Jutland, whose father was killed by his brother King Fengo, told in *Gesta Danorum* .

Main Characters
Hamlet
The young Prince of Denmark. Hamlet is a scholarly man with high principles; he wants to avenge the murder of his father but knows that this action is wrong. A loner, Hamlet is more than aware that the world in which he lives is dishonest but cannot see how he can improve things without becoming dishonest himself. He loves his mother deeply but is disgusted by her marriage to his father's brother and murderer. This revulsion plunges him into depression, easily allowing Claudius, the devious king, to outwit him. Hamlet often appears surly and the king and queen reproach him for his sulky behaviour. Following the meeting with the Ghost in Act 1, Scene 5, Hamlet decides to change his attitude.

> Remember thee?
> Ay, thou poor ghost, while memory holds a seat
> In this distracted globe. Remember thee?
> Yea, from the table of my memory
> I'll wipe away all trivial fond records,
> All saws of books, all forms, all pressures past,
> That youth and observation copied there.

Hamlet finally succumbs to the evil in the world that he so despises.

Polonius
The Lord Chamberlain, Polonius is the crafty father of Laertes and Ophelia. He is pompous and never uses one word when six will do. He doesn't trust Hamlet's love for Ophelia and has his own son spied on in Paris. Lord Polonius gets fixed ideas in his mind and once an idea is established nothing and no one can shift

it. Polonius is fully aware of the corruption around the court of King Claudius but is quite happy to use it for his own ends. His behaviour is always cynical and leads directly to his death.

Laertes

Polonius' son and Ophelia's brother, Laertes has inherited his father's cynicism: he is only too willing to believe that Hamlet's intentions towards Ophelia are not honourable. Grief-stricken at the deaths of both his father and sister, he believes that Hamlet is responsible (which, in at least one case, he is) and thus is easily persuaded to join the plot to murder the young Prince.

Ophelia

The daughter of Polonius, Ophelia is naive but in a touching way. Deeply in love with Hamlet, she rejects him because her father tells her that she must. However, the death of her father and the end of the affair with Hamlet upsets the balance of her mind. She dies by her own hand in a stream, although Gertrude says that the death was accidental. Dr Johnson describes her as 'the young, the beautiful, the harmless and the pious'.

Claudius

King Claudius, who murdered his brother, took his throne and then married his sister-in-law a month later. Claudius is manipulative and easily outmanoeuvres his nephew and stepson. Claudius is savvy enough to know that Hamlet is aware of the truth behind his father's death and sees through the young Prince's 'madness'. He plots to do away with Hamlet but comes unstuck, leading to his own death.

Gertrude

The queen of two kings, Gertrude is unaware that her brother-in-law murdered his own brother to assume the throne and marry her. She is truly shocked when Hamlet tells her. She is torn between her filial love and spousal love. In the end it is her love for her son that causes her to commit suicide.

Osric
A courtier. He is totally subservient to the king. (Osric was the name of Amleth's foster-brother in the Saxo Grammaticus story.)

Rosencrantz and Guildenstern
The inseparable courtiers. Two wanderers in life who have no function and no meaning, they are happy to spy on Hamlet when Claudius asks them to. On the trip to England that is supposed to take Hamlet to his death, he discovers they are carrying sealed orders for his murder. He artfully swaps their names for his and they are murdered.

Horatio
Hamlet's best friend. A true, loyal and devoted chum to the Prince of Denmark. Hamlet says of him:

> Give me that man
> That is not passion's slave, and I will wear him
> In my heart's core, ay, in my heart of heart,
> As I do thee.

Young Fortinbras
The nephew of the King of Norway, Prince Fortinbras is a glory hunter. He even seeks to gain possession of a plot of land that would be too small in which to bury the dead. He sees much in Hamlet that he admires.

The Plot
The play opens on the battlements of Elsinore, the castle that is home to the King of Denmark. King Hamlet has died (supposedly of a snakebite received while he was asleep in the orchard, but really poisoned by his brother) and Claudius, his brother, has taken the throne and married his widow, Queen Gertrude. Young Prince Hamlet is unhappy at what he sees as the usurpation of his father as both monarch and husband. Soldiers Francisco and Barnardo are on the battlements where Francisco

is to relieve Barnardo. As Francisco leaves he meets Horatio and Marcellus. When they arrive, Marcellus asks Barnardo, 'What, has this thing appear'd again to-night?' meaning the Ghost. Barnardo says no. Horatio is sceptical that the spectre exists at all, which is why he is on the battlements at midnight.

> MARCELLUS
> Horatio says 'tis but our fantasy
> And will not let belief take hold of him
> Touching this dreaded sight, twice seen of us;
> Therefore I have entreated him along
> With us to watch the minutes of this night;
> That if again this apparition come,
> He may approve our eyes and speak to it.

Horatio responds: 'Tush, tush, 'twill not appear.' Suddenly the Ghost appears – it is the spitting image of Hamlet's father. Horatio keeps his calm and asks it:

> What art thou that usurp'st this time of night,
> Together with that fair and warlike form
> In which the majesty of buried Denmark
> Did sometimes march? By heaven I charge thee speak.

The Ghost is offended and storms off.

Marcellus and Horatio fill in much of the plot: Denmark is preparing for war as Fortinbras of Norway is about to invade, wanting to reclaim land that his father lost to King Hamlet.

> MARCELLUS
> Good now, sit down, and tell me, he that knows,
> Why this same strict and most observant watch
> So nightly toils the subject of the land,
> And why such daily cast of brazen cannon,
> And foreign mart for implements of war;
> Why such impress of shipwrights, whose sore task

Does not divide the Sunday from the week;
What might be toward, that this sweaty haste
Doth make the night joint-labourer with the day,
Who is't that can inform me?

HORATIO
That can I
At least, the whisper goes so: our last king,
Whose image even but now appeared to us,
Was as you know by Fortinbras of Norway,
Thereto pricked on by a most emulate pride,
Dared to the combat; in which our valiant Hamlet -
For so this side of our known world esteemed him –
Did slay this Fortinbras, who by a sealed compact,
Well ratified by law and heraldry,
Did forfeit with his life all those his lands
Which he stood seized on, to the conqueror;
Against the which a moiety competent
Was gaged by our king; which had returned
To the inheritance of Fortinbras
Had he been vanquisher as, by the same covenant,
And carriage of the article design'd,
His fell to Hamlet. Now, sir, young Fortinbras,
Of unimproved mettle hot and full,
Hath in the skirts of Norway here and there
Shark'd up a list of landless resolutes,
For food and diet, to some enterprise
That hath a stomach in't; which is no other -
As it doth well appear unto our state -
But to recover of us, by strong hand
And terms compulsatory, those foresaid lands
So by his father lost: and this, I take it,
Is the main motive of our preparations,
The source of this our watch and the chief head
Of this post-haste and rummage in the land.

The Ghost reappears and is challenged by Horatio, who puts three questions to it. Before the Ghost can reply the cock heralds the advent of dawn and it disappears.

Horatio, Marcellus and Barnardo tell Hamlet about the Ghost and he says that he will join them on the battlements that night.

Hamlet is in love with Ophelia, the daughter of Lord Polonius, but Polonius and Laertes, her brother, order her to end the affair. Polonius says that Hamlet cannot be trusted and, anyway, his choice of bride is not a decision for him; the king will make it. Meekly, she obeys.

As he wanders on the battlements Hamlet sees the Ghost. It asks the Prince to follow him to somewhere more private where they can talk. Despite the vehement protestations of his friends, Hamlet follows.

HORATIO
It beckons you to go away with it,
As if it some impartment did desire
To you alone.

MARCELLUS
Look, with what courteous action
It waves you to a more removed ground:
But do not go with it

HORATIO
No, by no means.

HAMLET
It will not speak; then I will follow it.

HORATIO
Do not, my lord.

HAMLET
Why, what should be the fear?

I do not set my life at a pin's fee;
And for my soul, what can it do to that,
Being a thing immortal as itself?
It waves me forth again: I'll follow it.

When Hamlet goes with the Ghost, his companions follow him, Marcellus opining, 'Something is rotten in the state of Denmark.' The Ghost tells Hamlet that he is the ghostly spirit of his father, who was murdered – poison was poured into his ear as he slept – and the killer was his own brother. He is

Doom'd for a certain term to walk the night,
And for the day confined to fast in fires,
Till the foul crimes done in my days of nature
Are burnt and purged away.

He begs Hamlet to avenge his death and clean the stain of incest that is hanging over the throne. The Ghost is not sure whether Claudius bedded Gertrude before or after the king's murder.

The ever devious Lord Polonius sends a spy to France to see what his son, Laertes, is doing. As Reynaldo the agent leaves, Ophelia rushes in to see her father and tells him that she has just had a very strange meeting with Hamlet. She reports:

My lord, as I was sewing in my chamber,
Lord Hamlet, with his doublet all unbraced;
No hat upon his head; his stockings foul'd,
Ungarter'd, and down-gyved to his ankle;
Pale as his shirt; his knees knocking each other;
And with a look so piteous in purport
As if he had been loosed out of hell
To speak of horrors, he comes before me.

Polonius rushes off to tell Claudius the news. Meanwhile, Claudius becomes worried about Hamlet's behaviour and orders the Prince's old school friends Rosencrantz and

Guildenstern to spy on him. When Polonius tells Claudius that his daughter has dumped Hamlet, Claudius assumes that this is the reason for the odd behaviour. Hamlet has written a letter to Ophelia detailing his love for her, so Claudius and Polonius set up a meeting between the young lovers that they will be privy to.

Rosencrantz and Guildenstern tell Hamlet about their mission but Hamlet's favourite theatre troupe arrives and spoils the chat. Hamlet asks the company to put on *The Murder of Gonzalo,* a play that deals, indirectly, with the subject of his father's death. Hamlet decides to invite Claudius to the production and watch his reaction.

Meanwhile, the meeting is arranged between Hamlet and Ophelia. Claudius and Polonius hide to observe the outcome. Hamlet delivers the most famous soliloquy in theatre history:

> To be, or not to be, that is the question:
> Whether 'tis nobler in the mind to suffer
> The slings and arrows of outrageous fortune,
> Or to take arms against a sea of troubles
> And by opposing end them. To die – to sleep,
> No more; and by a sleep to say we end
> The heartache and the thousand natural shocks
> That flesh is heir to: 'tis a consummation
> Devoutly to be wish'd. To die, to sleep;
> To sleep, perchance to dream – ay, there's the rub:
> For in that sleep of death what dreams may come,
> When we have shuffled off this mortal coil,
> Must give us pause – there's the respect
> That makes calamity of so long life.
> For who would bear the whips and scorns of time,
> Th'oppressor's wrong, the proud man's contumely,
> The pangs of dispriz'd love, the law's delay,
> The insolence of office, and the spurns
> That patient merit of th'unworthy takes,
> When he himself might his quietus make
> With a bare bodkin? Who would fardels bear,

> To grunt and sweat under a weary life,
> But that the dread of something after death,
> The undiscover'd country, from whose bourn
> No traveller returns, puzzles the will,
> And makes us rather bear those ills we have
> Than fly to others that we know not of?
> Thus conscience does make cowards of us all,
> And thus the native hue of resolution
> Is sicklied o'er with the pale cast of thought,
> And enterprises of great pith and moment
> With this regard their currents turn awry
> And lose the name of action.

When Hamlet meets Ophelia, her manner lets him know that she is part of a conspiracy and he becomes angry, guessing that their conversation is being overheard. He observes:

> 'the power of beauty will sooner transform honesty from what it is to a bawd than the force of honesty can translate beauty into his likeness: this was sometime a paradox, but now the time gives it proof. I did love you once.'

He is disgusted and tells her,

> 'Get thee to a nunnery: why wouldst thou be a breeder of sinners? I am myself indifferent honest; but yet I could accuse me of such things that it were better my mother had not borne me: I am very proud, revengeful, ambitious, with more offences at my beck than I have thoughts to put them in, imagination to give them shape, or time to act them in. What should such fellows as I do crawling between heaven and earth? We are arrant knaves, all; believe none of us. Go thy ways to a nunnery.'

After Hamlet leaves, Ophelia is left alone and sad, but Claudius realizes that his nephew is not insane and decides to send him to England.

Polonius suggests that Hamlet should be watched again after the play and Claudius agrees to the request. Hamlet arranges for Horatio to watch Claudius' reaction during the performance. Hamlet positions himself next to Ophelia so that he, too, can keep an eye on Claudius. Before the action starts there is a mime, suggested by Hamlet, of the Ghost's story of the assassination. Neither the king nor the queen shows any reaction.

During the first act, the actress playing the queen says that she will be faithful to her husband forever. In the interval Hamlet asks Gertrude what she thinks of the play and specifically the declaration of undying wifely love. The Queen's reaction is cold: 'The lady doth protest too much, methinks.' In the second act the murder is once again shown, but Hamlet states that the killer was the king's nephew. He desperately hopes to provoke a reaction from Claudius, but for much of the performance there is none. Taking on the role of the chorus, Claudius finally loses patience and makes to leave, causing the play to end in chaos, much to Hamlet's delight.

After the play he goes to berate not his stepfather but his mother. Alone, Claudius decides that he will send Hamlet away. He falls to his knees to pray and is seen by Hamlet on his way to Gertrude's room. It is the perfect opportunity for Hamlet to avenge his father's murder, but the Prince cannot bring himself to kill a man at prayer, especially since it would mean that Claudius would go to heaven and not the hell that Hamlet believes he deserves. Hamlet continues to his mother's room, where she berates him for what she sees as his unseemly behaviour. Furious, he turns on her, prompting Gertrude to call for help. Hamlet hears a noise and, believing it to be Claudius, he lashes out with his sword and stabs Polonius instead. Gertrude accuses her son of committing 'a rash and bloody deed', to which Hamlet responds that what he did was nothing compared to what she has done: 'A bloody deed! almost as bad, good mother,

As kill a king, and marry with his brother.'

Gertrude's outraged reaction shows that she was blissfully unaware of the slaying. Hamlet continues shouting at his mother, silenced only by the reappearance of the Ghost. It appears to Gertrude that her son is addressing thin air and she again doubts his sanity. Hamlet persuades his mother that he is not mad and, realizing her enormous folly, she promises her son she will stand by him.

The shocking revelation has created a distance between husband and wife but both think that the other thinks that Hamlet is deranged. After Hamlet is packed off to England, Claudius admits that he is sending his stepson to an almost certain death.

Just before Hamlet leaves Denmark, he chances upon young Fortinbras and his army, off to fight for glory but nothing else in Poland – *dulce et decorum est pro patria mori* (it is noble and glorious to die for your country). Hamlet is initially sickened by what he sees as their vain glory, but upon reflection sees that young Fortinbras' actions and those of his men are in direct contrast to his own. He decides he will have 'bloody' thoughts from then on.

There follows another long soliloquy from Hamlet, which was cut by Laurence Olivier from his 1948 film version because he found it impossible to include without slowing down the story. For the sake of completeness, it is included here in full.

> How all occasions do inform against me,
> And spur my dull revenge! What is a man,
> If his chief good and market of his time
> Be but to sleep and feed? A beast, no more.
> Sure, he that made us with such large discourse,
> Looking before and after, gave us not
> That capability and god like reason
> To fust in us unused. Now, whether it be
> Bestial oblivion, or some craven scruple
> Of thinking too precisely on the event,

A thought which, quarter'd, hath but one part
   wisdom
And ever three parts coward, I do not know
Why yet I live to say 'This thing's to do';
Sith I have cause, and will, and strength, and means
To do't. Examples gross as earth exhort me:
Witness this army of such mass and charge
Led by a delicate and tender prince,
Whose spirit with divine ambition puff'd
Makes mouths at the invisible event,
Exposing what is mortal and unsure
To all that fortune, death and danger dare,
Even for an egg-shell. Rightly to be great
Is not to stir without great argument,
But greatly to find quarrel in a straw
When honour's at the stake. How stand I then,
That have a father kill'd, a mother stain'd,
Excitements of my reason and my blood,
And let all sleep? while, to my shame, I see
The imminent death of twenty thousand men,
That, for a fantasy and trick of fame,
Go to their graves like beds, fight for a plot
Whereon the numbers cannot try the cause,
Which is not tomb enough and continent
To hide the slain? O, from this time forth,
My thoughts be bloody, or be nothing worth!

King Claudius is worried about the people's reaction to the murder of Polonius. Laertes secretly returns from France and demands to know of Claudius how his father died.

Horatio receives a letter from Hamlet telling him that he has escaped from the ship taking him to his death. He reads it aloud: pirates attacked the ship and during the fighting Hamlet manoeuvred his way on to the pirate ship, which then sailed away. The pirates looked after Hamlet, while Rosencrantz and Guildenstern sail to England, where they are later murdered.

Meanwhile, Ophelia has suffered a total mental breakdown at the news of the death of her father. Laertes determines to seek vengeance for his father's death. Just before Claudius is about to tell Laertes how he disposed of Hamlet, a second missive arrives. Having been informed how his father met his death, the two men conspire to kill Hamlet. Death is in the air. Gertrude tells her husband that Ophelia has committed suicide by drowning.

> There is a willow grows aslant a brook,
> That shows his hoar leaves in the glassy stream;
> There with fantastic garlands did she make
> Of crow-flowers, nettles, daisies, and long purples
> That liberal shepherds give a grosser name,
> But our cold maids do dead men's fingers call them:
> There, on the pendent boughs her crownet weeds
> Clambering to hang, an envious sliver broke;
> When down the weedy trophies and herself
> Fell in the weeping brook. Her clothes spread wide;
> And, mermaid-like, awhile they bore her up:
> Which time she chanted snatches of old tunes;
> As one incapable of her own distress,
> Or like a creature native and endued
> Unto that element but long it could not be
> Till that her garments, heavy with their drink,
> Pull'd the poor wretch from her melodious lay
> To muddy death.

In the graveyard, two clowns gossip about Ophelia's death, wondering why a suicide would have a Christian burial. Hamlet approaches, oblivious to the machinations of his uncle and ex-girlfriend's brother. The clowns unearth the skull of Yorick. Alone, Hamlet talks about death and how it equalizes all the differences between rich and poor, clever and foolish, white and black. His speech features one of the most misquoted lines in Shakespeare:

Alas, poor Yorick! I knew him, Horatio: a fellow of infinite jest, of most excellent fancy: he hath borne me on his back a thousand times; and now, how abhorred in my imagination it is! My gorge rises at it. Here hung those lips that I have kissed I know not how oft. Where be your gibes now? your gambols? your songs? your flashes of merriment, that were wont to set the table on a roar? Not one now, to mock your own grinning? Quite chop-fallen? Now get you to my lady's chamber, and tell her, let her paint an inch thick, to this favour she must come; make her laugh at that. Prithee, Horatio, tell me one thing.

Yorick was the jester at his father's court and has been dead for twenty-three years. Ophelia's cortege arrives with Laertes as the chief mourner. His theatrical grief infuriates Hamlet, who insults the corpse's brother and the two end up in a bout of fisticuffs.

Hamlet tells Horatio that he believes Providence allowed him to escape from the ship. Hamlet now believes that he would not be damned by God for killing Claudius but would if he did not. Still smarting at the humiliation he suffered at the graveside, Laertes challenges Hamlet to a fencing match.

Hamlet apologizes to Laertes, who accepts, but the fencing match, a somewhat lopsided affair, goes on. Claudius provides Laertes with a poison-tipped rapier and, to be on the safe side, also prepares a drink that is laced with poison for Hamlet if he wins. Gertrude, realizing what is happening, drinks the poisoned draught despite the best efforts of Claudius to stop her. Laertes manages to wound Hamlet with the poisoned rapier but as they tussle their weapons are somehow swapped and Hamlet wounds Laertes. The poison works on Gertrude but not before she tells Hamlet that the wine was contaminated. Hamlet turns on Claudius and stabs him before making him drink the poisoned wine. Not long after, Laertes succumbs to the poison and his wound. Hamlet dies of his wounds and

the poison in the arms of his beloved friend, Horatio, who he
begs not to commit suicide.

> HAMLET
> The rest is silence.

> HORATIO
> Now cracks a noble heart. Good-night, sweet
>   prince,
> And flights of angels sing thee to thy rest!

The throne becomes vacant and the foreigner, young
Fortinbras, assumes power on the nomination of Hamlet.

Othello
Sources
First performed by the King's Men at the court of King James I
on 1 November 1604. Written during Shakespeare's great
tragic period, which also included the composition of *Hamlet*
(1600), *King Lear* (1604-05), *Macbeth* (1606) and *Antony and
Cleopatra* (1607-08), *Othello* is set against the backdrop of the
wars between Venice and Turkey that raged in the latter part of
the sixteenth century. Cyprus, the setting for most of the
action, was a Venetian outpost attacked by the Turks in 1570
and conquered the following year.

   Shakespeare's information on the Venetian-Turkish conflict
probably derives from Richard Knolles' *Generall Historie of the
Turkes*, which was published in England in the autumn of 1603.
The story of *Othello* is also derived from another source: an
Italian prose tale written in 1565 by Giovanni Battista Giraldi
Cinzio (usually referred to as Cinthio). The original story
contains the bare bones of Shakespeare's plot: a Moorish general
is deceived by his ensign into believing his wife is unfaithful. To
Cinthio's story Shakespeare added supporting characters such as
the rich young dupe Roderigo and the outraged and grief-stricken
Brabanzio, Desdemona's father. Shakespeare compressed the

action into the space of a few days and set it against the backdrop of military conflict. And, most memorably, he turned the ensign, a minor villain, into the arch-villain Iago.

The question of Othello's exact race is open to some debate. The word Moor refers to the Islamic Arabic inhabitants of North Africa who conquered Spain in the eighth century, but the term was used rather broadly in the period and was sometimes applied to Africans from other regions. George Abbott, for example, in his *A Brief Description of the Whole World* of 1599, made distinctions between 'blackish Moors' and 'black Negroes'; a 1600 translation of John Leo's *The History and Description of Africa* distinguishes 'white or tawny Moors' of the Mediterranean coast of Africa from the 'Negroes or black Moors' of the south. Othello's darkness or blackness is alluded to many times in the play, but Shakespeare and other Elizabethans frequently described brunette or darker-than-average Europeans as black. The opposition of black and white imagery that runs throughout *Othello* is certainly a marker of difference between Othello and his European peers, but the difference is never quite so racially specific as a modern reader might imagine it to be.

While Moor characters abound on the Elizabethan and Jacobean stage, none are given so major or heroic a role as Othello. Perhaps the most vividly stereotypical black character of the period is Aaron, the villain of Shakespeare's early play *Titus Andronicus*. The antithesis of Othello, Aaron is lecherous, cunning and vicious: his final words are: 'If one good deed in all my life I did/I do repent it to my very soul' (*Titus Andronicus*, V.3). Othello, by contrast, is a noble figure of great authority, respected and admired by the Duke and Senate of Venice as well as by those who serve him, such as Cassio, Montano, and Lodovico. Only Iago voices an explicitly stereotypical view of Othello, depicting him from the beginning as an animalistic, barbarous, foolish outsider.

Main Characters
Othello

Beginning with the opening lines of the play, Othello remains at a distance from much of the action that concerns and affects him. Roderigo and Iago refer ambiguously to a 'he' or 'him' for much of the first scene. When they begin to specify whom they are talking about, especially once they stand beneath Brabanzio's window, they do so with racial epithets, not names. These include 'the Moor', 'the thick-lips', 'an old black ram', and 'a Barbary horse'. Although Othello appears at the beginning of the second scene, we do not hear his name until well into the third scene of Act I. Later, Othello's ship will be the last of the three to arrive at Cyprus; Othello will stand apart while Cassio and Iago supposedly discuss Desdemona; and Othello will assume that Cassio is dead without being present when the fight takes place. Othello's status as an outsider may be the reason he is such easy prey for Iago.

Although Othello is a cultural and racial outsider in Venice, his skill as a soldier and leader is nevertheless valuable and necessary to the state, and he is an integral part of Venetian civic society. He is in great demand by the Duke and Senate, as evidenced by Cassio's comment that the Senate 'sent about three several quests' to look for Othello. The Venetian government trusts Othello enough to put him in full martial and political command of Cyprus; indeed, in his dying speech, Othello reminds the Venetians of the 'service' he has done their state.

Those who consider Othello their social and civic peer, such as Desdemona and Brabanzio, nevertheless seem drawn to him because of his exotic qualities. Othello admits as much when he tells the Duke about his friendship with Brabanzio, saying: '[Desdemona's] father loved me, oft invited me,/Still questioned me the story of my life/From year to year.' Othello is also able to captivate his peers with his speech. The Duke's reply to Othello's speech about how he wooed Desdemona with his tales of adventure is: 'I think this tale would win my daughter too.'

Othello sometimes makes a point of presenting himself as an

outsider, whether because he recognizes his exotic appeal or because he is self-conscious of, and defensive about, his difference from other Venetians. For example, in spite of his obvious eloquence, he protests: 'Rude am I in my speech,/And little blessed with the soft phrase of peace.' While Othello is never rude in his speech, he does allow his eloquence to suffer as he is put under increasing strain by Iago's plots. In the final moments of the play, Othello regains his composure and, once again, seduces both his onstage and offstage audiences with his words. The speech that precedes his suicide is a tale that could woo almost anyone. It is the tension between Othello's victimization at the hands of a foreign culture and his own willingness to torment himself that makes him a tragic figure rather than simply Iago's ridiculous puppet.

Desdemona

The daughter of the Venetian senator Brabanzio. Desdemona and Othello are secretly married before the play begins. Desdemona is a more plausible, well-rounded figure than much criticism has given her credit for. Arguments that see Desdemona as stereotypically weak and submissive ignore the conviction and authority of her first speech ('My noble father,/I do perceive here a divided duty') and her terse fury after Othello strikes her ('I have not deserved this'). Similarly, critics who argue that Desdemona's slightly bizarre, bawdy jesting with Iago is either an interpolation not written by Shakespeare or a mere vulgarity ignore the fact that Desdemona is young, sexual and recently married. She later displays the same chiding, almost mischievous wit when she attempts to persuade Othello to forgive Cassio.

Desdemona is at times a submissive character, most notably in her willingness to take credit for her own murder. In response to Emilia's question, 'O, who hath done this deed?' Desdemona's final words are: 'Nobody, I myself Farewell./Commend me to my kind lord. O, farewell.' The play, then, depicts Desdemona contradictorily as a self-effacing, faithful wife and as a bold, independent personality. This contradiction

may be intentional, meant to portray the way Desdemona
herself feels after defending to her father her choice of marriage,
and then almost immediately being put in the position of
defending her fidelity to her husband. She begins the play as a
supremely independent person, but midway through she must
struggle against all odds to convince Othello that she is not
'too' independent. The manner in which Desdemona is
murdered – smothered by a pillow in a bed covered in her
wedding sheets – seems to be symbolic: she is literally suffo-
cated beneath the demands put on her fidelity. Since her first
lines, Desdemona has seemed capable of meeting or even rising
above those demands. In the end, Othello stifles the speech
that made Desdemona so powerful.

Tragically, Desdemona is apparently aware of her imminent
death. She, not Othello, asks Emilia to put her wedding sheets
on the bed, and she asks Emilia to bury her in these sheets
should she die first. The last time we see Desdemona before she
awakens to find Othello standing over her with murder in his
eyes, she sings a song she learned from her mother's maid:

> She was in love, and he she loved proved mad
> And did forsake her: she had a song of Willow;
> An old thing 'twas, but it express'd her fortune,
> And she died singing it: that song to-night
> Will not go from my mind

Like the audience, Desdemona seems able only to watch as her
husband is driven insane with jealousy. Though she maintains
to the end that she is 'guiltless', Desdemona also forgives her
husband. Her forgiveness of Othello may help the audience to
forgive him as well.

Iago
Possibly the most heinous villain in Shakespeare's works, Iago
is fascinating for his most terrible characteristic: his utter lack
of convincing motivation for his actions. In the first scene, he

claims to be angry at Othello for having passed him over for the position of lieutenant. At the end of Act I, Scene 3, Iago says he thinks Othello may have slept with his wife Emilia: 'It is thought abroad that 'twixt my sheets/He has done my office.' Iago mentions this suspicion again at the end of Act II, Scene 1, explaining that he lusts after Desdemona because he wants to get even with Othello 'wife for wife'. None of these claims seem to adequately explain Iago's deep hatred of Othello, and Iago's lack of motivation – or his inability or unwillingness to express his true motivation – makes his actions all the more terrifying. He is willing to take revenge on anyone – Othello, Desdemona, Cassio, Roderigo, even Emilia – at the slightest provocation and enjoys the pain and damage he causes.

Iago is often funny, especially in his scenes with the foolish Roderigo, which serve as a showcase of Iago's manipulative abilities. He seems almost to wink at the audience as he revels in his own skill. As entertained spectators, we find ourselves on Iago's side when he is with Roderigo, but the interactions between the two also reveal a streak of cowardice in Iago – a cowardice that becomes manifest in the final scene, when Iago kills his own wife.

Iago's murder of Emilia could also stem from the general hatred of women that he displays. Some readers have suggested that Iago's true, underlying motive for persecuting Othello is his homosexual love for the general. He certainly seems to take great pleasure in preventing Othello from enjoying marital happiness, and he expresses his love for Othello frequently and effusively.

It is Iago's talent for understanding and manipulating the desires of those around him that makes him both a powerful and a compelling figure. Iago is able to take the handkerchief from Emilia and know that he can deflect her questions; he is able to tell Othello of the handkerchief and know that Othello will not doubt him; he is able to tell the audience: 'And what's he then that says I play the villain,' and know that they will laugh as though he were a clown. Though the most inveterate liar, Iago inspires in all of the play's characters the trait that is most lethal to Othello: trust.

Michael Cassio

Othello's lieutenant Cassio is a young and inexperienced soldier, whose high position is much resented by Iago. Truly devoted to Othello, Cassio is extremely ashamed after being implicated in a drunken brawl in Cyprus and losing his place as lieutenant. Iago uses Cassio's youth, good looks and friendship with Desdemona to play on Othello's insecurities about Desdemona's fidelity.

Emilia

Iago's wife and Desdemona's attendant. A cynical, worldly woman, she is deeply attached to her mistress and distrustful of her husband.

Roderigo

A jealous suitor of Desdemona. Young, rich and foolish, Roderigo is convinced that if he gives Iago all of his money, Iago will help him win Desdemona's hand. Repeatedly frustrated as Othello marries Desdemona and then takes her to Cyprus, Roderigo is ultimately desperate enough to agree to help Iago kill Cassio after Iago points out that Cassio is another potential rival for Desdemona.

Bianca

A courtesan, or prostitute, in Cyprus. Bianca's favourite customer is Cassio, who teases her with promises of marriage.

Brabanzio

Desdemona's father, a somewhat blustering and self-important Venetian senator. As a friend of Othello, Brabanzio feels betrayed when the general marries his daughter in secret.

Duke of Venice

The official authority in Venice, the Duke has great respect for Othello as a public and military servant. His primary role within the play is to reconcile Othello and Brabanzio, and then to send Othello to Cyprus.

Montano
The governor of Cyprus before Othello. We see him first as he recounts the status of the war and awaits the Venetian ships.

Lodovico
One of Brabanzio's kinsmen, Lodovico acts as a messenger from Venice to Cyprus. He arrives in Cyprus with letters announcing that Othello has been replaced by Cassio as governor.

Graziano
Brabanzio's kinsman who accompanies Lodovico to Cyprus. Amid the chaos of the final scene, Graziano mentions that Desdemona's father has died.

Clown
Othello's servant. Although the clown appears only in two short scenes, his appearances reflect and distort the action and words of the main plots: his puns on the word 'lie' in Act III, Scene 4, for example, anticipate Othello's confusion of two meanings of that word in Act IV, Scene 1.

The Plot
Othello begins on a street in Venice, in the midst of an argument between Roderigo and Iago. The rich Roderigo has been paying Iago to help him in his suit to Desdemona, but he has seen no progress, and he has just learned that Desdemona has married Othello, a general whom Iago serves as ensign. Iago reassures Roderigo that he hates Othello. Chief among Iago's reasons for this hatred is Othello's recent promotion of Michael Cassio to the post of lieutenant. In spite of Iago's service in battle and the recommendation of three 'great ones' of the city, Othello chose to give the position to a man with no experience of leading men in battle. As he waits for an opportunity to

further his own self-interest, Iago only pretends to serve Othello.

Iago advises Roderigo to spoil some of Othello's pleasure in his marriage by rousing Desdemona's family against the general. The two men come to the street outside the house of Desdemona's father, Brabanzio, and cry out that he has been robbed by 'thieves'. Brabanzio, who is a Venetian senator, comes to the window. At first he doesn't believe what he hears, because he has told Roderigo to stay away from his daughter before, and thinks Roderigo is merely scheming once again in order to see Desdemona. Iago speaks in inflammatory terms, vulgarly telling the senator that his daughter and Othello are having sex by saying that they are 'making the beast with two backs'. Brabanzio begins to take what he hears seriously and decides to search for his daughter. Seeing the success of his plan, Iago leaves Roderigo alone and goes to attend on Othello. Like Brabanzio, Othello has no idea of Iago's role in Roderigo's accusations. As Iago departs, Brabanzio comes out of his house, furious that his daughter has left him. Declaring that his daughter has been stolen from him by magic 'charms', Brabanzio and his men follow Roderigo to Othello.

Iago arrives at Othello's lodgings, where he warns the general that Brabanzio will not hesitate to attempt to force a divorce between Othello and Desdemona. Othello sees a party of men approaching, and Iago, thinking that Brabanzio and his followers have arrived, counsels Othello to retreat indoors. Othello stands his ground, but the party turns out to be Cassio and officers from the Venetian court. They bring Othello the message that he is wanted by the Duke of Venice about a matter concerning Cyprus, an island in the Mediterranean controlled by Venice. As Cassio and his men prepare to leave, Iago mentions that Othello is married, but before he can say any more, Brabanzio, Roderigo and Brabanzio's men arrive to accost Othello. Brabanzio orders his men to attack and subdue Othello. A struggle between Brabanzio's and Othello's followers seems imminent, but Othello brings the confrontation to a halt by calmly and authoritatively telling both sides to put up their swords. Hearing that the Duke has summoned Othello to the court, Brabanzio decides to bring his cause before the Duke himself.

The Duke's meeting with his senators about the imminent Turkish invasion of Cyprus takes an unexpected turn when a sailor arrives and announces that the Turks seem to have turned towards Rhodes, another island controlled by Venice. One of the senators guesses that the Turks' change of course is intended to mislead the Venetians, because Cyprus is more important to the Turks and is far more vulnerable than Rhodes. This guess proves to be correct, as another messenger arrives to report that the Turks have joined with more forces and are heading back toward Cyprus.

This military meeting is interrupted by the arrival of Brabanzio, Othello, Cassio, Iago, Roderigo and various officers. Brabanzio demands that all state business be put aside in order to address his own grievance: his daughter has been stolen from him by spells and potions purchased from charlatans. The Duke is initially eager to take Brabanzio's side, but he becomes more sceptical when he learns that Othello is the man accused. The Duke gives Othello the chance to speak for himself. Othello admits that he has married Desdemona, but he denies having used magic to woo her and claims that Desdemona will support his story. He explains that Brabanzio frequently invited him to his house and questioned him about his remarkable life story, full of harrowing battles, travels outside the civilized world and dramatic reversals of fortune. Desdemona overheard parts of the story and found a convenient time to ask Othello to retell it to her. Desdemona was moved to love Othello by his story.

The Duke is persuaded by Othello's tale, dismissing Brabanzio's claim by remarking that the story probably would win his own daughter. Desdemona enters, and Brabanzio asks her to tell those present to whom she owes the most obedience. Brabanzio clearly expects her to say her father. Desdemona, however, confirms that she married Othello of her own free will and that, like her own mother before her, she must shift her primary loyalty from father to husband. Brabanzio reluctantly resigns himself to her decision and allows the court to return to state affairs.

The Duke decides that Othello must go to Cyprus to defend the island from the Turks. Othello is willing and ready to go, and he asks that appropriate accommodations be provided for his wife. The Duke suggests that she stay with her father, but neither Desdemona nor Brabanzio nor Othello will accept this, and Desdemona asks to be allowed to go with Othello. The couple then leave to prepare for the night's voyage. The stage is cleared, leaving only Roderigo and Iago. Once again, Roderigo feels that his hopes of winning Desdemona have been dashed, but Iago insists that all will be well. Iago mocks Roderigo for threatening to drown himself, and Roderigo protests that he can't help being tormented by love. Iago contradicts him, asserting that people can choose at will what they want to be. 'Put but money in thy purse,' Iago tells Roderigo repeatedly, urging him to follow him to Cyprus. Iago promises to work everything out from there. When Roderigo leaves, Iago delivers his first soliloquy, declaring his hatred for Othello and his suspicion that Othello has slept with his wife Emilia. He lays out his plan to cheat Roderigo out of his money, to convince Othello that Cassio has slept with Desdemona, and to use Othello's honest and unsuspecting nature to bring him to his demise.

On the shores of Cyprus, Montano, the island's governor, watches a storm with two gentlemen. Just as Montano says that the Turkish fleet of ships could not survive the storm, a third gentleman comes to confirm his prediction: as his ship travelled from Venice, Cassio witnessed that the Turks lost most of their fleet in the tempest. It is still uncertain whether Othello's ship has survived. Hope lifts as voices offstage announce the sighting of a sail offshore, but the new ship turns out to be carrying Iago, Emilia, Desdemona and Roderigo. Desdemona disembarks, and no sooner does Cassio tell her that Othello has yet to arrive than a friendly shot announces the arrival of a third ship. While the company waits for the ship, Cassio and Desdemona tease Emilia about being a chatterbox, but Iago quickly takes the opportunity to criticize women in general as deceptive and hypocritical, saying they are lazy in all matters except sex: 'You rise to play and go to bed to work.' Desdemona plays along, laughing as Iago belittles women, whether beautiful or ugly, intelligent or stupid, as equally despicable. Cassio takes Desdemona away to speak with her privately about Othello's arrival. Iago notices that Cassio takes Desdemona's hand as he talks to her, and, in an aside, Iago plots to use Cassio's hand-holding to frame him so that he loses his newly gained promotion to lieutenant. 'With as little a web as this I will ensnare as great a fly as Cassio,' he asserts.

Othello arrives safely and greets Desdemona, expressing his devotion to her and giving her a kiss. He then thanks the Cypriots for their welcome and hospitality, and orders Iago to unload the ship. All but Roderigo and Iago head to the castle to celebrate the drowning of the Turks. Iago tells the despondent Roderigo that Desdemona will soon grow tired of being with Othello and will long for a more well-mannered and handsome man. But, Iago continues, the obvious first choice for Desdemona will be Cassio, whom Iago characterizes over and over again as a 'knave'. Roderigo tries to argue that Cassio was merely being polite by taking Desdemona's hand, but Iago convinces him of Cassio's ill intentions and convinces Roderigo to start a quarrel with Cassio that evening. He posits that the uproar the quarrel will cause in the still tense city will make Cassio fall out of favour with Othello. Left alone onstage again, Iago explains his actions to the audience in a soliloquy. He secretly lusts after Desdemona, partially because he suspects that Othello has slept with Emilia, and he wants to get even with the Moor 'wife for wife'. But, Iago continues, if he is unable to get his revenge by sleeping with Desdemona, Roderigo's accusation of Cassio will make Othello suspect his lieutenant of sleeping with his wife and eventually drive

Othello to madness.

A herald announces that Othello plans revelry for the evening in celebration of Cyprus' safety from the Turks, and also in celebration of his marriage to Desdemona.

Othello leaves Cassio on guard during the revels, reminding him to practise self-restraint during the celebration. Othello and Desdemona leave to consummate their marriage. Once Othello is gone, Iago enters and joins Cassio on guard. He tells Cassio that he suspects Desdemona to be a temptress, but Cassio maintains that she is modest. Then, despite Cassio's protestations, Iago persuades Cassio to take a drink and to invite some revellers to join them.

Once Cassio leaves to fetch the revellers, Iago tells the audience his plan: Roderigo and three other Cypriots, all of whom are drunk, are going to join Iago and Cassio on guard duty. Amid all the drunkards, Iago will lead Cassio into committing an action that will disgrace him. Cassio returns, already drinking, with Montano and his attendants. It is not long before he gets completely intoxicated and he wanders offstage, assuring his friends that he isn't drunk. Once Cassio leaves, Iago tells Montano that while Cassio is a wonderful soldier, he fears that Cassio may have too much responsibility for someone with such a serious drinking problem. Roderigo enters, and Iago points him in Cassio's direction. As Montano continues to suggest that something should be said to Othello of Cassio's drinking problem, Cassio chases Roderigo across the stage, threatening to beat him. Montano steps in to prevent the fight and is attacked by Cassio. Iago orders Roderigo to leave and 'cry a mutiny'. As Montano and others attempt to hold Cassio down, Cassio stabs Montano. An alarm bell is rung, and Othello bursts on to the scene with armed attendants.

Immediately taking control of the situation, Othello demands to know what happened, but both Iago and Cassio claim to have forgotten how the struggle began. Montano insists that he is in too much pain to speak and insists that Iago tell the story. At first Iago feigns reluctance to incriminate

Cassio, emphasizing the fact that he was chasing after Roderigo (to whom Iago does not refer by name) when the fight between Cassio and Montano began, and suggesting that the unknown man must have done something to upset Cassio. Othello falls into Iago's trap, stating that he can tell that Iago softened the story out of honest affection for Cassio. Othello dismisses Cassio from his service.

Desdemona has been awakened by the commotion, and Othello leads her back to bed, saying that he will look to Montano's wound. Iago and Cassio remain behind, and Cassio laments the permanent damage now done to his reputation by a quarrel, the cause of which he cannot even remember. Iago suggests that Cassio appeal to Desdemona, because she commands Othello's attention and goodwill. Iago argues that Desdemona's kindheartedness will prompt her to help Cassio if Cassio entreats her, and that she will persuade Othello to give Cassio back his lieutenantship.

When Cassio leaves, Iago jokes about the irony of the fact that his so-called villainy involves counselling Cassio to a course of action that would actually help him. He repeats what he told Cassio about Desdemona's generosity and Othello's devotion to her. However, as Iago reminds the audience, he does the most evil when he seems to do good. Now that Cassio will be spending time with Desdemona, Iago will find it all the easier to convince Othello that Desdemona is having an affair with Cassio, thus turning Desdemona's virtue to 'pitch'.

Roderigo enters, upset that he has been beaten and angry because Iago has taken all his money and left Roderigo nothing to show for it. Iago counsels him to be patient and not to return to Venice, reminding him that they have to work by their wits. He assures Roderigo that everything is going according to plan. After telling Roderigo to go, Iago finishes telling the audience the plot that is to come: he will convince Emilia to speak to Desdemona on Cassio's behalf, and he will arrange for Othello to witness Cassio's suit to Desdemona.

In an effort to win Othello's good grace, Cassio sends

musicians to play beneath the general's window. Othello sends his servant, a clown, to tell the musicians to go away. Cassio asks the clown to entreat Emilia to come speak with him, so that he can ask her for access to Desdemona. When the clown leaves, Iago enters and tells Cassio that he will send for Emilia straightaway and figure out a way to take Othello aside so that Cassio and Desdemona can confer privately. After Iago exits, Emilia enters and tells Cassio that Othello and Desdemona have been discussing his case. Desdemona has pleaded for Cassio, but Othello is worried that Montano's influence and popularity in Cyprus would make Cassio's reappointment impractical, no matter how much Othello cares for his former lieutenant. Emilia allows Cassio to come in and tells him to wait for Desdemona.

Iago, Othello, and a gentleman walk together at the citadel. Othello gives Iago some letters to deliver and decides to take a look at the town's fortifications.

Desdemona, Cassio and Emilia enter mid-conversation. Desdemona has just vowed to do everything she can on Cassio's behalf when Othello and Iago enter. Cassio quickly departs, protesting to Desdemona that he feels too uneasy to do himself any good. Othello asks whether it was Cassio he saw leaving the room, and Iago responds that surely Cassio would not behave like a guilty man at Othello's approach.

Desdemona entreats Othello to forgive Cassio and reinstate him as lieutenant. Othello assures her that he will speak to Cassio, but he answers evasively when she tries to arrange a meeting time. She criticizes Othello for responding to her request so grudgingly and hesitantly, and he tells her that he will deny her nothing but wishes to be left to himself for a little while.

Alone with Othello, Iago begins his insinuations of an affair between Cassio and Desdemona by reminding Othello that Cassio served as Othello and Desdemona's go-between during their courtship. Othello asks Iago whether he believes Cassio to be honest, and Iago feigns reluctance to answer. Iago plants in Othello's mind thoughts of adultery, cuckoldry and hypocrisy, until Othello screams at the ensign to speak his mind. Iago suggests that Othello observe his wife closely when she is with Cassio.

Othello tells Iago to have Emilia watch Desdemona when she is with Cassio. Iago appears to retreat from his accusations and suggests that Othello leave the matter alone; but he has already made his point. By himself, Othello muses that his wife no longer loves him, probably because he is too old for her, because he is black, and because he doesn't have the manners of a courtier. 'She's gone,' he laments.

Desdemona and Emilia enter to inform Othello that he is expected at dinner. Othello says that he has a pain in his forehead, and Desdemona offers to bind his head with her handkerchief. Othello pushes her handkerchief away, telling her that it is too small. The handkerchief drops to the floor, where it remains as Othello and Desdemona exit. Emilia, staying behind, picks up the handkerchief, remarking that her husband has asked her to steal it at least 100 times. Iago enters, and Emilia teases him with the promise of a surprise. He is ecstatic when she gives the handkerchief to him, and sends her away.

As Iago gleefully plots to plant the handkerchief in Cassio's room, Othello enters and flies into a rage at him. Othello declares that his soul is in torment, and that it would be better to be deceived completely than to suspect without proof. He demands that Iago bring him visual evidence that Desdemona is a whore. Iago protests that it would be impossible to actually witness Desdemona and Cassio having sex, even if the two were as lustful as animals. He promises that he can provide circumstantial evidence, however. First, he tells Othello that while Cassio and Iago were sharing a bed, Cassio called out Desdemona's name in his sleep, wrung Iago's hand, kissed him hard on the lips, and threw his leg over Iago's thigh. This story enrages Othello, and Iago reminds him that it was only Cassio's dream. Iago then claims to have witnessed Cassio wiping his

beard with the handkerchief Othello gave Desdemona as his
first gift to her. Furious, Othello cries out for blood. He kneels
and vows to heaven that he will take his revenge on Desdemona
and Cassio, and Iago kneels with him, vowing to help execute
his master's vengeance. Othello promotes Iago to lieutenant.

Desdemona orders the clown to find Cassio and bring him
the message that she has made her suit to Othello. As the clown
departs, Desdemona wonders to Emilia where her handkerchief might be. Othello enters and tells Desdemona to give him
her hand. She does so, and he chastises her for her hand's
moistness – a sign of sexual promiscuity. He then asks her to
lend him her handkerchief. When Desdemona cannot produce
the handkerchief, Othello explains the handkerchief's history.
An Egyptian sorceress gave it to his mother and told her that it
would make her desirable and keep Othello's father loyal, but
if she lost it or gave it away, Othello's father would leave her.
Othello's mother gave him the magic handkerchief on her
deathbed, instructing him to give it to the woman he desired to
marry. Desdemona is unsettled by the story and says that she
has the handkerchief but not with her. Othello does not believe
her. As he accuses her, demanding, 'The handkerchief!' with
increasing vehemence, she entreats for Cassio as a way of
changing the subject.

After Othello storms off, Emilia laments the fickleness of
men. Cassio and Iago enter, and Cassio immediately continues
with his suit to Desdemona for help in winning over her husband.
Desdemona tells Cassio that his timing is unfortunate, as Othello
is in a bad humour, and Iago promises to go and soothe his
master. Emilia speculates that Othello is jealous, but Desdemona
maintains her conviction that Othello is upset by some political
matter. She tells Cassio to wait while she goes to find Othello
and bring him to talk with his former lieutenant.

While Cassio waits, Bianca, a prostitute, enters. She reprimands him for not visiting her more frequently, and he apologizes, saying that he is under stress. He asks her to copy the
embroidery of a handkerchief he recently found in his room on

to another handkerchief. Bianca accuses him of making her copy the embroidery of a love gift from some other woman, but Cassio tells her she is being silly. They make a plan to meet later that evening.

Othello and Iago enter in mid-conversation. Iago goads Othello by arguing that it is no crime for a woman to be naked with a man, if nothing happens. Iago then remarks that if he were to give his wife a handkerchief, it would be hers to do as she wished with it. These persistent insinuations of Desdemona's unfaithfulness work Othello into an incoherent frenzy. He focuses obsessively on the handkerchief and keeps pumping Iago for information about Cassio's comments to Iago. Finally, Iago says that Cassio has told him he has lain with Desdemona, and Othello '[f]alls down in a trance'.

Cassio enters, and Iago mentions that Othello has fallen into his second fit of epilepsy in two days. He warns Cassio to stay out of the way but tells him that he would like to speak once Othello has gone. Othello comes out of his trance, and Iago explains that Cassio stopped by and that he has arranged to speak with the ex-lieutenant. Iago orders Othello to hide nearby and observe Cassio's face during their conversation. Iago explains that he will make Cassio retell the story of where, when, how and how often he has slept with Desdemona, and when he intends to do so again. When Othello withdraws, Iago informs the audience of his actual intention. He will joke with Cassio about the prostitute Bianca, so that Cassio will laugh as he tells the story of Bianca's pursuit of him. Othello will be driven mad, thinking that Cassio is joking with Iago about Desdemona.

The plan works: Cassio laughs uproariously as he tells Iago the details of Bianca's love for him, and even makes gestures in an attempt to depict her sexual advances. Just as Cassio says that he no longer wishes to see Bianca, she herself enters with the handkerchief and again accuses Cassio of giving her a love token given to him by another woman. Bianca tells Cassio that if he doesn't show up for supper with her that evening, he will never be welcome to come back again. Othello has recognized his handkerchief and, coming out of hiding when Cassio and Bianca are gone, wonders how he should murder his former lieutenant. Othello goes on to lament his hardheartedness and love for Desdemona, but Iago reminds him of his purpose. Othello has trouble reconciling his wife's delicacy, class, beauty and allure with her adulterous actions. He suggests that he will poison his wife, but Iago advises him to strangle her in the bed that she contaminated through her infidelity. Iago also promises to arrange Cassio's death.

Desdemona enters with Lodovico, who has come from Venice with a message from the Duke. Lodovico irritates Othello by inquiring about Cassio, and Desdemona irritates Othello by answering Lodovico's inquiries. The contents of the letter also upset Othello – he has been called back to Venice, with orders to leave Cassio as his replacement in Cyprus. When Desdemona hears the news that she will be leaving Cyprus, she expresses her happiness, whereupon Othello strikes her. Lodovico is horrified by Othello's loss of self-control, and asks Othello to call back Desdemona, who has left the stage. Othello does so, only to accuse her of being a false and promiscuous woman. He tells Lodovico that he will obey the Duke's orders, commands Desdemona to leave and storms off. Lodovico cannot believe that the Othello he has just seen is the same self-controlled man he once knew. He wonders whether Othello is mad, but Iago refuses to answer Lodovico's questions, telling him that he must see for himself.

Othello interrogates Emilia about Desdemona's behaviour, but Emilia insists that Desdemona has done nothing suspicious. Othello tells Emilia to summon Desdemona, implying while Emilia is gone that she is a 'bawd' or female pimp. When Emilia returns with Desdemona, Othello sends Emilia to guard the door. Alone with Desdemona, Othello weeps and proclaims that he could have borne any affliction other than the pollution of the 'fountain' from which his future children are to flow. When Desdemona fervently denies being unfaithful, Othello sarcastically replies that he begs her pardon: he took her for the 'cunning whore of Venice' who married Othello. Othello storms out of the room, and Emilia comes in to comfort her mistress. Desdemona tells Emilia to lay her wedding sheets on the bed for that night.

At Desdemona's request, Emilia brings in Iago, and Desdemona tries to find out from him why Othello has been treating her like a whore. Emilia says to her husband that Othello must have been deceived by some villain, the same sort of villain who made Iago suspect Emilia of sleeping with Othello. Iago assures Desdemona that Othello is merely upset by some official business, and a trumpet flourish calls Emilia and Desdemona away to dinner with the Venetian emissaries. Roderigo enters, furious that he is still frustrated in his love, and ready to make himself known in his suit to Desdemona so that she might return all of the jewels that Iago was supposed to have given her from him. Iago tells Roderigo that Cassio is being assigned to Othello's place. Iago also lies, saying that Othello is being sent to Mauritania, in Africa, although he is really being sent back to Venice. He tells Roderigo that the only way to prevent Othello from taking Desdemona away to Africa with him would be to get rid of Cassio. He sets about persuading Roderigo that he is just the man for 'knocking out [Cassio's] brains'.

After dinner, Othello proposes to walk with Lodovico, and sends Desdemona to bed, telling her that he will be with her shortly and that she should dismiss Emilia. Desdemona seems aware of her imminent fate as she prepares for bed. She says that if she dies before Emilia, that Emilia should use one of the wedding sheets for her shroud. As Emilia helps her mistress to undress, Desdemona sings a song called 'Willow', about a woman whose love forsook her. She says she learned the song from her mother's maid, Barbary, who died singing the song after she had been deserted by her lover. The song makes Desdemona think about adultery, and she asks Emilia whether she would cheat on her husband 'for all the world'. Emilia says that she would not deceive her husband for jewels or rich clothes, but that the whole world is a huge prize and would outweigh the offence. This leads Emilia to speak about the fact that women have appetites for sex and infidelity just as men do, and that men who deceive their wives have only themselves to blame if their wives cheat on them. Desdemona replies that she prefers to answer bad deeds with good deeds rather than with more bad deeds. She readies herself for bed.

Iago and Roderigo wait outside the brothel where Cassio visits Bianca. Iago positions Roderigo with a rapier in a place where he will be able to ambush Cassio. Iago then withdraws, although Roderigo asks him not to go too far in case he needs help killing Cassio. When Cassio enters, Roderigo stabs at him but fails to pierce Cassio's armour. Cassio stabs and wounds Roderigo. Iago darts out in the commotion, stabs Cassio in the leg and exits. Not knowing who has stabbed him, Cassio falls. At this moment, Othello enters. Hearing Cassio's cries of murder, Othello believes that Iago has killed him. Inspired by what he believes to be Iago's successful vengeance, Othello returns to his bedroom to kill Desdemona.

Lodovico and Graziano enter and hear Cassio's and Roderigo's cries. They can see nothing because of the darkness, and they are wary of helping the crying men in case it is a trap. Iago enters carrying a light. He first pretends to discover Cassio, who begs him for help, and then stumbles upon Cassio's assailant, Roderigo, whom Iago stabs without hesitation. Graziano and Lodovico are still unable to see Iago, and they are unaware of what he is doing. Finally, the three men come face-to-face, and they question Cassio about his injuries.

Bianca enters and begins to cry out when she sees the wounded Cassio. Iago questions Cassio about his assailant, but Cassio can provide no explanation for what has happened. Iago suggests that Roderigo is to blame. Cassio says that he does not know Roderigo. Attendants carry off Cassio, and Roderigo's corpse. Emilia enters and Iago tells her what has happened, adding the explanation, 'This is the fruits of whoring.' He and

Emilia chastise Bianca, at whose house Cassio had dined that evening. Iago puts Bianca under arrest, and sends Emilia to tell Othello and Desdemona what has happened. Iago ends the scene with an aside: 'This is the night/That either makes me or fordoes me quite.'

Holding a candle, Othello stands over the sleeping Desdemona and prepares to kill her. He bends down to kiss her once before he does the deed, she wakes, and he tells her to prepare to die. Growing frightened, Desdemona asks her husband why he means to kill her, and Othello responds that she has been unfaithful to him with Cassio – he has seen the proof in the handkerchief. Othello refuses to believe Desdemona's denial of the charge, saying that Cassio has confessed but will speak no more, since he has been killed by Iago. Desdemona begins to weep for Cassio, which only drives Othello into a greater rage. Wrestling with her as she begs to be allowed to live just a little longer, Othello finally succeeds in smothering his wife. Emilia calls from outside the door, and Othello, apparently delirious, confuses her cries with his wife's and concludes that Desdemona is not yet dead. Thinking himself to be merciful, and not wanting to have his wife linger in pain, he smothers her again.

Othello draws the bed curtains and lets Emilia in. Emilia informs Othello that Cassio has killed Roderigo. Othello asks if Cassio has been killed as well, and Emilia informs him that Cassio is alive. As Othello begins to realize that his plans have gone awry, Desdemona cries out that she has been murdered. She stays alive long enough to recant this statement, telling Emilia that she was not murdered but killed herself. She dies. Othello triumphantly admits to Emilia that he killed Desdemona, and when she asks him why, Othello tells her that Iago opened his eyes to Desdemona's falsehood. Unfazed by Othello's threat that she 'were best' to remain silent, Emilia calls out for help, bringing Montano, Graziano and Iago to the scene.

As the truth of Iago's villainy begins to come out through

Emilia's accusations, Othello falls weeping upon the bed that
contains the body of his dead wife. Almost to himself, Graziano
expresses relief that Brabanzio is dead – the first news the
audience has heard of this – and has not lived to see his daughter
come to such a terrible end. Othello still clings to his belief in
Iago's truth and Desdemona's guilt, mentioning the handkerchief and Cassio's 'confession'. When Othello mentions the
handkerchief, Emilia erupts, and Iago, no longer certain that he
can keep his plots hidden, attempts to silence her with his
sword. Graziano stops him and Emilia explains how she found
the handkerchief and gave it to Iago. Othello runs at Iago but is
disarmed by Montano. In the commotion, Iago is able to stab
his wife, who falls, apparently dying. Iago flees and is pursued
by Montano and Graziano. Left alone onstage with the bodies
of the two women, Othello searches for another sword.
Emilia's dying words provide eerie background music, as she
sings a snatch of the song 'Willow'. She tells Othello that
Desdemona was chaste and loved him.

Graziano returns to find Othello armed and defiant,
mourning the loss of his wife. They are joined shortly by
Montano, Lodovico, Cassio and Iago, who is being held
prisoner. Othello stabs Iago, wounding him, and Lodovico
orders some soldiers to disarm Othello. Iago sneers that he
bleeds but is not killed. He refuses to say anything more about
what he has done, but Lodovico produces a letter found in
Roderigo's pocket that reveals everything that has happened.
Seeking some kind of final reconciliation, Othello asks Cassio
how he came by the handkerchief, and Cassio replies that he
found it in his chamber.

Lodovico tells Othello that he must come with them back to
Venice, and that he will be stripped of his power and command
and put on trial. Refusing to be taken away before he has
spoken, Othello asks his captors: 'When you shall these
unlucky deeds relate,/Speak of me as I am.' He reminds them
of a time in Aleppo when he served the Venetian state and slew
a malignant Turk. 'I took by the throat the circumcised dog/

And smote him thus,' says Othello, pulling a third dagger from hiding and stabbing himself in demonstration. Pledging to 'die upon a kiss', Othello falls on to the bed with his wife's body.

Lodovico tells Iago to look at the results of his devious efforts, names Graziano as Othello's heir, and puts Montano in charge of Iago's execution. Lodovico prepares to leave for Venice to bear the news from Cyprus to the Duke and Senate.

King Lear
Sources
Shakespeare probably wrote *King Lear* in late 1605, between *Othello* and *Macbeth*, and it is usually ranked alongside *Hamlet* as one of Shakespeare's greatest plays. It was performed at court on Boxing Day 1606. Its sources include *The True Chronicle History of King Leir and his Three Daughters* (1590) as well as *Declaration of Egregious Popish Impostures* (1603).

The setting of *King Lear* is as far removed from Shakespeare's time as the setting of any of his other plays, dramatizing events from the eighth century BC. But the parallel stories of Lear's and Gloucester's sufferings at the hands of their own children reflect anxieties that would have been close to home for Shakespeare's audience. One possible event that may have influenced this play is a lawsuit that occurred not long before *King Lear* was written, in which the eldest of three sisters tried to have her elderly father, Sir Brian Annesley, declared insane so that she could take control of his property. Annesley's youngest daughter, Cordell, successfully defended her father against her sister. Another event that Shakespeare and his audience would have been familiar with is the case of William Allen, a mayor of London who was treated very poorly by his three daughters after dividing his wealth among them. Not least among relevant developments was the then recent transfer of power from Elizabeth I to James I, which occurred in March 1603. Elizabeth had produced no male heir, and the anxiety about who her successor would be was fuelled by fears that a dynastic struggle along the lines of the fifteenth-century Wars of the Roses might ensue.

Elizabethan England was an extremely hierarchical society, demanding that absolute deference be paid and respect be shown not only to the wealthy and powerful but also to parents and the elderly. *King Lear* demonstrates how vulnerable parents and noblemen are to the depredations of unscrupulous children, and thus how fragile the fabric of Elizabethan society actually was.

Main Characters
King Lear

The ageing King of Britain and the protagonist of the play. Lear is used to enjoying absolute power and to being flattered, and he does not respond well to being contradicted or challenged. At the beginning of the play, his values are notably hollow – he prioritizes the appearance of love over actual devotion and wishes to maintain the power of a king while unburdening himself of the responsibility. Nevertheless, he inspires loyalty in subjects such as Gloucester, Kent, Cordelia and Edgar, all of whom risk their lives for him.

According to my esteemed Mammoth colleague Mike Ashley, Lear or Leir or Llyr, the 'legendary king of Britain', was the son of Blaedud and was the founder of Leicester. He reigned for sixty years and was buried in a vault under the River Soar at Leicester. He was succeeded by Cordelia, Britain's first queen, who ruled for five years before being deposed by her nephews, Marganus and Cunedagius. Cordelia died in prison by her own hand.

Cordelia

Lear's youngest daughter, disowned by her father for refusing to flatter him. Cordelia is held in extremely high regard by all of the good characters in the play – the King of France marries her for her virtue alone, overlooking her lack of dowry. She remains loyal to Lear despite his cruelty towards her; she forgives him, and displays a mild and forbearing temperament even towards her evil sisters, Goneril and Regan. Despite her obvious virtues, Cordelia's reticence makes her motivations difficult to read, as in her refusal to declare her love for her father at the beginning of the play.

Goneril
Lear's ruthless oldest daughter and the wife of the Duke of Albany. Goneril is jealous, treacherous and amoral. Shakespeare's audience would have been particularly shocked at Goneril's aggressiveness, a quality that it would not have expected in a female character. She challenges Lear's authority, boldly initiates an affair with Edmund, and wrests military power away from her husband.

Regan
Lear's middle daughter and the wife of the Duke of Cornwall. Regan is as ruthless as Goneril and as aggressive in all the same ways. In fact, it is difficult to think of any quality that distinguishes her from her sister. When they are not egging each other on to further acts of cruelty, they jealously compete for the same man, Edmund.

Gloucester
A nobleman loyal to King Lear whose rank, earl, is below that of duke. The first thing we learn about Gloucester is that he is an adulterer, having fathered a bastard son, Edmund. His fate is in many ways parallel to that of Lear: he misjudges which of his children to trust. He appears weak and ineffectual in the early acts, when he is unable to prevent Lear from being turned out of his own house, but he later demonstrates that he is also capable of great bravery.

Edgar
Gloucester's older, legitimate son, Edgar plays many different roles, starting out as a gullible fool easily tricked by his brother, then assuming a disguise as a mad beggar to evade his father's

men, then carrying his impersonation further to aid Lear and Gloucester, and finally appearing as an armoured champion to avenge his brother's treason. Edgar's propensity for disguises and impersonations makes it difficult to characterize him effectively.

Edmund
Gloucester's younger, illegitimate son, Edmund resents his status as a bastard and schemes to usurp Gloucester's title and possessions from Edgar. He is a formidable character, succeeding in almost all of his schemes and wreaking destruction upon virtually all of the other characters.

Kent
A nobleman of the same rank as Gloucester who is loyal to King Lear. Kent spends most of the play disguised as a peasant, calling himself 'Caius', so that he can continue to serve Lear even after Lear banishes him. He is extremely loyal, but he gets himself into trouble throughout the play by being overly blunt and outspoken.

Albany
The husband of Lear's daughter Goneril, Albany is good at heart, and he eventually denounces and opposes the cruelty of Goneril, Regan and Cornwall. Yet he is indecisive and lacks foresight, realizing the evil of his allies only quite late in the play.

Cornwall
The husband of Lear's daughter Regan. Unlike Albany, Cornwall is domineering, cruel and violent, and he works with his wife and sister-in-law Goneril to persecute Lear and Gloucester.

Fool
Lear's jester, who uses double-talk and seemingly frivolous songs to give Lear important advice.

Oswald

The steward, or chief servant, in Goneril's house. Oswald obeys his mistress' commands and helps in her conspiracies.

The Plot

The play begins with two noblemen, Gloucester and Kent, discussing the fact that King Lear is about to divide his kingdom. Their conversation quickly changes, however, when Kent asks Gloucester to introduce his son. Gloucester introduces Edmund, explaining that Edmund is a bastard being raised away from home, but that he nevertheless loves his son dearly.

Lear, the ruler of Britain, enters his throne room and announces his plan to divide the kingdom among his three daughters. He intends to give up the responsibilities of government and spend his old age visiting his children. He commands his daughters to say which of them loves him the most, promising to give the greatest share of his kingdom to that daughter.

Lear's scheming older daughters, Goneril and Regan, respond to his test with flattery, telling him in wildly overblown terms that they love him more than anything else. But Cordelia, Lear's youngest (and favourite) daughter, refuses to speak. When pressed, she says that she cannot 'heave her heart into her mouth', that she loves him exactly as much as a daughter should love her father, and that her sisters wouldn't have husbands if they loved their father as much as they say. In response, Lear flies into a rage, disowns Cordelia and divides her share of the kingdom between her two sisters.

The Earl of Kent, a nobleman who has served Lear faithfully for many years, is the only courtier who dares to disagree with the king's actions. Kent tells Lear that he is insane to reward the flattery of his older daughters and disown Cordelia, who loves him more than her sisters do. Lear now turns his anger on Kent, banishing him from the kingdom forever and telling him that he must be gone within six days.

The King of France and Duke of Burgundy are at Lear's court, awaiting his decision as to which of them will marry Cordelia. Lear calls them in and tells them that Cordelia no longer has any title or land. Burgundy withdraws his offer of marriage, but the King of France is impressed by Cordelia's honesty and decides to make her his queen. Lear sends her away without his blessing.

Goneril and Regan scheme together in secrecy. Although they recognize that they now have complete power over the kingdom, they agree that they must act to reduce their father's remaining authority.

Edmund enters and delivers a soliloquy expressing his dissatisfaction with society's attitude towards bastards. He bitterly resents his legitimate half-brother, Edgar, who stands to inherit their father's estate. He resolves to do away with Edgar and seize the privileges that society has denied him.

Edmund begins his campaign to discredit Edgar by forging a letter in which Edgar appears to plot the death of their father, Gloucester. Edmund makes a show of hiding this letter from his father, so, naturally, Gloucester demands to read it. Edmund answers his father with careful lies, so that Gloucester ends up thinking that his legitimate son, Edgar, has been scheming to kill him in order to hasten his inheritance of Gloucester's wealth and lands. Later, when Edmund talks to Edgar, he tells him that Gloucester is very angry with him and that Edgar should avoid him as much as possible and carry a sword with him at all times. Thus, Edmund carefully arranges circumstances so that Gloucester will be certain that Edgar is trying to murder him.

Lear is spending the first portion of his retirement at Goneril's castle. Goneril complains to her steward, Oswald, that Lear's knights are becoming 'riotous' and that Lear himself is an obnoxious guest. Seeking to provoke a confrontation, she orders her servants to behave rudely toward Lear and his attendants.

Disguised as a simple peasant, Kent appears in Goneril's

castle, calling himself Caius. He puts himself in Lear's way, and after an exchange of words in which Caius emphasizes his frankness and honesty, Lear accepts him into service.

Lear's servants and knights notice that Goneril's servants no longer obey their commands. When Lear asks Oswald as to Goneril's whereabouts, Oswald rudely leaves the room without replying. Oswald soon returns, but his disrespectful replies to Lear's questions induce Lear to strike him. Kent steps in to aid Lear and trips Oswald.

Lear's Fool arrives and, in a series of puns and double entendres, tells him that he has made a great mistake in handing over his power to Goneril and Regan. After a long delay, Goneril herself arrives to speak with Lear. She tells him that his servants and knights have been so disorderly that he will have to send some of them away whether he likes it or not.

Lear is shocked at Goneril's treasonous betrayal. Nonetheless, Goneril remains adamant in her demand that Lear send away half of his 100 knights. An enraged Lear repents ever handing over his power to Goneril. He curses his daughter, calling on nature to make her childless. Surprised by his own tears, he calls for his horses. He declares that he will stay with Regan, whom he believes will be a true daughter and give him the respect that he deserves. When Lear has gone, Goneril argues with her husband, Albany, who is upset at the harsh way she has treated Lear. She says that she has written a letter to her sister Regan, who is likewise determined not to house Lear's 100 knights.

Lear sends Kent to deliver a message to Gloucester. The Fool needles Lear further about his bad decisions, foreseeing that Regan will treat Lear no better than Goneril did. Lear calls on heaven to keep him from going mad. Lear and his attendants leave for Regan's castle.

In Gloucester's castle, Gloucester's servant Curan tells Edmund that he has informed Gloucester that the Duke of Cornwall and his wife, Regan, are coming to the castle that very night. Curan also mentions vague rumours about trouble brewing between the Duke of Cornwall and the Duke of Albany.

Edmund is delighted to hear of Cornwall's visit, realizing that he can make use of him in his scheme to get rid of Edgar. Edmund calls Edgar out of his hiding place and tells him that Cornwall is angry with him for being on Albany's side of their disagreement. Edgar has no idea what Edmund is talking about. Further, Edmund tells Edgar that Gloucester has discovered his hiding place and that he ought to flee the house immediately under cover of night. When he hears Gloucester coming, Edmund draws his sword and pretends to fight with Edgar, while Edgar runs away. Edmund cuts his arm with his sword and lies to Gloucester, telling him that Edgar wanted him to join a plot against Gloucester's life and that Edgar tried to kill him for refusing. The unhappy Gloucester praises Edmund and vows to pursue Edgar, sending men out to search for him.

Cornwall and Regan arrive at Gloucester's house. They believe Edmund's lies about Edgar, and Regan asks if Edgar is one of the disorderly knights that attend Lear. Edmund replies that he is, and Regan speculates further that these knights put Edgar up to the idea of killing Gloucester in order to acquire Gloucester's wealth. Regan then asks Gloucester for his advice in answering letters from Lear and Goneril.

Outside Gloucester's castle, Kent, still in peasant disguise, meets Oswald, the chief steward of Goneril's household. Oswald doesn't recognize Kent from their earlier scuffle. Kent abuses Oswald, describing him as cowardly, vain, boastful, overdressed, servile and grovelling. Oswald still maintains that he doesn't know Kent, then Kent draws his sword and attacks him.

Oswald's cries for help bring Cornwall, Regan and Gloucester to the scene. Kent replies rudely to their calls for explanation, and Cornwall orders him to be punished in the stocks, a wooden device that shackles a person's ankles and renders them immobile. Gloucester objects that inflicting this humiliating punishment on Lear's messenger will be seen as disrespectful of Lear himself and that the former king will take offence. But Cornwall and Regan maintain that Kent deserves this treatment for assaulting Goneril's servant, and they put him in the stocks.

After everyone leaves, Kent reads a letter that he has received from Cordelia in which she promises that she will find some way, from her current position in France, to help improve conditions in Britain. The unhappy and resigned Kent dozes off in the stocks.

As Kent sleeps in the stocks, Edgar enters. He has thus far escaped the manhunt for him, but he is afraid that he will soon be caught. Stripping off his fine clothing and covering himself with dirt, he turns himself into 'poor Tom'. He states that he will pretend to be one of the beggars who, having been released from insane asylums, wander the countryside constantly seeking food and shelter.

Lear, accompanied by the Fool and a knight, arrives at Gloucester's castle. Lear spies Kent in the stocks and is shocked that anyone would treat one of his servants so badly. When Kent tells him that Regan and Cornwall put him there, Lear cannot believe it and demands to speak with them. Regan and Cornwall refuse to speak with Lear, however, excusing themselves on the grounds that they are sick and weary from travelling. Lear insists. He has difficulty controlling his emotions, but he finally acknowledges to himself that sickness can make people behave strangely. When Regan and Cornwall eventually appear, Lear starts to tell Regan about Goneril's 'sharp-toothed unkindness' toward him. Regan suggests that Goneril may have been justified in her actions, that Lear is growing old and unreasonable, and that he should return to Goneril and beg her forgiveness.

On his knees, Lear begs Regan to shelter him, but she refuses. He complains more strenuously about Goneril and falls to cursing her. Much to Lear's dismay, Goneril herself arrives at Gloucester's castle. Regan, who had known from Goneril's letters that she was coming, takes her sister's hand and allies herself with Goneril against their father. They both tell Lear that he is getting old and weak and that he must give up half of his men if he wants to stay with either of his daughters.

Lear, confused, says that he and his 100 men will stay with Regan. However, Regan responds that she will allow him only twenty-five men. Lear turns back to Goneril, saying that he will be willing to come down to fifty men if he can stay with her. But Goneril is no longer willing to allow him even that many. A moment later, things get even worse for Lear: both Goneril and Regan refuse to allow him any servants.

Outraged, Lear curses his daughters and goes outside, where a wild storm is brewing. Gloucester begs Goneril and Regan to bring Lear back inside, but the daughters prove unyielding and state that it is best to let him do as he will. They order that the doors be shut and locked, leaving their father outside in the threatening storm.

A storm rages on the heath. Kent, seeking Lear in vain, runs into one of Lear's knights and learns that Lear is somewhere in the area, accompanied only by his Fool. Kent gives the knight secret information: he has heard that there is unrest between Albany and Cornwall and that there are spies for the French in the English courts. Kent tells the knight to go to Dover, the city in England nearest to France, where he may find friends who will help Lear's cause. He gives the knight a ring and orders him to give it to Cordelia, who, when she sees the ring, will know who has sent the knight. Kent leaves to search for Lear.

Meanwhile, Lear wanders around in the storm, cursing the weather and challenging it to do its worst against him. He seems slightly irrational, his thoughts wandering from idea to idea but always returning to fixate on his two cruel daughters. The Fool, who accompanies him, urges him to humble himself before his daughters and seek shelter indoors, but Lear ignores him. Kent finds Lear and the Fool and urges them to take shelter inside a nearby hovel. Lear finally agrees and follows Kent towards the hovel. The Fool makes a strange and confusing prophecy.

Inside his castle, a worried Gloucester speaks with Edmund. The loyal Gloucester recounts how he became uncomfortable when Regan, Goneril and Cornwall shut Lear out in the storm. But when he urged them to give him permission to go out and help Lear, they became angry, took possession of his castle and ordered him never to speak to Lear or plead on his behalf.

Gloucester tells Edmund that he has received news of a conflict between Albany and Cornwall. He also informs him that a French army, is invading and that part of it has already landed in England. Gloucester feels that he must take Lear's side and now plans to go seek him out in the storm. He tells Edmund that locked in his room, there is a letter with news of the French army and he asks his son to go and distract the Duke of Cornwall while he, Gloucester, goes on to the heath to search for Lear. He adds that it is imperative that Cornwall does not notice his absence; otherwise, Gloucester might die for his treachery.

When Gloucester leaves, Edmund privately rejoices at the opportunity that has presented itself. He plans to betray his father immediately, going to Cornwall to tell him about both Gloucester's plans to help Lear and the location of the traitorous letter from the French. Edmund expects to inherit his father's title, land and fortune as soon as Gloucester is put to death.

Kent leads Lear through the storm to the hovel. He tries to get him to go inside, but Lear resists, saying that his own mental anguish makes him hardly feel the storm. He sends his Fool inside to take shelter and then kneels and prays. He reflects that, as king, he took too little care of the wretched and homeless, who have scant protection from storms such as the one in which he finds himself.

The Fool runs out of the hovel, claiming that there is a spirit inside. The spirit turns out to be Edgar in his disguise as Tom O'Bedlam. Edgar plays the part of the madman by complaining that he is being chased by a devil. He adds that fiends possess and inhabit his body. Lear, whose grip on reality is loosening, sees nothing strange about these statements. He sympathizes with Edgar, asking him whether bad daughters have been the ruin of him as well.

Lear asks the disguised Edgar what he used to be before he went mad and became a beggar. Edgar replies that he was once a wealthy courtier who spent his days having sex with many women and drinking wine. Observing Edgar's nakedness, Lear tears off his own clothes in sympathy.

Gloucester, carrying a torch, comes looking for the King. He is unimpressed by Lear's companions and tries to bring Lear back inside the castle with him, despite the possibility of evoking Regan and Goneril's anger. Kent and Gloucester finally convince Lear to go with Gloucester, but Lear insists on bringing with him the disguised Edgar, whom he has begun to like.

Inside Gloucester's castle, Cornwall vows revenge against Gloucester, whom Edmund has betrayed by showing Cornwall a letter that proves Gloucester's secret support of a French invasion. Edmund pretends to be horrified at the discovery of his father's 'treason' but he is actually delighted, since the powerful Cornwall, now his ally, confers upon him the title of Earl of Gloucester. Cornwall sends Edmund to find Gloucester, and Edmund reasons to himself that if he can catch his father in the act of helping Lear, Cornwall's suspicions will be confirmed.

Gloucester, Kent, Lear and the Fool take shelter in a small building (perhaps a shed or farmhouse) on Gloucester's property. Gloucester leaves to find provisions for King Lear. His mind wandering ever more widely, Lear holds a mock trial of his wicked daughters, with Edgar, Kent and the Fool presiding. Both Edgar and the Fool speak like madmen, and the trial is an exercise in hallucination and eccentricity.

Gloucester hurries back to tell Kent that he has overheard a plot to kill Lear. Gloucester begs Kent to quickly transport Lear toward Dover, where allies will be waiting for him. Gloucester, Kent and the Fool leave. Edgar remains behind for a moment and speaks in his own undisguised voice about how much less important his own suffering feels now that he has seen Lear's far worse suffering.

Back in Gloucester's castle, Cornwall gives Goneril the treasonous letter concerning the French army at Dover and tells her to take it and show it to her husband Albany. He then sends his servants to apprehend Gloucester, so that he can be punished. He orders Edmund to go with Goneril to Albany's palace, so that Edmund will not have to witness the violent punishment of his father.

Oswald brings word that Gloucester has helped Lear escape to Dover. Gloucester is found and brought before Regan and Cornwall. They treat him cruelly, binding him like a thief, insulting him and pulling his white beard. Cornwall remarks to himself that he cannot put Gloucester to death without holding a formal trial, but he can still punish him brutally and get away with it.

Admitting that he helped Lear escape, Gloucester swears that he will see Lear's wrongs avenged. Cornwall replies, 'See 't shalt thou never,' and proceeds to dig out one of Gloucester's eyes, throw it on the floor and step on it. Gloucester screams, and Regan demands that Cornwall put out the other eye, too.

One of Cornwall's servants suddenly steps in, saying that he cannot stand by and let this outrage happen. Cornwall draws his sword and the two fight. The servant wounds Cornwall, but Regan grabs a sword from another servant and kills the first servant before he can injure Cornwall further. Irate, the wounded Cornwall gouges out Gloucester's remaining eye.

Gloucester calls out for his son Edmund to help him, but Regan triumphantly tells him that it was Edmund who betrayed him to Cornwall in the first place. Gloucester, realizing immediately that Edgar was the son who really loved him, laments his folly and prays to the gods to help Edgar. Regan and Cornwall order that Gloucester be thrown out of the house to 'smell/His way to Dover'. Cornwall, aware that his wound is bleeding heavily, exits with Regan's aid.

Left alone with Gloucester, Cornwall and Regan's servants

express their shock and horror at what has just happened. They decide to treat Gloucester's bleeding face and hand him over to the mad beggar to lead Gloucester where he will.

Edgar talks to himself on the heath, reflecting that his situation is not as bad as it could be. He is immediately presented with the horrifying sight of his blinded father. Gloucester is led by an old man who has been a tenant of both Gloucester and Gloucester's father for eighty years. Edgar hears Gloucester tell the old man that if he could only touch his son Edgar again, it would be worth more to him than his lost eyesight. But Edgar chooses to remain disguised as Poor Tom rather than reveal himself to his father. Gloucester asks the old man to bring some clothing to cover Tom, and he asks Tom to lead him to Dover. Edgar agrees. Specifically, Gloucester asks to be led to the top of the highest cliff.

Goneril and Edmund arrive outside her palace, and Goneril expresses surprise that Albany did not meet them on the way. Oswald tells her that Albany is displeased with Goneril and Regan's actions, glad to hear that the French army had landed, and sorry to hear that Goneril is returning home.

Goneril realizes that Albany is no longer her ally and criticizes his cowardice, resolving to assert greater control over her husband's military forces. She directs Edmund to return to Cornwall's house and raise Cornwall's troops for the fight against the French. She informs him that she will likewise take over power from her husband. She promises to send Oswald with messages. She bids Edmund goodbye with a kiss, strongly hinting that she wants to become his mistress.

As Edmund leaves, Albany enters. He harshly criticizes Goneril. He has not yet learned about Gloucester's blinding, but he is outraged at the news that Lear has been driven mad by Goneril and Regan's abuse. Goneril angrily insults Albany, accusing him of being a coward. She tells him that he ought to be preparing to fight against the French invaders. Albany retorts by calling her monstrous and condemns the evil that she has done to Lear.

A messenger arrives and delivers the news that Cornwall has died from the wound that he received while putting out Gloucester's eyes. Albany reacts with horror to the report of Gloucester's blinding and interprets Cornwall's death as divine retribution. Meanwhile, Goneril displays mixed feelings about Cornwall's death: on the one hand, it makes her sister Regan less powerful; on the other hand, it leaves Regan free to pursue Edmund herself. Goneril leaves to answer her sister's letters.

Albany demands to know where Edmund was when his father was being blinded. When he hears that it was Edmund who betrayed Gloucester and that Edmund left the house specifically so that Cornwall could punish Gloucester, Albany resolves to take revenge upon Edmund and help Gloucester.

Kent, still disguised as an ordinary serving man, speaks with a gentleman in the French camp near Dover. The gentleman tells Kent that the King of France landed with his troops but quickly departed to deal with a problem at home. Kent's letters have been brought to Cordelia, who is now the Queen of France and who has been left in charge of the army. Kent questions the gentleman about Cordelia's reaction to the letters, and the gentleman gives a moving account of Cordelia's sorrow upon reading about her father's mistreatment.

Kent tells the gentleman that Lear, who now wavers unpredictably between sanity and madness, has also arrived safely in Dover. Lear, however, refuses to see Cordelia because he is ashamed of the way he treated her. The gentleman informs Kent that the armies of both Albany and the late Cornwall are on the march, presumably to fight against the French troops.

Cordelia enters, leading her soldiers. Lear has hidden from her in the cornfields, draping himself in weeds and flowers and singing madly to himself. Cordelia sends 100 of her soldiers to find Lear and bring him back. She consults with a doctor about Lear's chances for recovering his sanity. The doctor tells her that what Lear most needs is sleep and that there are medicines that can make him sleep. A messenger brings Cordelia the news that the British armies of Cornwall and Albany are marching toward them. Cordelia expected this news, and her army stands ready to fight.

Back at Gloucester's castle, Oswald tells Regan that Albany's army has set out, although Albany has been dragging his feet about the expedition. It seems that Goneril is a 'better soldier' than Albany. Regan is extremely curious about the letter that Oswald carries from Goneril to Edmund, but Oswald refuses to show it to her. Regan guesses that the letter concerns Goneril's love affair with Edmund, and she tells Oswald plainly that she wants Edmund for herself. Regan reveals that she has already spoken with Edmund about this possibility; it would be more appropriate for Edmund to get involved with her, now a widow, than with Goneril, with whom such involvement would constitute adultery. She gives Oswald a token or a letter (the text doesn't specify which) to deliver to Edmund, whenever he may find him. Finally, she promises Oswald a reward if he can find and kill Gloucester.

Still disguised, Edgar leads Gloucester toward Dover. Edgar pretends to take Gloucester to the cliff, telling him that they are going up steep ground and that they can hear the sea. Finally, he tells Gloucester that they are at the top of the cliff and that looking down from the great height gives him vertigo. He waits quietly nearby as Gloucester prays to the gods to forgive him. Gloucester can no longer bear his suffering and intends to commit suicide. He falls to the ground, fainting.

Edgar wakes Gloucester. He no longer pretends to be Poor Tom but now acts like an ordinary gentleman, although he still doesn't tell Gloucester that he is his son. Edgar says that he saw him fall all the way from the cliffs of Dover and that it is a miracle that he is still alive. Clearly, Edgar states, the gods do not want Gloucester to die just yet. Edgar also informs Gloucester that he saw the creature who had been with him at the top of the cliff and that this creature was not a human being but a devil. Gloucester accepts Edgar's explanation that the gods have preserved him and resolves to endure his sufferings patiently.

Lear, wandering across the plain, stumbles upon Edgar and Gloucester. Crowned with wild flowers, he is clearly mad. He babbles to Edgar and Gloucester, speaking both irrationally and with a strange perceptiveness. He recognizes Gloucester, alluding to Gloucester's sin and source of shame – his adultery. Lear pardons Gloucester for this crime, but his thoughts then follow a chain of associations from adultery to copulation to womankind, culminating in a tirade against women and sexuality in general. Lear's disgust carries him to the point of incoherence, as he deserts iambic pentameter (the verse form in which his speeches are written) and spits out the words: 'Fie, fie, fie! pah! pah!'

Cordelia's people enter, seeking King Lear. Relieved to find him at last, they try to take him into custody to bring him to Cordelia. When Lear runs away, Cordelia's men follow him.

Oswald comes across Edgar and Gloucester on the plain. He does not recognize Edgar, but he plans to kill Gloucester and collect the reward from Regan. Edgar adopts yet another persona, imitating the dialect of a peasant from the west of England. He defends Gloucester and kills Oswald with a cudgel. As he dies, Oswald entrusts Edgar with his letters.

Gloucester is disappointed not to have been killed. Edgar reads with interest the letter that Oswald carries to Edmund. In the letter, Goneril urges Edmund to kill Albany if he gets the opportunity, so that Edmund and Goneril can be together. Edgar is outraged; he decides to keep the letter and show it to Albany when the time is right. Meanwhile, he buries Oswald nearby and leads Gloucester to temporary safety.

In the French camp, Cordelia speaks with Kent. She knows his real identity, but he wishes it to remain a secret to everyone else. Lear, who has been sleeping, is brought in to Cordelia. He only partially recognizes her. He says that he knows now that he is senile and not in his right mind, and he assumes that Cordelia hates him and wants to kill him, just as her sisters do. Cordelia tells him that she forgives him for banishing her.

Meanwhile, the news of Cornwall's death is repeated in the

camp, and we learn that Edmund is now leading Cornwall's troops. The battle between France and England rapidly approaches.

In the British camp near Dover, Regan asks Edmund if he loves Goneril and if he has found his way into her bed. Edmund responds in the negative to both questions. Regan expresses jealousy of her sister and beseeches Edmund not to be familiar with her.

Abruptly, Goneril and Albany enter with their troops. Albany states that he has heard that the invading French army has been joined by Lear and unnamed others who may have legitimate grievances against the present government. Despite his sympathy toward Lear and these other dissidents, Albany declares that he intends to fight alongside Edmund, Regan and Goneril to repel the foreign invasion. Goneril and Regan jealously spar over Edmund, neither willing to leave the other alone with him. The three exit together.

Just as Albany begins to leave, Edgar, now disguised as an ordinary peasant, catches up to him. He gives Albany the letter that he took from Oswald's body – the letter in which Goneril's involvement with Edmund is revealed and in which Goneril asks Edmund to kill Albany. Edgar tells Albany to read the letter and says that if Albany wins the upcoming battle, he can sound a trumpet and Edgar will provide a champion to defend the claims made in the letter. Edgar vanishes and Edmund returns. Edmund tells Albany that the battle is almost upon them, and Albany leaves. Alone, Edmund addresses the audience, stating that he has sworn his love to both Regan and Goneril. He debates what he should do, reflecting that choosing either one would anger the other. He decides to put off the decision until after the battle, observing that if Albany survives it, Goneril can take care of killing him herself. He asserts menacingly that if the British win the battle and he captures Lear and Cordelia, he will show them no mercy.

The battle begins. Edgar, in peasants' clothing, leads Gloucester to the shelter of a tree and goes into battle to fight on Lear's side. He soon returns, shouting that Lear's side has lost and that Lear and Cordelia have been captured. Gloucester states that he will stay where he is and wait to be captured or killed, but Edgar says that one's death occurs at a predestined time. Persuaded, Gloucester goes with Edgar.

Edmund leads in Lear and Cordelia as his prisoners. Cordelia expects to confront Regan and Goneril, but Lear vehemently refuses to do so. He describes a vividly imagined fantasy, in which he and Cordelia live alone together like birds in a cage, hearing about the outside world but observed by no one. Edmund sends them away, giving the captain who guards them a note with instructions as to what to do with them. He doesn't make the note's contents clear to the audience, but he speaks ominously. The captain agrees to follow Edmund's orders.

Albany enters, accompanied by Goneril and Regan. He praises Edmund for his brave fighting on the British side and orders that he produce Lear and Cordelia. Edmund lies to Albany, claiming that he sent Lear and Cordelia far away because he feared that they would excite the sympathy of the British forces and create a mutiny. Albany rebukes him for getting above himself, but Regan breaks in to declare that she plans to make Edmund her husband. Goneril tells Regan that Edmund will not marry her, but Regan, who is unexpectedly beginning to feel sick, claims Edmund as her husband and lord.

Albany intervenes, arresting Edmund on a charge of treason. Albany challenges Edmund to defend himself against the charge in a trial by combat, and he sounds the trumpet to summon his champion. While Regan, who is growing ill, is helped to Albany's tent, Edgar appears in full armour to accuse Edmund of treason and face him in single combat. Edgar defeats Edmund, and Albany cries out to Edgar to leave Edmund alive for questioning. Goneril tries to help the wounded Edmund, but Albany brings out the treacherous letter to show that he knows of her conspiracy against him. Goneril rushes off in desperation.

Edgar takes off his helmet and reveals his identity. He reconciles with Albany.

Goneril, Regan and Edmund are dead. Edgar is too late to save Cordelia, who is carried on stage by Lear crying, 'Howl!' Lear dies of a broken heart after mentioning that his Fool is hanged. Kent announces he cannot stay but must set out on a journey. Albany ends the play by saying: 'The oldest have borne most. We that are young shall never see so much, nor live so long.'

Macbeth
Sources
Like *Hamlet*, *Macbeth* is one of Shakespeare's most popular plays, yet is also one to which much superstition is attached. Actors traditionally refuse to refer to the play by name, instead calling it the 'Scottish Play'. *Macbeth* was written between 1603 and 1606, supposedly with the recently crowned James I in the forefront of the playwright's mind.

James VI of Scotland had become James I of England in 1603 following the death of Queen Elizabeth I. James was an interesting man. The son of Mary, Queen of Scots, he loathed smoking, even going so far as to write a treatise *A Counterblaste to Tobacco*, in which he labelled smoking a 'filthie noveltie ... loathsome to the eye, hatefull to the nose, harmefull to the braine, dangerous to the lungs'. He disliked Puritans and Catholics equally and escaped death in the Gunpowder Plot when about to pass anti-Catholic laws. He was superstitious and, believing Christian Europe was about to be taken over by witches, he set about persecuting Scottish 'witches' and personally supervised the interrogation of the 'North Berwick witches'. He was called 'the wisest fool in Christendom' by Count Gondomar, the Spanish ambassador.

Shakespeare, aware of James' interests, incorporated many of them into *Macbeth*. The play was first performed on 7 August 1606. Some believe that the existing text was an abridgement of the full play, edited because James I didn't like

long plays. Shakespeare took much of his background information from Holinshed's *Chronicles* of 1577. Holinshed took
his knowledge from Hector Boece's *Scotorum Historiae*,
published in the 1520s.

Main Characters
Macbeth
The Thane of Cawdor. A brave, resourceful general who, when
promoted, finds that he has a desire for greater power and his
loyalty is compromised. He is undoubtedly a man of action,
even when those actions are wrong. He is also led when he
wants to be: first the witches then Lady Macbeth persuade him
to do things that ordinarily he might not be happy to do,
knowing that they are immoral. However, Macbeth cannot be
persuaded to do things against his nature, to go to places that
he secretly doesn't really want to go to. His determination is
tempered with a violent and ruthless streak. He does have a
conscience but, as we shall see, this can be easily overridden.
He is also vain: Lady Macbeth's appeals to his manhood often
persuade him to do something when he is having serious
doubts. Macbeth has a need to prove himself, to be sure of
himself, to be 'manly'.

In real life, Macbeth ruled Scotland rather well for seventeen
years before he was slain on 15 August 1057.

Lady Macbeth
Macbeth's devious wife. The granddaughter of King Kenneth
IV of Scotland through his eldest son, she is described by
Holinshed as 'very ambitious, burning in unquenchable desire
to have the name of queen'. She is excited by Macbeth's plan to
do away with King Duncan and, when he has second thoughts,
she is the driving force behind the murder. She is cunning,
dominating, practical and probably thinks that all men are
weak fools who can be manipulated. When we first encounter
Macbeth, he is a hero who has proved himself in battle. Lady
Macbeth is nothing more than a schemer who sees opportunities

and, through her manipulation of her husband, seizes them. She is the catalyst that causes Macbeth to become completely amoral. She uses her 'weaker' sex to her advantage – when Macbeth is being questioned over the murder of Duncan's bodyguards, she faints in order to draw attention away from him. She suffers a total mental breakdown following her actions and kills herself.

Duncan

King of Scotland. Duncan places his trust in the wrong people and pays for it with his life. Duncan is apparently everything a king should be – dedicated, open, honest, honourable, devoted and admired by his subjects. The real Duncan was by all accounts a good king. Known as 'Duncan the Meek', he died not in his castle but on the field of battle.

Banquo

Macbeth's captain in the battle against the rebels, he is with Macbeth on his first encounter with the three witches. While they tell Macbeth that he will be king, they also tell Banquo that while he will never gain the crown, his descendants will. He represents Macbeth's opposite – having the ability to resist temptation, although the actual Banquo, as shown in Holinshed's *Chronicles*, was an accomplice in Macbeth's crimes. He is murdered by Macbeth, who is jealous of the witches' prophecy, and at the height of Macbeth's paranoia Banquo's ghost haunts the banquet.

Macduff

Macbeth's nemesis. It is Macduff who discovers the murdered body of King Duncan and flees to England for safety, and to persuade Malcolm to revenge his father's death. In retaliation, Macbeth kills Macduff's wife and children in one of the most dramatic scenes in the play. In the final battle, Macbeth faces Macduff and the witches' final prophecy comes to pass:

MACBETH
Let fall thy blade on vulnerable crests;
I bear a charmed life, which must not yield
To one of woman born.

MACDUFF
Despair thy charm,
And let the angel whom thou still hast served
Tell thee, Macduff was from his mother's womb
Untimely ripp'd.

Malcolm

Prince of Cumberland; the Scottish heir to Duncan. He flees
Scotland and the flight saves his life. He is less trusting than his
father, as is evidenced by his testing of Macduff to ensure the
nobleman is not one of Macbeth's secret agents. The real person
was known as Malcolm Canmore, meaning 'great head'. He
was crowned in 1057 following Macbeth's death, but his reign
was anything but peaceful; he spent much of his time fighting
to keep his kingdom.

The Three Witches

Mysterious apparitions. They are sometimes called the 'Weird
Sisters'. They symbolize evil but they do not actually tell
Macbeth to do anything bad, leaving it to his character.

Donalbain

The second son of King Duncan, he too flees from Macbeth.

Lady Macduff

Macduff's brave and loyal wife. She attacks him for 'cowardice',
but when Macbeth sends ruffians to kill her she refuses to
divulge any information about Macduff's whereabouts.

Ross
Thane who always manages to be on the right side.

Siward
Earl of Northumberland, a brave soldier who leads the English army dispatched by Edward the Confessor to defeat Macbeth.

Lennox
Courtier who serves Macbeth but changes side as soon as it is safe to do so.

The Plot
The action takes place in eleventh-century Scotland. In the middle of a storm three witches (or 'weird sisters') are discussing their forthcoming meeting with Macbeth.

> THIRD WITCH
> That will be ere the set of sun.

> FIRST WITCH
> Where the place?

> SECOND WITCH
> Upon the heath.

> THIRD WITCH
> There to meet with Macbeth.

Meanwhile, King Duncan has heard from a wounded sergeant that the bravery of General Macbeth and General Banquo has resulted in a seeming victory over the traitorous Macdonald.

> Doubtful it stood;
> As two spent swimmers, that do cling together
> And choke their art. The merciless Macdonald –
> Worthy to be a rebel, for to that

The multiplying villainies of nature
Do swarm upon him – from the western isles
Of kerns and gallowglasses is supplied;
And fortune, on his damned quarry smiling,
Show'd like a rebel's whore: but all's too weak:
For brave Macbeth – well he deserves that name –
Disdaining fortune, with his brandish'd steel,
Which smoked with bloody execution,
Like valour's minion
Carved out his passage till he faced the slave;
Which ne'er shook hands, nor bade farewell to him,
Till he unseem'd him from the nave to the chops,
And fix'd his head upon our battlements.

Much of his army has been routed but at the final moments
Macdonald's men receive reinforcements from King Sweno of
Norway and the Thane of Cawdor, a traitor. The sergeant has
left the battlefield to receive medical treatment and so is not
sure who actually won the battle.

The Thane of Ross appears at court and informs the assembly
that victory is assured, thanks to Macbeth's bravery. Macbeth
killed Macdonald by ripping him open from lips to belly and
beheading him. Duncan is pleased and announces that the Thane
of Cawdor is to be executed and his title given to Macbeth.

No more that Thane of Cawdor shall deceive
Our bosom interest: go pronounce his present
    death,
And with his former title greet Macbeth.

The storm still breaks around the witches on a heath near
Forres and they cast a spell. Macbeth and Banquo approach.
They call out to Macbeth, calling him Thane of Glamis, Thane
of Cawdor and King of Scotland. Banquo is put out that the
witches don't predict his future. They tell him:

FIRST WITCH
Lesser than Macbeth, and greater.

SECOND WITCH
Not so happy, yet much happier.

THIRD WITCH
Thou shalt get kings, though thou be none.

Macbeth is bemused by the comments of the witches and asks them to tell him how they know these things will occur:

> Stay, you imperfect speakers, tell me more:
> By Sinel's death I know I am Thane of Glamis;
> But how of Cawdor? The Thane of Cawdor lives,
> A prosperous gentleman; and to be king
> Stands not within the prospect of belief,
> No more than to be Cawdor. Say from whence
> You owe this strange intelligence? or why
> Upon this blasted heath you stop our way
> With such prophetic greeting? Speak, I charge you.

The witches disappear in the proverbial puff of smoke before Macbeth can find the answers to his questions. Macbeth and Banquo discuss the witches' predictions: Macbeth will be Thane of Cawdor and King of Scotland; Banquo's children will be kings. It is plainly too ridiculous for words. Then Ross and Angus enter and tell Macbeth that King Duncan is pleased with him and has made him Thane of Cawdor. Macbeth and Banquo look at each other in amazement and Macbeth points out that the Thane of Cawdor is still very much in the land of the living. Angus has the answer:

> Who was the Thane lives yet;
> But under heavy judgement bears that life

Which he deserves to lose. Whether he was
    combined
With those of Norway, or did line the rebel
With hidden help and vantage, or that with both
He labour'd in his country's wrack, I know not;
But treasons capital, confess'd and proved,
Have overthrown him.

We can immediately see the wheels of Macbeth's mind begin to slowly but inexorably turn: 'Glamis, and Thane of Cawdor! The greatest is behind.' Macbeth thanks the messengers but Banquo warns him not to place too much emphasis on what the witches have said. Macbeth cannot or will not listen:

[Aside] This supernatural soliciting
Cannot be ill, cannot be good: if ill,
Why hath it given me earnest of success,
Commencing in a truth? I am Thane of Cawdor:
If good, why do I yield to that suggestion
Whose horrid image doth unfix my hair
And make my seated heart knock at my ribs,
Against the use of nature? Present fears
Are less than horrible imaginings:
My thought, whose murder yet is but fantastical,
Shakes so my single state of man that function
Is smother'd in surmise and nothing is
But what is not.

Macbeth sets off to see the King but is still concerned by what the witches have told him and says to Banquo: 'Think upon what hath chanced, and, at more time, the interim having weigh'd it, let us speak.' Banquo agrees to discuss the events later.

Malcolm tells his father, King Duncan, that the Thane of Cawdor died with 'deep repentance' and begged forgiveness for his sins.

Macbeth, Banquo, Ross and Angus are received by the King, who is very pleased with what has happened:

DUNCAN
O worthiest cousin!
The sin of my ingratitude even now
Was heavy on me: thou art so far before
That swiftest wing of recompense is slow
To overtake thee. Would thou hadst less deserved,
That the proportion both of thanks and payment
Might have been mine! Only I have left to say,
More is thy due than more than all can pay.

MACBETH
The service and the loyalty I owe,
In doing it, pays itself. Your highness' part
Is to receive our duties; and our duties
Are to your throne and state children and servants,
Which do but what they should, by doing everything
Safe toward your love and honour.

Duncan reveals his line of succession. His successor is to be his son Malcolm, the Prince of Cumberland. Duncan also announces that he is planning to visit Macbeth at his castle in Inverness. The new hero leaves to prepare his home for the royal visit and to make sure Lady Macbeth puts out the best silver, but as he leaves he reveals to us that he is very unhappy at the selection of Malcolm as the heir apparent. Meanwhile, the King praises Macbeth to Banquo.

MACBETH
[Aside] The Prince of Cumberland! that is a step
On which I must fall down, or else o'erleap,
For in my way it lies. Stars, hide your fires;
Let not light see my black and deep desires:
The eye wink at the hand; yet let that be,

Which the eye fears, when it is done, to see.
[Exit]

DUNCAN
True, worthy Banquo; he is full so valiant,
And in his commendations I am fed;
It is a banquet to me. Let's after him,
Whose care is gone before to bid us welcome:
It is a peerless kinsman.

Macbeth writes to Lady Macbeth to tell her of his news and to expect the arrival of the King: he does not want it to come as a complete shock. He also mentions his encounter with the witches. The letter reads:

They met me in the day of success: and I have learned by the perfectest report, they have more in them than mortal knowledge. When I burned in desire to question them further, they made themselves air, into which they vanished. Whiles I stood rapt in the wonder of it, came missives from the king, who all-hailed me 'Thane of Cawdor'; by which title, before, these weird sisters saluted me, and referred me to the coming on of time, with 'Hail, king that shalt be!' This have I thought good to deliver thee, my dearest partner of greatness, that thou mightst not lose the dues of rejoicing, by being ignorant of what greatness is promised thee. Lay it to thy heart, and farewell.

Macbeth believes that the witches were correct and that he will be king and, therefore, Lady Macbeth will be queen. Lady Macbeth believes her husband does not have the necessary steel in his backbone to be king: 'I fear thy nature; It is too full o' the milk of human kindness'. She decides that she will be the power behind the throne. When she learns that Duncan will be

staying overnight that very day at their home, she is excited
and calls upon dark powers to strengthen her resolve.

> Come, you spirits
> That tend on mortal thoughts, unsex me here,
> And fill me from the crown to the toe top-full
> Of direst cruelty! Make thick my blood;
> Stop up the access and passage to remorse,
> That no compunctious visitings of nature
> Shake my fell purpose, nor keep peace between
> The effect and it! Come to my woman's breasts,
> And take my milk for gall, you murdering ministers,
> Wherever in your sightless substances
> You wait on nature's mischief! Come, thick night,
> And pall thee in the dunnest smoke of hell,
> That my keen knife see not the wound it makes,
> Nor heaven peep through the blanket of the dark,
> To cry 'Hold, hold!

When her husband comes home, Lady Macbeth immediately
goes to work to ensure he doesn't falter. Lady Macbeth insists
that this is a golden opportunity to see off Duncan.

MACBETH
My dearest love,
Duncan comes here tonight.

LADY MACBETH
And when goes hence?

MACBETH
Tomorrow, as he purposes.

LADY MACBETH
O, never
Shall sun that morrow see!

Your face, my Thane, is as a book where men
May read strange matters. To beguile the time,
Look like the time; bear welcome in your eye,
Your hand, your tongue: look like the innocent
    flower,
But be the serpent under't. He that's coming
Must be provided for: and you shall put
This night's great business into my dispatch;
Which shall to all our nights and days to come
Give solely sovereign sway and masterdom.

The King arrives at the castle with his hautboys and torches,
Malcolm, Donalbain, Banquo, Lennox, Macduff, Ross, Angus
and various attendants, and is impressed by the bracing
Inverness air: 'This castle hath a pleasant seat; the air Nimbly
and sweetly recommends itself Unto our gentle senses.'
Duncan is met at the keep by Lady Macbeth. There is no sight
of her husband, the new Thane of Cawdor.

Macbeth is alone, contemplating the act he is about to
commit. He weighs up the pros and cons: Duncan is a relative;
Duncan is his king; Duncan is his guest; Duncan is a good
monarch; Duncan likes him; Duncan has only recently
promoted him; Macbeth wants to be king; Macbeth has been
told he will be king by the witches. The cons outweigh the pros
so he decides to abandon his murderous plan. When his wife
comes to find him, he tells her of his new resolve. Lady Macbeth
is not a woman to stand by her husband when he is going
against her wishes. She is unimpressed and tells him that she
thinks he is a coward. Macbeth is swayed by the powerful
arguments of his wife. Lady Macbeth says that she will get the
two lords of the bedchamber drunk so that they will not be in a
position to defend Duncan. Macbeth changes his mind once
more. The murder plot is back on.

Unable to sleep in a strange bed, Banquo goes for a walk
with his son, Fleance. Banquo has a premonition that something is amiss but cannot quite put his finger on what it is.

Meeting Macbeth, he hands him a diamond that the King has brought for Lady Macbeth. Then he tells him that he had dreamt of the three weird sisters, but Macbeth says that it is best to speak of them at some other time.

MACBETH
I think not of them:
Yet, when we can entreat an hour to serve,
We would spend it in some words upon that
    business,
If you would grant the time.

BANQUO
At your kind'st leisure.

MACBETH
If you shall cleave to my consent, when 'tis,
It shall make honour for you.

Macbeth bids Banquo and Fleance a good night and is left alone in his castle. He looks ahead of him and observes a knife – or does he?

Is this a dagger which I see before me,
The handle toward my hand? Come, let me clutch
    thee.
I have thee not, and yet I see thee still.
Art thou not, fatal vision, sensible
To feeling as to sight? Or art thou but
A dagger of the mind, a false creation,
Proceeding from the heat-oppressed brain?
I see thee yet, in form as palpable
As this which now I draw.
Thou marshall'st me the way that I was going;
And such an instrument I was to use.
Mine eyes are made the fools o' the other senses,

Or else worth all the rest; I see thee still,
And on thy blade and dudgeon gouts of blood,
Which was not so before. There's no such thing:
It is the bloody business which informs
Thus to mine eyes. Now o'er the one half-world
Nature seems dead, and wicked dreams abuse
The curtain'd sleep; witchcraft celebrates
Pale Hecate's offerings, and wither'd murder,
Alarum'd by his sentinel, the wolf,
Whose howl's his watch, thus with his stealthy pace.
With Tarquin's ravishing strides, towards his design
Moves like a ghost. Thou sure and firm-set earth,
Hear not my steps, which way they walk, for fear
Thy very stones prate of my whereabout,
And take the present horror from the time,
Which now suits with it. Whiles I threat, he lives:
Words to the heat of deeds too cold breath gives.

Macbeth considers the enormity of what he is about to do and is horrified, but then he hears a bell ring and is shaken from his thoughts and sets his sights on carrying out his foul task:

I go, and it is done; the bell invites me.
Hear it not, Duncan; for it is a knell
That summons thee to heaven or to hell.

Lady Macbeth is waiting for the return of her murderous husband in their bedroom. She is nervous but at the same time excited. She is proud to have drugged the guards and almost wishes that she could have murdered Duncan herself, but as he lay sleeping she was reminded of her father. Macbeth returns to their room, carrying two bloodied daggers. He is upset but also appears to be more distressed by the fact that he was unable to reply when Duncan's son called out for him to bless them:

But wherefore could not I pronounce 'Amen'?
I had most need of blessing, and 'Amen'
Stuck in my throat.

Lady Macbeth tells him not to worry about it, but it continues to play on his mind. She is still callous and tells Macbeth to go back to the murder scene and place the bloodied weapons by the sleeping bodyguards so as to place the blame on them. But Macbeth is unable to do so, such is his distress. Instead Lady Macbeth goes to implicate the guards and then retires to bed. She says that they both should be in bed when the corpse of Duncan is discovered and then no one will suspect them. Macbeth constantly hears a knocking but cannot tell whether it is real or his imagination playing tricks on him.

The knocking continues and a porter with a hangover goes to open the gate and admits Lennox and Macduff, who asks how the porter comes to be in the state he is. The porter confesses that it was the previous night's revelry. The knocking has supposedly awoken Macbeth and he comes down to the front gate to see what is happening. Typical of British people, Lennox mentions the stormy weather, while Macduff goes off to see the King.

LENNOX
The night has been unruly: where we lay,
Our chimneys were blown down; and, as they say,
Lamentings heard i' the air; strange screams of
   death,
And prophesying with accents terrible
Of dire combustion and confused events
New hatch'd to the woeful time: the obscure bird
Clamour'd the livelong night: some say, the earth
Was feverous and did shake.

MACBETH
'Twas a rough night.

LENNOX
My young remembrance cannot parallel
A fellow to it.

Macduff hurries back to Macbeth and Lennox in a frightful
state. They ask him what has happened but he is unable to
speak and tells them to go and see for themselves. Lady
Macbeth appears and demands to know what the commotion
is that has disturbed the household. Banquo then appears and
the pair are told what has happened.

MACDUFF
O horror, horror, horror!
Tongue nor heart cannot conceive nor name thee!

MACBETH, LENNOX
What's the matter.

MACDUFF
Confusion now hath made his masterpiece!
Most sacrilegious murder hath broke ope
The Lord's anointed temple, and stole thence
The life o' the building!

MACBETH
What is 't you say? The life?

LENNOX
Mean you his majesty?

MACDUFF
Approach the chamber, and destoy your sight
With a new Gorgon: do not bid me speak;
See, and then speak yourselves.
[Exeunt Macbeth and Lennox]
Awake, awake!

Ring the alarum-bell. Murder and treason!
Banquo and Donalbain! Malcolm! Awake!
Shake off this downy sleep, death's counterfeit,
And look on death itself! Up, up, and see
The great doom's image! Malcolm! Banquo!
As from your graves rise up, and walk like sprites,
To countenance this horror!
[Bell rings] [Enter Lady Macbeth]

LADY MACBETH
What's the business,
That such a hideous trumpet calls to parley
The sleepers of the house? – Speak, speak!

MACDUFF
O gentle lady,
'Tis not for you to hear what I can speak:
The repetition, in a woman's ear,
Would murder as it fell.
[Enter Banquo]
O Banquo, Banquo,
Our royal master's murder'd!

LADY MACBETH
Woe, alas!
What, in our house?

BANQUO
Too cruel anywhere.
Dear Duff, I prithee, contradict thyself,
And say it is not so.
[Re-enter Macbeth and Lennox, with Ross]

MACBETH
Had I but died an hour before this chance,
I had lived a blessed time; for, from this instant,

> There's nothing serious in mortality:
> All is but toys: renown and grace is dead;
> The wine of life is drawn, and the mere lees
> Is left this vault to brag of.

When Duncan's sons Malcolm and Donalbain awake they, too, ask what has happened and are told by Macduff that their father has been murdered. When Lennox suggests that Duncan's guards may have been behind the plot, Macbeth announces that he has killed them. Macduff is puzzled by this and asks Macbeth why. As the Thane attempts to justify his actions, his wife helps him out by conveniently fainting. Banquo is a man of action and he suggests that they have a meeting to discuss what should be their next move. Macbeth and the rest agree, apart from Duncan's sons Malcolm and Donalbain. They fear for their own lives, believing that the murderer was someone the King trusted who may seek to destroy them, too. They decide that they will be safer in Ireland and make plans to leave immediately.

Outside the castle, Ross and an old man are chatting about the events of the bloody night. The old man's memory goes back seventy years, but in all that time he cannot remember anything so terrible happening. Macduff arrives and Ross asks him what is the latest news. Macduff tells him that Duncan's sons, Malcolm and Donalbain, have indeed fled and the belief is that they bribed the guards to murder their father so that they could ascend the throne earlier. Macbeth has gone to the ancient place of Scottish kings, Scone, where he will be proclaimed the new monarch. Ross wonders if Macduff will be attending the coronation but is told that he will go home to Fife instead. However, Ross plans to go.

Alone at the castle at Forres, Banquo thinks of the witches: although he did not take their prophecies seriously, he is worried that Macbeth did. He begins to think that perhaps Macbeth's ascendancy to the throne was not quite as smooth as it seemed. But if the witches' prophecies have all come true for

Macbeth, it is likely that they will for Banquo and then he will
be safe.

> Thou hast it now: King, Cawdor, Glamis, all,
> As the weird women promised, and, I fear,
> Thou play'dst most foully for't: yet it was said
> It should not stand in thy posterity,
> But that myself should be the root and father
> Of many kings. If there come truth from them -
> As upon thee, Macbeth, their speeches shine -
> Why, by the verities on thee made good,
> May they not be my oracles as well,
> And set me up in hope? But hush! no more.

King Macbeth and his queen enter with their courtiers and
remind Banquo that he is the star guest at the feast being held
that night. Macbeth also tells Banquo that he will need to speak
privately to him because he wants his advice on what he should
do about Donalbain and Malcolm.

> We hear, our bloody cousins are bestow'd
> In England and in Ireland, not confessing
> Their cruel parricide, filling their hearers
> With strange invention: but of that tomorrow,
> When therewithal we shall have cause of state

Macbeth asks whether Fleance will be travelling with Banquo
later that night and is told that he will be. Banquo leaves and
Macbeth tells him to take care and that he looks forward to
seeing him at dinner that night. He tells his courtiers that he
needs some time alone and sends them all away apart from one
servant. He bids the minion to bring him two murderers for
whom he has a plan. Alone, Macbeth broods on his worries
about Banquo and especially about the witches' prediction that
Banquo's sons will be kings:

To be thus is nothing;
But to be safely thus. Our fears in Banquo
Stick deep; and in his royalty of nature
Reigns that which would be fear'd: 'tis much he
   dares;
And, to that dauntless temper of his mind,
He hath a wisdom that doth guide his valour
To act in safety. There is none but he
Whose being I do fear: and, under him,
My Genius is rebuked; as, it is said,
Mark Antony's was by Caesar. He chid the sisters
When first they put the name of king upon me,
And bade them speak to him: then prophet-like
They hail'd him father to a line of kings:
Upon my head they placed a fruitless crown,
And put a barren sceptre in my grip,
Thence to be wrench'd with an unlineal hand,
No son of mine succeeding. If't be so,
For Banquo's issue have I filed my mind;
For them the gracious Duncan have I murder'd;
Put rancours in the vessel of my peace
Only for them; and mine eternal jewel
Given to the common enemy of man,
To make them kings, the seed of Banquo kings!
Rather than so, come fate into the list.
And champion me to the utterance! Who's there?

The murderers are brought before the King and he persuades them that Banquo is an enemy of the state and that they would be doing the King an enormous favour if they were to ensure that he did not make the journey to Macbeth's castle for dinner that night.

Lady Macbeth is not privy to Macbeth's latest outrage and is troubled by fears of what she and her husband have done and what might happen to them. However, she hides her fears and tells off Macbeth for constantly contemplating their deeds.

They chat about the night's feast and decide to toast and praise Banquo. However, Macbeth tells his queen that he is worried about Banquo and Fleance and hints that another accident is to occur. Lady Macbeth is surprised but goes along with her husband's plans.

MACBETH
There's comfort yet; they are assailable;
Then be thou jocund: ere the bat hath flown
His cloister'd flight, ere to black Hecate's summons
The shard-borne beetle with his drowsy hums
Hath rung night's yawning peal, there shall be done
A deed of dreadful note.

LADY MACBETH
What's to be done?

MACBETH
Be innocent of the knowledge, dearest chuck,
Till thou applaud the deed. Come, seeling night,
Scarf up the tender eye of pitiful day;
And with thy bloody and invisible hand
Cancel and tear to pieces that great bond
Which keeps me pale! Light thickens; and the crow
Makes wing to the rooky wood:
Good things of day begin to droop and drowse;
While night's black agents to their preys do rouse.
Thou marvell'st at my words: but hold thee still;
Things bad begun make strong themselves by ill.
So, prithee, go with me.

The two murderers wait in a park near the palace, where they are joined by a third whom Macbeth sent to help them. The two are not sure that they need any help but as they talk they hear the approach of horses and realize that Banquo is on his way. They attack him and Fleance; the boy manages to escape but Banquo's throat is cut by the three villains.

Macbeth is greeting his guests when he spots one of the murderers. He takes the man aside and asks what has happened. He is told that Banquo is dead but is concerned when he learns that Fleance has escaped. When he returns to greeting his guests, Lady Macbeth nags him for leaving her alone to welcome the visitors. Macbeth insists that the feasting should begin but, as he stands to speak, the ghost of Banquo appears and sits in Macbeth's chair. Only Macbeth can see the apparition and is clearly terrified. He begins to see terrors around him, and Lady Macbeth tells the assembly that her husband is suffering from an old illness. When the ghost disappears Macbeth regains some semblance of normality but the meal has been ruined and Lady Macbeth bids all the guests depart. Alone with his wife, Macbeth tells her that he has placed spies in every place in his court and around the country and intends to see the three weird sisters to see what they have to say on the matters that have occurred.

> I will tomorrow,
> And betimes I will, to the weird sisters:
> More shall they speak; for now I am bent to know,
> By the worst means, the worst. For mine own good,
> All causes shall give way: I am in blood
> Stepp'd in so far that, should I wade no more,
> Returning were as tedious as go o'er:
> Strange things I have in head, that will to hand;
> Which must be acted ere they may be scann'd.

The three witches meet Hecate, the goddess of witchcraft, who demands to know why the sisters did not include her when they first met Macbeth. She orders them to prepare a spell that will ensure that Macbeth is unable to think straight when he meets them.

In the palace, Lennox is talking to another nobleman, piecing together what has been happening in Scotland. Lennox believes that Macbeth is behind the recent spate of murders. Malcolm is in England trying to drum up support for a bid to retake his throne. Macduff is also in England after falling out with Macbeth and is attempting to ally himself with Malcolm.

The three witches sit around a bubbling cauldron in a cavern: they are cooking up a spell to cast on Macbeth. Hecate approves of their work.

FIRST WITCH
Thrice the brinded cat hath mew'd.

SECOND WITCH
Thrice and once the hedge-pig whined.

THIRD WITCH
Harpier cries 'Tis time, 'tis time.

FIRST WITCH
Round about the cauldron go;
In the poison'd entrails throw.
Toad, that under cold stone
Days and nights has thirty-one
Swelter'd venom sleeping got,
Boil thou first i' the charmed pot.

ALL
Double, double toil and trouble;
Fire burn, and cauldron bubble.

SECOND WITCH
Fillet of a fenny snake,
In the cauldron boil and bake;
Eye of newt and toe of frog,
Wool of bat and tongue of dog,
Adder's fork and blind-worm's sting,
Lizard's leg and owlet's wing,

For a charm of powerful trouble,
Like a hell-broth boil and bubble.

ALL:
Double, double toil and trouble;
Fire burn, and cauldron bubble.

THIRD WITCH
Scale of dragon, tooth of wolf,
Witches' mummy, maw and gulf
Of the ravin'd salt-sea shark,
Root of hemlock digg'd i' the dark,
Liver of blaspheming Jew,
Gall of goat, and slips of yew
Silver'd in the moon's eclipse,
Nose of Turk and Tartar's lips,
Finger of birth-strangled babe
Ditch-deliver'd by a drab,
Make the gruel thick and slab:
Add thereto a tiger's chaudron,
For the ingredients of our cauldron.

ALL
Double, double toil and trouble;
Fire burn, and cauldron bubble.

SECOND WITCH
Cool it with a baboon's blood,
Then the charm is firm and good.

Macbeth arrives and demands the witches answer his questions.
They call upon three apparitions to respond to him. The apparitions make three prophecies: beware Macduff; none of woman
born shall harm Macbeth; and Macbeth shall never vanquish'd
be until Great Birnam Wood to high Dunsinane Hill shall come
against him. Macbeth is not satisfied and asks what will become

of Banquo's children. A show of eight kings appears, the last with a glass in his hand with the ghost of Banquo following. The apparitions and then the witches all vanish. Lennox appears and Macbeth asks if he saw the witches. Lennox says that he didn't; Macbeth insists he must have but Lennox is adamant that he saw nothing. He tells Macbeth that Macduff has fled to England. Macbeth, furious, orders Lady Macduff, her children and all members of his family to be killed.

Lady Macduff, her son and Ross are chatting in her castle in Fife. She is upset that her husband has fled and accuses him of cowardice. Ross leaves and the son and his mother continue talking. He asks about treason.

MACDUFF'S SON
Was my father a traitor, mother?

LADY MACDUFF
Ay, that he was.

MACDUFF'S SON
What is a traitor?

LADY MACDUFF
Why, one that swears and lies.

MACDUFF'S SON
And be all traitors that do so?

LADY MACDUFF
Everyone that does so is a traitor, and must be
    hanged.

MACDUFF'S SON
And must they all be hanged that swear and lie?

LADY MACDUFF
Every one.

A messenger enters and warns Lady Macduff that she is in danger then quickly leaves. She considers what she has been told and wonders why her life should be in danger since she is not a traitor, she has stayed at home and she hasn't fled to England or plotted against the king. Some ruffians appear and ask Lady Macduff for the whereabouts of her husband. She defends him, saying that wherever he is, she hopes that they will not be able to find him. One of the ruffians calls him a traitor but her son defends Macduff: 'Thou liest, thou shag-hair'd villain!' This was a dangerous thing to say to someone with a knife because the youngster is immediately stabbed. The boy begs his mother to flee for her life: 'He has kill'd me, mother: Run away, I pray you!' Lady Macduff runs off screaming, 'Murderers!'

At the court of the English king (Edward the Confessor), Malcolm and Macduff discuss what has happened. Malcolm, fearful of Macbeth's perfidy, is worried that Macduff may be a spy and tests him, but is then convinced that Macduff is no friend of Macbeth. This belief is confirmed when a messenger arrives and informs Macduff that his family has been murdered. Macduff swears that he will avenge them and kill Macbeth.

In an ante-room in the castle of Dunsinane, a waiting-gentlewoman and a doctor discuss Lady Macbeth but the waiting-gentlewoman won't say what Lady Macbeth mumbled in her sleep, because there were no other witnesses. The doctor encourages her to repeat what was said.

GENTLEWOMAN
That, sir, which I will not report after her.

DOCTOR
You may to me: and 'tis most meet you should.

GENTLEWOMAN
Neither to you nor anyone; having no witness to confirm my speech.

Then Lady Macbeth appears, sleepwalking and talking to herself. They watch as she confesses her guilt and then tries to wash the 'blood' off her hands.

> Out, damned spot! out, I say! – One: two: why,
> then, 'tis time to do't. – Hell is murky! – Fie, my
> lord, fie! a soldier, and afeard? What need we
> fear who knows it, when none can call our power to
> account? – Yet who would have thought the old
> man to have had so much blood in him.

Lady Macbeth has clearly had a mental breakdown caused by her actions and those of her husband and the stress of trying to keep them secret. The doctor feels helpless to help his mistress.

> This disease is beyond my practice: yet I have
> known those which have walked in their sleep who
> have died holily in their beds.

In the countryside outside Dunsinane the armies of the thanes are gathering for the final push against Macbeth. They know that Malcolm is on his way with English troops and the plan is to meet at Birnam Wood.

Inside the castle Macbeth is confident of victory. After all, he has been told that he cannot be killed by a man 'born of woman'. A servant enters and tells Macbeth that the English are gathering. Macbeth is not pleased by the news.

> MACBETH
> Bring me no more reports; let them fly all:
> Till Birnam Wood remove to Dunsinane,
> I cannot taint with fear. What's the boy Malcolm?
> Was he not born of woman? The spirits that know
> All mortal consequences have pronounced me thus:
> 'Fear not, Macbeth; no man that's born of woman

Shall e'er have power upon thee.' Then fly,
false thanes,
And mingle with the English epicures:
The mind I sway by and the heart I bear
Shall never sag with doubt nor shake with fear.
[Enter a Servant]
The devil damn thee black, thou cream-faced loon!
Where got'st thou that goose look?

SERVANT
There is ten thousand-

MACBETH
Geese, villain!

SERVANT
Soldiers, sir.

MACBETH
Go prick thy face, and over-red thy fear,
Thou lily-liver'd boy. What soldiers, patch?
Death of thy soul! those linen cheeks of thine
Are counsellors to fear. What soldiers, whey-face?

SERVANT
The English force, so please you.

MACBETH
Take thy face hence.

Macbeth tells the doctor to cure Lady Macbeth but takes no notice of the advice he is given about his stricken wife.

In the countryside near Birnam Wood, the armies have gathered. Malcolm tells his soldiers to cut down a length of tree that they can hide behind so Macbeth will be unsure of their number. Macbeth's plan is to stay behind the walls of his castle and endure a siege because his soldiers are demoralized.

Inside the castle Macbeth is confident that he can withstand the siege and will emerge victorious. Obviously, he would like to go out and fight the enemy face to face but he is unable to do so because too many of his men have deserted. A woman cries out and one of his aides goes to investigate. When he returns he tells Macbeth that Lady Macbeth has died by her own hand. A messenger tells Macbeth that Birnam Wood is 'moving' towards Dunsinane. Macbeth becomes worried about the prophecies and, changing his mind, orders an outright attack on his enemies.

Battle commences and Macbeth encounters Siward's son. They fight and the youngster is killed by Macbeth. Just as Macbeth's army appears to be routed he meets Macduff. Macbeth doesn't want to fight but Macduff insists. They clash swords and Macbeth taunts his opponent with the witches' prediction that Macbeth cannot be killed by a man born of woman. As they continue to fight Macduff tells Macbeth that he was born via Caesarean section and thus wasn't technically born of a woman in the usual way. Macbeth refuses to fight but again, Macduff insists. They resume fighting and Macbeth is killed.

When Malcolm is proclaimed the victor, Siward is told that his son is dead. Macduff arrives with Macbeth's head and calls Malcolm his king:

> Hail, King! for so thou art: behold, where stands
> The usurper's cursed head: the time is free:
> I see thee compass'd with thy kingdom's pearl,
> That speak my salutation in their minds;
> Whose voices I desire aloud with mine:
> Hail, King of Scotland!

Malcolm accepts the acclamation and promises to be a good king and right all of Macbeth's wrongs. He ennobles his thanes and invites them to his coronation at Scone.

Romeo and Juliet
Sources

Probably the most famous romantic play in the world, let alone the Shakespeare canon. Written in the mid-1590s and first published in 1597, *Romeo and Juliet* is Shakespeare's first non-historical tragedy, and it is in many ways the richest and most mature of his early works. The writing bears many of the characteristics of Shakespeare's early work, with frequent use of end-rhymes and an abundance of descriptive, metaphoric imagery.

Shakespeare did not invent the story of *Romeo and Juliet*. He did not, in fact, even introduce the story into the English language. The generally, and understandably, forgotten Arthur Brooks first brought the story of *The Tragicall Historye of Romeus and Juliet* (1562) to an English-speaking audience in a long and plodding poem that was itself not original, but rather an adaptation of adaptations that stretched across nearly 100 years and two languages. They included a 1559 French poem written by Pierre Boaisteau, which in turn was based on a 1554 Italian story by Mateo Bandello, who in turn lifted from Luigi da Porto's 1530 version. Many of the details of Shakespeare's plot are lifted directly from Brooks' poem, including the meeting of Romeo and Juliet at the ball, their secret marriage, Romeo's fight with Tybalt, the sleeping potion, and the timing of the lover's eventual suicides.

Such appropriation of other stories is characteristic of Shakespeare, who often wrote plays based on earlier works. Two examples are *Richard III*, which Shakespeare based in large part on Thomas More's excellent history of that English king, and *Hamlet*, which is based on two known sources: one from France, another from medieval Denmark. Shakespeare's use of existing material as fodder for his plays should not be taken as a lack of originality. Instead, readers should note how Shakespeare crafts his sources in new ways while displaying a remarkable understanding of the literary tradition in which he is working. Shakespeare's version of *Romeo and Juliet* is no exception. The play distinguishes itself from its predecessors in several important aspects: the subtlety and originality of its characterization (Shakespeare almost wholly created Mercutio); the intense pace of its action, which is compressed from nine months into four frenetic days; a powerful enrichment of the story's thematic aspects; and, above all, an extraordinary use of language.

Contemporary readers often view Shakespeare as having invented literature, and thus see Shakespeare as having occupied an enviable position in which he could create his masterpieces upon a blank and impressionable slate. This is not true. By the time of Shakespeare, a rich and ancient tradition of literature already existed. *Romeo and Juliet*, in fact, bears a resemblance not only to the works on which it is based; it is also quite similar in plot, theme and its dramatic ending to the story of Pyramus and Thisbe, told by the great Roman poet Ovid in his *Metamorphoses*. Shakespeare was quite aware of this; he includes a reference to Thisbe in *Romeo and Juliet*.

Shakespeare also includes scenes from the story of Pyramus and Thisbe in the comically awful play-within-a-play put on by Bottom and his friends in *A Midsummer Night's Dream* – a play Shakespeare wrote at around the same time he was composing *Romeo and Juliet*. Indeed, one can look at the play-within-a-play in *A Midsummer Night's Dream* as parodying the very story that Shakespeare seeks to tell in *Romeo and Juliet*. If *A Midsummer Night's Dream* and *Romeo and Juliet* are looked at as a pair, as the simultaneity of their writing implies they could be, it appears likely that Shakespeare wrote *Romeo and Juliet* in full knowledge that the story he was telling was old, clichéd and an easy target for parody. In writing *Romeo and Juliet*, then, Shakespeare implicitly set himself the task of telling a love story despite the considerable forces he knew were stacked against its success. Through the incomparable intensity of his language Shakespeare succeeded in this effort, writing a play that is universally accepted in Western culture as the pre-eminent, archetypal love story.

Main Characters
Romeo

The only son of the Montagues, when Romeo first appears on stage, he is a moody lover, rejected and dejected and wanting to do nothing but pine for his unrequited love. The fact that his friends and family comment on how changed he is, indicates that this behaviour is very out of character; once Romeo meets Juliet and becomes lively and witty again, his friends are relieved to see him back to his usual self, with Mercutio telling him: 'Now art thou sociable/Now art thou Romeo.'

Very well thought of in Verona, even by his enemy Lord Capulet who acknowledges his nobility, Romeo is a hugely passionate and impetuous lover who, however deep his love for Juliet, is not particularly practical. When Tybalt challenges him to fight, he is too much taken up with thoughts of Juliet to deal well with the situation and, although his impetuous killing of Tybalt in revenge for Mercutio's death demonstrates a fearless courage and loyalty, it is typical of Romeo, who is quick to action but thinks little of ways, means and consequences. As he stands over Tybalt's slain body, it is his friends who have the presence of mind to drag him away, mindful of the danger he is now in.

Once banished, Romeo loses all self-control and embraces his tragedy wholeheartedly, throwing himself to the ground and threatening to kill himself. Once he hears of Juliet's death, it is typical of Romeo that his first thought is to rush to her side and join her in death. Highly vocal in his woes, it is Romeo's passionate and impetuous nature that creates much of the tragedy; his hastiness is a large contributing factor to the final tragic end of the play. He is, however, one of Shakespeare's greatest lovers and the lyrical language in which he expresses his love is all-pervasive.

Juliet

The only daughter of the Capulets, Juliet, though no less passionate than Romeo, is a quieter character. At the beginning of the play she is a young girl who has led a sheltered life, the obedient and submissive only daughter of the house. From the first, she is the more practical of the lovers. It is she who suggests arranging their marriage, while Romeo is quite content to rhapsodize on her beauty. The passion of their love – and the predicament it throws them both into – forces Juliet to mature greatly throughout the play, so that she moves from a young sheltered child to a passionate and resolute woman at the end of the play.

While Romeo's nature can be shown to be fickle (he quickly swaps his infatuation with Rosaline for his love for Juliet) Juliet, above all, is honest and always speaks her mind. When her furiously angry and violent father threatens to cast her off if she will not marry Paris, she courageously remains steadfast, and when she deceives her father by agreeing to the match, she is being no less true to herself. It is only because her love for Romeo is so great that she is forced to take drastic action. Let down by both her mother and father, it is her nurse's desertion that compounds the bitterness of Juliet's situation, leaving her alone and friendless, a truly tragic heroine. Her courage is paramount throughout, shown in her drinking of the potion with a final toast – 'To my love' – and effecting her swift death when she discovers Romeo's body.

Mercutio

Witty, lively and loud, Mercutio's sense of humour is the perfect foil for Romeo's fits of passion. A kinsman of the Prince, Mercutio is unaffected by romantic love himself. He has a winning personality and he loves to talk and entertain. Fearless and argumentative, he is greatly liked by his friends but his witty remarks, which threaten to turn the play into a comedy early on, have deeper meanings. Even as he dies, Mercutio is joking, telling his friends: 'Ask for me tomorrow and you shall find me a grave man,' But beneath the laughter run deep feelings and he dies with a sincere curse: 'A plague on both your houses!'

Benvolio

Quiet and rational, Benvolio is the ultimate peacemaker. Romeo's cousin, he is totally loyal to Romeo and withstands his moods and passionate outbursts with equanimity. He is the friend most in Romeo's confidence and it is Benvolio that Lord and Lady Montague call on to find out what is the matter with their son. Benvolio's attempts at preserving peace form a pattern throughout the play. When he sees the mood Mercutio is in, he tries to persuade him to withdraw from the streets, knowing that the Capulets are also abroad; when fighting threatens to break out, Benvolio is constantly pleading for peace. Quick-thinking, level-headed and sensitive, it is he who makes sure Romeo flees the scene after killing Tybalt, and it is Benvolio who the Prince turns to, as a responsible subject, to give him a full account of the fray.

Balthazar

Romeo's faithful servant. When Balthazar learns of the death of Juliet, his first thought is to rush with the news to his master, who is in exile in Mantua. Scared by Romeo's reaction and fearing the worst, he courageously agrees to accompany him to Capulet's monument where Juliet lies and, when a wretched but resolute Romeo dismisses him from the scene, he courageously resolves on staying close by.

Montague

Romeo's father, the head of the house of Montague is of noble character, but his obvious hatred for his enemy Capulet makes him blind to many things. When they first appear together, his wife has to physically restrain him from attacking Capulet in the street. He is obviously fond of, and proud of, his son, but they have a distant relationship. When Romeo appears sullen and moody, Montague asks Benvolio to find out what is wrong with him instead of tackling the problem himself.

Lady Montague

Submissive to her husband in everything, Lady Montague shares his concerns for Romeo but is content to let his friends deal with the problem. Although her relationship with her son is not apparent in the play, her deep love for him is clear when she dies, broken-hearted with grief that he must be banished from Verona.

Capulet

A more imposing figure than Montague, Capulet appears a genial, fun-loving lord who jokes with his servants, dotes on his daughter, delights in company and playing the host and exercises a laissez-faire attitude towards party gatecrashers. But beneath this, he is made of sterner stuff. Although he may acknowledge Romeo's good reputation, his hatred of Montague is intense and his fury at the death of Tybalt is deeply felt. His love for Juliet, too, is not unconditional and, although when the play opens he talks of only letting her marry Paris if she chooses, when she refuses to obey him his anger is so violent that he shocks even the nurse and his wife with his fierceness towards her. At the close of the play, he is a broken man and is able to acknowledge Juliet's virtues in death as he never did while she lived.

Capulet's wife

Vain, proud and independent, Capulet hints strongly that the love between him and his wife died long ago, commenting wryly that giving birth to Juliet at such a young age has done little to increase his wife's qualities, leaving Juliet as his main pleasure in life. As he tells Paris: 'Too soon marred are those so early made/Earth hath swallowed all my hopes but she.' Strong-willed and impatient, Lady Capulet is disdainful of Juliet's nurse and clearly annoyed by her prattling. When

Tybalt is killed she publicly begs the Prince to kill Romeo in return, and though she, like her husband, weeps bitterly for her daughter when she is dead, she is as unyielding as Capulet over the subject of her marriage to Paris.

Tybalt

Referred to by Mercutio as 'Prince of Cats', Tybalt is undoubtedly one of the Capulet family's finest assets. A cousin to Juliet, he is proud, very arrogant, powerful and smooth-talking. Unlike Mercutio, who fights with words and wit as much as by action, Tybalt is a man of few words but quick to action. Vengeful and aggressive, his pride is so offended at seeing Romeo has infiltrated a Capulet party that he instantly begs leave to fight him then and there. His death, by Romeo's hand, comes as a great blow to the Capulets, who mourn him grievously.

Juliet's nurse

The character of the nurse, who did not appear in any previous versions of *Romeo and Juliet*, is used by Shakespeare to provide a great deal of the comedy in the play. Blissfully unaware of her lowly position in the household, the nurse is Juliet's closest confidante, having been her constant companion since she was born. Bawdy, coarse and garrulous, the nurse speaks a good deal but says very little. Her favourite topic of conversation is sex. She is a much better talker than she is a listener, infuriating Juliet with her babbling and evasive answers to her questions. She is important as a go-between between the lovers and comforts Juliet without always appearing to sympathize sincerely with her plight, for she changes her opinions constantly, first upbraiding Juliet for taking Romeo's part against Tybalt, then, moments later, agreeing to help Juliet reunite with Romeo in secret. Vulgar and immoral, she helps arrange Juliet's marriage to Romeo, even though she had previously approved of Juliet marrying Paris. Even after Romeo and Juliet are married, the nurse is still praising Paris as a suitable husband for her charge. When the nurse lets down Juliet at her most crucial hour, their relationship shifts dramatically and Juliet, now no longer a girl but a woman, realizes she can no longer call on her nurse for help or comfort.

Friar Laurence

Resourceful and reliable, Friar Laurence is vital to the plot, being the orchestrator of Romeo and Juliet's marriage, their wedding night and Juliet's subsequent fake death to escape marriage to Paris. One of the few people in the play to have no allegiance to either family, he sees the marriage of Romeo and Juliet as a way to restore peace between the warring Capulets and Montagues; when filled with misgivings over the plans he is formulating for the lover, he always calls on this peaceful goal to support his reasoning.

Friar John

A fellow friar who is entrusted by Friar Laurence to deliver his letter to Romeo. Although clearly reliable and conscientious, Friar John is unable to do this, accelerating the tragedy.

Paris

As Romeo's rival in love, Count Paris could not offer more of a contrast. Where Romeo is headstrong and passionate, stealing in by night to woo Juliet at her balcony and rushing into marriage, Paris' methods of courtship are much more restrained. He is calm and decorous, he approaches Juliet's father to discuss marriage to her, and throughout the play he speaks but few words to Juliet directly – all his wooing is made to her father. But although Paris' romantic and passionate involvement is cold and weak compared to Romeo's, Shakespeare does present him as a man of honour and courage, who, when he sees the desperate Romeo in Act V, does not hesitate to fight him off to protect what he sees as a threat to his lost bride.

Prince Escalus

Elevated above all in Verona, the Prince's power is such that even the most headstrong of his subjects must bow to him. With one word he can still a violent street fight and his authority is never questioned. The Prince is authoritative, thoughtful and quick to judgement; although he is, by his own admission, not infallible. At the close of the play when, once again he, reigns over his subject, he upbraids himself for letting the tragedy happen:

> I, for winking at your discords, too
> Have lost a brace of kinsmen. All are punished.

The Plot

The play opens, as does many of Shakespeare's, with the Chorus, who delivers a summary of the play the audience are about to see. The Chorus speaks of a long-standing feud between the Capulets and Montagues, two prominent families of Verona. The feud has broken out anew and will only be healed through the death of a pair of ill-fated lovers, Romeo and Juliet, children of these families. The Chorus asks the audience to watch with patience while the actors do their best to entertain them.

The action then opens on two Capulet servants, Samson and Gregory, who are discussing the feud between the two families. They are loud, bawdy and spoiling for a fray, so that when they spy two Montague servants enter the marketplace, Samson's challenge to Gregory – 'Quarrel, I will back thee' – is all that is needed to start a fight. Benvolio, arriving on the scene, tries to stop the quarrel but is taunted to fight in earnest with Tybalt, the Capulet. The uproar caused by the people of Verona, who join in the fray, brings Lord and Lady Capulet and Lord and Lady Montague to the scene and, finally, Escalus, Prince of Verona, arrives, silencing the crowd. Furious at the fighting of his people, the Prince commands peace and decrees that any further fighting between the two families will be punished by death.

The crowd disperses, leaving Lord and Lady Montague alone with Benvolio, who explains to Montague how the fight broke out. Lady Montague expresses relief that her son Romeo was not involved in the fighting, and the talk turns to how Romeo has changed so much of late. He has become unusually solitary, locking himself in his room and stealing out in the early morning, moping about in fits of depression that his parents are at a loss to understand. Benvolio agrees to try to find out what ails Romeo and, seeing him approach, Lord and Lady Montague quickly depart, leaving their son alone with his friend.

Romeo, melancholy and disconsolate, confesses to Benvolio that he is desolate that Rosaline, the lady he loves, does not return his affection, for she has sworn to live a chaste life. Benvolio encourages him to try to forget Rosaline by seeking out other women, but Romeo wails that this would only demonstrate how much more beautiful Rosaline is than any other woman.

The action then moves to the house of the Capulets, where Paris, a noble young count, is talking with Lord Capulet. Paris asks permission of Lord Capulet to marry his daughter Juliet. Capulet hesitates at first, arguing that his daughter is very young to be married, but Paris reminds him that there are younger girls in Verona who are already happily married with children. Capulet tells Paris he will agree to the match if Juliet consents and invites him to the feast that is to be held that night in his house. He advises Paris to look at all the ladies there to be sure it is Juliet he wants as his bride. Capulet then gives his servant a list of names, bidding him go and invite them all to the feast. Left alone with a list of names he is unable to read, the servant asks Romeo, who has entered with Benvolio, to read them for him. Rosaline, the lady Romeo loves, is, as Lord Capulet's niece, one of the guests and, on discovering this, Romeo and Benvolio decide to go, uninvited, to the feast. Benvolio hopes that Romeo will see ladies more beautiful than Rosaline and therefore forget about his infatuation. Romeo dismisses such an idea and insists he will never love anyone else.

Back in the Capulet home, Lady Capulet goes to see her daughter Juliet. Constantly interrupted by the nurse, who prattles on with fond recollections of Juliet's childhood, she tells her daughter that Count Paris wishes to marry her. Juliet, much taken aback by the news, agrees to her mother's suggestion that she study him at the feast to see if she likes him. The nurse, thrilled at the news and full of praise for Paris, bids her 'go, seek happy nights to happy days'.

Romeo, Benvolio and their friend Mercutio are headed to the feast, wearing masks and bearing torches. Mercutio, a kinsman of the Prince, has been invited but, as they arrive, Romeo falters and tells them he doesn't want to go – because of a dream he has had. Mercutio laughs at his fears but, as his friends go in, Romeo lingers, suddenly overcome by a feeling of foreboding that the evening's revelry shall have bitter consequences.

Inside Capulet's house, the servants are busy clearing the hall for the dancing that will follow the meal. Capulet welcomes his masked guests and recollects his own dancing days with his cousin. Romeo, who has entered along with the other masked revellers, sees Juliet dancing and immediately falls in love with her, renouncing all his other feigned affections as he wonders: 'Did my heart love till now? Forswear it, sight/For I ne'er saw true beauty till this night.'

Juliet's cousin Tybalt, on overhearing Romeo, realizes that the son of their great enemy has strayed into the Capulet feast. Furious at his audacity, Tybalt sends his servant to fetch his rapier so he can fight him off. Lord Capulet, apprehending what is happening, forbids Tybalt to disturb his party with fighting and orders him to behave civilly to Romeo, who has a fine reputation throughout Verona. Romeo, meanwhile, has approached Juliet and, in holy symbolism, declares his love for her. In their first exchange, the lovers form an English sonnet, the traditional fourteen-line form of verse so often used for love poetry.

ROMEO
If I profane with my unworthiest hand
This holy shrine, the gentler sin is this:
My lips, two blushing pilgrims, ready stand
To smooth that rough touch with a tender kiss.

JULIET
Good pilgrim, you do wrong your hand too much,
Which mannerly devotion shows in this;
For saints have hands that pilgrims' hands do touch,
And palm to palm is holy palmers' kiss.

ROMEO
Have not saints lips, and holy palmers too?

JULIET
Ay, pilgrim, lips that they must use in prayer.

ROMEO
O, then, dear saint, let lips do what hands do;
They pray, grant thou, lest faith turn to despair.

JULIET
Saints do not move, though grant for prayers' sake.

ROMEO
Then move not, while my prayer's effect I take. [He
    kisses her)

The nurse interrupts the two, telling Juliet that her mother
wants to speak to her. Left alone with the nurse, Romeo asks
who is Juliet's mother and, on learning that she is Lady Capulet,
the sworn enemy of his own family, curses fate that this should
be so. The guests begin to leave, Romeo and his friends among
them, but Juliet, watching with her nurse, bids her tell who a
number of men are, among them Romeo. On hearing that he is

a Montague, she, too, curses fate that she should have 'my only love sprung from my only hate'. The nurse, overhearing her, asks her what she is talking about. She tells her it is nothing and goes to bed.

At this point in the play, the Chorus returns to set the scene for night, stressing the predicament of Romeo and Juliet, who cannot easily meet for fear of their families' wrath. Romeo enters, caught in a dilemma. He cannot bear to leave the house where Juliet lives, even though it is not safe for him to stay. He withdraws as Benvolio and Mercutio arrive looking for him. Benvolio thinks he has seen Romeo jump over the wall that surrounds the Capulet's estate, and Mercutio, still in high party spirits and unaware of Romeo's love for Juliet, tries to lure him out by shouting out bawdy suggestions about his love for Rosaline. Romeo, however, does not respond and the two friends go home without him.

Left alone in the darkness, Romeo dismisses the jokes of Mercutio, who has never been in love so does not know its pain. Advancing towards the house, he sees Juliet step out on to her balcony and, in one of the most famous soliloquies in all of Shakespeare, he pays homage to her beauty:

> But, soft! What light through yonder window breaks?
> It is the east, and Juliet is the sun.
> Arise, fair sun, and kill the envious moon,
> Who is already sick and pale with grief,
> That thou, her maid, art far more fair than she:
> Be not her maid, since she is envious;
> Her vestal livery is but sick and green
> And none but fools do wear it; cast it off.
> It is my lady, O, it is my love!
> O, that she knew she were!
> She speaks yet she says nothing: what of that?
> Her eye discourses; I will answer it.
> I am too bold, 'tis not to me she speaks:

Two of the fairest stars in all the heaven,
Having some business, do entreat her eyes
To twinkle in their spheres till they return.
What if her eyes were there, they in her head?
The brightness of her cheek would shame those
    stars,
As daylight doth a lamp; her eyes in heaven
Would through the airy region stream so bright
That birds would sing and think it were not night.
See, how she leans her cheek upon her hand!
O, that I were a glove upon that hand,
That I might touch that cheek!

Not realizing Romeo is below, Juliet confesses her love for him, despite the fact that he is a Montague. Her soliloquy begins with the most famous line in the play:

O Romeo, Romeo, wherefore art thou Romeo?
Deny thy father and refuse thy name;
Or, if thou wilt not, be but sworn my love
And I'll no longer be a Capulet.

She is shocked out of her reverie by hearing Romeo's voice. Once she has realized it is him, she begs him to leave, afraid for his safety in her house, but he stands firm, insisting his life were better ended in her company than continued elsewhere. They both declare their love to each other, and then Juliet is called away by her nurse. Rushing back, she tells Romeo that if his intention is to marry her, and he can send word the next day as to how they will be married, she will happily become his wife. She arranges to send a go-between to Romeo by 9 a.m. to learn what plans he has made and, on hearing the nurse repeatedly call for her, she finally drags herself away from him. When she's gone, Romeo, delirious with happiness, decides to go and see Friar Laurence to find out if he can help arrange the marriage.

Friar Laurence is out gathering herbs in the dawn when he meets Romeo. Glad to hear he is no longer infatuated with Rosaline, he is astonished to hear of Romeo's new-found love for Juliet and chides him for being so inconstant in his affections. He does, however, agree to marry the pair, thinking that the union may finally put an end to the feud between their two families.

Benvolio and Mercutio, who went to bed after the Capulet feast without finding Romeo, are still looking for him the next morning. They talk of how Tybalt has carried out his threat to make Romeo pay for intruding on a Capulet party and has sent a challenge to Montague, which Benvolio believes Romeo will accept. When they run into Romeo, who is coming from his meeting with the friar, he is in high spirits and engages in such a skirmish of wit with Mercutio, who, thrilled to see him returned to his old self, tells him: 'Is this not better now than groaning for love?/Now art thou sociable, now art thou Romeo.' Juliet's nurse, and her man Peter, approach the friends, who, thoroughly enjoying themselves, loudly mock her appearance. The nurse, who has been sent by Juliet, asks which one of them is Romeo. He makes himself known and Mercutio and Benvolio depart. The nurse, after she has expressed her disapproval of Mercutio's taunts, warns him that if he ever hurts Juliet he will live to regret it, before asking if he has managed to make any plans for the marriage. Romeo tells her to arrange for Juliet to go that afternoon to confession at Friar Laurence's, where he will marry them. He also arranges for his servant to give the nurse a rope ladder that he can use to enter Juliet's room that night. The nurse agrees to the plans and hurries away to take the news to her charge.

Back at the Capulet home Juliet, racked with anticipation, is waiting impatiently for the return of her nurse, who has been gone for three hours. When the nurse finally arrives Juliet falls on her, begging to hear the news from Romeo, and she is worked up into a vexation of fury by the nurse's continual evasion of the question. Eventually Juliet hears of the wedding plan and, thrilled, rushes off to prepare herself.

At Friar Laurence's cell, the friar, who is waiting there with Romeo, prays for God's blessing that the wedding will bring peace. Romeo argues that any disasters are worth the joy of knowing that he is to be Juliet's husband and, as Juliet arrives, the lovers once again declare their devotion to each other before the friar rushes them to the altar, telling them the ceremony must be swift.

In a street in Verona, Mercutio, who has entered with Benvolio and some of their men, is in a very quarrelsome mood. Disgruntled by the extremely hot day, he rejects Benvolio's suggestion that they should leave the streets because the Capulets are also at large in Verona that day. He playfully mocks Benvolio's attempt to prevent any fighting by telling Benvolio he is extraordinarily quarrelsome. Yet when Tybalt arrives, it is Mercutio who deliberately provokes him. As they argue, Benvolio once again urges Mercutio to take his quarrel with Tybalt somewhere more private, but Mercutio steadfastly refuses. Tybalt, however, is still looking for Romeo and when Romeo arrives, Tybalt insults him and repeats his challenge for Romeo to 'turn and draw'. Romeo, still delirious with happiness from his marriage, and unwilling to fight his new cousin, insists he wants only peace with Tybalt, hinting he now has a very good reason to love him, but Mercutio, annoyed at Romeo's cowardice, goads Tybalt into action once more and the two draw their swords and begin to fight. Romeo, appalled, tries to intervene and persuade them to put down their weapons, reminding them that the Prince has expressly forbidden any fighting in the streets. Tybalt stabs Mercutio under the arm before being whisked away by his frightened followers. Left alone, Romeo and Benvolio help the wounded Mercutio into a nearby house. Mercutio, though insisting the wound is just 'a scratch', jokes about his impending death, while simultaneously proclaiming: 'A plague on both your houses!' Romeo, realizing his friend has been mortally wounded, curses his former cowardice that had led Mercutio to die on his behalf, insisting it is the power of Juliet's beauty that has made him so effeminate. In a moment of grim foreboding, he tells Benvolio that the day's tragedy foreshadows many more tragic days and, setting aside all thoughts that he is now Tybalt's cousin, he draws his sword and challenges him to a fight to avenge Mercutio's death. They fight and Tybalt falls, killed by Romeo's sword. Benvolio, realizing the danger Romeo is now in, urges him to leave the scene at once before the Prince and the crowds have him put to death. As Romeo runs away, the Prince himself appears on the scene, along with Capulet, Montague and their wives. Lady Capulet breaks down in grief upon seeing Tybalt's body, and the Prince commands Benvolio to tell him what has been happening. On hearing the whole story, the Prince demands that Romeo should be banished immediately from Verona, decreeing that if he be found within the city limits, he shall be put to death.

Unaware of the dramas on the streets, Juliet is waiting impatiently for night and Romeo's appearance, full of joyful thoughts of the consummation of their marriage. Her ecstatic reverie is halted by the appearance of her nurse, who arrives wringing her hands in grief over Tybalt's death. She does not name Tybalt and, in reply to Juliet's questions, speaks only of his bloody body so that Juliet, immediately believing Romeo to be dead, wills the world to end if it is so.

The nurse assures her that Romeo lives, and tells her that it was Romeo who slew her cousin Tybalt and is now banished. Distraught, Juliet laments the tragedy yet angrily upbraids her nurse when she wishes: 'Shame come to Romeo!' The nurse, amazed, asks Juliet how she can speak so well of one who killed her cousin, but Juliet tells her: 'Shall I speak ill of him who is my husband?' Juliet then lingers on the subject of Romeo's banishment, overcome with grief that she will not see him again. The nurse, telling her that she knows where Romeo is hidden, promises to arrange for him to come to her that night as arranged and Juliet, much cheered at this news, sends her on her way with a ring to give to him.

At Friar Laurence's cell, Romeo hears of his fate as decreed by the Prince and, overcome with despair, reflects how death would have been preferable to banishment, if he cannot see Juliet again. A knocking from the door rouses the friar and, with much difficulty, he persuades the weeping Romeo to hide. The nurse enters, telling the friar that Juliet is in much the same condition as Romeo, who lies sobbing on the floor of the friar's study. Romeo asks the nurse if Juliet hates him for killing her cousin, but the nurse replies only that she is caught in a paroxysm of grief. Romeo once again bitterly laments his name of Montague and, impetuously seizing his dagger, tries to stab himself: to get rid of that 'vile part of my anatomy' in which his name lives. The friar tells him to pull himself together, reminding him that he has much to be thankful for and that, by killing himself, he will surely kill Juliet. He tells Romeo that he will arrange for him to visit Juliet that night and then be taken to Mantua outside Verona, where he will live until they can make their marriage public and beg pardon from the Prince and their families. Much comforted, Romeo agrees to be guided by them.

In Capulet's house, Lord Capulet and his wife are talking with Paris, who is reiterating his desire to marry Juliet. Earlier, Capulet had said he would follow Juliet's wishes in the matter, but now that Tybalt's death has so disturbed the family, there has been no time for discussion. He tells Paris he is sure Juliet will obey him in the matter and arranges the marriage for next Thursday, resolving to tell Juliet the next morning of her impending wedding.

In the dawning light, Romeo and Juliet reluctantly admit that the bird they thought was a nightingale is the lark and that Romeo must leave for Mantua, for his own safety. The nurse, rushing in to tell Juliet her mother is coming to see her, forces his departure and Romeo finally tears himself away with great regret, as Juliet, filled with sudden misgivings, wonders if they shall ever see each other again. Left alone, Juliet is confronted by her mother, who tells her that she must marry Paris in two days' time and that the wedding has been arranged by her father to stop her grieving for Tybalt. Juliet, horrified at this suggestion, flatly refuses, and when she is forced to reiterate this response to her father he is consumed by fury at her disobedience, shocking both the nurse and Lady Capulet with the violence of his anger and the insults he hurls at his daughter. He swears that, unless Juliet obeys him, he will disown her as his daughter. Finding no help from her mother, Juliet, overcome with desolation, throws herself on her nurse when her parents have left, begging for help. The nurse replies that she thinks it best for Juliet to marry Paris, since Romeo is banished and it is unlikely she will ever see him again. Juliet, appalled by this suggestion, quietly thanks the nurse for her suggestion and bids her tell her parents that she repents her wilful behaviour and has gone to Friar Laurence for confession. Let down by even the nurse, she hurries towards the friar's cell for help.

Arriving at the friar's cell, Juliet finds him talking with Paris, who has come to tell the friar of his impending marriage to Juliet. On meeting Paris, Juliet carefully avoids answering his questions about her love for him and their marriage and, thinking she is there for confession, he leaves her alone with the friar with a final vow of affection. Left alone, Juliet dissolves into tears, bidding the friar: 'Shut the door, and when thou hast done so/Come weep with me, past hope, past care, past help.' The friar, who is already aware of Juliet's dilemma, tells her there is a faint hope for her, for he has a plan. Eagerly, she tells him that she would rather undergo many torments than marry Paris, and implores his help. The friar advises that she should tell her father she has consented to marry Paris and that tomorrow night – the night before her wedding – she should take a potion he can give her that will make her appear dead, but from the effects of which she will awaken, unharmed, as if from a sleep. When she is found on her wedding day, they will all think her dead and she will be placed in the Capulet vault. Meanwhile, the friar will get a letter to Romeo informing him of the plan and he and Romeo will be there when Juliet awakens, when Romeo can then take her back to Mantua with him. Juliet readily agrees to this desperate plan.

In the Capulet house, preparations are going forward for the wedding. Juliet submits entirely to her father and he is so pleased at her submission that he moves the wedding forward a day with a heart made 'wondrous light' by her obedience. Since the change of day won't leave much time for the preparations, Capulet resolves to stay up all night to work on getting everything ready for his daughter's marriage.

In her bedroom the night before the wedding, Juliet dismisses both her mother and the nurse from her company, telling them she is sure they must have work to do for the wedding. Left alone, she wonders if she will ever see them again and, suddenly overcome by panic, nearly calls the nurse back to comfort her. As she holds the potion, it crosses her mind that the friar may have actually given her a poison to kill her in earnest, to save him risking his honour by marrying an already married woman. She comforts herself with the thought that a holy man would not do such a thing and, struggling with fears of being placed while still alive in a vault full of dead bodies, she finally sets her resolve and drinks the potion with a final toast to Romeo.

Meanwhile, Capulet, with great excitement, is busying himself with preparations for the wedding feast, joking with the servants and good-naturedly hurrying everyone as much as he can. The nurse, who is unaware of the potion, goes in to wake Juliet and finds her charge apparently dead. Overcome with grief, her loud sobs draw Lady Capulet who, devastated to see her daughter lying dead, quickly brings Capulet, Paris and Friar Laurence to the scene. Among his own and the family's grief, Capulet decrees that Juliet should be borne to the family vault. He also commands that all their festive decorations be turned to solemn black. The friar bids the family and Paris go ahead to the vault.

Exiled in Mantua, Romeo is aroused out of his usual melancholy by a dream he has had in which he was found dead by Juliet, who awoke him with kisses, whereupon he lived to be an emperor. His musings are interrupted by his servant Balthazar, who he seizes upon to ask if she has any news from Juliet: 'For nothing can be ill if she is well.' Balthazar tells Romeo she is dead, that he has just seen her buried in Capulet's monument and begs for pardon in bringing such ill news. Romeo, in torment, defies the world and resolves to return to Verona and Capulet's monument. Ironically, he asks Balthazar if he has any letters for him from the friar – the letter that the friar was to have sent by the hand of Friar John has obviously not reached him – but Balthazar replies that he has not. Romeo orders him to get the horses ready for the journey and, left alone, resolves to seek out the apothecary he has seen in the area, to buy poison with which to kill himself at Juliet's grave. The apothecary proves reluctant to sell Romeo the poison, since it is forbidden by the law of Mantua, but, on seeing the sum of money Romeo is offering him, he eventually concedes.

Back in Verona, Friar John explains to Friar Laurence that he was not able to deliver his letter to Romeo because he was shut up by health officers in a house in Verona, thought to be plague-ridden and could not convey anything to Mantua. Greatly worried, Friar Laurence hastens to the vault alone, for Juliet will soon be waking.

When the scene opens on Juliet's tomb it is Paris, not Romeo, by her side. Paris, who has come to grieve at the deathbed of his would-be bride, performs solemn funeral rites over her body. He is disturbed by the arrival of Romeo, who gives Balthazar, who has attended him, a letter to deliver to his father, before charging him not to intervene with any action he is about to take. Balthazar, agreeing, dismisses himself from his presence and Romeo enters the vault alone. Paris, recognizing him as the banished Montague son who killed Tybalt, thinks he has now come to mutilate the dead bodies of Tybalt and Juliet. Romeo, not recognizing him – his sights set only on Juliet and his impending suicide – urges him to leave, but Paris, leaping into action, tries to arrest Romeo who, quickly provoked, draws his sword. In the ensuing fight, Paris is killed and it is only after he lies dead that Romeo recognizes Paris as the one who was to marry Juliet. Moving into the monument, he falters as he once again beholds Juliet, over whose beauty death has had no power. In a paroxysm of grief, Romeo holds her in his arms and kisses her for the last time before swallowing the poison with a final declaration of love. Moments after he dies, Friar Laurence arrives with Balthazar and, finding the bodies of Paris and Romeo, urges the waking Juliet to fly the scene. When she realizes that Romeo is dead, Juliet steadfastly refuses to leave and the despairing friar, hearing the noise of the approaching watch summoned by Paris' servant, hurries away. Left alone with Romeo's body, Juliet's only thought is of how to join him. Kissing his lips to try and share his poison has no effect so, on hearing the noise of intruders draw near, she grabs his dagger and stabs herself.

Two watchmen, arriving on the scene, find the bodies of Paris, Romeo and Juliet, who appear to be freshly dead. They have just apprehended Balthazar and Friar Laurence when the Prince, followed by Capulet and Montague, arrives on the scene to take charge. Amid the general confusion, the Prince commands the friar to tell them what he knows and Friar Laurence unfolds the whole story of the lovers. The Prince takes charge of Romeo's letter to his father, which explains the story the friar has just told, and Montague tells the Prince his wife is also dead, killed by grief over their son's exile. United in grief, Capulet and Montague agree to make amends, Montague telling Capulet he will erect a statue of pure gold to Juliet while Capulet agrees to do the same for Romeo. It is the Prince who closes the play, summing up the effects of the morning's tragedy:

> A glooming peace this morning with it brings;
> The sun, for sorrow, will not show his head:
> Go hence, to have more talk of these sad things;
> Some shall be pardon'd, and some punished:
> For never was a story of more woe
> Than this of Juliet and her Romeo.

THE ROMANCES

Shakespeare's romances are a relatively late element of his repertoire. They are intimately connected with the use of the indoor theatre at Blackfriars, where soft music and lowered voices became possible upon the stage. They are as much masques as plays; they induce happiness and awaken hope in the audience. Lost children are found, and those who are supposedly dead return to life. They are plays of magic and enchantment, where the language is suffused with a wild poetry of sustained feeling. Shakespeare seems to transcribe the process of thought itself as it turns into expression.

Towards the end of Shakespeare's writing career, he created new worlds of magic and mystery. These dark romances speak of endings, death, jealousy and pain, but there is always some resolution, as in a fairytale. Abandoned babies are discovered alive and well; wives thought dead are found to be living; statues come to life; terrible storms turn out not to have harmed shipwrecked mariners.

The Tempest, in particular, is often seen as Shakespeare's farewell, when he breaks his staff and drowns his books. Though not literally true – Shakespeare did write plays after

The Tempest – there is an elegiac feel to this great play of love, death and reconciliation set on an island where even the monsters speak poetry.

Pericles, Prince of Tyre
Sources

Pericles, probably written in 1607–08 (a copy of the play was entered at the Stationers' Register on 20 May 1608), came late in Shakespeare's career, after some of his most powerful dramas, such as *Hamlet*, *Macbeth*, *King Lear* and *Othello*. Yet this play is very different from those previous tours de force. This character-laden tale of families fragmented by shipwreck and mistaken deaths harks back to some of Shakespeare's earliest work, such as *The Comedy of Errors*.

As in most of Shakespeare's other plays and the writings of his contemporaries, Shakespeare used earlier authors and common stories as source material for the play. The fourteenth-century poet John Gower, who appears in the play itself as a kind of chorus, wrote the most important direct source for *Pericles*, a story about Apollonius of Tyre, in his *Confessio Amantis* (1385–99). Via intermediaries, this story probably dates back to a fifth- or sixth-century Latin text, and before that perhaps from a Greek romance influenced by *The Odyssey*. Other sources, including that of Pericles' name, may have been Sir Philip Sidney's *Arcadia* and Plutarch's *Lives*, one of Shakespeare's favourite sources. Shakespeare may also have used Laurence Twine's *The Pattern of Painful Adventures* (1576).

The actual authorship of *Pericles* has long been debated and never resolved. It is probable that another playwright named George Wilkins wrote the first nine scenes and Shakespeare wrote the remaining thirteen. Dual authorship is a good explanation for the stylistic differences between the two parts of the play. In the first part, the language closely reflects John Gower's fourteenth-century language, rather than that of Shakespeare or his contemporaries. Though both Wilkins and

Shakespeare use iambic pentameter, Wilkins uses more rhyming couplets ending with the end of the line, while Shakespeare relies on his characteristic use of enjambment, where a phrase or idea doesn't end at the end of a line, but carries over to the next. Structurally the dual-author theory works well, since the actions of the first half of the play repeat themselves for the most part in the second half, with various episodes repeating or reflecting each other.

Another interesting problem about *Pericles* is the unreliability of its source text. Almost all of Shakespeare's other plays, first published in quarto form, draw directly on the author's manuscript or the actor's promptbooks. *Pericles*, however, was assembled out of reports by actors and spectators. Elizabethan citizens and actors lived in a world where far less printed text was available, so memorizing was common. Their memory capacities were probably much greater than our own – but certainly they were not flawless. For this reason, no really authoritative text of *Pericles* exists. It was one of three plays printed in quarto during Shakespeare's lifetime with his name on the title page but which were not included in the First Folio of 1623. The other two were *The London Prodigal* and *A Yorkshire Tragedy*. All three, plus four others known not to have been written by Shakespeare, were included in the Third Folio of 1664, but only *Pericles* is still considered to be – at least in part – Shakespeare's work.

Main Characters
Pericles, Prince of Tyre
Pericles is the wanderer who survives many dangers and whose 'recognition scene' with Marina in Act V is reminiscent of that between King Lear and Cordelia.

Antiochus
The King of Antioch. Pericles stumbles upon the King's shameful secret and sets sail for Tarsus to escape his anger.

Cleon
Cleon is the Governor of Tarsus whose first scene is sincerity in distress. Later he is punished for his wife's crime and burnt with his wife in their palace.

Dionyza
The villainess of the play, Cleon's wife Dionyza is not a convincing portrait of evil. Dionyza pledges to care for Pericles' child, Marina, but falls prey to jealousy and envy when her own daughter is less praised than his. Hence she makes a plot to have Marina killed. Cleon is stunned by Dionyza's cruelty, yet they are both punished in the end.

Simonides
King of Pentapolis, father of Thaisa. Pericles is shipwrecked in Pentapolis, and wins a jousting contest for the hand of Simonides' daughter, Thaisa. Simonides is impressed with Pericles and tries to jolt him out of his melancholy by offering to be his friend. Later, when he finds out his daughter wants to marry Pericles, Simonides tests Pericles by insulting his honour, and then marries the couple.

Thaisa
Daughter of Simonides, mother of Marina. Thaisa expects to marry whoever wins the jousting contest in Pentapolis. She is very impressed with Pericles, and writes to her father that she wants to marry him. Simonides sends away the other knights and challenges Thaisa, saying that Pericles is not a good catch since they don't know his lineage. She insists she will have him, and they are married. Later, at sea with Pericles on the way back to Tyre, Thaisa gives birth to Marina but is thought to die during the birth. She is tossed off the boat in a wooden chest, but is later discovered and revived in Ephesus by Cerimon. She becomes a priestess in Diana's temple in Ephesus.

Marina

Daughter of Pericles and Thaisa, Marina was born at sea during a tempest. Pericles leaves her in Tarsus with Cleon and Dionyza because he believes the child won't survive the journey to Tyre. Raised like royalty, Marina is astonished when faced with a murderer hired by Dionyza to kill her. Before she can be killed, though, she is saved by pirates, but they sell her into prostitution in Mytilene. Her virtue prevails, and she convinces every man who wants to buy her that it would be a crime to take her honour. Eventually she is assigned to a more honourable household and becomes a teacher. The governor of Mytilene, Lysimachus, is smitten with her.

Leonine

The murderer hired by Dionyza to kill Marina. When the pirates take Marina, Leonine plans to tell Dionyza that he killed her anyway. Dionyza poisons Leonine.

Lychordia

Thaisa's nurse, who reveals to Pericles that Marina has died. Later Marina's nurse, Lychordia lives with Marina in Tarsus until her death, prior to Dionyza's murder plot.

Cerimon

A kindly physician in Ephesus, Cerimon helps the destitute and has miraculous healing powers, bringing Thaisa back from the brink of death. When she wants to become a priestess, he helps her. He is a model of charity.

Philemon

Cerimon's assistant.

Lysimachus

Governor of Mytilene, Lysimachus comes in disguise to the brothel where Marina works, but she convinces him to leave her alone. When Pericles comes into port, Lysimachus goes out to greet him and wants to relieve Pericles' suffering. When he discovers that Marina is his daughter, he has Marina brought to talk to Pericles. Later, he and Marina are engaged to be married.

Pander
A generic name for one who runs a brothel. This Pander buys Marina from the pirates who took her from Tarsus.

Boult
Servant to Pander and Bawd, Boult, too, falls under the virtuous spell of Marina and offers to help her find a more honourable place to work.

Diana
The goddess of chastity, Diana appears to Pericles in a dream after he discovers Marina is alive, urging him to go to her temple in Ephesus and reveal all his misfortune. Since Thaisa lives in that same temple, Diana sets up the eventual reunion of Pericles' family.

Shipmaster
Captain of the ship on which Thaisa allegedly dies. He insists that the body be thrown overboard, following a superstition that the sea can't be calm with a dead body on board a ship.

The Plot
Gower – as prologue – comes on stage and addresses the audience, saying that he has donned mortal flesh for the purpose of telling a diverting story. He tells of the story's setting in Antioch, a city in Syria where King Antioch rules. His sources, he says, relate that the King's wife died, leaving a daughter so attractive that the king took a liking to her and enticed her into incest. Eventually young princes began approaching the king to request marriage with his daughter. In order to keep her for himself, the King made a law that whoever

asked for her hand had to answer a riddle correctly or face execution. Many have already tried and died. Gower exits.

King Antiochus and Pericles, the Prince of Tyre, come on stage. Antiochus asks Pericles if he understands the danger he places himself in by trying the riddle, and Pericles says that he does. Antiochus' daughter enters, and Pericles speaks of her apparent virtues: 'Her face the book of praises, where is read nothing but curious pleasures.' Antiochus reminds Pericles of the other princes who have tried the riddle and died, but Pericles says that he is ready to die if he must. Antiochus, frustrated at the willingness of Pericles to throw away his life, hurls the written riddle on the floor. Antiochus' daughter wishes him well.

Pericles reads the riddle and realizes that it refers to Antiochus' daughter finding a father and lover in the same body. Recognizing that the secret of the court, and the riddle, is incest, Pericles rejects his feelings for Antiochus' daughter. When Antiochus asks for Pericles' answer, Pericles says that he knows the truth, but it is a truth better kept concealed. Antiochus understands that Pericles has unravelled the riddle but does not publicly admit it. Thus Pericles is doomed to die, having not answered the riddle correctly – but Antiochus allows him forty days' grace before his sentence will be completed. The court departs, leaving Pericles alone.

Pericles speaks with scorn of the sinful incest between Antiochus and his daughter, and thinks that surely his life is in danger if he remains in Antioch, now that he knows the truth. He determines to flee the city, and exits.

Antiochus enters and admits that he wants Pericles' head before Pericles tells his secret to the world. The villian Thaliart enters, and Antiochus offers him gold to kill the Prince of Tyre. They receive news that Pericles has fled. Antiochus tells Thaliart to hurry after him, and Thaliart exits. Antiochus concludes, saying he will not be calm until Pericles is dead.

Pericles is back in Tyre, overwhelmed by melancholy. In a monologue, he reveals that his mind is occupied with worry about the dangers of Antioch; he is convinced that Antiochus will not be content to see that Pericles has remained silent, and will probably take action against him. He imagines Antiochus will invade Tyre, threatening a war that Pericles is sure his people will lose. Several lords enter with Helicanus, one of Pericles' counsellors. Helicanus scolds Pericles for languishing in his gloom, and offers his advice. Pericles sends the lords away and listens as Helicanus suggests that Pericles bear his grief with patience.

Pericles tells Helicanus about his trip to Antioch, his discovery that Antiochus and Antiochus' daughter are engaged in incest, his flight, and his worry that Antiochus' tyrannical nature and fears will lead him to invade Tyre. Pericles has been trying to think of ways to 'stop this tempest ere it came'. Helicanus says that he understands Pericles' fear of either a public war or a private treason, and urges Pericles to travel away from Tyre until Antiochus' anger is past, passing the throne temporarily to Helicanus himself. Pericles agrees, and decides to depart for Tarsus, believing Helicanus is a trustworthy adviser.

Meanwhile, Thaliart enters Tyre intending to kill Pericles, though he will be hanged in Tyre for it. He reasons, simply, that if he doesn't commit the crime he will be hanged at home. Helicanus and Aeschines, Pericles' other adviser, enter with some lords. Thaliart overhears them talking about how the king has departed. Thaliart introduces himself to the court saying he has come with a message from Antiochus for Pericles, but will have to take it back to Antioch since Pericles is gone. Thaliart determines to tell Antiochus that Pericles perished in the sea.

Cleon, governor of Tarsus, enters with his wife Dionyza. Cleon and Dionyza try to tell each other sad stories to distract themselves from their own sadness, but fail. Instead they relate their misfortune: that for several years famine has devastated Tarsus, decimating the country's former riches. While they complain about their bad luck, one of the lords of Tarsus enters, and explains that a ship has been spotted off the coast. Cleon thinks it must mean a neighbouring nation has come to conquer Tarsus, now that it is too weak to defend itself. The lord says that the ship flies a white flag of peace, but Cleon has doubts.

Pericles enters and allays Cleon's fears, saying his ships are not the Trojan horse, but are stored with corn to feed the hungry of Tarsus. The residents of Tarsus are grateful; Pericles explains that in return he merely wants a safe harbour for his ships and men. Cleon welcomes them.

Gower re-enters, and recounts the action we have already seen, noting the contrast between the bad king (Antiochus) and the good prince (Pericles). Gower introduces a dumb show, a brief pantomime used to advance the plot. As Gower relates, Helicanus has sent word to Pericles about the arrival of Thaliart in Tyre, and recommends Pericles' return. While sailing home, Pericles is caught in a storm and shipwrecked. Pericles clambers ashore and speaks of his misfortune. Then several fishermen and their master enter the scene.

The fishermen talk about fish in the sea, and how the bigger ones eat the littler ones – just like men do on land. Pericles listens and notes how the fishermen assess well the infirmities of man, using the metaphor of the sea. He comes forward and talks to them, and asks them for help, saying he is not one used to begging. They ask him if he can fish, he says no, and faints. The master helps Pericles up, tells him he is in the city of Pentapolis, where Simonides is King of a peaceful nation. The master tells him that on the following day Simonides' daughter celebrates her birthday, and many knights will joust in a tournament for her love. Pericles says that he wishes he could be there, too.

The fishermen pull Pericles' armour out of the sea, which pleases Pericles, as his dead father bequeathed it to him. Pericles begs it from the fishermen, so he can go and joust for the King's daughter. They give it to him, asking only that he remember they did him a good turn. The fishermen offer to take him to the court.

King Simonides and his daughter, Thaisa, sit in a reviewing stand at a tournament ground with several lords. In turn, each of the knights passes the reviewing stand to show off their coat of arms, each with a motto in Latin or Italian. The king reads each one aloud, translates it and comments on it. Five knights pass the reviewing stand; Pericles is the sixth, in rusty armour, without the gaudy trappings of the others. His shield says: 'I live in this hope', which the king reads while the other lords mock his rusty outfit. The king scolds the lords for judging the interior of a man by his outward appearance.

Later, in the palace at Pentapolis, a banquet is prepared. King Simonides and Thaisa enter, along with Pericles and other knights. Simonides and Thaisa congratulate Pericles on winning the tournament, and Thaisa gives him the wreath of victory. While dining, both Simonides and Thaisa find they are so taken with Pericles that they lose their appetite. Pericles sees similarities between Simonides and his own father's glorious reign, and notes that his condition is now much changed from his life in Tyre – unrecognized as a prince, now he must take things as they come.

A melancholy Pericles sits at the table, so Simonides sends Thaisa to him with a glass of wine, telling her to ask him about his parentage. He says that he is Pericles of Tyre, recently ship-wrecked; Thaisa relates that to her father, who pities his misfortune and offers himself as a friend to Pericles. Dancing follows the banquet, and then the knights go to bed to prepare to woo Thaisa the next day.

Back in Tyre, Helicanus and Aeschines discuss how Antiochus and his daughter were magically burnt to a crisp in a fire from heaven that punished them for their sins. Helicanus says that justice has been done. Several lords enter, saying that Pericles has been gone for so long they wonder if they have a real king. They want to crown Helicanus, but Helicanus resists, suggesting they wait twelve months before making any decisions about the ownership of the crown. The lords leave to seek out Pericles.

In the palace at Pentapolis, Pericles is led to his lodgings by a gentleman. Pericles asks for a musical instrument, which he plays while he sings to himself.

The next day, King Simonides tells his knights that his daughter has written him a letter saying that she intends not to marry. The knights decide to leave. Simonides, once alone, reveals that Thaisa's letter says that she wants to marry the stranger, Pericles. When Pericles enters, Simonides commends his singing from the night before, and asks him what he thinks of Thaisa. Simonides shows him Thaisa's letter, and Pericles immediately thinks he has caused offence. Simonides plays along, calling him a traitor, and accuses him of having bewitched his child. Pericles is offended, saying he came to the court in search of honour, and intends to defend it with his sword.

Thaisa enters, and Pericles asks her to tell her father that he never said a word of love to her. Thaisa doesn't understand who would take offence at something she wants him to do. Simonides takes his daughter aside to ask if Pericles is the right man for her, since they don't know about his lineage. Thaisa responds that Pericles is virtuous even if he may be of base birth, and she says that she is in love with him and won't be controlled. Simonides threatens to banish Pericles, but Thaisa defends him. Simonides says that he will tame her, or he will punish her by making Thaisa and Pericles man and wife. He clasps their hands together; they kiss and are married. Simonides is pleased that they are both happy with the match.

Gower enters. He says that Thaisa is now pregnant, and introduces a dumb show. Gower relates how news of the death of Antiochus and his daughter at last reached Pericles in Pentapolis. Pericles hears, too, of the plan of some in Tyre to crown Helicanus, and determines that he must go home to halt a mutiny. In Pentapolis, people rejoice that their heir apparent is already a king, and hurry him off to Tyre. Pericles boards a ship for Tyre with Thaisa and Lychordia, a nurse. Out at sea, a tempest besets the ship, threatening to destroy it.

On deck, Pericles bemoans his fate in becoming caught up in

another tempest. Lychordia comes on deck with an infant baby and tells Pericles that Thaisa is dead. Pericles cries to the gods that they make him love their creations, yet snatch them away cruelly soon. Lychordia hands him his child, saying that her future life will surely be calm in contrast to a birth in the middle of such violence. The shipmaster declares that the body of Thaisa must be tossed overboard, following a sailor's superstition that the sea will not be calm until the dead are off the ship.

Pericles goes to Thaisa's room and speaks over her body, expressing his regret that he cannot give her a proper burial. The shipmaster offers a chest to put the body in, with some of Pericles' jewels and spices and a note. The shipmaster says that the boat is near Tarsus, and Pericles orders the ship to land there. He intends to give the child to Cleon, believing it will not survive until Tyre.

In Ephesus, Cerimon, a kindly doctor, and his aid Philemon provide fire and food to those suffering from the wicked storm. Two gentlemen enter and discuss how well-known Cerimon is for his charity. Then Philemon enters with a chest that has been discovered floating on the sea. Inside they find what appears to be a corpse, with a note attached written by Pericles, asking any who find the body of Thaisa to give her a proper burial, since she was the daughter of a king.

Cerimon looks at the body and determines that she is not yet dead, and he brings in some medicines. Soon she stirs and wakes. Meanwhile, Pericles arrives in Tarsus, and tells Cleon and Dionyza about his misfortune, saying:

> Should I rage and roar
> as doth the sea [Thaisa] lies in, yet the end
> Must be as 'tis.

He lands at Tarsus and charges Cleon and Dionyza with the care of his child, and asks them to raise her as a noble. Cleon promises that he will, wanting to repay Pericles for the good he did Tarsus during the famine. Pericles leaves, swearing he will not cut his hair until his daughter, whom he names Marina, marries.

In Ephesus, Cerimon explains to Thaisa that some jewels and Pericles' letter lay in the chest with her. She recognizes the writing as that of Pericles, and believes she will never see him again. Thus she expresses a desire to take holy orders and become one of the goddess Diana's vestal virgins. Cerimon offers to help her, and she thanks him.

Gower enters, narrating the passage of time. Now Pericles is settled as a king in Tyre, Thaisa is a priestess in Ephesus, and Marina has become a young woman in Tarsus. Cleon has another daughter who spends all her time with Marina, but Cleon's daughter, now of marriageable age, does not match up to the nearly perfect young Marina. Marina receives all the praise, and Dionyza is wildly envious; she makes plans to murder Marina so that her daughter alone may receive praise. When Marina's nurse Lychordia dies, Dionyza is ready. She hires Leonine, a murderer.

With Gower's monologue finished, Dionyza makes Leonine swear to never tell who ordered the death of Marina. Marina enters to strew flowers on Lychordia's grave, moaning:

> Ay me, poor maid,
> Born in a tempest when my mother died,
> This world to me is but a ceaseless storm
> Whirring me from my friends.

Dionyza notes how pale she is, and suggests she takes a walk along the sea with Leonine. Marina agrees grudgingly.

As they walk, Marina speaks of the tempest in which she was born, and what her nurse had told her of her father. Leonine tells her to say her prayers, and that he is going to kill her. Marina asks why Dionyza would have her killed when she has never done a bad thing to anyone. Leonine says that he doesn't know the reason; it's just his duty. Marina asks him to come between Dionyza and herself and spare her, rather than killing her. Then several pirates enter, scaring Leonine. The pirates take Marina, and Leonine decides to tell Dionyza that he killed Marina and threw her in the sea.

In Mytilene on the island of Lesbos, Pander, who runs the brothel, and Bawd, who supplies the prostitutes, enter with their man Boult. They discuss their need to get women for the brothel, having already raised a number of girls to the profession. Boult goes to look in the market, and Pander and Bawd discuss retiring, since prostitution is a bad vocation.

Then Boult enters with the pirates and Marina. Pander decides to buy Marina for the brothel, and Bawd and Marina talk. Marina wishes that Leonine had succeeded in killing her. Bawd says that she will be content to live in pleasure with gifts from all the gentlemen. Since she is a virgin, Bawd has Boult advertise Marina in the marketplace, assuming many men will line up for the opportunity to take her virginity.

Bawd tells Marina that she must not weep, as none will have a good opinion of her then. Bawd promises Boult that he will be allowed to sleep with Marina, too, and sends him off to advertise her more thoroughly. Marina swears to Diana that she will stay a virgin.

In Tarsus, Cleon and Dionyza discuss the apparent death of Marina. Cleon wishes that he could undo Marina's murder, which he did not have a hand in planning. Dionyza has poisoned Leonine in order to keep her plot secret. Cleon asks what they'll say to Pericles when he comes looking for his daughter; Dionyza says that they should tell him Marina died by foul play. Dionyza says that no one knows what happened, and reiterates that Marina threatened her own child by drawing all the attention. And as for Pericles, she insists that he will see they have done right by Marina, by mourning her and building a monument to her. Cleon calls Dionyza a harpy, smiling while she digs her talons in deeper, and Dionyza scorns him for being so afraid of the gods.

Gower enters and tells that Pericles is again on the sea,

coming with Helicanus to Tarsus to see his daughter. Gower narrates another dumb show, wherein Pericles arrives in Tarsus and Cleon and Dionyza show him Marina's tomb. Pericles puts on sackcloth and swears never to wash his face or cut his hair again, and: 'he bears/A tempest which his mortal vessel tears.'

Gower reads Marina's epitaph, which declares that she was a good, virtuous person. Pericles, believing his daughter is dead, determines to bear this new bereavement and whatever else fortune throws in his path.

In Mytilene, two gentlemen emerge from the brothel, remarking on the divinity they have heard preached within. Determined to be virtuous, they go looking for religious entertainment.

Pander and Bawd come on stage, saying they wish they had never bought Marina, who is botching up their entire operation by making anyone who meets her suddenly want to be virtuous. Someone must ravish her, or they'll be done for. Lysimachus, the disguised governor of Mytilene, arrives at the brothel, and Bawd offers Marina to him. Marina is brought in, and Bawd assures Marina that Lysimachus is an honourable man; Marina retorts that he can't be if he wants to seduce her.

Left alone with Marina, Lysimachus finds Marina is a clever conversationalist. He asks her how long she has been in the business, but she understands him to mean the business of being honourable, and declares she has always been at it. He explains that he is the governor, and has the power to punish or overlook corruption as he sees fit, and he is drawn to her beauty. Marina, touched by his seemingly honourable nature, asks him to govern himself, as he was born to govern, and not to take her honour from her. Comparing her honour to a house, she asks him not to deface it, or burn it to the ground. He is impressed by her impassioned pleas, and admits that his impure intentions have been cleansed by her words. He gives her gold, and leaves.

Pander and Bawd return to discover that Marina has talked

Lysimachus into virtuous perceptions of her, too, and they send Boult to rape her, so that she can at last be useful to the brothel. Alone with her, Boult, too, is swayed by her insistence that to take her honour is the worst thing anyone could do to her. She tells him that she can become a teacher, and undertake other money-making activities in the city. Boult promises to do what he can to move her to a more honourable house.

Gower enters, telling that Marina escaped the brothel and was sold to an honest house. She thrives, working with her needle and teaching others, and giving her extra money to the Bawd. Meanwhile, Pericles has been at sea, and comes to Mytilene. Lysimachus sets out to meet Pericles on his ship.

On Pericles' ship to Mytilene, Helicanus and several sailors discuss the arrival of Lysimachus. Helicanus explains to Lysimachus where they are from, and that the king on board has not spoken for three months. Lysimachus sees Pericles and tries to speak to him, but Pericles will not respond. Lysimachus says that there is a woman in Mytilene who he believes can convince Pericles to talk, and sends one of his men to get Marina.

When Marina arrives, Lysimachus comments on her beauty, and sends her in with her maid to talk to Pericles. Marina tells Pericles that she, too, has endured great grief, having been born of kings, but now being bound in servitude. Pericles speaks to her, and notes in an aside that she seems very like his wife Thaisa. He asks her to tell him about her parentage, saying that if her story is a fraction as horrible as his own has been, then he will deem himself to have been weak in his suffering.

She tells him that her name is Marina, but Pericles interrupts her, saying he is being mocked. She goes on to tell about her father the King, and how she was born at sea. Pericles can't believe it, and asks about her mother. Marina says that her mother died in childbirth, and that she was cared for by a nurse named Lychordia. Pericles believes he must be dreaming, and listens as Marina tells about Cleon and Dionyza plotting her death in Tarsus, and of the fortuitous intervention of the pirates. Finally, Marina says that she is the daughter of King Pericles.

Pericles calls in Helicanus to tell him if he sees anything unique about Marina, but he doesn't. Pericles tells Marina that he is Pericles, and demands Marina to say the name of her mother. She names Thaisa, and Pericles is overjoyed.

Left alone, Pericles sleeps and is visited by the goddess Diana, who tells Pericles to go to her temple in Ephesus and, before all who are assembled there, to tell the story of the loss of his wife and discovery of Marina. When he wakes, Pericles declares his intention to go to Ephesus. Before leaving, he promises Marina to Lysimachus.

Gower enters and tells about the reception Pericles received in Mytilene, where Lysimachus was promised to wed Marina upon Marina's and Pericles' return from Ephesus. Gower explains that Pericles and his company have arrived in Ephesus, and stands aside.

Pericles goes to Diana's temple and makes a speech, saying that he married Thaisa at Pentapolis but she died at sea, giving birth to a child named Marina. He explains how Marina lived at Tarsus until Cleon ordered her killed. He told of his arrival in Mytilene, where Marina miraculously arrived on his ship and made herself known to him. Thaisa herself is in attendance as a priestess, and she faints. Cerimon tells Pericles that this is his wife, and tells how he found the chest and revived the woman inside.

When Thaisa recovers, she is reunited with Pericles and Marina. Pericles says that he will offer daily oblations to Diana, and adds that when Marina is married, he can finally cut his hair. Thaisa tells Pericles that she has heard about the death of her father, Simonides; Pericles decides that he and Thaisa should go to the wedding of his daughter and then spend the rest of their days in Pentapolis, leaving Marina and her husband to rule Tyre.

All exit but Gower, who speaks of Antiochus. Gower has told of the monstrous corruption of that nation, and how they received their just reward. And, he adds, we have seen Pericles, Thaisa and Marina assailed with terrible misfortune, but they preserved their virtue intact, and thus are rewarded with joy at last. Helicanus, he notes, is a figure of truth, faith and loyalty, and Cerimon of charity. As for Cleon and Dionyza, once the story of their evil deed had spread, their city revolted and burned them to death in their palace. Gower notes the gods for murder were content to punish a deed that was not completed but planned.

Cymbeline
Sources
Cymbeline is one of Shakespeare's final plays. Composed and performed around 1609-10, probably on the indoor Blackfriars stage rather than at the more famous Globe, it joins *Pericles*, *The Winter's Tale* and *The Tempest* in the list of genre-defying later plays that are usually referred to as romances or tragicomedies. The happy ending of each of these productions distinguishes them from the earlier histories and tragedies, but each play emphasizes the danger and power of evil in the world – and death, while never victorious in the end, looms as an ever-present force in the stories. Indeed, the plot of *Cymbeline* bears a striking resemblance at various points to a number of the great tragedies: the Imogen-Cymbeline relationship suggests Lear and Cordelia in *King Lear*, while Iachimo plays a role similar to that of Iago in *Othello,* and the sleeping potion taken by Imogen reminds us of a similar device in *Romeo and Juliet.* In *Cymbeline*, however, disaster may threaten but it never strikes: only the wicked characters die, and the end of the play treats us to a joyous reconciliation.

There is no obvious source for *Cymbeline.* The titular king and his sons Guiderius and Arviragus are quasi-historical figures: Cymbeline, according to a dubious source available during Shakespeare's time, ruled in Britain around the time of Christ. (The same source was used for the title character in *King Lear*, another play set in pre-Christian Britain.) The

Iachimo plot, in which a seduction is attempted on a virtuous wife, may have its roots in the celebrated *Decameron*, a collection of stories by the Renaissance author Boccaccio. And the scenes in the Welsh wilderness, especially Imogen's death-like slumber, bear a striking resemblance to fairytales like *Snow White*. The bulk of the plot and most of the characters, however, can be attributed directly to Shakespeare's imagination; such pure originality was rare for the playwright, who adored lifting and reworking plots from other authors, writing in dialogue with older stories.

Main Characters

Imogen

Cymbeline's daughter, the British princess. Wise, beautiful, and resourceful, she incurs her father's displeasure when she chooses to marry the low-born Posthumus instead of Cymbeline's oafish stepson, Cloten.

Posthumus

An orphaned gentleman, he is adopted and raised by Cymbeline, and he marries Imogen in secret, against her father's will. He is deeply in love with her but is nevertheless willing to think the worst of her when she is accused of infidelity.

Cymbeline

The King of Britain and Imogen's father. A wise and gracious monarch, he is led astray by the machinations of his wicked Queen.

Queen

Cymbeline's wife and Imogen's stepmother. A villainous woman, she will stop at nothing – including murder – to see her son Cloten married to Imogen and, thus, made the eventual King of Britain.

Cloten

The Queen's son, he was betrothed to Imogen before her secret wedding to Posthumus. Her unwillingness to marry him is understandable, since he is an arrogant, clumsy fool.

Iachimo

A clever and dishonest Italian gentleman. He makes a wager with Posthumus that he can seduce Imogen and, when his attempt at seduction fails, resorts to trickery to make Posthumus believe that he has succeeded.

Pisanio

Posthumus' loyal servant, he is left behind in Britain when his master goes into exile, and he acts as a servant to Imogen and the Queen.

Belarius

A British nobleman, unjustly banished by Cymbeline. He kidnapped Cymbeline's infant sons to revenge himself on the King and, under the name of Morgan, he has raised them as his own sons in the Welsh wilderness.

Guiderius

Cymbeline's eldest son and Imogen's brother, he was kidnapped and raised by Belarius under the name of Polydore.

Arviragus

Cymbeline's younger son and Imogen's brother, he was kidnapped and raised by Belarius under the name of Cadwal.

Philario

An Italian gentleman. Posthumus stays at his home during his exile from Britain.

Caius Lucius

The Roman ambassador to Britain and, later, the general of the

Roman invasion force.

Cornelius
A doctor at the court of Cymbeline.

Soothsayer
A seer in the service of Caius Lucius.

Jupiter
The thunder-god and King of Olympus in Roman myth.

The Plot
In Britain, two noblemen discuss recent events at King Cymbeline's court. We learn that his daughter, Imogen, was betrothed to Cloten, the son of Cymbeline's new Queen. However, the Princess secretly married Posthumus, an Italian-born orphan who was raised as a ward of the King. Infuriated by the young people's disobedience, Cymbeline banished Posthumus and imprisoned Imogen – an action made even more tragic considering that she is his only remaining child: his two sons, Guiderius and Arviragus, were kidnapped years ago.

The Queen meets with Posthumus and Imogen and she promises to be kind to them, not 'evil-eyed' as most step-mothers would be in such circumstances. She swears that she will work to convince Cymbeline to relent and then allows them to take one last walk together around the garden before Posthumus goes into exile. When she has gone, Imogen declares that she sees through the Queen, whose kindness is all an act. The two lovers then agree to be faithful to one another, and they exchange love tokens – a ring and a bracelet – and promise to wear them forever. As they speak, however, Cymbeline enters with his court, and Posthumus departs in haste. The King begins berating his daughter for her conduct, and while she defends herself vigorously, he orders her to be locked away, despite the Queen's protests. Pisanio, Posthumus' servant, comes in, bringing word that as his master departed he was assaulted by Cloten; however, the two men were separated before anyone was hurt. He now offers his services to Imogen, saying that Posthumus wished him to serve the Princess during his exile.

Outside, Cloten boasts to two gentlemen of the court about how he would have cut Posthumus to pieces had they been allowed to fight. The lords flatter him to his face, but their conversation with each other makes it clear that the Queen's son is a strutting fool and a poor swordsman who would have had no chance against Posthumus. Meanwhile, Pisanio tells Imogen of how much Posthumus will miss her, and he promises that they will hear from him soon. Then, Imogen goes to attend to the Queen.

The scene now shifts to Italy, where Posthumus has gone into exile. In the home of his friend Philario, he debates with a large company of men from around Europe on the respective virtue of their countries' women. One of the company, Iachimo, declares that there is no woman born who cannot be seduced. Posthumus angrily disagrees and declares that his Imogen is invulnerable – that she would never betray him with another man. Iachimo says that he will take this as a challenge and go to England to attempt the seduction, and he convinces Posthumus to make a bet with him: if Imogen succumbs to Iachimo, Posthumus will give him his ring; if Imogen chastely refuses, Iachimo will pay Posthumus 10,000 ducats.

In Britain, the Queen has ordered a doctor named Cornelius to prepare for her a deadly poison, which she claims will be used for scientific purposes, on small animals and the like. Cornelius is suspicious of her, however, and tells the audience that he has given her not a poison, but a sleeping potion that will effect the appearance of death. When he has gone, the Queen confirms his suspicions of her by giving the 'poison' to Pisanio and telling him that it is a soothing medicine. She hopes that he will take it and die: Pisanio, as Posthumus' servant, supports and champions his master, and when he is dead, it will be easier to convince Imogen to marry Cloten. Thus, we see that her earlier honeyed words to Imogen and Posthumus were indeed nothing but lies, just as Imogen thought, concealing her malicious and selfish purposes.

Meanwhile, Iachimo arrives from Italy and gives Imogen a letter from Posthumus. He immediately begins to compliment her grace and beauty, and when she asks about her exiled husband, Iachimo tells her that Posthumus has all but forgotten her, and is enjoying himself – and, he implies, enjoying other women – while in Italy. Imogen is horrified, and Iachimo attempts to play upon her injured feelings by suggesting that she might revenge herself on the unfaithful Posthumus by being unfaithful herself – with him, naturally. The Princess, taken aback, rebuffs him, and declares that she does not believe his malicious stories about her husband's conduct. Iachimo quickly admits that it was all a lie and says that he only attempted to seduce her because he loves Posthumus so much and wanted to test Imogen to make certain that he had a faithful and worthy wife. After begging her pardon profusely, he offers to carry her letters to her husband, and he then asks her permission to store a large trunk in her chambers – he claims that it contains his most valued possessions – and she grants his request.

Meanwhile, Cloten is behaving typically, complaining about his poor luck in a game of bowling, while the two gentlemen who attend on him make fun of him behind his back. When he has gone, one of them remarks on how peculiar it is that such a crafty mother should have borne such a foolish son, and he then expresses his sympathy for Imogen's predicament and hopes that she will weather her current problems and find happiness with her husband.

That night, when Imogen goes to bed, Iachimo's trunk sits stored in her room. After she has fallen asleep, the trunk opens and Iachimo himself slips out. He watches her as she sleeps and then makes careful note of all the furnishings in her bedchamber, as well as a particular birthmark on her left breast. Then, he slips from her wrist the bracelet that Posthumus gave to her and slips back into the trunk, planning to present the item of jewellery, as well as his new familiarity with her bedchamber, as evidence of a successful seduction.

In Britain, Cymbeline, the Queen and Cloten meet with Caius Lucius, the Roman ambassador, who demands the continuation of a tribute that was begun in Julius Caesar's time. Britain pays this tribute in exchange for Rome's promise not to invade. Supported by his wife and stepson, Cymbeline refuses to pay it, declaring that Britain is an independent isle and will remain so – which leads Lucius to say, regretfully, that a state of war must thus exist between Rome and Britain.

Meanwhile, Pisanio has received a letter from Posthumus, accusing Imogen of infidelity and asking his servant to lead her away from London and murder her. Pisanio is horrified and cannot believe what he is being asked to do. Nevertheless, he begins to carry out his master's orders: he gives Imogen another letter, also from Posthumus, in which her husband asks her to meet him at Milford Haven, on the coast of Wales. Imogen is transported with joy at the thought of seeing him again, and she immediately makes preparations to slip away from her father's palace.

The scene now shifts to the wilderness of Wales, where an old shepherd named Belarius instructs his two sons, Guiderius and Arviragus, in the wonders of nature. The young men are restless because they have never been allowed to leave their wilderness home and see the wider world; Belarius insists, however, that there is nothing in the city but treachery and wickedness, and he recounts how he was once a nobleman in Cymbeline's court but was banished for crimes he did not commit. When his sons exit the stage, he tells the audience that the boys are actually the sons of Cymbeline himself; Belarius kidnapped them when they were very young in order to avenge his unjust exile. They remain ignorant of their true identity; they believe that Belarius' name is Morgan and that they themselves are named Polydore and Cadwal.

Imogen and Pisanio arrive in Milford Haven, and the Princess, seeing no sign of her husband, becomes perturbed. The unhappy servant then reveals the deception, and he shows her Posthumus' letter accusing her of infidelity. Imogen falls to weeping, cursing her husband's lack of trust in her, and she then begs Pisanio to follow his master's orders and kill her, since her life is no longer worth living. He refuses, however, and she asks why he bothered to bring her to Milford Haven if not to kill her. Pisanio replies that by maintaining the appearance of having followed through with the plan – by faking Imogen's death – they may instill guilt in Posthumus and restore his love for her. Posthumus must have been deceived by some villain into thinking Imogen unfaithful; perhaps the villain, too, will become contrite upon hearing of Imogen's 'death' and turn himself in. He therefore suggests that she disguise herself as a boy, with clothes that he has brought for this purpose, and enter the service of Caius Lucius, who will soon be leaving England from the Milford Haven port. In this way, she can make her way to Italy, where Posthumus resides. She agrees to his plan, and she changes clothes – and as a parting gift, he presents her with the potion that the Queen gave to him, telling her what he believes to be true: it is a soothing cordial that will help her if she grows sick on the voyage.

Back at Cymbeline's court, the disappearance of the Queen's son, Cloten, has stricken her with a wasting fever. Cymbeline threatens Pisanio with torture in an attempt to find out where Imogen has fled to, but the Roman invasion of Britain intervenes, and Cymbeline must prepare his army to meet the new threat. Meanwhile, Guiderius, Arviragus and Belarius hear armies moving through the wilderness; Belarius wants to lie low, since he is afraid that some of the Britons may recognize him from his days at court, but his adoptive sons are eager to fight, and they insist that they go down to assist Cymbeline's forces.

Posthumus returns to Britain, after having been conscripted

– as an Italian resident – into the Roman forces. He has received a bloody handkerchief from Pisanio, ostensibly a token of Imogen's death, and he is overcome with remorse, resolving that ''Tis enough/That, Britain, I have killed thy mistress; peace,/I'll give no wound to thee'. He takes off his Roman uniform and dresses himself as a British peasant for the battle.

During the fight, Iachimo, fighting on the side of the Romans, loses his sword in a duel with the disguised Posthumus. Left alone, he expresses his remorse for having lied about Imogen's faithlessness. Meanwhile, the battle goes badly for the British until the sudden arrival of Belarius, Guiderius and Arviragus, who save Cymbeline from capture and turn the tide. The Romans are beaten; Caius Lucius is taken prisoner – along with Posthumus who, although he fought for the victorious Britons, is trying to punish himself for his supposed murder of Imogen, and he has quickly changed back into Roman garb in order to be taken prisoner. He is thrown into a British stockade and, desiring death, falls asleep.

While he sleeps, a collection of spirits ascends from the netherworld and gathers around him. They are Posthumus' dead ancestors, and they plead with Jupiter, the king of the gods, to take pity on their descendant and restore his fortunes. After a time, Jupiter himself arrives from the heavens, surrounded in thunder and lightning and riding on the back of an eagle. He berates the spirits for troubling him, but he grudgingly agrees to bring about happiness for Posthumus. Then, all the supernatural creatures depart and Posthumus awakens, feeling strangely refreshed, and finds a written oracle on the ground beside him, which he is unable to interpret. The jailer comes to take him to be hanged, but then a messenger arrives, summoning Posthumus to stand before Cymbeline.

Cymbeline brings Guiderius, Arviragus and Belarius before him to reward them for their valour in battle. He regrets that the unknown peasant who fought so well for Britain (who is, of course, Posthumus) cannot be found, and he then proceeds to knight Belarius and the two young men (who are his own sons, though he does not know it) in gratitude for their service.

Just then, Cornelius comes in, bringing word that the Queen has died of her fever. Before she died, he reports, she confessed that she never loved Cymbeline and planned to gradually poison him so that the crown would devolve upon her son, Cloten. The King, amazed, says that she managed to deceive him completely, and he attributes her success in this to her great beauty.

The Roman prisoners, including Caius Lucius, Iachimo and Posthumus, with Imogen (still disguised as the boy Fidele) following at the rear, are all brought in together. The Roman general asks that Cymbeline treat them mercifully – and asks especially that his servant, a British boy (who is, of course, the disguised Imogen), be ransomed and freed. Imogen is then brought before her father, who does not recognize her but orders her to be freed and even offers her any privilege within his power to grant. She asks to speak with him in private, and father and daughter separate themselves from the rest of the company. When they return, Imogen asks Iachimo to step forward, and she demands to know where he got the ring that encircles his finger (the audience knows that Imogen gave the ring to Posthumus and that Posthumus lost it to Iachimo in the wager). Iachimo, feeling pangs of remorse, confesses how he used trickery to win the bet with Posthumus, describing his entire scheme to gain entrance to Imogen's bedroom. Hearing the story, Posthumus attempts to assault Iachimo, but Imogen hastily reveals her true identity, stripping off her boy's disguise, and the reunited couple embrace.

Through dialogue, the characters piece together the story of how Imogen came to the cave, how she only appeared dead after taking the Queen's potion, and how Cloten met actual death. Cymbeline declares that Guiderius must die for killing a prince, but Belarius hastily reveals himself as the banished courtier and tells the King that Guiderius and Arviragus are the sons that were stolen from him long ago. Cymbeline, overcome with happiness, forgives Belarius and welcomes him back to court; meanwhile, Iachimo offers his life to Posthumus as payment for his sins, but Posthumus graciously forgives him. Caius Lucius' soothsayer comes forward and interprets the prophecy that Posthumus found beside him that morning (left by Zeus), which is revealed to refer to the reunion of Imogen with her husband and the return of Cymbeline's two sons. Caught up in the abiding joyful spirit, the King promises to free the Romans, to allow them to return home unpunished, and even to resume the tribute, which was the issue over which the war was fought in the first place. Rejoicing, the entire company exits together to make a great feast and offer sacrifices to the gods.

The Winter's Tale
Sources
One of Shakespeare's final plays. Composed and performed around 1610-11, it joins *Pericles*, *Cymbeline* and *The Tempest* in the list of genre-defying later plays that are usually referred to as the romances or tragicomedies. In *The Winter's Tale* we are given the joyous ending that sets these plays apart from the earlier histories and tragedies, but the playwright demands that we endure the savage madness of Leontes, and the deaths of three innocent people before we reach the happy resolution.

There is no single source for *The Winter's Tale*, although Shakespeare relies heavily on the works of Richard Greene, a London writer in the 1580s and 1590s. (Greene may have been the author of a 1592 pamphlet attacking Shakespeare, which makes the Bard's borrowings from the deceased writer particularly appropriate.) From *Pandosto*, Greene's 1588 prose romance, Shakespeare borrowed most of the characters and events of the first three acts; and the character and habits of Autolycus seem to be drawn from Greene's pamphlet accounts of criminals in Elizabethan London. The story of the abandoned royal baby, meanwhile, owes much to popular folklore of the time, and the seasonal themes touched on in Act IV echo Ovid's *Metamorphoses* – Perdita is associated with Proserpina, whose emergence from the Underworld in Greek myth was supposed to herald the return of spring. Finally, the resurrection of Hermione in Act V owes an obvious debt to the *Pygmalion* story, in which a sculptor's work comes to life through divine intervention.

In terms of strength of character, unity of plot and audience satisfaction, *The Winter's Tale* may be the best of the later romances, and it has been a favourite of directors and audiences up to the present day.

Main Characters

Leontes
The King of Sicilia, and the childhood friend of Polixenes, the King of Bohemia. He is gripped by jealous fantasies that convince him Polixenes has been having an affair with his wife, Hermione; his jealousy leads to the destruction of his family.

Hermione
The virtuous and beautiful Queen of Sicilia. Falsely accused of infidelity by her husband, Leontes, she apparently dies of grief just after being vindicated by the Oracle of Delphi, but is restored to life at the play's close.

Perdita
The daughter of Leontes and Hermione. Because her father believes her to be illegitimate, she is abandoned as a baby on the coast of Bohemia, and brought up by a shepherd. Unaware of her royal lineage, she falls in love with Florizel, the Prince of Bohemia.

Polixenes
The King of Bohemia, and the boyhood friend of Leontes. He is falsely accused of having an affair with Leontes' wife, and barely escapes Sicilia with his life. Much later, he sees his only son fall in love with a lowly shepherd's daughter – who is, in fact, a Sicilian princess.

Florizel
Polixenes' only son and heir; he falls in love with Perdita, unaware of her royal ancestry, and defies his father by eloping with her.

Camillo
An honest Sicilian nobleman, he refuses to follow Leontes' order to poison Polixenes, deciding instead to flee Sicily and enter the Bohemian King's service.

Paulina
A noblewoman of Sicilia, she is fierce in her defence of Hermione's virtue, and unrelenting in her condemnation of Leontes after Hermione's death. She is also the agent of the (apparently) dead Queen's resurrection.

Autolycus
A 'snapper-up of unconsidered trifles'. A roguish peddler, vagabond and pickpocket; he steals the clown's purse and does a great deal of pilfering at the shepherd's sheepshearing, but ends by assisting in Perdita and Florizel's escape.

Shepherd
An old and honourable sheep-tender, he finds Perdita as a baby and raises her as his own daughter.

Antigonus
Paulina's husband, and also a loyal defender of Hermione. He is given the unfortunate task of abandoning the baby Perdita on the Bohemian coast.

Clown
The shepherd's buffoonish son, and Perdita's adopted brother.

Mamillus
The young prince of Sicilia, Leontes and Hermione's son. He

dies, perhaps of grief, after his father wrongly imprisons his mother.

Cleomenes
A lord of Sicilia, sent to Delphi to ask the Oracle about Hermione's guilt.

Dion
A Sicilian lord, he accompanies Cleomenes to Delphi.

Emilia
One of Hermione's ladies-in-waiting.

Archidamus
A lord of Bohemia.

The Plot
In the kingdom of Sicilia, King Leontes is visited by his childhood friend, King Polixenes of Bohemia. One of Leontes' lords, Camillo, discusses the striking differences between the two kingdoms with a Bohemian nobleman, Archidamus. The conversation then turns to the great and enduring friendship between the two kings, and the beauty and promise of Leontes' young son, Mamillus.

These two lords go out, and Leontes comes in, along with his wife Hermione (who is pregnant), Mamillus and Polixenes, who is making ready to depart for home. Leontes pleads with him to stay a little longer in Sicilia, but his friend refuses, declaring that he has been away from Bohemia for nine months, which is long enough. Hermione then takes up the argument, and Polixenes yields to her entreaties, promising to stay for a little longer. He tells the Sicilian queen how wonderful his childhood with Leontes was – how 'we were, fair queen/Two lads that thought there was no more behind/But such a day tomorrow as today/And to be boy eternal.'

Leontes, meanwhile, tells Hermione that she has never

spoken to better effect than in convincing Polixenes to stay –
save for once, when she agreed to marry him. But as his wife
and his friend walk together, apart from him, he feels stirrings
of jealousy, and tells the audience that he suspects them of
being lovers. He turns to his son and notes that the boy
resembles him, and this reassures him that Mamillus is, in fact,
his son and not someone else's; his suspicion of his wife
remains, however, and grows quickly, until he is certain that
she is sleeping with Polixenes. He sends the two of them to
walk in the garden together, promising to join them later, and
then calls Camillo over, asking if he has noticed anything
peculiar about Polixenes' behaviour lately. Camillo says that
he has not, and Leontes accuses him of being negligent, and
then declares that Hermione and Polixenes have made him a
cuckold – that is, a betrayed husband. Camillo, appalled,
refuses to believe it, but his king insists that it is true, and
orders the lord to act as cupbearer to Polixenes – and then
poison him at the first opportunity.

Camillo promises to obey, but his conscience is greatly
troubled, and when Leontes has gone and Polixenes reappears,
the Bohemian King realizes that something is amiss. Saying
that Leontes just gave him a peculiar and threatening look, he
demands to know what is going on, and Camillo, after a
moment of anguish, tells him of the Sicilian King's suspicions
and desire to have him poisoned. He begs protection of
Polixenes, who accepts him as a servant, and they decide to
flee the country immediately by sneaking out of the castle
and taking ship for Bohemia. Camillo promises to use his
authority in Sicilia to aid their escape, and the two men slip
away together.

Hermione asks her little boy, Mamillus, to sit by her and tell
her a story. Meanwhile, Leontes storms in, having just learned
of Polixenes' escape and Camillo's role in accomplishing it. To
his diseased mind, this is proof positive that his suspicions
were correct – he decides that Camillo must have been in
Polixenes' pay from the beginning. He orders Mamillus to be

taken away from Hermione, and then accuses his wife of being pregnant with the King of Bohemia's child. Hermione, astonished, denies it vigorously, but to no avail; her husband orders her to be taken away to jail, along with her ladies-in-waiting. When she has been dragged off, the lords of Sicilia plead with Leontes, declaring that he is mistaken and his queen is innocent; Hermione's most vocal defender is a lord named Antigonus. The King will have none of it, however – he is certain of his own rightness, and says that the matter is none of their concern. However, he does promise to ask the celebrated Oracle of Apollo, at Delphi, for a verdict before proceeding against his wife.

Antigonus' wife Paulina attempts to visit Hermione in prison, but is rebuffed by the guards. She is, however, allowed to speak with one of the queen's ladies, Emilia, who reports that her mistress has given birth to a beautiful daughter. Overriding the uncertain jailer, Paulina decides to take the child from the cell and bring it to Leontes, in the hopes that the sight of his new-born daughter will release the King from his madness.

Meanwhile, Mamillus has fallen ill since Hermione's imprisonment. Leontes, of course, attributes his son's ailment to shame over his mother's infidelity; meanwhile, he angrily wishes that Polixenes had not managed to escape his wrath. Paulina brings the child to the King, and he grows furious with her, demanding of Antigonus why he cannot manage to control his wife better. Paulina, instead of falling silent, argues with Leontes, defending Hermione's honour and then laying the baby before the angry King before she departs. When she is gone, Leontes orders Antigonus to take the child away and throw it into the fire, so that he will never have to see another man's bastard call him father. His lords are horrified by this order, and beg him to reconsider. He relents after a moment, but only a little – instead of burning the infant, he tells Antigonus to carry it into the wilderness and leave it there. As the unhappy nobleman takes the child and departs, word arrives that his messengers to the Oracle of Delphi have returned, bringing with them the divine verdict on the matter.

Making their way back from Delphi, the lords Dion and Cleomenes discuss events in their native Sicilia and express their hope that the message they bring from the Oracle will vindicate the unfortunate Hermione. Meanwhile, Leontes convenes a court, with himself as judge, in order to give his wife a fair trial. She is brought from the prison to appear before him, and the indictment, charging her with adultery and conspiracy in the escape of Polixenes and Camillo, is read to the entire court. Hermione defends herself eloquently, saying that she loved the Bohemian King 'as in honour he required', but no more, certainly not in a sexual fashion; that she is ignorant of any conspiracy; and that Camillo is an honest man. Leontes, paying little heed to her words, declares that she is guilty, and that her punishment must be death. Hermione laughs bitterly at this and says that given her sufferings so far, death would be a blessed release.

At this juncture, the two lords arrive with the Oracle's message which is unsealed and read aloud. 'Hermione is chaste,' it reports, 'Polixenes blameless, Camillo a true subject, Leontes a jealous tyrant, his innocent babe truly begotten, and the King shall live without an heir if that which is lost be not found.' The courtiers rejoice, while Leontes refuses to believe it; at that moment, however, a servant rushes in with word that Mamillus has died, and the enormity of the King's mistake suddenly comes crashing down on him. Hermione faints, and she is quickly carried away by her ladies and Paulina, who are frantically attempting to revive her. Leontes, now grief-stricken, pours curses upon his own head, and Paulina re-enters and tells him that Hermione, too, has died, and that he has murdered her. One of the lords rebukes her, but Leontes accepts her accusation as no more than his due. Ordering a single grave for the body of his wife and son, he pledges to spend the rest of his life doing penance for his sin.

Unaware of the Oracle's revelations, Antigonus has arrived on the desolate Bohemian coast, bearing the infant princess. He tells the audience how Hermione appeared to him in a dream, telling him to name the babe Perdita, and declaring that he would never see his home, or his wife Paulina, again. He lays the infant down in the woods, and places gold and jewels beside her, and a note bearing the child's name, and then makes ready to depart. A storm has risen, however, and a bear appears and chases him off. After a time, a shepherd finds the baby; he is joined by his son, a clown, who reports seeing a man (Antigonus) killed by a bear, and a ship (Antigonus' vessel) go down in the storm. The two men then discover the wealth left with Perdita, and they rejoice in their good fortune and vow to raise the child themselves.

On the empty stage, an actor appears, playing Time, and announces that in the space between acts, sixteen years have passed. The scene shifts to Polixenes' castle in Bohemia, where the King is conversing with Camillo. The nobleman asks leave of Polixenes to return to his native Sicilia, since sixteen years away have made him homesick – and besides, the still-grieving Leontes would welcome him home with open arms. Polixenes replies that he cannot manage the kingdom without Camillo's assistance, and the two men discuss the King's son, Florizel, who has been spending a great deal of time away from court, at the house of a wealthy shepherd – a shepherd whose daughter is reputed to be a great beauty. Somewhat worried, Polixenes decides that they will visit this shepherd's house, but in disguise, to see what Florizel is up to.

Meanwhile, in the Bohemian countryside, a jovial vagabond, pedlar and thief named Autolycus is wandering along a highway and singing loudly. He comes upon a clown on his way to market, counting a substantial sum of money with which he plans to buy supplies for a country sheep-shearing (a great event in the area). Autolycus accosts him and pretends to be the victim of a robbery. As the clown commiserates with him, the crafty thief picks his pocket, and when his victim has

gone on his way, Autolycus resolves to make an appearance at
the sheep-shearing – in a different disguise, of course.

On the day of the sheep-shearing, Perdita and Florizel walk
together outside her home. She is decked out in flowers, and he
compliments her on her grace and beauty. It quickly becomes
apparent that the couple are deeply in love, but Perdita
expresses concern over the possibility of their eventual union,
pointing out that Florizel's father is bound to oppose it. The
Prince reassures her, declaring: 'I'll be thine, my fair,/Or not
my father's'. As they talk together, the shepherd comes in with
a huge crowd, including the clown, a group of shepherdesses,
and the disguised Polixenes and Camillo. The shepherd tells his
adoptive daughter to act the hostess, as is proper, and so she
busies herself distributing flowers to the new arrivals, which
leads to a discussion of horticulture with Polixenes. Watching
and listening to her, Florizel is inspired to another effusive
declaration of his love. At this point, we learn that he is going
by the alias of Doricles.

Polixenes remarks to Camillo that Perdita is 'the prettiest
low-born lass that ever/Ran on the greensward. Nothing she
does or seems/But smacks of something greater than herself.
Too noble for this place.' He asks the shepherd about 'Doricles',
and the shepherd tells him that his daughter's suitor is some
high-born fellow, and that the two are deeply in love – 'I think
there is not half a kiss to choose/Who loves another best.'
Meanwhile, a pedlar arrives, with the promise of entertaining
the company with songs. He is allowed in – it is Autolycus, in
a pedlar's costume – and sets about selling ballads to the clown
and the shepherdesses, and then singing for the entire group.
As he does so, Polixenes asks Doricles why he has not bought
anything for his love, and the Prince replies that he knows that
Perdita does not desire such silly things as the pedlar is offering.
He then decides to take this moment to ask the shepherd to seal
their betrothal, and the old man gladly agrees to do so.

Before they make the compact, however, Polixenes asks
Doricles why he does not consult his father before getting

engaged, and the Prince (still unaware of whom he is speaking with) replies that there are reasons, which he dares not share, why his father cannot know of his betrothal. He urges the shepherd to 'mark our contract', but the King now casts aside his disguise and declares that the betrothal shall not go forward: the shepherd will be executed for allowing a prince to court his daughter; Perdita's beauty shall be 'scratched with briers'; and Florizel will be disinherited if he ever speaks of her again. Polixenes relents slightly, after a moment, and decides to spare the life of the shepherd and the face of his daughter, but tells them that if they ever see the Prince again, their lives will be forfeit. Polixenes then departs, ordering his son to follow him to court, and leaving everyone horrified.

Both Perdita and the shepherd despair, with the latter cursing Florizel for deceiving him and then storming off. The Prince is remarkably unfazed, however, and assures Perdita that he will not be separated from her – that he is willing to give up the succession and flee Bohemia immediately. Camillo advises him against it, but Florizel insists that he will not break his oath to Perdita for anything in the world. This resolve gives Camillo an idea, and he advises the Prince to flee at once to Sicilia, where Leontes, believing him sent from Polixenes, will give him a good welcome. In the meantime, Camillo promises to bring Polixenes round to the notion of his son marrying a commoner. In truth, however, Camillo hopes that the King will follow his son to Sicilia, and bring him along, thus allowing him to return to his native land.

Florizel agrees to the old lord's plan, but points out that he does not have an appropriate retinue to appear in the court of Sicilia as Polixenes' son. While they discuss this problem, with Camillo promising to furnish the necessary attendants and letters, Autolycus comes in, bragging to himself about all the cheap goods he sold and all the purses he stole during the sheep-shearing. Noticing him, Camillo asks the rascal to exchange clothes with Florizel. Autolycus, baffled, agrees, and the Prince puts on the pedlar's rags, which, he hopes, will enable him to reach a ship undetected by his father. This done, Florizel, Perdita and Camillo leave Autolycus alone on stage. The crafty pedlar/thief declares that he has figured out their business from listening to them, but will not go and tell the king, since that would be a good deed – and good deeds are against his nature.

As Autolycus talks to himself, the clown and the shepherd come in. Seeing an opportunity for mischief, he pretends to be a nobleman (he is still wearing Florizel's clothing). The clown is advising the shepherd to tell King Polixenes how he found Perdita in the forest years before – since if she was a foundling, he is not her real father and therefore not responsible for her actions. Hearing this, Autolycus tells them that the King has gone aboard a nearby ship, and sends them in that direction. In fact, he sends them to the ship that Florizel and Perdita are taking to Sicilia.

In Sicilia, Leontes is still in mourning for Hermione and Mamillus, although some of his lords urge him to forget the past, forgive himself and marry again. Paulina, however, encourages his continued contrition, and extracts from him a promise that he will never take another wife until she gives him leave. Word comes of the arrival of Prince Florizel and his new wife Perdita from Bohemia, and the couple is ushered into Leontes' presence and greeted eagerly – since the Sicilian king has had no word from Bohemia for years. Everyone remarks on the beauty and grace of Perdita, and Florizel pretends to be on a diplomatic mission from his father. As they talk, however, a lord brings news that Polixenes himself, along with Camillo, are in the city, in pursuit of Florizel – and that they have the shepherd and the clown (who came to Sicilia on Florizel's ship) in their custody. Leontes, stunned, immediately resolves to go down and meet his former friend, bringing the despairing Florizel and Perdita with him.

What follows is told secondhand, by several lords of Leontes' court to the newly arrived Autolycus. Briefly, once the shepherd has told everyone his story of finding Perdita on the Bohemian coast and reveals the tokens that were left on her, Leontes and Polixenes realize who she is; both kings – but especially Leontes – are overcome with joy, and there is general rejoicing. The lords also tell Autolycus that the happy group has not yet returned to court, since Perdita expressed a wish to see a statue of her mother, recently finished in Paulina's country house. Then the clown and shepherd come in, having both been made gentlemen, and Autolycus pledges to amend his life and become their loyal servant.

The scene shifts to Paulina's home, and she unveils the statue, which impresses everyone with its realism and attention to detail – as well as the fact that the sculptor made Hermione look exactly sixteen years older than she was when she died. Leontes is overcome by the sight of her, and tries to touch the statue's hand. Paulina holds him back, saying that she did not expect it to move him to such grief, and offers to draw the curtain, but the King refuses to allow it. Paulina then offers to make the statue come down from the pedestal – and, to everyone's amazement, there is music and the statue moves. It steps down, and embraces Leontes: it is the real Hermione, alive again. She blesses her daughter, saying that she hoped to see her again, and Leontes, now overcome with happiness, betroths Paulina and Camillo and then leads the company out, rejoicing in the apparent miracle.

The Tempest
Sources
Shakespeare's final play, written around 1610–11, it is also one of the few plays to almost adhere to the classical unities of 'time, place and action', whereby the play is performed in real time, the location remains unchanged and there is only one plot. *The Tempest* generally lasts around two hours (the action actually takes four); it is set in one location (apart from the opening scene at sea); and the action centres mainly around Prospero.

On 27 May 1606 the government passed a law 'for the

preventing and avoiding of the great abuse of the Holy Name
of God in Stage playes, Interludes, Maygames, Shows, and
such like'. If a playwright was foolhardy enough to use the
name of God, Jesus Christ, the Holy Ghost or the Holy Trinity
in his work, he could face a fine of £10 (a vast sum of money in
the seventeenth century). Consequently, Shakespeare makes
little mention of the Christian deities, contenting himself with
alluding to gods of classical mythology.

The Tempest was first performed on 1 November 1611 in
the Banqueting Hall 'at Whithall before ye Kinges Maiestie'.
James I liked the play so much that it was again presented in the
winter of 1612-13. The King chose the play as a Royal
Command Performance since it was part of the celebrations
for the marriage of his daughter, Princess Elizabeth, to
Frederick, the Elector of Germany's Palatine States.

Shakespeare used material from a number of sources in
writing *The Tempest.* These included Montaigne's 1603 essay
Of Cannibals, the 1610 pamphlet *A Discovery of the Barmudas
otherwise called the Ile of Divels* by Sir Thomas Gates, Sir
George Sommers and Captain Newport 'with divers others',
and a German play, *Die Schöne Sidea* (The Lovely Sidea). In
William Thomas' *History of Italy* (1549) he recounts the tale of
Prospero Adorno, the Duke of Genoa who is deposed in 1460
and returns to his dukedom seventeen years later. Deposed
again, he was replaced by his brother, Anthony Adorno. It is
more than likely that Shakespeare was aware of the story and
used the names and part of the tale as the basis for *The Tempest.*

Many scholars have seen parallels between the play and
Shakespeare's own life. Prospero's farewell is seen as
Shakespeare's own valediction.

Main Characters
Prospero
The former Duke of Milan. A kindly, generous, studious man
who was not interested in playing politics, with the result that
he fell victim to the machinations of his scheming brother,

Antonio. The critic Lytton Strachey, however, in an essay on Shakespeare (in 1904?) called him 'opinionated and sour ... there is no character in the play to whom, during some part of it, he is not studiously disagreeable'. Prospero spends his time on the island learning magic so that he can get revenge on his enemies. However, he is not malicious and wants to use the magic for the common good: to improve and teach his foes rather than simply punish them. He is very protective of his daughter, Miranda, and although he likes Prince Ferdinand he is rather suspicious of the young man's intentions. 'They are both in either's pow'rs: but this swift business/I must uneasy make, lest too light winning/ Make the prize light.' He can see the political advantage of an alliance between Milan and Naples. He watches over events on the island from his cell, controlling as he goes.

Caliban

A 'freckled whelp, hag-born', the fish-like Caliban is the 'savage and deformed' son of a devil and Sycorax, a witch. (In Shakespeare's day savage meant wild or uncivilized, rather than cruel.) At twenty-four, Caliban is just one step removed from the beasts of the jungle, but he is able to talk. A violent creature, he is incapable of being taught the difference between good and bad. Despite Prospero's best efforts, he tries to rape Miranda, Prospero's daughter. Caliban is resentful of authority and is easily swayed, pledging loyalty to anyone who he thinks can give him a better life. He promises allegiance to Stephano and Trinculo if they kill Prospero, little realizing he is swapping one master, albeit a good one, for another. Caliban was probably based on tales of West Indian savages that Shakespeare had heard and it is possible that the name Caliban is derived from the word cannibal. Shakespeare certainly intended Caliban to be black: Prospero calls him a 'thing of darkness'.

Ariel

An 'ayrie sprite' discovered by Prospero on the island. Ariel is desperate to be free but owes an allegiance to Prospero, who liberated him from the cloven pine tree where he had been held captive for twelve years for refusing to take orders from Sycorax. Unlike Caliban, Ariel serves Prospero and Miranda gladly – he caused the storm of the title. Not human, Ariel can move among humans unnoticed (cf. Puck in *A Midsummer Night's Dream*). Unemotional by nature, Ariel has almost developed feelings due to the time he has spent with humans.

Miranda

Prospero's fifteen-year-old daughter. An innocent girl uncorrupted by the evils of the world because she has had only her father for company for the previous twelve years. Her complexion is thus unsullied and affects even the evil Caliban when he tries to rape her. Like many teenage girls she feels the suffering of others; if living today, she would probably be a vegetarian. She falls in love with Prince Ferdinand at first sight, but thinks that he is a spirit because 'nothing natural I ev'r saw no noble'. When Prospero makes Ferdinand haul logs, Miranda offers to do the work for him, telling him that she loves him.

Ferdinand

A Neapolitan prince, the handsome and brave son of King Alonso. As he swims ashore he believes he is the only survivor of the shipwreck, but when he is led to Prospero's cell he is mesmerized by the sight of the virginal Miranda, 'the goddess on whom these airs attend'. He is so taken with her that he willingly undertakes the menial tasks set by her father, Prospero, to test his spirit and manliness.

Alonso

The King of Naples. Alonso is a monarch who is too easily led by his advisers. He suggests that Milan becomes a fiefdom of Naples when Prospero is deposed and cast adrift. Once on the island he is distraught at the death of his son and later feels guilt at what he did to Prospero. Alonso even considers dying by his own hand. Unlike some of the other characters, he learns and develops during the course of the play. He is delighted to learn that Ferdinand is not only alive but also in love, and his son's relationship cements his friendship with Prospero.

Gonzalo

'An honest old counsellor', Gonzalo is an ageing aristocrat with a good heart and comparable optimism. It is Gonzalo who helps Prospero when the Duke is set adrift. Courageous and dignified, Gonzalo accepts his fate on the island. It is Ariel's intervention that prevents Gonzalo being murdered. His view of the situation on the island – he wants to build a utopian society – is, however, unrealistic and unworkable. Prospero likes him immensely – 'good Gonzalo, my true preserver' – and with obvious good reason. Samuel Johnson opined, 'It may be observed of Gonzalo that, being the only good Man that appears with the King, he is the only Man that preserves his cheerfulness in the wreck, and his Hope on the island.'

Antonio

The heartless and cruel Duke of Milan incumbent who, with the aid of King Alonso, to whom he subsequently pays an annual fee deposed his elder brother, Prospero, to take the title. He also, so he thought, condemned his brother and niece to certain death by drowning. On the island, his cruelty is again in evidence as, with Sebastian, Antonio plots to murder Alonso. The King learns from his behaviour and repents but Antonio is irredeemably evil.

Sebastian

The younger brother of King Alonso. He is a power-hungry coward who restrains his behaviour out of fear that he will be caught, rather than the knowledge that what he is doing is wrong. He is quite happy to join Antonio (who has already, so he thinks, murdered his brother) in killing his sibling and assuming the throne. Like Antonio, he is unrepentant about his actions.

Trinculo

Alonso's jester. Trinculo is unusual for a jester in that he seems to have no sense of humour, only a bullying manner. He is fearful of Caliban until he realizes that the spirit can do him no evil – then Trinculo reverts to form and verbally and physically bullies Caliban.

Stephano

Alonso's butler. A drunken friend of Trinculo, Stephano shares the jester's bullying ways. Stephano is a typical drunk, quiet when sober and loud and bragging when 'in his cups'. Stephano has a vivid imagination: he agrees to join the plot to kill Prospero because he thinks that he will be able to take Miranda as his bride.

The Plot

King Alonso of Naples has just seen his beloved daughter, Princess Claribel, married to the King of Tunis and is returning home when a massive storm blows up. The monarch's ship is separated from the rest of his fleet and the wind and tide force his ship towards an island. The ship is dashed on to the rocks and is abandoned by crew and passengers, hoping to swim to safety on the island.

Prospero was once the Duke of Milan but, as he forlornly tells his daughter Miranda, he was more interested in his books than watching his back: his 'library was dukedom large enough'. Twelve years earlier, with the aid of King Alonso's army, Prospero's own brother, Antonio, had usurped him (cf. *As You Like It*). The two conspirators then told Gonzalo, an ageing aristocrat, to put Prospero and his young daughter to sea in a boat that was not seaworthy. In fact, it was said that the rats had deserted it just in case. Gonzalo was not a mean man and helped Prospero and Miranda by giving them 'rich garments, linens, stuffs and necessaries' and also Prospero's beloved library. Washed ashore on the seemingly uninhabited island, Prospero and Miranda come across a twelve-year-old black boy, Caliban. The child's mother, Sycorax, a witch, had died not long after parent and child arrived, banished by the ruler of Algiers. Prospero took to the boy and tried to teach him all manner of things, but Caliban's savage ways got the better of him and he tried to rape Miranda. Prospero made Caliban his slave. Before she died, Sycorax imprisoned in a tree a spirit called Ariel, but Prospero researches magic in his library and discovers how to free Ariel. It is Ariel (invisible to everyone except Prospero) who causes the violent storm and shipwreck at Prospero's behest. Miranda tells Prospero:

> 'O my dear father if by your art you have raised this dreadful storm, have pity on their sad distress. See! the vessel will be dashed to pieces. Poor souls! they will all perish. If I had power, I would sink the sea beneath the earth, rather than the good ship should be destroyed, with all the precious souls within her.'

Prospero calms her fears:

> 'Be not so amazed, daughter Miranda. There is no harm done. I have ordered it that no person in the ship shall receive any hurt. What I have done has been in care of you, my dear child.'

Disguised as a sea nymph, Ariel leads Alonso's son, Prince Ferdinand, away from the others and towards Prospero. When Ferdinand sees Miranda he thinks that she is a goddess. She is quite smitten with him as well but, until disavowed of the notion by her father, she thinks that Ferdinand 'is a spirit … a beautiful creature'. She was just three years old when she was put to sea and has seen no man other than her father. Prospero is pleased that Ferdinand and his daughter like each other but he is determined to test their love, to indeed ensure that the path of true love doesn't run smoothly. He takes Ferdinand prisoner and, in spite of Miranda's pleas, makes the young Prince fetch and carry logs.

King Alonso is convinced that his son has drowned (cf. Viola in *Twelfth Night*) and is inconsolable. Gonzalo does his best to comfort his monarch, but Alonso doesn't want to hear his kind words. Despite this, the two men decide to search for Ferdinand but the effort tires them and they fall asleep – thanks in no small part to Ariel's spell. Antonio, ever the opportunist, tells Prince Sebastian that they could kill Alonso as he sleeps and take his throne. Ariel overhears them and wakes Gonzalo by whispering in his ear. Antonio and Sebastian explain their drawn swords by telling the King that they were protecting them all from attack by wild animals. Alonso believes their tale and the search for Ferdinand continues.

Trinculo, the king's jester, swims ashore and is seen by Caliban, who hides, thinking that Trinculo must be a spirit. The rain is becoming heavier and he crawls under Caliban's cloak for shelter. Stephano, Alonso's butler, arrives on the scene having floated on to the island on a barrel of wine, some of which he has obviously drunk to calm his nerves. After the men recognize each other, Caliban is given alcohol by Stephano. Since Caliban has never tasted liquor before, he assumes that anyone who has it must be a god. Caliban tells Stephano that he will become his servant if he agrees to murder Prospero. The merry trio set off to commit the foul deed, but the seemingly ever-present Ariel leads them into a 'filthy-mantled pool', where they become trapped neck-deep in the mud. Ariel leaves them to their own devices while he goes off to inform Prospero of what has happened.

The hunting party fail to locate Ferdinand, but they come across some spirits who prepare a feast for them. Yet before they can eat a morsel, Ariel disguises himself as a harpy (a foul, malign character from Greek mythology with the wings and claws of a bird and the body of a woman) and reminds the 'three men of sin' of their behaviour towards Prospero and Miranda more than a decade earlier. The sumptuous meal disappears and Alonso is sorry for his actions. The faithless Antonio and Sebastian have no such remorse.

Prospero is impressed by Ferdinand and agrees to him marrying Miranda. He holds a solemn masque, arranged by Ariel and performed by ghostly actors, to celebrate the nuptials. They disguise themselves as Greek gods Iris (the messenger of the gods and goddess of the rainbow), Juno (the queen of the gods) and Ceres (the goddess of fertility). Towards the end of the festivities Prospero remembers Caliban's plan to murder him but easily thwarts it.

Prospero gathers everyone together and, dressed as the Duke of Milan, confronts his old enemies but grudgingly forgives them their sins. He restores King Alonso's son to him and tells Alonso that Ferdinand, thinking his father was dead, has engaged himself to Miranda without his permission. The union is blessed.

The sailors and the ship are discovered unharmed – the tempest was just an illusion – and preparations are made to return to the real world. Prospero breaks his staff, releases Ariel and becomes an ordinary mortal once again.

The Two Noble Kinsmen
Sources
Written by John Fletcher and William Shakespeare. It was entered in the Stationers' Register on 8 April 1634 by the printer John Waterson. It was first performed in 1613 or 1614. Ben Jonson referred to it in his *Bartholomew's Fair*, which was first performed in October 1614, and it may have been played at court in 1619. *The Two Noble Kinsmen* was not included in any of the seventeenth-century folio editions of Shakespeare's works and it is possible Shakespeare's name was added to Fletcher's to attract more interest.

Contrary to legend, when Shakespeare talks in *The Tempest* of breaking his staff and drowning his books, he did not mean he never intended to write again. He went on to write most of *Henry VIII*, possibly with John Fletcher (fifteen years Shakespeare's junior), and at least some of *The Two Noble Kinsmen*. *Henry VIII* was performed at the Globe on 29 June 1613, when the Globe caught fire and was burned to the ground. Shakespeare went on to collaborate on other plays for the King's Men.

Some critics argue against Shakespeare having much to do with *The Two Noble Kinsmen* on the grounds that it includes sexual vulgarity and, more convincingly, that Fletcher's showy style is very different from Shakespeare's. However, the characterization is similar to that of Shakespeare's later plays; some of the imagery is characteristic of Shakespeare; and there are passages similar in tone to passages in other plays by Shakespeare.

The source of *The Two Noble Kinsmen* is Chaucer's *The Knight's Tale*; Chaucer based his story on Boccaccio's *Il Teseida*. Shakespeare also drew for some details on Plutarch's *Life of Theseus*, which he also used in *A Midsummer Night's Dream*.

The play has seldom been performed since it was written. Pepys enjoyed the singing and dancing in a performance given on 10 September 1664. The Restoration added song and dance to many plays and Sir William Davenant reworked it under the title of *The Rivals*. Thereafter, *The Two Noble Kinsmen* has languished unseen until very recently (The Royal Shakespeare Company produced it at the Swan Theatre in 1986).

Main Characters
Theseus, Duke of Athens
The wise lord to whom everyone appeals.

Hippolyta
Theseus' Amazon bride.

Emilia
Hippolyta's sister, with whom the noble kinsmen are in love.

Palamon and Arcite
Creon's nephews, captured by Theseus and in love with Emilia.

The Gaoler's Daughter

In love with Palamon, she helps him escape – then goes mad but regains her sanity when she is wooed by someone pretending to be Palamon.

The Plot

Three queens urge Theseus, Duke of Athens, to attack Creon, King of Thebes, who killed their husbands. Theseus is about to marry Hippolyta, but he agrees to make war against Creon. Palamon and Arcite, Creon's nephews – the play's two noble kinsmen – are captured by Theseus. From their prison they see Hippolyta's sister Emilia and both fall in love with her.

Arcite is released and banished from Athens. In disguise, he takes service with Emilia. The gaoler's daughter falls in love with Palamon and helps him escape and later goes mad when she finds he does not love her.

The two noble kinsmen fight an inconclusive duel and Theseus insists they return a month later to conclude it. The winner will have Emilia and the loser will be executed. Emilia cannot decide which of the two she loves.

Arcite wins the duel but falls from his horse and is mortally wounded. He gives Emilia to Palamon. The gaoler's daughter regains her sanity.

THE POEMS

Shakespeare was celebrated as a poet before he was praised as a dramatist. At the time *Venus and Adonis* was written, in the early months of 1593, none of his plays had been published under his own name. The poem itself was immensely popular, and only one copy of the first edition survives; the first print run had been read and re-read until it fell apart. It is in essence a piece of dramatic oratory that moves rapidly and energetically, filled with the play of words as much as the play of allusion. The subsequent poem, *The Rape of Lucrece*, was equally splendid and theatrical; the torrid drama of Tarquin's lust is balanced by the moving anguish of his victim. Their words, in Shakespeare's own phrase, do 'ravish like inchaunting harmonie'.

Shakespeare's 154 sonnets, once despised for their artificiality, are now considered his greatest poetic achievement. They celebrate love with a fervour, but often with a realism, that speaks to us today. For whom they were written remains an enigma. Who was the 'dark lady' and who was Mr W.H.? We shall never know for sure but, far from being a literary exercise, these sonnets are works of great beauty and the emotions they express are all the more intense for being constricted by the strict rhyming pattern of three four-line groups with a final clinching couplet.

Venus and Adonis
Entered in the Stationers' Register on 18 April 1593, and dedicated to the Earl of Southampton. It was printed by Richard Field, who had originally come from Stratford-upon-Avon,

and was a respected, high-quality printer. *Venus and Adonis* proved popular: there were several editions in the next decade and there are references to it in the works of other poets. It is funny, erotic and compassionate. It tells the story of a female in pursuit of a male – not a subject often treated in the literature of the period. Its popularity waned but the Romantics rediscovered it, notably Coleridge and Keats.

The poem is written in six-line stanzas, the rhyme scheme being ababcc. This had been used by Spenser in *The Shepherd's Calendar* but it was still unusual. Its most famous expression was in Marlowe's *Hero and Leander*.

The story of Venus' love for Adonis was well known and Shakespeare probably drew on Ovid's version in his *Metamorphoses*. It is also told in Spenser's *Faerie Queene*. Adonis prefers hunting to love. Venus pulls him off his horse in order to kiss him. Adonis protests but Venus says she will only stop kissing him if he kisses her back. He promises to do so but later refuses.

Venus woos him, saying he must be in love with himself and he ought to have children to pass on his beauty. Adonis remains obdurate and is indifferent to Venus' tears and pleading. He tries to get back on his horse but it runs after a mare and he cannot catch it. Venus pretends to faint and, to revive her, Adonis kisses her. She revives but still Adonis says he is too young to love, though he promises to kiss her farewell. However, he says it will not be 'tomorrow' as he is going hunting.

Adonis is killed by a boar during the hunt. Venus weeps over him and his body becomes a purple flower. Venus retires to Cyprus to mourn him.

The poem begins:

> Even as the sun with purple-coloured face
> Had ta'en his last leave of the weeping morn,
> Rose-cheeked Adonis hied him to the chase.
> Hunting he loved, but love he laughed to scorn.

Sick-thoughted Venus makes amain unto him,
And like a bold-faced suitor 'gins to woo him.

In line 5, 'makes amain' means hastens.

The Rape of Lucrece

Entered in the Stationers' Register on 9 May 1594 under the title *The Ravishment of Lucrece*. It was printed by Richard Field for John Harrison, to be sold at the sign of the White Greyhound in Paul's Churchyard. The poem was a success and was reprinted several times in the two decades after it was first published.

The story of Lucrece is told by Livy, the Roman historian, and by Ovid in his *Fasti* (Chronicles). Chaucer tells the story in his *The Legend of Good Women* and it was well-known in Elizabethan times.

Shakespeare's version is written in a metre known as rhyme royal, which consists of stanzas of seven lines, rhymed ababbcc.

The poem is dedicated to 'The Right Honourable Henry Wriothesley, Earl of Southampton and Baron of Tichfield'. It is prefaced by a long prose 'argument' in which Shakespeare tells the story of Lucrece, including details not in the poem.

King Tarquin has obtained the throne of Rome by murdering his father-in-law. The King's son, also Tarquin, is besieging the town of Ardea. They decide to test their wives' virtue by riding back to Rome to check on what they are doing while their husbands are away. All the wives are enjoying themselves except Collatinus' wife Lucretia, or, as she is known in the poem, Lucrece. She is spinning with her women. Tarquin lusts after her and rapes her. Lucrece tells her father and husband what has happened and then stabs herself to death.

Seeking revenge, husband and father rouse the people of Rome, who chase the Tarquins out of the city. The monarchy is replaced by a republic.

The poem begins:

> From the besieged Ardea all in post,
> Borne by the trustless wings of false desire,
> Lust-breathed Tarquin leaves the Roman host,
> And to Collatium bears the lightless fire
> Which, in pale embers hid, lurks to aspire,
> And girdle with embracing flames the waist
> Of Collatine's fair love, Lucrece the chaste.

The Passionate Pilgrim

By W. Shakespeare, as the title of this pocket book has it, was published in 1599 by W. Leake, at the Greyhound in Paul's Churchyard. It was only 4½ × 2¾ inches in size.

It contains twenty-one poems of which only five are certainly by Shakespeare – I, a version of Sonnet 138; III, a version of Sonnet 144; and numbers III, V and XVI I, poems from *Love's Labour's Lost* first printed in 1598.

One of the other poems is a version of Christopher Marlowe's famous poem 'Come live with me and be my love'.

In 1612 a new edition of *The Passionate Pilgrim* included pirated poems written by Thomas Heywood and printed without permission.

The Phoenix and Turtle

Published in 1601, an anthology of poems by several 'modern' poets was published called *Love's Martyr: Or Rosalins Complaint Allegorically shadowing the truth of Love, in the Constant Fate of the Phoenix and Turtle.* The authors included Shakespeare, John Marston, George Chapman and Benjamin Jonson. Shakespeare's offering – a total of sixty-eight lines – makes little sense and is clearly some coded message or allegory that we cannot now decipher. The following is an extract:

> Here the anthem doth commence:
> Love and constancy is dead,

Phoenix and the turtle fled
In a mutual flame from hence.

So they loved, as love in twain
Had the essence but in one;
Two distincts, division none.
Number there in love was slain.

Hearts remote, yet not asunder;
Distance, and no space was seen
'Twixt this turtle and his Queen.
But in them it were a wonder.

A Lover's Complaint

Printed as an appendix to the *Sonnets* (1609) and, like other
Elizabethan poems such as Samuel Daniel's *Complaint of
Rosamond* (1592), tells the story of a girl betrayed by her lover.
It is a long poem – 329 lines – and the first stanza gives a taste of
the whole: awkward, artificial and rather absurd.

From off a hill whose concave womb reworded
A plaintful story from a sistering vale,
My spirits to attend this double voice accorded,
And down I laid to list the sad-tuned tale;
Ere long espied a fickle maid full pale,
Tearing of papers, breaking rings atwain,
Storming her world with sorrow's wind and rain.

The Sonnets

The complexities of the sonnets have never been resolved. Are they an intimation of Shakespeare's true feelings, or are they an exercise in dramatic projection? Were they circulated to a strictly private audience, or were they intended for publication? They are intimate but unidentifiable, a compound of lament and celebration, love and guilt. There have been attempts to impose order upon the entire sequence, but the abrupt changes in tone and mood do not make a convincing case for unity. The poems are perhaps best seen as a performance. In the process, Shakespeare has created original and marvellous poetry but, as the clown says in *As You Like It*, 'the truest poetrie is the most faining'.

Sources, Form and Subject Matter

Shakespeare's sonnets will always remain a mystery. To whom were they written and on which occasions? Were they written to honour a woman or a man or for two different people? Are they intimate love poems or exercises in style to show off Shakespeare's literary expertise?

There are, however, some definite facts among the questions

we can never answer definitively. On 20 May 1609, Thomas
Thorpe entered in the Stationers' Register 'a Booke called
Shakespeare's Sonnettes'. The title on Thorpe's quarto reads:
'Shakespeare's Sonnets – Never before imprinted at London
by G. Eld for T.T. and are to be solde by John Wright, dwelling
at Christ Church gate 1609'. The enigmatic dedication is as
follows:

> TO. THE. ONLY. BEGETTER.OF.
> THESE. ENSUING. SONNETS.
> Mr W.H. ALL. HAPPINESS.
> AND. THAT. ETERNITY.
> PROMISED.
> BY.
> OUR. EVER-LIVING. POET.
> WISHETH.
> THE. WELL-WISHING.
> ADVENTURER. IN.
> SETTING.
> FORTH.
> T.T.

On 19 June, Edward Alleyn noted among his purchases
'Shakespeare's sonnettes 5d'. In 1598, Francis Meres, the
author of *Palladis Tamia*, refers to Shakespeare's 'sugared
Sonnets'. The following year, William Jaggard had issued a
book called *The Passionate Pilgrime* by W. Shakespeare, which
included versions of Sonnets 138 and 144, some poems from
Love's Labour's Lost and poems by other authors. This proves
some of the sonnets were circulating at least eleven years before
they were first printed. Thorpe's edition of the *Sonnets* is
arranged in definable sections. The first seventeen are addressed
to a beautiful youth, calling on him to marry so that his beauty
is preserved in his children.

From Sonnet 18 to Sonnet 126, admiration is seen to turn to
love and the sonnets become ever more intimate. They cover a

range of moods from jealousy to ecstasy, and lovingly rebuke the young man for stealing the poet's mistress (Sonnets 40-42) and his wantonness (Sonnet 96). The poet says he wears the youth's picture (Sonnets 47-49) and apologizes for giving away the 'tables' the youth has given him (Sonnet 122). There follow twenty-six sonnets addressed to a mysterious 'dark lady'. She is faithless, wanton, ugly and yet irresistible. The collection ends with two sonnets to Cupid.

We may assume that T.T. is Thomas Thorpe but who is Mr W.H.? Who is the beautiful youth and who is the dark lady? Hundreds of books have been written on this subject, but one can assume that no final answer will ever be arrived at.

The reader has to bear in mind that the order in which Thorpe printed the sonnets may not be in any sense Shakespeare's. They may have been written in a quite different order and for several different people. (There was an edition of the *Sonnets* in 1640 in a different order, with changes to the text including substituting 'she' for 'he' and 'he' for 'she' in some poems.)

The sonnet form – artificial and highly stylized – was very popular in the age of Queen Elizabeth 1. The sonnet is a fourteen-line lyric poem, traditionally written in iambic pentameter, that is in lines ten-syllables long with accents falling on every second syllable, as in: 'Shall I compare thee to a summer's day?'

The sonnet became popular during the Italian Renaissance, when the poet Petrarch published a sequence of love sonnets addressed to Laura. The poets Wyatt and Surrey translated Petrarch's sonnets in the 1530s, but it was with Sir Philip Sidney's *Astrophel and Stella* that the sonnet form really became fashionable. Shakespeare's sonnets remind the reader of his *Venus and Adonis*, *Love's Labour's Lost* and the other plays written in or around 1595.

As for Mr W.H., many suggestions have been made about whom he might be. One possible candidate is Sir William Harvey, who married the mother of the Earl of Southampton in 1598. If the Earl of Southampton was Shakespeare's beautiful youth, then it makes sense to identify Harvey as Mr W.H. Another suggestion is William Herbert, Earl of Pembroke; but an earl would not relish being called 'Mr'.

Henry Wriothesley, Earl of Southampton, is the most likely subject of the 'beautiful youth' sonnets. He was born on 6 October 1573. He was a ward of Lord Burghley, the Queen's great minister of state, and Burghley was angered when Wriothesley refused to marry his granddaughter. He was almost too beautiful and though he did marry, eventually, Mistress Elizabeth Vernon, one of the Queen's ladies-in-waiting, he was in no hurry to attach himself to a woman. Shakespeare dedicated *Venus and Adonis* (1593) to him and *The Rape of Lucrece* a year later, which shows that he regarded Southampton as his patron.

Among many other less likely candidates is a boy actor called William Hughes, but there is no record of such an actor in Elizabethan acting companies.

After 1609 the sonnets were largely forgotten until the eighteenth century, when Malone prepared his edition of Shakespeare's work.

THE COMPLETE SONNETS

TO. THE. ONLY. BEGETTER.OF.
THESE. ENSUING. SONNETS.
Mr W.H. ALL. HAPPINESS.
AND. THAT. ETERNITY.
PROMISED.
BY.
OUR. EVER-LIVING. POET.
WISHETH.
THE. WELL-WISHING.
ADVENTURER. IN.
SETTING.
FORTH.

T.T.

I.
From fairest creatures we desire increase,
That thereby beauty's rose might never die,
But as the riper should by time decease,
His tender heir might bear his memory:
But thou, contracted to thine own bright eyes,

Feed'st thy light's flame with self-substantial fuel,
Making a famine where abundance lies,
Thyself thy foe, to thy sweet self too cruel.
Thou that art now the world's fresh ornament
And only herald to the gaudy spring,
Within thine own bud buriest thy content
And, tender churl, makest waste in niggarding.
　　Pity the world, or else this glutton be,
　　To eat the world's due, by the grave and thee.

II.
When forty winters shall besiege thy brow,
And dig deep trenches in thy beauty's field,
Thy youth's proud livery, so gazed on now,
Will be a tatter'd weed, of small worth held:
Then being ask'd where all thy beauty lies,
Where all the treasure of thy lusty days,
To say, within thine own deep-sunken eyes,
Were an all-eating shame and thriftless praise.
How much more praise deserved thy beauty's use,
If thou couldst answer 'This fair child of mine
Shall sum my count and make my old excuse,'
Proving his beauty by succession thine!
　　This were to be new made when thou art old,
　　And see thy blood warm when thou feel'st it
　　cold.

III.
Look in thy glass, and tell the face thou viewest
Now is the time that face should form another;
Whose fresh repair if now thou not renewest,
Thou dost beguile the world, unbless some mother.
For where is she so fair whose unear'd womb
Disdains the tillage of thy husbandry?
Or who is he so fond will be the tomb
Of his self-love, to stop posterity?

Thou art thy mother's glass, and she in thee
Calls back the lovely April of her prime:
So thou through windows of thine age shalt see
Despite of wrinkles this thy golden time.
 But if thou live, remember'd not to be,
 Die single, and thine image dies with thee.

IV.
Unthrifty loveliness, why dost thou spend
Upon thyself thy beauty's legacy?
Nature's bequest gives nothing but doth lend,
And being frank she lends to those are free.
Then, beauteous niggard, why dost thou abuse
The bounteous largess given thee to give?
Profitless usurer, why dost thou use
So great a sum of sums, yet canst not live?
For having traffic with thyself alone,
Thou of thyself thy sweet self dost deceive.
Then how, when nature calls thee to be gone,
What acceptable audit canst thou leave?
 Thy unused beauty must be tomb'd with thee,
 Which, usèd, lives th' executor to be.

V.
Those hours, that with gentle work did frame
The lovely gaze where every eye doth dwell,
Will play the tyrants to the very same
And that unfair which fairly doth excel:
For never-resting time leads summer on
To hideous winter and confounds him there;
Sap check'd with frost and lusty leaves quite gone,
Beauty o'ersnow'd and bareness everywhere:
Then, were not summer's distillation left,
A liquid prisoner pent in walls of glass,
Beauty's effect with beauty were bereft,
Nor it nor no remembrance what it was:

But flowers distill'd though they with winter
   meet,
Lose but their show; their substance still lives
   sweet.

VI.
Then let not winter's ragged hand deface
In thee thy summer, ere thou be distill'd:
Make sweet some vial; treasure thou some place
With beauty's treasure, ere it be self-kill'd.
That use is not forbidden usury,
Which happies those that pay the willing loan;
That's for thyself to breed another thee,
Or ten times happier, be it ten for one;
Ten times thyself were happier than thou art,
If ten of thine ten times refigured thee:
Then what could death do, if thou shouldst depart,
Leaving thee living in posterity?
   Be not self-will'd, for thou art much too fair
      To be death's conquest and make worms thine
         heir.

VII.
Lo, in the orient when the gracious light
Lifts up his burning head, each under eye
Doth homage to his new-appearing sight,
Serving with looks his sacred majesty;
And having climb'd the steep-up heavenly hill,
Resembling strong youth in his middle age,
Yet mortal looks adore his beauty still,
Attending on his golden pilgrimage;
But when from highmost pitch, with weary car,
Like feeble age, he reeleth from the day,
The eyes, 'fore duteous, now converted are
From his low tract and look another way:
   So thou, thyself outgoing in thy noon,

Unlook'd on diest, unless thou get a son.

VIII.

Music to hear, why hear'st thou music sadly?
Sweets with sweets war not, joy delights in joy.
Why lovest thou that which thou receivest not
    gladly,
Or else receivest with pleasure thine annoy?
If the true concord of well-tunèd sounds,
By unions married, do offend thine ear,
They do but sweetly chide thee, who confounds
In singleness the parts that thou shouldst bear.
Mark how one string, sweet husband to another,
Strikes each in each by mutual ordering,
Resembling sire and child and happy mother
Who all in one, one pleasing note do sing:
    Whose speechless song, being many, seeming
      one,
    Sings this to thee: 'Thou single wilt prove none.'

IX.

Is it for fear to wet a widow's eye
That thou consum'st thyself in single life?
Ah, if thou issueless shalt hap to die.
The world will wail thee, like a makeless wife;
The world will be thy widow and still weep
That thou no form of thee hast left behind,
When every private widow well may keep
By children's eyes her husband's shape in mind.
Look, what an unthrift in the world doth spend
Shifts but his place, for still the world enjoys it;
But beauty's waste hath in the world an end,
And kept unused, the user so destroys it.
    No love toward others in that bosom sits
    That on himself such murderous shame commits.

X.

For shame deny that thou bear'st love to any,
Who for thyself art so unprovident.
Grant, if thou wilt, thou art beloved of many,
But that thou none lov'st is most evident;
For thou art so possess'd with murderous hate
That 'gainst thyself thou stick'st not to conspire.
Seeking that beauteous roof to ruinate
Which to repair should be thy chief desire.
O, change thy thought, that I may change my mind!
Shall hate be fairer lodged than gentle love?
Be, as thy presence is, gracious and kind,
Or to thyself at least kind-hearted prove:
　　Make thee another self, for love of me,
　　That beauty still may live in thine or thee.

XI.

As fast as thou shalt wane, so fast thou grow'st
In one of thine, from that which thou departest;
And that fresh blood which youngly thou bestow'st
Thou mayst call thine when thou from youth
　　convertest.
Herein lives wisdom, beauty and increase:
Without this, folly, age and cold decay:
If all were minded so, the times should cease
And threescore year would make the world away.
Let those whom nature hath not made for store,
Harsh, featureless, and rude, barrenly perish:
Look, whom she best endow'd she gave the more;
Which bounteous gift thou shouldst in bounty
　　cherish:
　　She carved thee for her seal, and meant thereby
　　Thou shouldst print more, not let that copy die.

XII.

When I do count the clock that tells the time,

And see the brave day sunk in hideous night;
When I behold the violet past prime,
And sable curls all silver'd o'er with white;
When lofty trees I see barren of leaves
Which erst from heat did canopy the herd,
And summer's green all girded up in sheaves
Borne on the bier with white and bristly beard,
Then of thy beauty do I question make,
That thou among the wastes of time must go,
Since sweets and beauties do themselves forsake
And die as fast as they see others grow;
    And nothing 'gainst time's scythe can make
      defence
    Save breed, to brave him when he takes thee
      hence.

XIII.

O, that you were yourself! But, love, you are
No longer yours than you yourself here live:
Against this coming end you should prepare,
And your sweet semblance to some other give.
So should that beauty which you hold in lease
Find no determination: then you were
Yourself again after your self's decease,
When your sweet issue your sweet form should
    bear.
Who lets so fair a house fall to decay,
Which husbandry in honour might uphold
Against the stormy gusts of winter's day
And barren rage of death's eternal cold?
    O, none but unthrifts! Dear my love, you know
    You had a father: let your son say so.

XIV.

Not from the stars do I my judgement pluck;
And yet methinks I have astronomy,

But not to tell of good or evil luck,
Of plagues, of dearths, or seasons' quality;
Nor can I fortune to brief minutes tell,
Pointing to each his thunder, rain and wind,
Or say with princes if it shall go well,
By oft predict that I in heaven find:
But from thine eyes my knowledge I derive,
And, constant stars, in them I read such art
As truth and beauty shall together thrive,
If from thyself to store thou wouldst convert;
  Or else of thee this I prognosticate:
  Thy end is truth's and beauty's doom and date.

XV.
When I consider every thing that grows
Holds in perfection but a little moment,
That this huge stage presenteth nought but shows
Whereon the stars in secret influence comment;
When I perceive that men as plants increase,
Cheerèd and check'd even by the self-same sky,
Vaunt in their youthful sap, at height decrease,
And wear their brave state out of memory;
Then the conceit of this inconstant stay
Sets you most rich in youth before my sight,
Where wasteful time debateth with decay,
To change your day of youth to sullied night;
  And all in war with time for love of you,
  As he takes from you, I engraft you new.

XVI.
But wherefore do not you a mightier way
Make war upon this bloody tyrant, time?
And fortify yourself in your decay
With means more blessèd than my barren rhyme?
Now stand you on the top of happy hours,
And many maiden gardens yet unset

With virtuous wish would bear your living flowers,
Much liker than your painted counterfeit:
So should the lines of life that life repair,
Which this, time's pencil, or my pupil pen,
Neither in inward worth nor outward fair,
Can make you live yourself in eyes of men.
  To give away yourself keeps yourself still,
  And you must live, drawn by your own sweet
  skill.

XVII.
Who will believe my verse in time to come,
If it were fill'd with your most high deserts?
Though yet, heaven knows, it is but as a tomb
Which hides your life and shows not half your parts.
If I could write the beauty of your eyes
And in fresh numbers number all your graces,
The age to come would say, 'This poet lies:
Such heavenly touches ne'er touch'd earthly faces.'
So should my papers yellow'd with their age
Be scorn'd like old men of less truth than tongue,
And your true rights be term'd a poet's rage
And stretchèd metre of an antique song:
  But were some child of yours alive that time,
  You should live twice; in it and in my rhyme.

XVIII.
Shall I compare thee to a summer's day?
Thou art more lovely and more temperate:
Rough winds do shake the darling buds of May,
And summer's lease hath all too short a date:
Sometime too hot the eye of heaven shines,
And often is his gold complexion dimm'd;
And every fair from fair sometime declines,
By chance or nature's changing course untrimm'd;
But thy eternal summer shall not fade

Nor lose possession of that fair thou ow'st;
Nor shall death brag thou wander'st in his shade,
When in eternal lines to time thou grow'st:
　　So long as men can breathe or eyes can see,
　　So long lives this, and this gives life to thee.

XIX.

Devouring time, blunt thou the lion's paws,
And make the earth devour her own sweet brood;
Pluck the keen teeth from the fierce tiger's jaws,
And burn the long-lived phoenix in her blood;
Make glad and sorry seasons as thou fleets,
And do whate'er thou wilt, swift-footed time,
To the wide world and all her fading sweets;
But I forbid thee one most heinous crime:
O, carve not with thy hours my love's fair brow,
Nor draw no lines there with thine antique pen;
Him in thy course untainted do allow
For beauty's pattern to succeeding men.
　　Yet, do thy worst, old time: despite thy wrong,
　　My love shall in my verse ever live young.

XX.

A woman's face with nature's own hand painted
Hast thou, the master-mistress of my passion;
A woman's gentle heart, but not acquainted
With shifting change, as is false women's fashion;
An eye more bright than theirs, less false in rolling,
Gilding the object whereupon it gazeth;
A man in hue, all 'hues' in his controlling,
Much steals men's eyes and women's souls amazeth.
And for a woman wert thou first created;
Till nature, as she wrought thee, fell a-doting,
And by addition me of thee defeated,
By adding one thing to my purpose nothing.

But since she pricked thee out for women's
   pleasure,
Mine be thy love and thy love's use their treasure.

XXI.

So is it not with me as with that muse
Stirr'd by a painted beauty to his verse,
Who heaven itself for ornament doth use
And every fair with his fair doth rehearse
Making a couplement of proud compare,
With sun and moon, with earth and sea's rich gems,
With April's first-born flowers, and all things rare
That heaven's air in this huge rondure hems.
O' let me, true in love, but truly write,
And then believe me, my love is as fair
As any mother's child, though not so bright
As those gold candles fix'd in heaven's air:
   Let them say more than like of hearsay well;
   I will not praise that purpose not to sell.

XXII.

My glass shall not persuade me I am old,
So long as youth and thou are of one date;
But when in thee time's furrows I behold,
Then look I death my days should expiate.
For all that beauty that doth cover thee
Is but the seemly raiment of my heart,
Which in thy breast doth live, as thine in me:
How can I then be elder than thou art?
O, therefore, love, be of thyself so wary
As I, not for myself, but for thee will;
Bearing thy heart, which I will keep so chary
As tender nurse her babe from faring ill.
   Presume not on thy heart when mine is slain;
   Thou gav'st me thine, not to give back again.

XXIII.

As an unperfect actor on the stage
Who with his fear is put besides his part,
Or some fierce thing replete with too much rage,
Whose strength's abundance weakens his own
    heart.
So I, for fear of trust, forget to say
The perfect ceremony of love's rite,
And in mine own love's strength seem to decay,
O'ercharged with burden of mine own love's might.
O, let my books be then the eloquence
And dumb presagers of my speaking breast,
Who plead for love and look for recompense
More than that tongue that more hath more
    express'd.
    O, learn to read what silent love hath writ:
    To hear with eyes belongs to love's fine wit.

XXIV.

Mine eye hath play'd the painter and hath steeled
Thy beauty's form in table of my heart;
My body is the frame wherein 'tis held,
And perspective it is the painter's art.
For through the painter must you see his skill,
To find where your true image pictured lies;
Which in my bosom's shop is hanging still,
That hath his windows glazèd with thine eyes.
Now see what good turns eyes for eyes have done:
Mine eyes have drawn thy shape, and thine for me
Are windows to my breast, wherethrough the sun
Delights to peep, to gaze therein on thee;
    Yet eyes this cunning want to grace their art;
    They draw but what they see, know not the heart.

XXV.

Let those who are in favour with their stars

Of public honour and proud titles boast,
Whilst I, whom fortune of such triumph bars,
Unlook'd-for joy in that I honour most.
Great princes' favourites their fair leaves spread
But as the marigold at the sun's eye,
And in themselves their pride lies buried,
For at a frown they in their glory die.
The painful warrior famousèd for might,
After a thousand victories once foil'd,
Is from the book of honour razèd quite,
And all the rest forgot for which he toil'd:
    Then happy I, that love and am belov'd
    Where I may not remove nor be remov'd.

XXVI.
Lord of my love, to whom in vassalage
Thy merit hath my duty strongly knit,
To thee I send this written embassage,
To witness duty, not to show my wit:
Duty so great, which wit so poor as mine
May make seem bare in wanting words to show it,
But that I hope some good conceit of thine
In thy soul's thought, all naked, will bestow it;
Till whatsoever star that guides my moving
Points on me graciously with fair aspect
And puts apparel on my tatter'd loving,
To show me worthy of thy sweet respect:
    Then may I dare to boast how I do love thee;
    Till then not show my head where thou mayst
        prove me.

XXVII.
Weary with toil, I haste me to my bed,
The dear repose for limbs with travel tired;
But then begins a journey in my head,
To work my mind, when body's work's expir'd:

For then my thoughts, from far where I abide,
Intend a zealous pilgrimage to thee,
And keep my drooping eyelids open wide,
Looking on darkness which the blind do see
Save that my soul's imaginary sight
Presents thy shadow to my sightless view,
Which, like a jewel hung in ghastly night,
Makes black night beauteous and her old face new.
    Lo, thus, by day my limbs, by night my mind,
      For thee and for myself no quiet find.

XXVIII.

How can I then return in happy plight,
That am debarr'd the benefit of rest?
When day's oppression is not eas'd by night,
But day by night, and night by day, oppress'd?
And each, though enemies to either's reign,
Do in consent shake hands to torture me;
The one by toil, the other to complain
How far I toil, still farther off from thee.
I tell the day, to please him thou art bright
And dost him grace when clouds do blot the heaven:
So flatter I the swart-complexion'd night,
When sparkling stars twire not thou gild'st the even.
    But day doth daily draw my sorrows longer
      And night doth nightly make grief's strength
        seem stronger.

XXIX.

When, in disgrace with fortune and men's eyes,
I all alone beweep my outcast state
And trouble deaf heaven with my bootless cries
And look upon myself and curse my fate,
Wishing me like to one more rich in hope,
Featur'd like him, like him with friends possess'd,
Desiring this man's art and that man's scope,

With what I most enjoy contented least;
Yet in these thoughts myself almost despising,
Haply I think on thee, and then my state,
Like to the lark at break of day arising
From sullen earth, sings hymns at heaven's gate;
>For thy sweet love remember'd such wealth
>brings
>That then I scorn to change my state with kings.

XXX.

When to the sessions of sweet silent thought
I summon up remembrance of things past,
I sigh the lack of many a thing I sought,
And with old woes new wail my dear time's waste:
Then can I drown an eye, unus'd to flow,
For precious friends hid in death's dateless night,
And weep afresh love's long-since cancell'd woe,
And moan the expense of many a vanish'd sight:
Then can I grieve at grievances foregone,
And heavily from woe to woe tell o'er
The sad account of fore-bemoaned moan,
Which I new pay as if not paid before.
>But if the while I think on thee, dear friend,
>All losses are restored and sorrows end.

XXXI.

Thy bosom is endearèd with all hearts,
Which I by lacking have supposèd dead,
And there reigns love and all love's loving parts,
And all those friends which I thought buried.
How many a holy and obsequious tear
Hath dear religious love stol'n from mine eye
As interest of the dead, which now appear
But things remov'd that hidden in thee lie!
Thou art the grave where buried love doth live,
Hung with the trophies of my lovers gone,

Who all their parts of me to thee did give;
That due of many now is thine alone:
    Their images I lov'd I view in thee,
    And thou, all they, hast all the all of me.

XXXII.

If thou survive my well-contented day,
When that churl death my bones with dust shall
    cover,
And shalt by fortune once more re-survey
These poor rude lines of thy deceasèd lover,
Compare them with the bettering of the time,
And though they be outstripp'd by every pen,
Reserve them for my love, not for their rhyme,
Exceeded by the height of happier men.
O, then vouchsafe me but this loving thought:
'Had my friend's muse grown with this growing
    age,
A dearer birth than this his love had brought,
To march in ranks of better equipage:
    But since he died and poets better prove,
    Theirs for their style I'll read, his for his love.'

XXXIII.

Full many a glorious morning have I seen
Flatter the mountain tops with sovereign eye,
Kissing with golden face the meadows green,
Gilding pale streams with heavenly alchemy;
Anon permit the basest clouds to ride
With ugly rack on his celestial face,
And from the forlorn world his visage hide,
Stealing unseen to west with this disgrace:
Even so my sun one early morn did shine
With all triumphant splendor on my brow;
But out, alack, he was but one hour mine;
The region cloud hath mask'd him from me now.

Yet him for this my love no whit disdaineth;
Suns of the world may stain when heaven's sun
    staineth.

XXXIV.

Why didst thou promise such a beauteous day,
And make me travel forth without my cloak,
To let base clouds o'ertake me in my way,
Hiding thy bravery in their rotten smoke?
'Tis not enough that through the cloud thou break,
To dry the rain on my storm-beaten face,
For no man well of such a salve can speak
That heals the wound and cures not the disgrace:
Nor can thy shame give physic to my grief;
Though thou repent, yet I have still the loss:
The offender's sorrow lends but weak relief
To him that bears the strong offence's cross.
    Ah! but those tears are pearl which thy love
        sheds,
    And they are rich and ransom all ill deeds.

XXXV.

No more be griev'd at that which thou hast done:
Roses have thorns, and silver fountains mud;
Clouds and eclipses stain both moon and sun,
And loathsome canker lives in sweetest bud.
All men make faults, and even I in this,
Authorizing thy trespass with compare,
Myself corrupting, salving thy amiss,
Excusing thy sins more than thy sins are;
For to thy sensual fault I bring in sense--
Thy adverse party is thy advocate--
And 'gainst myself a lawful plea commence:
Such civil war is in my love and hate
    That I an accessory needs must be
    To that sweet thief which sourly robs from me.

XXXVI.

Let me confess that we two must be twain,
Although our undivided loves are one:
So shall those blots that do with me remain
Without thy help by me be borne alone.
In our two loves there is but one respect,
Though in our lives a separable spite,
Which though it alter not love's sole effect,
Yet doth it steal sweet hours from love's delight.
I may not evermore acknowledge thee,
Lest my bewailèd guilt should do thee shame,
Nor thou with public kindness honour me,
Unless thou take that honour from thy name:
    But do not so; I love thee in such sort
    As, thou being mine, mine is thy good report.

XXXVII.

As a decrepit father takes delight
To see his active child do deeds of youth,
So I, made lame by fortune's dearest spite,
Take all my comfort of thy worth and truth.
For whether beauty, birth, or wealth, or wit,
Or any of these all, or all, or more,
Entitled in thy parts do crowned sit,
I make my love engrafted to this store:
So then I am not lame, poor, nor despis'd,
Whilst that this shadow doth such substance give
That I in thy abundance am suffic'd
And by a part of all thy glory live.
    Look, what is best, that best I wish in thee:
    This wish I have; then ten times happy me!

XXXVIII.

How can my muse want subject to invent,
While thou dost breathe, that pour'st into my verse
Thine own sweet argument, too excellent

For every vulgar paper to rehearse?
O, give thyself the thanks, if aught in me
Worthy perusal stand against thy sight;
For who's so dumb that cannot write to thee,
When thou thyself dost give invention light?
Be thou the tenth muse, ten times more in worth
Than those old nine which rhymers invocate;
And he that calls on thee, let him bring forth
Eternal numbers to outlive long date.
    If my slight muse do please these curious days,
    The pain be mine, but thine shall be the praise.

XXXIX.

O, how thy worth with manners may I sing,
When thou art all the better part of me?
What can mine own praise to mine own self bring?
And what is 't but mine own when I praise thee?
Even for this let us divided live,
And our dear love lose name of single one,
That by this separation I may give
That due to thee which thou deserv'st alone.
O absence, what a torment wouldst thou prove,
Were it not thy sour leisure gave sweet leave
To entertain the time with thoughts of love,
Which time and thoughts so sweetly doth deceive,
    And that thou teachest how to make one twain,
    By praising him here who doth hence remain.

XL.

Take all my loves, my love, yea, take them all;
What hast thou then more than thou hadst before?
No love, my love, that thou mayst true love call;
All mine was thine before thou hadst this more.
Then if for my love thou my love receivest,
I cannot blame thee for my love thou usest;
But yet be blamed, if thou thyself deceivest

By wilful taste of what thyself refusest.
I do forgive thy robbery, gentle thief,
Although thou steal thee all my poverty;
And yet, love knows, it is a greater grief
To bear love's wrong than hate's known injury.
    Lascivious grace, in whom all ill well shows,
    Kill me with spites; yet we must not be foes.

XLI.
Those pretty wrongs that liberty commits,
When I am sometime absent from thy heart,
Thy beauty and thy years full well befits,
For still temptation follows where thou art.
Gentle thou art and therefore to be won,
Beauteous thou art, therefore to be assail'd;
And when a woman woos, what woman's son
Will sourly leave her till he have prevail'd?
Ay me, but yet thou mightst my seat forbear,
And chide thy beauty and thy straying youth,
Who lead thee in their riot even there
Where thou art forced to break a twofold truth,
    Hers by thy beauty tempting her to thee,
    Thine, by thy beauty being false to me.

XLII.
That thou hast her, it is not all my grief,
And yet it may be said I lov'd her dearly;
That she hath thee, is of my wailing chief,
A loss in love that touches me more nearly.
Loving offenders, thus I will excuse ye:
Thou dost love her, because thou know'st I love
    her;
And for my sake even so doth she abuse me,
Suffering my friend for my sake to approve her.
If I lose thee, my loss is my love's gain,
And losing her, my friend hath found that loss;

Both find each other, and I lose both twain,
And both for my sake lay on me this cross:
    But here's the joy; my friend and I are one;
    Sweet flattery! Then she loves but me alone.

XLIII.
When most I wink, then do mine eyes best see,
For all the day they view things unrespected;
But when I sleep, in dreams they look on thee,
And darkly bright are bright in dark directed.
Then thou, whose shadow shadows doth make
    bright,
How would thy shadow's form form happy show
To the clear day with thy much clearer light,
When to unseeing eyes thy shade shines so!
How would, I say, mine eyes be blessed made
By looking on thee in the living day,
When in dead night thy fair imperfect shade
Through heavy sleep on sightless eyes doth stay!
    All days are nights to see till I see thee,
    And nights bright days when dreams do show
      thee me.

XLIV.
If the dull substance of my flesh were thought,
Injurious distance should not stop my way;
For then despite of space I would be brought,
From limits far remote where thou dost stay.
No matter then although my foot did stand
Upon the farthest earth removed from thee;
For nimble thought can jump both sea and land
As soon as think the place where he would be.
But ah, thought kills me that I am not thought,
To leap large lengths of miles when thou art gone,
But that so much of earth and water wrought
I must attend time's leisure with my moan,

Receiving naught by elements so slow
But heavy tears, badges of either's woe.

XLV.

The other two, slight air and purging fire,
Are both with thee, wherever I abide;
The first my thought, the other my desire,
These present-absent with swift motion slide.
For when these quicker elements are gone
In tender embassy of love to thee,
My life, being made of four, with two alone
Sinks down to death, oppress'd with melancholy;
Until life's composition be recured
By those swift messengers return'd from thee,
Who even but now come back again, assur'd
Of thy fair health, recounting it to me:
　　This told, I joy; but then no longer glad,
　　I send them back again and straight grow sad.

XLVI.

Mine eye and heart are at a mortal war
How to divide the conquest of thy sight;
Mine eye my heart thy picture's sight would bar,
My heart mine eye the freedom of that right.
My heart doth plead that thou in him dost lie,
A closet never pierced with crystal eyes;
But the defendant doth that plea deny
And says in him thy fair appearance lies.
To 'cide this title is empannelled
A quest of thoughts, all tenants to the heart,
And by their verdict is determinèd
The clear eye's moiety and the dear heart's part:
　　As thus; mine eye's due is thy outward part,
　　And my heart's right thy inward love of heart.

XLVII.

Betwixt mine eye and heart a league is took,
And each doth good turns now unto the other:
When that mine eye is famish'd for a look,
Or heart in love with sighs himself doth smother,
With my love's picture then my eye doth feast
And to the painted banquet bids my heart;
Another time mine eye is my heart's guest
And in his thoughts of love doth share a part:
So, either by thy picture or my love,
Thyself away art present still with me;
For thou no farther than my thoughts canst move,
And I am still with them and they with thee;
    Or, if they sleep, thy picture in my sight
    Awakes my heart to heart's and eye's delight.

XLVIII.

How careful was I, when I took my way,
Each trifle under truest bars to thrust,
That to my use it might unusèd stay
From hands of falsehood, in sure wards of trust!
But thou, to whom my jewels trifles are,
Most worthy of comfort, now my greatest grief,
Thou, best of dearest and mine only care,
Art left the prey of every vulgar thief.
Thee have I not lock'd up in any chest,
Save where thou art not, though I feel thou art,
Within the gentle closure of my breast,
From whence at pleasure thou mayst come and part;
    And even thence thou wilt be stol'n, I fear,
    For truth proves thievish for a prize so dear.

XLIX.

Against that time, if ever that time come,
When I shall see thee frown on my defects,
Whenas thy love hath cast his utmost sum,

Call'd to that audit by advised respects;
Against that time when thou shalt strangely pass
And scarcely greet me with that sun thine eye,
When love, converted from the thing it was,
Shall reasons find of settled gravity;
Against that time do I ensconce me here
Within the knowledge of mine own desert,
And this my hand against myself uprear,
To guard the lawful reasons on thy part:
  To leave poor me thou hast the strength of laws,
  Since why to love I can allege no cause.

L.
How heavy do I journey on the way,
When what I seek, my weary travel's end,
Doth teach that ease and that repose to say
'Thus far the miles are measured from thy friend!'
The beast that bears me, tired with my woe,
Plods dully on, to bear that weight in me,
As if by some instinct the wretch did know
His rider lov'd not speed, being made from thee:
The bloody spur cannot provoke him on
That sometimes anger thrusts into his hide;
Which heavily he answers with a groan,
More sharp to me than spurring to his side;
  For that same groan doth put this in my mind;
  My grief lies onward and my joy behind.

LI.
Thus can my love excuse the slow offence
Of my dull bearer when from thee I speed:
From where thou art why should I haste me thence?
Till I return, of posting is no need.
O, what excuse will my poor beast then find,
When swift extremity can seem but slow?
Then should I spur, though mounted on the wind;

In wingèd speed no motion shall I know:
Then can no horse with my desire keep pace;
Therefore desire of perfect'st love being made,
Shall rein no dull flesh in his fiery race;
But love, for love, thus shall excuse my jade;
    Since from thee going he went wilful-slow,
    Towards thee I'll run, and give him leave to go.

LII.
So am I as the rich, whose blessèd key
Can bring him to his sweet up-lockèd treasure,
The which he will not every hour survey,
For blunting the fine point of seldom pleasure.
Therefore are feasts so solemn and so rare,
Since, seldom coming, in the long year set,
Like stones of worth they thinly placèd are,
Or captain jewels in the carcanet.
So is the time that keeps you as my chest,
Or as the wardrobe which the robe doth hide,
To make some special instant special blest,
By new unfolding his imprison'd pride.
    Blessèd are you, whose worthiness gives scope,
    Being had, to triumph, being lack'd, to hope.

LIII.
What is your substance, whereof are you made,
That millions of strange shadows on you tend?
Since every one hath, every one, one shade,
And you, but one, can every shadow lend.
Describe Adonis, and the counterfeit
Is poorly imitated after you;
On Helen's cheek all art of beauty set,
And you in Grecian tires are painted new:
Speak of the spring and foison of the year;
The one doth shadow of your beauty show,
The other as your bounty doth appear;

And you in every blessèd shape we know.
   In all external grace you have some part,
   But you like none, none you, for constant heart.

LIV.
O, how much more doth beauty beauteous seem
By that sweet ornament which truth doth give!
The rose looks fair, but fairer we it deem
For that sweet odour which doth in it live.
The canker blooms have full as deep a dye
As the perfumèd tincture of the roses,
Hang on such thorns and play as wantonly
When summer's breath their maskèd buds discloses:
But, for their virtue only is their show,
They live unwoo'd and unrespected fade,
Die to themselves. Sweet roses do not so;
Of their sweet deaths are sweetest odours made:
   And so of you, beauteous and lovely youth,
   When that shall fade, my verse distils your truth.

LV.
Not marble, nor the gilded monuments
Of princes, shall outlive this powerful rhyme;
But you shall shine more bright in these contents
Than unswept stone besmear'd with sluttish time.
When wasteful war shall statues overturn,
And broils root out the work of masonry,
Nor Mars his sword nor war's quick fire shall burn
The living record of your memory.
'Gainst death and all-oblivious enmity
Shall you pace forth; your praise shall still find room
Even in the eyes of all posterity
That wear this world out to the ending doom.
   So, till the judgement that yourself arise,
   You live in this, and dwell in lover's eyes.

LVI.

Sweet love, renew thy force; be it not said
Thy edge should blunter be than appetite,
Which but today by feeding is allay'd,
Tomorrow sharpen'd in his former might:
So, love, be thou; although today thou fill
Thy hungry eyes even till they wink with fullness,
Tomorrow see again, and do not kill
The spirit of love with a perpetual dullness.
Let this sad interim like the ocean be
Which parts the shore, where two contracted new
Come daily to the banks, that, when they see
Return of love, more blessed may be the view;
    Or call it winter, which being full of care
      Makes summer's welcome thrice more wish'd,
        more rare.

LVII.

Being your slave, what should I do but tend
Upon the hours and times of your desire?
I have no precious time at all to spend,
Nor services to do, till you require.
Nor dare I chide the world-without-end hour
Whilst I, my sovereign, watch the clock for you,
Nor think the bitterness of absence sour
When you have bid your servant once adieu;
Nor dare I question with my jealous thought
Where you may be, or your affairs suppose,
But, like a sad slave, stay and think of naught
Save, where you are how happy you make those.
    So true a fool is love that in your will,
      Though you do anything, he thinks no ill.

LVIII.

That god forbid that made me first your slave,
I should in thought control your times of pleasure,

Or at your hand the account of hours to crave,
Being your vassal, bound to stay your leisure!
O, let me suffer, being at your beck,
The imprison'd absence of your liberty;
And patience, tame to sufferance, bide each check,
Without accusing you of injury.
Be where you list, your charter is so strong
That you yourself may privilege your time
To what you will; to you it doth belong
Yourself to pardon of self-doing crime.
    I am to wait, though waiting so be hell;
    Not blame your pleasure, be it ill or well.

LIX.

If there be nothing new, but that which is
Hath been before, how are our brains beguiled,
Which, labouring for invention, bear amiss
The second burden of a former child!
O, that record could with a backward look,
Even of five hundred courses of the sun,
Show me your image in some antique book,
Since mind at first in character was done!
That I might see what the old world could say
To this composèd wonder of your frame;
Whether we are mended, or whether better they,
Or whether revolution be the same.
    O, sure I am, the wits of former days
    To subjects worse have given admiring praise.

LX.

Like as the waves make towards the pebbled shore,
So do our minutes hasten to their end;
Each changing place with that which goes before,
In sequent toil all forwards do contend.
Nativity, once in the main of light,
Crawls to maturity, wherewith being crown'd,

Crookèd eclipses 'gainst his glory fight,
And time that gave doth now his gift confound.
Time doth transfix the flourish set on youth
And delves the parallels in beauty's brow,
Feeds on the rarities of nature's truth,
And nothing stands but for his scythe to mow:
    And yet to times in hope my verse shall stand,
    Praising thy worth, despite his cruel hand.

LXI.

Is it thy will thy image should keep open
My heavy eyelids to the weary night?
Dost thou desire my slumbers should be broken,
While shadows like to thee do mock my sight?
Is it thy spirit that thou send'st from thee
So far from home into my deeds to pry,
To find out shames and idle hours in me,
The scope and tenor of thy jealousy?
O, no; thy love, though much, is not so great:
It is my love that keeps mine eye awake;
Mine own true love that doth my rest defeat,
To play the watchman ever for thy sake:
    For thee watch I whilst thou dost wake else-
        where,
    From me far off, with others all too near.

LXII.

Sin of self-love possesseth all mine eye
And all my soul and all my every part;
And for this sin there is no remedy,
It is so grounded inward in my heart.
Methinks no face so gracious is as mine,
No shape so true, no truth of such account;
And for myself mine own worth do define,
As I all other in all worths surmount.
But when my glass shows me myself indeed,

Beated and chopp'd with tann'd antiquity,
Mine own self-love quite contrary I read;
Self so self-loving were iniquity.
    'Tis thee, myself, that for myself I praise,
    Painting my age with beauty of thy days.

LXIII.
Against my love shall be, as I am now,
With time's injurious hand crush'd and o'er-worn;
When hours have drain'd his blood and fill'd his
    brow
With lines and wrinkles; when his youthful morn
Hath travell'd on to age's steepy night,
And all those beauties whereof now he's king
Are vanishing or vanish'd out of sight,
Stealing away the treasure of his spring;
For such a time do I now fortify
Against confounding age's cruel knife,
That he shall never cut from memory
My sweet love's beauty, though my lover's life:
    His beauty shall in these black lines be seen,
    And they shall live, and he in them still green.

LXIV.
When I have seen by time's fell hand defaced
The rich proud cost of outworn buried age;
When sometime lofty towers I see down-razed
And brass eternal slave to mortal rage;
When I have seen the hungry ocean gain
Advantage on the kingdom of the shore,
And the firm soil win of the watery main,
Increasing store with loss and loss with store;
When I have seen such interchange of state,
Or state itself confounded to decay;
Ruin hath taught me thus to ruminate,
That time will come and take my love away.

This thought is as a death, which cannot choose
But weep to have that which it fears to lose.

LXV.

Since brass, nor stone, nor earth, nor boundless sea,
But sad mortality o'er-sways their power,
How with this rage shall beauty hold a plea,
Whose action is no stronger than a flower?
O, how shall summer's honey breath hold out
Against the wreckful siege of battering days,
When rocks impregnable are not so stout,
Nor gates of steel so strong, but time decays?
O fearful meditation! Where, alack,
Shall time's best jewel from time's chest lie hid?
Or what strong hand can hold his swift foot back?
Or who his spoil of beauty can forbid?
    O, none, unless this miracle have might,
    That in black ink my love may still shine bright.

LXVI.

Tired with all these, for restful death I cry,
As to behold desert a beggar born,
And needy nothing trimm'd in jollity,
And purest faith unhappily forsworn,
And gilded honour shamefully misplaced,
And maiden virtue rudely strumpeted,
And right perfection wrongfully disgraced,
And strength by limping sway disablèd,
And art made tongue-tied by authority,
And folly doctor-like controlling skill,
And simple truth miscall'd simplicity,
And captive good attending captain ill:
    Tired with all these, from these would I be gone,
    Save that, to die, I leave my love alone.

LXVII.

Ah, wherefore with infection should he live,
And with his presence grace impiety,
That sin by him advantage should achieve
And lace itself with his society?
Why should false painting imitate his cheek
And steal dead seeming of his living hue?
Why should poor beauty indirectly seek
Roses of shadow, since his rose is true?
Why should he live, now nature bankrupt is,
Beggar'd of blood to blush through lively veins?
For she hath no exchequer now but his,
And, proud of many, lives upon his gains.
    O, him she stores, to show what wealth she had
    In days long since, before these last so bad.

LXVIII.

Thus is his cheek the map of days outworn,
When beauty lived and died as flowers do now,
Before the bastard signs of fair were born,
Or durst inhabit on a living brow;
Before the golden tresses of the dead,
The right of sepulchres, were shorn away,
To live a second life on second head;
Ere beauty's dead fleece made another gay:
In him those holy antique hours are seen,
Without all ornament, itself and true,
Making no summer of another's green,
Robbing no old to dress his beauty new;
    And him as for a map doth nature store,
    To show false art what beauty was of yore.

LXIX.

Those parts of thee that the world's eye doth view
Want nothing that the thought of hearts can mend;
All tongues, the voice of souls, give thee that due,

Uttering bare truth, even so as foes commend.
Thy outward thus with outward praise is crown'd;
But those same tongues that give thee so thine own
In other accents do this praise confound
By seeing farther than the eye hath shown.
They look into the beauty of thy mind,
And that, in guess, they measure by thy deeds;
Then, churls, their thoughts, although their eyes
    were kind,
To thy fair flower add the rank smell of weeds:
    But why thy odour matcheth not thy show,
    The soil is this, that thou dost common grow.

LXX.
That thou art blamed shall not be thy defect,
For slander's mark was ever yet the fair;
The ornament of beauty is suspect,
A crow that flies in heaven's sweetest air.
So thou be good, slander doth but approve
Thy worth the greater, being wooed of time;
For canker vice the sweetest buds doth love,
And thou present'st a pure unstainèd prime.
Thou hast pass'd by the ambush of young days,
Either not assail'd or victor being charged;
Yet this thy praise cannot be so thy praise,
To tie up envy evermore enlarged:
    If some suspect of ill mask'd not thy show,
    Then thou alone kingdoms of hearts shouldst
        owe.

LXXI.
No longer mourn for me when I am dead
Than you shall hear the surly sullen bell
Give warning to the world that I am fled
From this vile world, with vilest worms to dwell:
Nay, if you read this line, remember not

The hand that writ it; for I love you so
That I in your sweet thoughts would be forgot
If thinking on me then should make you woe.
O, if, I say, you look upon this verse
When I perhaps compounded am with clay,
Do not so much as my poor name rehearse.
But let your love even with my life decay,
  Lest the wise world should look into your moan
  And mock you with me after I am gone.

LXXII.
O, lest the world should task you to recite
What merit lived in me, that you should love
After my death, dear love, forget me quite,
For you in me can nothing worthy prove;
Unless you would devise some virtuous lie,
To do more for me than mine own desert,
And hang more praise upon deceasèd I
Than niggard truth would willingly impart:
O, lest your true love may seem false in this,
That you for love speak well of me untrue,
My name be buried where my body is,
And live no more to shame nor me nor you.
  For I am shamed by that which I bring forth,
  And so should you, to love things nothing worth.

LXXIII.
That time of year thou mayst in me behold
When yellow leaves, or none, or few, do hang
Upon those boughs which shake against the cold,
Bare ruin'd choirs, where late the sweet birds sang.
In me thou seest the twilight of such day
As after sunset fadeth in the west,
Which by and by black night doth take away,
Death's second self, that seals up all in rest.
In me thou see'st the glowing of such fire

That on the ashes of his youth doth lie,
As the death-bed whereon it must expire
Consumed with that which it was nourish'd by.
    This thou perceiv'st, which makes thy love more
        strong,
    To love that well which thou must leave ere long.

LXXIV.
But be contented: when that fell arrest
Without all bail shall carry me away,
My life hath in this line some interest,
Which for memorial still with thee shall stay.
When thou reviewest this, thou dost review
The very part was consecrate to thee:
The earth can have but earth, which is his due;
My spirit is thine, the better part of me:
So then thou hast but lost the dregs of life,
The prey of worms, my body being dead,
The coward conquest of a wretch's knife,
Too base of thee to be rememberèd.
    The worth of that is that which it contains,
    And that is this, and this with thee remains.

LXXV.
So are you to my thoughts as food to life,
Or as sweet-seasoned showers are to the ground;
And for the peace of you I hold such strife
As 'twixt a miser and his wealth is found;
Now proud as an enjoyer and anon
Doubting the filching age will steal his treasure,
Now counting best to be with you alone,
Then better'd that the world may see my pleasure;
Sometime all full with feasting on your sight
And by and by clean starvèd for a look;
Possessing or pursuing no delight,
Save what is had or must from you be took.

Thus do I pine and surfeit day by day,
Or gluttoning on all, or all away.

LXXVI.
Why is my verse so barren of new pride,
So far from variation or quick change?
Why with the time do I not glance aside
To new-found methods and to compounds strange?
Why write I still all one, ever the same,
And keep invention in a noted weed,
That every word doth almost tell my name,
Showing their birth and where they did proceed?
O, know, sweet love, I always write of you,
And you and love are still my argument;
So all my best is dressing old words new,
Spending again what is already spent:
　　For as the sun is daily new and old,
　　So is my love still telling what is told.

LXXVII.
Thy glass will show thee how thy beauties wear,
Thy dial how thy precious minutes waste;
The vacant leaves thy mind's imprint will bear,
And of this book this learning mayst thou taste.
The wrinkles which thy glass will truly show
Of mouthèd graves will give thee memory;
Thou by thy dial's shady stealth mayst know
Time's thievish progress to eternity.
Look, what thy memory cannot contain
Commit to these waste blanks, and thou shalt find
Those children nursed, deliver'd from thy brain,
To take a new acquaintance of thy mind.
　　These offices, so oft as thou wilt look,
　　Shall profit thee and much enrich thy book.

LXXVIII.

So oft have I invoked thee for my muse
And found such fair assistance in my verse
As every alien pen hath got my use
And under thee their poesy disperse.
Thine eyes that taught the dumb on high to sing
And heavy ignorance aloft to fly
Have added feathers to the learned's wing
And given grace a double majesty.
Yet be most proud of that which I compile,
Whose influence is thine and born of thee:
In others' works thou dost but mend the style,
And arts with thy sweet graces gracèd be;
    But thou art all my art and dost advance
    As high as learning my rude ignorance.

LXXIX.

Whilst I alone did call upon thy aid,
My verse alone had all thy gentle grace,
But now my gracious numbers are decay'd
And my sick muse doth give another place.
I grant, sweet love, thy lovely argument
Deserves the travail of a worthier pen,
Yet what of thee thy poet doth invent
He robs thee of and pays it thee again.
He lends thee virtue and he stole that word
From thy behaviour; beauty doth he give
And found it in thy cheek; he can afford
No praise to thee but what in thee doth live.
    Then thank him not for that which he doth say,
    Since what he owes thee thou thyself dost pay.

LXXX.

O, how I faint when I of you do write,
Knowing a better spirit doth use your name,
And in the praise thereof spends all his might,

To make me tongue-tied, speaking of your fame!
But since your worth, wide as the ocean is,
The humble as the proudest sail doth bear,
My saucy bark inferior far to his
On your broad main doth wilfully appear.
Your shallowest help will hold me up afloat,
Whilst he upon your soundless deep doth ride;
Or being wreck'd, I am a worthless boat,
He of tall building and of goodly pride:
    Then if he thrive and I be cast away,
    The worst was this; my love was my decay.

LXXXI.

Or I shall live your epitaph to make,
Or you survive when I in earth am rotten;
From hence your memory death cannot take,
Although in me each part will be forgotten.
Your name from hence immortal life shall have,
Though I, once gone, to all the world must die:
The earth can yield me but a common grave,
When you entombèd in men's eyes shall lie.
Your monument shall be my gentle verse,
Which eyes not yet created shall o'er-read,
And tongues to be your being shall rehearse
When all the breathers of this world are dead;
    You still shall live – such virtue hath my pen -
    Where breath most breathes, even in the mouths
      of men.

LXXXII.

I grant thou wert not married to my muse
And therefore mayst without attaint o'erlook
The dedicated words which writers use
Of their fair subject, blessing every book
Thou art as fair in knowledge as in hue,
Finding thy worth a limit past my praise,

And therefore art enforced to seek anew
Some fresher stamp of the time-bettering days
And do so, love; yet when they have devised
What strainèd touches rhetoric can lend,
Thou truly fair wert truly sympathized
In true plain words by thy true-telling friend;
   And their gross painting might be better used
   Where cheeks need blood; in thee it is abused.

LXXXIII.
I never saw that you did painting need
And therefore to your fair no painting set;
I found, or thought I found, you did exceed
The barren tender of a poet's debt;
And therefore have I slept in your report,
That you yourself being extant well might show
How far a modern quill doth come too short,
Speaking of worth, what worth in you doth grow.
This silence for my sin you did impute,
Which shall be most my glory, being dumb;
For I impair not beauty, being mute,
When others would give life and bring a tomb.
   There lives more life in one of your fair eyes
   Than both your poets can in praise devise.

LXXXIV.
Who is it that says most? Which can say more
Than this rich praise, that you alone are you?
In whose confine immurèd is the store
Which should example where your equal grew.
Lean penury within that pen doth dwell
That to his subject lends not some small glory;
But he that writes of you, if he can tell
That you are you, so dignifies his story,
Let him but copy what in you is writ,
Not making worse what nature made so clear,

And such a counterpart shall fame his wit,
Making his style admirèd everywhere.
    You to your beauteous blessings add a curse,
        Being fond on praise, which makes your praises
        worse.

LXXXV.

My tongue-tied muse in manners holds her still,
While comments of your praise, richly compiled,
Reserve thy character with golden quill
And precious phrase by all the muses filed.
I think good thoughts whilst other write good
    words,
And like unletter'd clerk still cry 'Amen'
To every hymn that able spirit affords
In polish'd form of well-refinèd pen.
Hearing you praised, I say ''Tis so, 'tis true,'
And to the most of praise add something more;
But that is in my thought, whose love to you,
Though words come hindmost, holds his rank
    before.
    Then others for the breath of words respect,
    Me for my dumb thoughts, speaking in effect.

LXXXVI.

Was it the proud full sail of his great verse,
Bound for the prize of all-too-precious you,
That did my ripe thoughts in my brain inhearse,
Making their tomb the womb wherein they grew?
Was it his spirit, by spirits taught to write
Above a mortal pitch, that struck me dead?
No, neither he, nor his compeers by night
Giving him aid, my verse astonishèd.
He, nor that affable familiar ghost
Which nightly gulls him with intelligence
As victors of my silence cannot boast;

I was not sick of any fear from thence:
> But when your countenance fill'd up his line,
> Then lack'd I matter; that enfeebled mine.

LXXXVII.

Farewell – thou art too dear for my possessing,
And like enough thou know'st thy estimate:
The charter of thy worth gives thee releasing;
My bonds in thee are all determinate.
For how do I hold thee but by thy granting?
And for that riches where is my deserving?
The cause of this fair gift in me is wanting,
And so my patent back again is swerving.
Thyself thou gav'st, thy own worth then not
> knowing,
Or me, to whom thou gav'st it, else mistaking;
So thy great gift, upon misprision growing,
Comes home again, on better judgement making.
> Thus have I had thee, as a dream doth flatter,
> In sleep a king, but waking no such matter.

LXXXVIII.

When thou shalt be dispos'd to set me light,
And place my merit in the eye of scorn,
Upon thy side against myself I'll fight,
And prove thee virtuous, though thou art forsworn.
With mine own weakness being best acquainted,
Upon thy part I can set down a story
Of faults conceal'd, wherein I am attainted,
That thou in losing me shalt win much glory:
And I by this will be a gainer too;
For bending all my loving thoughts on thee,
The injuries that to myself I do,
Doing thee vantage, double-vantage me.
> Such is my love, to thee I so belong,
> That for thy right myself will bear all wrong.

LXXXIX.

Say that thou didst forsake me for some fault,
And I will comment upon that offence;
Speak of my lameness, and I straight will halt,
Against thy reasons making no defence.
Thou canst not, love, disgrace me half so ill,
To set a form upon desirèd change,
As I'll myself disgrace: knowing thy will,
I will acquaintance strangle and look strange,
Be absent from thy walks, and in my tongue
Thy sweet belovèd name no more shall dwell,
Lest I, too much profane, should do it wrong
And haply of our old acquaintance tell.
For thee against myself I'll vow debate,
For I must ne'er love him whom thou dost hate.

XC.

Then hate me when thou wilt; if ever, now;
Now, while the world is bent my deeds to cross,
Join with the spite of fortune, make me bow,
And do not drop in for an after-loss:
Ah, do not, when my heart hath 'scaped this sorrow,
Come in the rearward of a conquer'd woe;
Give not a windy night a rainy morrow,
To linger out a purposed overthrow.
If thou wilt leave me, do not leave me last,
When other petty griefs have done their spite
But in the onset come; so shall I taste
At first the very worst of fortune's might,
    And other strains of woe, which now seem woe,
    Compared with loss of thee will not seem so.

XCI.

Some glory in their birth, some in their skill,
Some in their wealth, some in their body's force,
Some in their garments (though new-fangled ill),

Some in their hawks and hounds, some in their
    horse;
And every humour hath his adjunct pleasure,
Wherein it finds a joy above the rest:
But these particulars are not my measure;
All these I better in one general best.
Thy love is better than high birth to me,
Richer than wealth, prouder than garments' cost,
Of more delight than hawks or horses be;
And having thee, of all men's pride I boast:
    Wretched in this alone, that thou mayst take
    All this away and me most wretched make.

XCII.

But do thy worst to steal thyself away,
For term of life thou art assurèd mine,
And life no longer than thy love will stay,
For it depends upon that love of thine.
Then need I not to fear the worst of wrongs,
When in the least of them my life hath end.
I see a better state to me belongs
Than that which on thy humour doth depend;
Thou canst not vex me with inconstant mind,
Since that my life on thy revolt doth lie.
O, what a happy title do I find,
Happy to have thy love, happy to die!
    But what's so blessèd-fair that fears no blot?
    Thou mayst be false, and yet I know it not.

XCIII.

So shall I live, supposing thou art true,
Like a deceivèd husband; so love's face
May still seem love to me, though altered new;
Thy looks with me, thy heart in other place:
For there can live no hatred in thine eye,
Therefore in that I cannot know thy change.

In many's looks the false heart's history
Is writ in moods and frowns and wrinkles strange,
But heaven in thy creation did decree
That in thy face sweet love should ever dwell;
Whate'er thy thoughts or thy heart's workings be,
Thy looks should nothing thence but sweetness tell.
    How like Eve's apple doth thy beauty grow,
    If thy sweet virtue answer not thy show!

XCIV.
They that have power to hurt and will do none,
That do not do the thing they most do show,
Who, moving others, are themselves as stone,
Unmovèd, cold, and to temptation slow,
They rightly do inherit heaven's graces
And husband nature's riches from expense;
They are the lords and owners of their faces,
Others but stewards of their excellence.
The summer's flower is to the summer sweet,
Though to itself it only live and die,
But if that flower with base infection meet,
The basest weed outbraves his dignity:
    For sweetest things turn sourest by their deeds;
    Lilies that fester smell far worse than weeds.

XCV.
How sweet and lovely dost thou make the shame
Which, like a canker in the fragrant rose,
Doth spot the beauty of thy budding name!
O, in what sweets dost thou thy sins enclose!
That tongue that tells the story of thy days,
Making lascivious comments on thy sport,
Cannot dispraise but in a kind of praise;
Naming thy name blesses an ill report.
O, what a mansion have those vices got
Which for their habitation chose out thee,

Where beauty's veil doth cover every blot,
And all things turn to fair that eyes can see!
   Take heed, dear heart, of this large privilege;
   The hardest knife ill-used doth lose his edge.

XCVI.

Some say thy fault is youth, some wantonness;
Some say thy grace is youth and gentle sport;
Both grace and faults are loved of more and less;
Thou makest faults graces that to thee resort.
As on the finger of a thronèd queen
The basest jewel will be well esteem'd,
So are those errors that in thee are seen
To truths translated and for true things deem'd.
How many lambs might the stern wolf betray,
If like a lamb he could his looks translate!
How many gazers mightst thou lead away,
If thou wouldst use the strength of all thy state!
   But do not so; I love thee in such sort
   As, thou being mine, mine is thy good report.

XCVII.

How like a winter hath my absence been
From thee, the pleasure of the fleeting year!
What freezings have I felt, what dark days seen!
What old December's bareness everywhere!
And yet this time removed was summer's time,
The teeming autumn, big with rich increase,
Bearing the wanton burden of the prime,
Like widow'd wombs after their lords' decease:
Yet this abundant issue seem'd to me
But hope of orphans and unfather'd fruit;
For summer and his pleasures wait on thee,
And, thou away, the very birds are mute;
   Or, if they sing, 'tis with so dull a cheer
   That leaves look pale, dreading the winter's near.

XCVIII.

From you have I been absent in the spring,
When proud-pied April dressed in all his trim
Hath put a spirit of youth in everything,
That heavy Saturn laughed and leapt with him.
Yet nor the lays of birds nor the sweet smell
Of different flowers in odour and in hue
Could make me any summer's story tell,
Or from their proud lap pluck them where they
    grew;
Nor did I wonder at the lily's white,
Nor praise the deep vermilion in the rose;
They were but sweet, but figures of delight,
Drawn after you, you pattern of all those.
    Yet seem'd it winter still, and, you away,
    As with your shadow I with these did play.

XCIX.

The forward violet thus did I chide:
Sweet thief, whence didst thou steal thy sweet that
    smells,
If not from my love's breath? The purple pride
Which on thy soft cheek for complexion dwells
In my love's veins thou hast too grossly dyed.
The lily I condemnèd for thy hand,
And buds of marjoram had stol'n thy hair:
The roses fearfully on thorns did stand,
One blushing shame, another white despair;
A third, nor red nor white, had stol'n of both
And to his robbery had annex'd thy breath;
But, for his theft, in pride of all his growth
A vengeful canker ate him up to death.
    More flowers I noted, yet I none could see
    But sweet or colour it had stol'n from thee.

C.

Where art thou, muse, that thou forget'st so long
To speak of that which gives thee all thy might?
Spend'st thou thy fury on some worthless song,
Darkening thy power to lend base subjects light?
Return, forgetful muse, and straight redeem
In gentle numbers time so idly spent;
Sing to the ear that doth thy lays esteem
And gives thy pen both skill and argument.
Rise, resty muse, my love's sweet face survey,
If time have any wrinkle graven there;
If any, be a satire to decay,
And make time's spoils despisèd every where.
     Give my love fame faster than time wastes life;
     So thou prevent'st his scythe and crookèd knife.

CI.

O truant muse, what shall be thy amends
For thy neglect of truth in beauty dyed?
Both truth and beauty on my love depends;
So dost thou too, and therein dignified.
Make answer, muse: wilt thou not haply say
'Truth needs no colour, with his colour fixed;
Beauty no pencil, beauty's truth to lay;
But best is best, if never intermixed?'
Because he needs no praise, wilt thou be dumb?
Excuse not silence so; for't lies in thee
To make him much outlive a gilded tomb,
And to be praised of ages yet to be.
Then do thy office, muse; I teach thee how
To make him seem long hence as he shows now.

CII.

My love is strengthen'd, though more weak in
     seeming;
I love not less, though less the show appear:

That love is merchandized whose rich esteeming
The owner's tongue doth publish everywhere.
Our love was new and then but in the spring
When I was wont to greet it with my lays,
As Philomel in summer's front doth sing
And stops her pipe in growth of riper days:
Not that the summer is less pleasant now
Than when her mournful hymns did hush the night,
But that wild music burdens every bough
And sweets grown common lose their dear delight.
    Therefore like her I sometime hold my tongue,
    Because I would not dull you with my song.

CIII.

Alack, what poverty my muse brings forth,
That having such a scope to show her pride,
The argument all bare is of more worth
Than when it hath my added praise beside!
O, blame me not, if I no more can write!
Look in your glass, and there appears a face
That overgoes my blunt invention quite,
Dulling my lines and doing me disgrace.
Were it not sinful then, striving to mend,
To mar the subject that before was well?
For to no other pass my verses tend
Than of your graces and your gifts to tell;
    And more, much more, than in my verse can sit
    Your own glass shows you when you look in it.

CIV.

To me, fair friend, you never can be old,
For as you were when first your eye I eyed,
Such seems your beauty still. Three winters cold
Have from the forests shook three summers' pride,
Three beauteous springs to yellow autumn turned
In process of the seasons have I seen,

Three April perfumes in three hot Junes burned,
Since first I saw you fresh, which yet are green.
Ah yet doth beauty, like a dial-hand,
Steal from his figure and no pace perceived;
So your sweet hue, which methinks still doth stand,
Hath motion and mine eye may be deceived:
    For fear of which, hear this, thou age unbred;
    Ere you were born was beauty's summer dead.

CV.
Let not my love be called idolatry,
Nor my belovèd as an idol show,
Since all alike my songs and praises be
To one, of one, still such, and ever so.
Kind is my love today, tomorrow kind,
Still constant in a wondrous excellence;
Therefore my verse to constancy confined,
One thing expressing, leaves out difference.
'Fair, kind and true,' is all my argument,
'Fair, kind, and true,' varying to other words;
And in this change is my invention spent,
Three themes in one, which wondrous scope
    affords.
    'Fair, kind, and true,' have often lived alone,
    Which three till now never kept seat in one.

CVI.
When in the chronicle of wasted time
I see descriptions of the fairest wights,
And beauty making beautiful old rhyme
In praise of ladies dead and lovely knights,
Then, in the blazon of sweet beauty's best,
Of hand, of foot, of lip, of eye, of brow,
I see their antique pen would have expressed
Even such a beauty as you master now.
So all their praises are but prophecies

Of this our time, all you prefiguring;
And, for they look'd but with divining eyes,
They had not skill enough your worth to sing:
 For we, which now behold these present days,
  Had eyes to wonder, but lack tongues to praise.

CVII.

Not mine own fears, nor the prophetic soul
Of the wide world dreaming on things to come,
Can yet the lease of my true love control,
Supposed as forfeit to a confined doom.
The mortal moon hath her eclipse endured
And the sad augurs mock their own presage;
Incertainties now crown themselves assured
And peace proclaims olives of endless age.
Now with the drops of this most balmy time
My love looks fresh, and death to me subscribes,
Since, spite of him, I'll live in this poor rhyme,
While he insults o'er dull and speechless tribes:
 And thou in this shalt find thy monument,
  When tyrants' crests and tombs of brass are
  spent.

CVIII.

What's in the brain that ink may character
Which hath not figured to thee my true spirit?
What's new to speak, what new to register,
That may express my love or thy dear merit?
Nothing, sweet boy; but yet, like prayers divine,
I must, each day say o'er the very same,
Counting no old thing old, thou mine, I thine,
Even as when first I hallow'd thy fair name.
So that eternal love in love's fresh case
Weighs not the dust and injury of age,
Nor gives to necessary wrinkles place,
But makes antiquity for aye his page,

Finding the first conceit of love there bred
Where time and outward form would show it
   dead.

CIX.

O, never say that I was false of heart,
Though absence seem'd my flame to qualify.
As easy might I from myself depart
As from my soul, which in thy breast doth lie:
That is my home of love: if I have ranged,
Like him that travels I return again,
Just to the time, not with the time exchanged,
So that myself bring water for my stain.
Never believe, though in my nature reigned
All frailties that besiege all kinds of blood,
That it could so preposterously be stained,
To leave for nothing all thy sum of good;
    For nothing this wide universe I call,
    Save thou, my rose; in it thou art my all.

CX.

Alas, 'tis true I have gone here and there
And made myself a motley to the view,
Gored mine own thoughts, sold cheap what is most
   dear,
Made old offences of affections new;
Most true it is that I have looked on truth
Askance and strangely: but, by all above,
These blenches gave my heart another youth,
And worse essays proved thee my best of love.
Now all is done, have what shall have no end:
Mine appetite I never more will grind
On newer proof, to try an older friend,
A god in love, to whom I am confined.
    Then give me welcome, next my heaven the best,
    Even to thy pure and most most loving breast.

CXI.

O, for my sake do you with fortune chide,
The guilty goddess of my harmful deeds,
That did not better for my life provide
Than public means which public manners breeds.
Thence comes it that my name receives a brand,
And almost thence my nature is subdued
To what it works in, like the dyer's hand:
Pity me then and wish I were renewed;
Whilst, like a willing patient, I will drink
Potions of eisel 'gainst my strong infection
No bitterness that I will bitter think,
Nor double penance, to correct correction.
    Pity me then, dear friend, and I assure ye
    Even that your pity is enough to cure me.

CXII.

Your love and pity doth the impression fill
Which vulgar scandal stamped upon my brow;
For what care I who calls me well or ill,
So you o'er-green my bad, my good allow?
You are my all-the-world, and I must strive
To know my shames and praises from your tongue:
None else to me, nor I to none alive,
That my steeled sense or changes, right or wrong.
In so profound abyss I throw all care
Of others' voices, that my adder's sense
To critic and to flatterer stoppèd are.
Mark how with my neglect I do dispense:
    You are so strongly in my purpose bred
    That all the world besides, methinks, they're dead.

CXIII.

Since I left you, mine eye is in my mind;
And that which governs me to go about
Doth part his function and is partly blind,

Seems seeing, but effectually is out;
For it no form delivers to the heart
Of bird of flower, or shape, which it doth latch:
Of his quick objects hath the mind no part,
Nor his own vision holds what it doth catch:
For if it see the rudest or gentlest sight,
The most sweet favour or deformèd'st creature,
The mountain or the sea, the day or night,
The crow or dove, it shapes them to your feature:
 Incapable of more, replete with you,
 My most true mind thus makes mine eye untrue.

CXIV.

Or whether doth my mind, being crown'd with
 you,
Drink up the monarch's plague, this flattery?
Or whether shall I say, mine eye saith true,
And that your love taught it this alchemy,
To make of monsters and things indigest
Such cherubins as your sweet self resemble,
Creating every bad a perfect best,
As fast as objects to his beams assemble?
O! 'tis the first; 'tis flattery in my seeing,
And my great mind most kingly drinks it up:
Mine eye well knows what with his gust is 'greeing,
And to his palate doth prepare the cup:
 If it be poison'd, 'tis the lesser sin
 That mine eye loves it and doth first begin.

CXV.

Those lines that I before have writ do lie,
Even those that said I could not love you dearer:
Yet then my judgement knew no reason why
My most full flame should afterwards burn clearer.
But reckoning time, whose millioned accidents
Creep in 'twixt vows and change decrees of kings,

Tan sacred beauty, blunt the sharp'st intents,
Divert strong minds to the course of altering things;
Alas, why, fearing of time's tyranny,
Might I not then say 'Now I love you best',
When I was certain o'er incertainty,
Crowning the present, doubting of the rest?
    Love is a babe; then might I not say so,
      To give full growth to that which still doth grow?

CXVI.

Let me not to the marriage of true minds
Admit impediments. Love is not love
Which alters when it alteration finds,
Or bends with the remover to remove:
O no! it is an ever-fixèd mark
That looks on tempests and is never shaken;
It is the star to every wandering barque,
Whose worth's unknown, although his height be
    taken.
Love's not time's fool, though rosy lips and cheeks
Within his bending sickle's compass come:
Love alters not with his brief hours and weeks,
But bears it out even to the edge of doom.
    If this be error and upon me proved,
      I never writ, nor no man ever loved.

CXVII.

Accuse me thus: that I have scanted all
Wherein I should your great deserts repay,
Forgot upon your dearest love to call,
Whereto all bonds do tie me day by day;
That I have frequent been with unknown minds
And given to time your own dear-purchased right
That I have hoisted sail to all the winds
Which should transport me farthest from your
    sight.

Book both my wilfulness and errors down
And on just proof surmise accumulate;
Bring me within the level of your frown,
But shoot not at me in your wakened hate;
    Since my appeal says I did strive to prove
    The constancy and virtue of your love.

CXVIII.

Like as, to make our appetites more keen,
With eager compounds we our palate urge,
As, to prevent our maladies unseen,
We sicken to shun sickness when we purge,
Even so, being full of your ne'er-cloying sweetness,
To bitter sauces did I frame my feeding
And, sick of welfare, found a kind of meetness
To be diseased ere that there was true needing.
Thus policy in love, to anticipate
The ills that were not, grew to faults assured
And brought to medicine a healthful state
Which, rank of goodness, would by ill be cured:
    But thence I learn, and find the lesson true,
    Drugs poison him that so fell sick of you.

CXIX.

What potions have I drunk of siren tears,
Distilled from limbecks foul as hell within,
Applying fears to hopes and hopes to fears,
Still losing when I saw myself to win!
What wretched errors hath my heart committed,
Whilst it hath thought itself so blessèd never!
How have mine eyes out of their spheres been fitted
In the distraction of this madding fever!
O benefit of ill! Now I find true
That better is by evil still made better;
And ruin'd love, when it is built anew,
Grows fairer than at first, more strong, far greater.

So I return rebuked to my content
And gain by ills thrice more than I have spent.

CXX.

That you were once unkind befriends me now,
And for that sorrow, which I then did feel,
Needs must I under my transgression bow,
Unless my nerves were brass or hammered steel.
For if you were by my unkindness shaken,
As I by yours, you've passed a hell of time;
And I, a tyrant, have no leisure taken
To weigh how once I suffered in your crime.
O! that our night of woe might have remembered
My deepest sense, how hard true sorrow hits,
And soon to you, as you to me, then tendered
The humble salve, which wounded bosoms fits!
    But that your trespass now becomes a fee;
    Mine ransoms yours, and yours must ransom me.

CXXI.

'Tis better to be vile than vile esteemed,
When not to be receives reproach of being;
And the just pleasure lost, which is so deemed
Not by our feeling, but by others' seeing:
For why should others' false adulterate eyes
Give salutation to my sportive blood?
Or on my frailties why are frailer spies,
Which in their wills count bad what I think good?
No, I am that I am, and they that level
At my abuses reckon up their own:
I may be straight though they themselves be bevel;
By their rank thoughts, my deeds must not be
    shown;
    Unless this general evil they maintain,
    All men are bad and in their badness reign.

CXXII.

Thy gift, thy tables, are within my brain
Full charactered with lasting memory,
Which shall above that idle rank remain,
Beyond all date, even to eternity:
Or, at the least, so long as brain and heart
Have faculty by nature to subsist;
Till each to razed oblivion yield his part
Of thee, thy record never can be missed.
That poor retention could not so much hold,
Nor need I tallies thy dear love to score;
Therefore to give them from me was I bold,
To trust those tables that receive thee more:
    To keep an adjunct to remember thee
     Were to import forgetfulness in me.

CXXIII.

No, time, thou shalt not boast that I do change:
Thy pyramids built up with newer might
To me are nothing novel, nothing strange;
They are but dressings of a former sight.
Our dates are brief, and therefore we admire
What thou dost foist upon us that is old;
And rather make them born to our desire
Than think that we before have heard them told.
Thy registers and thee I both defy,
Not wondering at the present nor the past,
For thy records and what we see doth lie,
Made more or less by thy continual haste.
    This I do vow and this shall ever be;
    I will be true despite thy scythe and thee.

CXXIV.

If my dear love were but the child of state,
It might for fortune's bastard be unfathered,
As subject to time's love or to time's hate,

Weeds among weeds, or flowers with flowers
   gathered.
No, it was builded far from accident;
It suffers not in smiling pomp, nor falls
Under the blow of thrallèd discontent,
Whereto th' inviting time our fashion calls:
It fears not policy, that heretic,
Which works on leases of short-numbered hours,
But all alone stands hugely politic,
That it nor grows with heat, nor drowns with
   showers.
    To this I witness call the fools of time,
    Which die for goodness, who have lived for
      crime.

CXXV.
Were 't aught to me I bore the canopy,
With my extern the outward honouring,
Or laid great bases for eternity,
Which proves more short than waste or ruining?
Have I not seen dwellers on form and favour
Lose all and more by paying too much rent
For compound sweet, forgoing simple savour,
Pitiful thrivers, in their gazing spent?
No; let me be obsequious in thy heart,
And take thou my oblation, poor but free,
Which is not mixed with seconds, knows no art,
But mutual render, only me for thee.
    Hence, thou suborned informer! A true soul
    When most impeached stands least in thy control.

CXXVI.
O thou, my lovely boy, who in thy power
Dost hold time's fickle glass, his sickle-hour;
Who hast by waning grown, and therein showest
Thy lovers withering, as thy sweet self growest.

If nature, sovereign mistress over wrack,
As thou goest onwards still will pluck thee back,
She keeps thee to this purpose, that her skill
May time disgrace and wretched minutes kill.
Yet fear her, O thou minion of her pleasure!
She may detain, but not still keep, her treasure:
    Her audit (though delayed) answer'd must be,
    And her quietus is to render thee.

CXXVII.

In the old age black was not counted fair,
Or if it were, it bore not beauty's name;
But now is black beauty's successive heir,
And beauty slandered with a bastard shame:
For since each hand hath put on nature's power,
Fairing the foul with art's false borrow'd face,
Sweet beauty hath no name, no holy bower,
But is profaned, if not lives in disgrace.
Therefore my mistress' eyes are raven-black,
Her eyes so suited, and they mourners seem
At such who, not born fair, no beauty lack,
Sland'ring creation with a false esteem:
    Yet so they mourn becoming of their woe,
    That every tongue says beauty should look so.

CXXVIII.

How oft when thou, my music, music play'st,
Upon that blessèd wood whose motion sounds
With thy sweet fingers when thou gently sway'st
The wiry concord that mine ear confounds,
Do I envy those jacks that nimble leap,
To kiss the tender inward of thy hand,
Whilst my poor lips which should that harvest reap,
At the wood's boldness by thee blushing stand!
To be so tickled, they would change their state
And situation with those dancing chips,

O'er whom thy fingers walk with gentle gait,
Making dead wood more blessed than living lips.
   Since saucy jacks so happy are in this,
    Give them thy fingers, me thy lips to kiss.

CXXIX.

The expense of spirit in a waste of shame
Is lust in action: and till action, lust
Is perjured, murd'rous, bloody, full of blame,
Savage, extreme, rude, cruel, not to trust;
Enjoyed no sooner but despisèd straight;
Past reason hunted; and no sooner had,
Past reason hated, as a swallowed bait,
On purpose laid to make the taker mad.
Mad in pursuit and in possession so;
Had, having, and in quest to have extreme;
A bliss in proof, and proved, a very woe;
Before, a joy proposed; behind a dream.
   All this the world well knows; yet none knows well
    To shun the heaven that leads men to this hell.

CXXX.

My mistress' eyes are nothing like the sun;
Coral is far more red than her lips' red:
If snow be white, why then her breasts are dun;
If hairs be wires, black wires grow on her head.
I have seen roses damasked, red and white,
But no such roses see I in her cheeks;
And in some perfumes is there more delight
Than in the breath that from my mistress reeks.
I love to hear her speak, yet well I know
That music hath a far more pleasing sound:
I grant I never saw a goddess go,
My mistress, when she walks, treads on the ground:
   And yet by heaven, I think my love as rare,

As any she belied with false compare.

CXXXI.
Thou art as tyrannous, so as thou art,
As those whose beauties proudly make them cruel;
For well thou know'st to my dear doting heart
Thou art the fairest and most precious jewel.
Yet, in good faith, some say that thee behold,
Thy face hath not the power to make love groan;
To say they err I dare not be so bold,
Although I swear it to myself alone.
And to be sure that is not false I swear,
A thousand groans, but thinking on thy face,
One on another's neck, do witness bear
Thy black is fairest in my judgement's place.
    In nothing art thou black save in thy deeds,
        And thence this slander, as I think, proceeds.

CXXXII.
Thine eyes I love, and they, as pitying me,
Knowing thy heart torments me with disdain,
Have put on black and loving mourners be,
Looking with pretty ruth upon my pain.
And truly not the morning sun of heaven
Better becomes the grey cheeks of the east,
Nor that full star that ushers in the even,
Doth half that glory to the sober west,
As those two mourning eyes become thy face:
O! let it then as well beseem thy heart
To mourn for me since mourning doth thee grace,
And suit thy pity like in every part.
    Then will I swear beauty herself is black,
        And all they foul that thy complexion lack.

CXXXIII.
Beshrew that heart that makes my heart to groan

For that deep wound it gives my friend and me!
Is 't not enough to torture me alone,
But slave to slavery my sweet'st friend must be?
Me from myself thy cruel eye hath taken,
And my next self thou harder hast engrossed:
Of him, myself, and thee I am forsaken;
A torment thrice threefold thus to be crossed.
Prison my heart in thy steel bosom's ward,
But then my friend's heart let my poor heart bail;
Whoe'er keeps me, let my heart be his guard;
Thou canst not then use rigour in my jail:
    And yet thou wilt; for I, being pent in thee,
    Perforce am thine, and all that is in me.

CXXXIV.

So now I have confess'd that he is thine,
And I myself am mortgaged to thy will,
Myself I'll forfeit, so that other mine
Thou wilt restore to be my comfort still:
But thou wilt not, nor he will not be free,
For thou art covetous, and he is kind;
He learn'd but surety-like to write for me,
Under that bond that him as fast doth bind.
The statute of thy beauty thou wilt take,
Thou usurer, that putt'st forth all to use,
And sue a friend came debtor for my sake;
So him I lose through my unkind abuse.
    Him have I lost; thou hast both him and me:
    He pays the whole, and yet am I not free.

CXXXV.

Whoever hath her wish, thou hast thy Will,
And Will to boot, and Will in overplus;
More than enough am I that vex thee still,
To thy sweet will making addition thus.
Wilt thou, whose will is large and spacious,

Not once vouchsafe to hide my will in thine?
Shall will in others seem right gracious,
And in my will no fair acceptance shine?
The sea, all water, yet receives rain still,
And in abundance addeth to his store;
So thou, being rich in Will, add to thy Will
One will of mine, to make thy large Will more.
     Let no unkind, no fair beseechers kill;
     Think all but one, and me in that one Will.

CXXXVI.
If thy soul check thee that I come so near,
Swear to thy blind soul that I was thy Will,
And will, thy soul knows, is admitted there;
Thus far for love, my love-suit, sweet, fulfil.
Will will fulfil the treasure of thy love,
Ay, fill it full with wills, and my will one.
In things of great receipt with ease we prove
Among a number one is reckoned none:
Then in the number let me pass untold,
Though in thy store's account I one must be;
For nothing hold me, so it please thee hold
That nothing me, a something sweet to thee:
     Make but my name thy love, and love that still,
     And then thou lovest me for my name is Will.

CXXXVII.
Thou blind fool, love, what dost thou to mine eyes,
That they behold, and see not what they see?
They know what beauty is, see where it lies,
Yet what the best is take the worst to be.
If eyes, corrupt by over-partial looks,
Be anchored in the bay where all men ride,
Why of eyes' falsehood hast thou forgèd hooks,
Whereto the judgement of my heart is tied?
Why should my heart think that a several plot,

Which my heart knows the wide world's common
　　place?
Or mine eyes, seeing this, say this is not,
To put fair truth upon so foul a face?
　　In things right true my heart and eyes have erred,
　　And to this false plague are they now transferred.

CXXXVIII.

When my love swears that she is made of truth,
I do believe her though I know she lies,
That she might think me some untutored youth,
Unlearnèd in the world's false subtleties.
Thus vainly thinking that she thinks me young,
Although she knows my days are past the best,
Simply I credit her false-speaking tongue:
On both sides thus is simple truth suppressed:
But wherefore says she not she is unjust?
And wherefore say not I that I am old?
O! love's best habit is in seeming trust,
And age in love, loves not to have years told:
　　Therefore I lie with her, and she with me,
　　And in our faults by lies we flattered be.

CXXXIX.

O, call not me to justify the wrong
That thy unkindness lays upon my heart;
Wound me not with thine eye, but with thy tongue:
Use power with power, and slay me not by art,
Tell me thou lov'st elsewhere; but in my sight,
Dear heart, forbear to glance thine eye aside:
What need'st thou wound with cunning, when thy
　　might
Is more than my o'erpressed defence can bide?
Let me excuse thee: ah! my love well knows
Her pretty looks have been mine enemies;
And therefore from my face she turns my foes,

That they elsewhere might dart their injuries:
    Yet do not so; but since I am near slain,
    Kill me outright with looks, and rid my pain.

CXL.
Be wise as thou art cruel; do not press
My tongue-tied patience with too much disdain;
Lest sorrow lend me words, and words express
The manner of my pity-wanting pain.
If I might teach thee wit, better it were,
Though not to love, yet, love to tell me so;
As testy sick men, when their deaths be near,
No news but health from their physicians know;
For, if I should despair, I should grow mad,
And in my madness might speak ill of thee;
Now this ill-wresting world is grown so bad,
Mad slanderers by mad ears believèd be.
    That I may not be so, nor thou belied,
    Bear thine eyes straight, though thy proud heart
        go wide.

CXLI.
In faith I do not love thee with mine eyes,
For they in thee a thousand errors note;
But 'tis my heart that loves what they despise,
Who, in despite of view, is pleas'd to dote.
Nor are mine ears with thy tongue's tune delighted;
Nor tender feeling, to base touches prone,
Nor taste, nor smell, desire to be invited
To any sensual feast with thee alone:
But my five wits nor my five senses can
Dissuade one foolish heart from serving thee,
Who leaves unswayed the likeness of a man,
Thy proud heart's slave and vassal-wretch to be:
    Only my plague thus far I count my gain,
    That she that makes me sin awards me pain.

CXLII.

Love is my sin, and thy dear virtue hate,
Hate of my sin, grounded on sinful loving:
O! but with mine compare thou thine own state,
And thou shalt find it merits not reproving;
Or, if it do, not from those lips of thine,
That have profaned their scarlet ornaments
And sealed false bonds of love as oft as mine,
Robbed others' beds' revenues of their rents.
Be it lawful I love thee, as thou lov'st those
Whom thine eyes woo as mine importune thee:
Root pity in thy heart, that when it grows,
Thy pity may deserve to pitied be.
    If thou dost seek to have what thou dost hide,
    By self-example mayst thou be denied!

CXLIII.

Lo, as a care-full housewife runs to catch
One of her feathered creatures broke away,
Sets down her babe, and makes all swift dispatch
In pursuit of the thing she would have stay;
Whilst her neglected child holds her in chase,
Cries to catch her whose busy care is bent
To follow that which flies before her face,
Not prizing her poor infant's discontent;
So runn'st thou after that which flies from thee,
Whilst I thy babe chase thee afar behind;
But if thou catch thy hope, turn back to me,
And play the mother's part, kiss me, be kind;
    So will I pray that thou mayst have thy 'Will',
    If thou turn back and my loud crying still.

CXLIV.

Two loves I have of comfort and despair,
Which like two spirits do suggest me still:
The better angel is a man right fair,

The worser spirit a woman coloured ill.
To win me soon to hell, my female evil,
Tempteth my better angel from my side,
And would corrupt my saint to be a devil,
Wooing his purity with her foul pride.
And whether that my angel be turned fiend,
Suspect I may, yet not directly tell;
But being both from me, both to each friend,
I guess one angel in another's hell:
    Yet this shall I ne'er know, but live in doubt,
    Till my bad angel fire my good one out.

CXLV.

Those lips that love's own hand did make,
Breathed forth the sound that said 'I hate',
To me that languished for her sake:
But when she saw my woeful state,
Straight in her heart did mercy come,
Chiding that tongue that ever sweet
Was used in giving gentle doom;
And taught it thus anew to greet;
'I hate' she altered with an end,
That followed it as gentle day,
Doth follow night, who like a fiend
From heaven to hell is flown away.
    'I hate', from hate away she threw,
    And saved my life, saying 'not you'.

CXLVI.

Poor soul, the centre of my sinful earth,
Fool'd by these rebel powers that thee array,
Why dost thou pine within and suffer dearth,
Painting thy outward walls so costly gay?
Why so large cost, having so short a lease,
Dost thou upon thy fading mansion spend?
Shall worms, inheritors of this excess,

Eat up thy charge? Is this thy body's end?
Then soul, live thou upon thy servant's loss,
And let that pine to aggravate thy store;
Buy terms divine in selling hours of dross;
Within be fed, without be rich no more:
　So shall thou feed on death, that feeds on men,
　And death once dead, there's no more dying
　　then.

CXLVII.
My love is as a fever, longing still,
For that which longer nurseth the disease;
Feeding on that which doth preserve the ill,
The uncertain sickly appetite to please.
My reason, the physician to my love,
Angry that his prescriptions are not kept,
Hath left me, and I desperate now approve
Desire is death, which physic did except.
Past cure I am, now reason is past care,
And frantic-mad with evermore unrest;
My thoughts and my discourse as madmen's are,
At random from the truth vainly expressed;
　For I have sworn thee fair, and thought thee
　　bright,
　Who art as black as hell, as dark as night.

CXLVIII.
O me, what eyes hath love put in my head,
Which have no correspondence with true sight;
Or, if they have, where is my judgement fled,
That censures falsely what they see aright?
If that be fair whereon my false eyes dote,
What means the world to say it is not so?
If it be not, then love doth well denote
Love's eye is not so true as all men's: no,
How can it? O, how can love's eye be true,

That is so vexed with watching and with tears?
No marvel then, though I mistake my view;
The sun itself sees not, till heaven clears.
   O cunning love, with tears thou keep'st me blind,
   Lest eyes well-seeing thy foul faults should find.

CXLIX.
Canst thou, O cruel! say I love thee not,
When I against myself with thee partake?
Do I not think on thee, when I forgot
Am of myself, all tyrant, for thy sake?
Who hateth thee that I do call my friend,
On whom frown'st thou that I do fawn upon,
Nay, if thou lour'st on me, do I not spend
Revenge upon myself with present moan?
What merit do I in myself respect,
That is so proud thy service to despise,
When all my best doth worship thy defect,
Commanded by the motion of thine eyes?
   But, love, hate on, for now I know thy mind,
   Those that can see thou lov'st, and I am blind.

CL.
O, from what power hast thou this powerful might,
With insufficiency my heart to sway?
To make me give the lie to my true sight,
And swear that brightness doth not grace the day?
Whence hast thou this becoming of things ill,
That in the very refuse of thy deeds
There is such strength and warrantise of skill,
That, in my mind, thy worst all best exceeds?
Who taught thee how to make me love thee more,
The more I hear and see just cause of hate?
O! though I love what others do abhor,
With others thou shouldst not abhor my state.

If thy unworthiness raised love in me,
More worthy I to be beloved of thee.

CLI.

Love is too young to know what conscience is,
Yet who knows not conscience is born of love?
Then, gentle cheater, urge not my amiss,
Lest guilty of my faults thy sweet self prove:
For, thou betraying me, I do betray
My nobler part to my gross body's treason;
My soul doth tell my body that he may
Triumph in love; flesh stays no farther reason,
But rising at thy name doth point out thee,
As his triumphant prize. Proud of this pride,
He is contented thy poor drudge to be,
To stand in thy affairs, fall by thy side.
    No want of conscience hold it that I call
    Her love, for whose dear love I rise and fall.

CLII.

In loving thee thou know'st I am forsworn,
But thou art twice forsworn, to me love swearing;
In act thy bed-vow broke, and new faith torn,
In vowing new hate after new love bearing:
But why of two oaths' breach do I accuse thee,
When I break twenty? I am perjured most;
For all my vows are oaths but to misuse thee,
And all my honest faith in thee is lost:
For I have sworn deep oaths of thy deep kindness,
Oaths of thy love, thy truth, thy constancy;
And, to enlighten thee, gave eyes to blindness,
Or made them swear against the thing they see;
    For I have sworn thee fair; more perjured eye,
    To swear against the truth so foul a lie!

CLIII.

Cupid laid by his brand and fell asleep:
A maid of Dian's this advantage found,
And his love-kindling fire did quickly steep
In a cold valley-fountain of that ground;
Which borrowed from this holy fire of love,
A dateless lively heat, still to endure,
And grew a seething bath, which yet men prove
Against strange maladies a sovereign cure.
But at my mistress' eye love's brand new-fired,
The boy for trial needs would touch my breast;
I, sick withal, the help of bath desired,
And thither hied, a sad distempered guest,
But found no cure, the bath for my help lies
Where Cupid got new fire; my mistress' eyes.

CLIV.

The little love-god lying once asleep,
Laid by his side his heart-inflaming brand,
Whilst many nymphs that vowed chaste life to keep
Came tripping by; but in her maiden hand
The fairest votary took up that fire
Which many legions of true hearts had warmed;
And so the general of hot desire
Was sleeping by a virgin hand disarmed.
This brand she quenchèd in a cool well by,
Which from love's fire took heat perpetual,
Growing a bath and healthful remedy,
For men diseased; but I, my mistress' thrall,
Came there for cure and this by that I prove,
Love's fire heats water, water cools not love.

THE WIT AND WISDOM OF SHAKESPEARE

On Love
How do you recognize a person in love?

SPEED
Marry, by these special marks: first, you have learned, like Sir Proteus, to wreath your arms, like a malcontent; to relish a love-song, like a robin redbreast; to walk alone, like one that had the pestilence; to sigh, like a schoolboy that had lost his ABC; to weep, like a young wench that had buried her grandam; to fast, like one that takes diet; to watch, like one that fears robbing; to speak puling, like a beggar at Hallowmas. You were wont, when you laughed, to crow like a cock; when you walked, to walk like one of the lions. When you fasted, it was presently after dinner; when you looked sadly, it was for want of money. And now you are metamorphosed with a mistress, that when I look on you I can hardly think you my master.
(*The Two Gentlemen of Verona*, II.1)

Benedick is bewildered to see the effect of love on his friend.

I do much wonder that one man, seeing how much
another man is a fool when he dedicates his behav-
iours to love, will, after he hath laughed at such
shallow follies in others, become the argument of
his own scorn by falling in love. And such a man is
Claudio. I have known when there was no music
with him but the drum and the fife, and now had he
rather hear the tabor and the pipe. I have known
when he would have walked ten mile afoot to see a
good armour, and now will he lie ten nights awake
carving the fashion of a new doublet. He was wont
to speak plain and to the purpose, like an honest
man and a soldier, and now is he turned to orthog-
raphy. His words are a very fantastical banquet, just
so many strange dishes. May I be so converted, and
see with these eyes? I cannot tell; I think not: I will
not be sworn but love may transform me to an
oyster, but I'll take my oath on it, till he have made
an oyster of me he shall never make me such a fool.
One woman is fair, yet I am well. Another is wise,
yet I am well. Another virtuous, yet I am well. But
till all the graces be in one woman, one woman shall
not come in my grace. Rich she shall be, that's
certain. Wise, or I'll none. Virtuous, or I'll never
cheapen her. Fair, or I'll never look on her. Mild, or
come not near me. Noble, or not I for an angel. Of
good discourse, an excellent musician, and her hair
shall be of what colour it please God.
(*Much Ado About Nothing*, II.3)

Here is the power of love at first sight.

O, she doth teach the torches to burn bright!
It seems she hangs upon the cheek of night

Like a rich jewel in an Ethiope's ear –
Beauty too rich for use, for earth too dear!
So shows a snowy dove trooping with crows
As yonder lady o'er her fellows shows.
The measure done, I'll watch her place of stand
And, touching hers, make blessed my rude hand.
Did my heart love till now? Forswear it, sight!
For I ne'er saw true beauty till this night.
(*Romeo and Juliet*, I.5)

Juliet's mother may not recognize true love, but she knows what a husband should look like.

What say you? Can you love the gentleman?
This night you shall behold him at our feast.
Read o'er the volume of young Paris' face,
And find delight writ there with beauty's pen.
Examine every married lineament,
And see how one another lends content.
And what obscured in this fair volume lies
Find written in the margin of his eyes.
This precious book of love, this unbound lover,
To beautify him only lacks a cover.
The fish lives in the sea, and 'tis much pride
For fair without the fair within to hide.
That book in many's eyes doth share the glory,
That in gold clasps locks in the golden story.
So shall you share all that he doth possess.
By having him, making yourself no less.
(*Romeo and Juliet*, I.3)

Is love real if there are no difficulties to be overcome in its pursuit?

LYSANDER
How now, my love? Why is your cheek so pale?

How chance the roses there do fade so fast?

HERMIA
Belike for want of rain, which I could well
Beteem them from the tempest of my eyes.

LYSANDER
Ay me! For aught that I could ever read,
Could ever hear by tale or history,
The course of true love never did run smooth;
But either it was different in blood –

HERMIA
O cross! – too high to be enthralled to low.

LYSANDER
Or else misgrafted in respect of years –

HERMIA
O spite! – too old to be engaged to young.

LYSANDER
Or merit stood upon the choice of friends –

HERMIA
O hell! – to choose love by another's eyes.

LYSANDER
Or if there were a sympathy in choice,
War, death, or sickness did lay siege to it,
Making it momentary as a sound,
Swift as a shadow, short as any dream,
Brief as the lightning in the collied night,
That in a spleen unfolds both heaven and earth,
And – ere a man hath power to say 'Behold!' –
The jaws of darkness do devour it up.

So quick bright things come to confusion.
(*A Midsummer Night's Dream*, I.1)

But the lover must be bold. Romeo risks death standing in
Capulet's garden making love to his daughter.

But, soft! What light through yonder window
    breaks?
It is the east and Juliet is the sun.
Arise, fair sun, and kill the envious moon,
Who is already sick and pale with grief,
That thou, her maid, are far more fair than she:
Be not her maid, since she is envious;
Her vestal livery is but sick and green
And none but fools do wear it; cast it off.
It is my lady, O, it is my love!
O, that she knew she were!
She speaks, yet she says nothing: what of that?
Her eye discourses; I will answer it.
I am too bold, 'tis not to me she speaks:
Two of the fairest stars in all the heaven,
Having some business, do entreat her eyes
To twinkle in their spheres till they return.
What if her eyes were there, they in her head?
The brightness of her cheek would shame those
    stars,
As daylight doth a lamp; her eyes in heaven
Would through the airy region stream so bright
That birds would sing and think it were not night.
See, how she leans her cheek upon her hand!
O, that I were a glove upon that hand,
That I might touch that cheek!
(*Romeo and Juliet*, II.1)

Henry V claims to be a blunt soldier, not used to mouthing pretty speeches, but when he has to woo Katharine, the French king's daughter, he is eloquent, in prose not verse.

Marry, if you would put me to verses, or to dance for your sake, Kate, why, you undid me. For the one l have neither words nor measure, and for the other I have no strength in measure – yet a reasonable measure in strength. If I could win a lady at leap-frog, or by vaulting into my saddle with my armour on my back, under the correction of bragging be it spoken, I should quickly leap into a wife. Or I might buffet for my love, or bound my horse for her favours, I could lay on like a butcher, and sit like a jackanapes, never off. But before God, Kate, I cannot look greenly, nor gasp out my eloquence, nor I have no cunning in protestation – only down-right oaths, which I never use till urged, nor never break for urging. If thou canst love a fellow of this temper, Kate, whose face is not worth sunburning, that never looks in his glass for love of anything he sees there, let thine eye be thy cook. I speak to thee plain soldier: if thou canst love me for this, take me. If not, to say to thee that I shall die, is true – but for thy love, by the Lord, no. Yet I love thee, too. And while thou livest, dear Kate, take a fellow of plain and uncoined constancy, for he perforce must do thee right, because he hath not the gift to woo in other places. For these fellows of infinite tongue, that can rhyme themselves into ladies' favours, they do always reason themselves out again. What! A speaker is but a prater, a rhyme is but a ballad; a good leg will fall, a straight back will stoop, a black beard will turn white, a curled pate will grow bald, a fair face will wither, a full eye will wax hollow, but a good heart, Kate, is the sun and the moon – or rather

the sun and not the moon, for it shines bright and
never changes, but keeps his course truly. If thou
would have such a one, take me; and take me, take a
soldier; take a soldier, take a king.
(*Henry V*, V.2)

**To make love one must be in the right mood. In The
Merchant of Venice *Lorenzo and Jessica agree that it is the
right kind of night for love.***

LORENZO
The moon shines bright: in such a night as this,
When the sweet wind did gently kiss the trees
And they did make no noise – in such a night
Troilus, methinks, mounted the Trojan walls,
And sighed his soul towards the Grecian tents
Where Cressid lay that night.

JESSICA
In such a night
Did Thisbe fearfully o'ertrip the dew
And saw the lion's shadow ere himself,
And ran dismayed away.

LORENZO
In such a night
Stood Dido with a willow in her hand
Upon the wild sea banks, and waft her love
To come again to Carthage.

JESSICA
In such a night
Medea gathered the enchanted herbs
That did renew old Aeson.

LORENZO
In such a night
Did Jessica steal from the wealthy Jew,
And with an unthrift love did run from Venice
As far as Belmont.

JESSICA
In such a night
Did young Lorenzo swear he loved her well,
Stealing her soul with many vows of faith,
And ne'er a true one.

LORENZO
In such a night
Did pretty Jessica, like a little shrew,
Slander her love, and he forgave it her.
(*The Merchant of Venice*, V.1)

Staying with nature – or maybe it is a more fleshly landscape Shakespeare describes here.

'Fondling,' she saith, 'since I have hemmed thee
  here
Within the circuit of this ivory pale,
I'll be a park, and thou shalt be my deer:
Feed where thou wilt, on mountain or in dale;
Graze on my lips; and if those hills be dry,
Stray lower, where the pleasant fountains lie.

Within this limit is relief enough,
Sweet bottom-grass, and high delightful plain,
Round rising hillocks, brakes obscure and rough,
To shelter thee from tempest and from rain.
Then be my deer, since I am such a park.
No dog shall rouse thee, though a thousand bark.'
(*Venus and Adonis*)

On Death

Shakespeare writes better than any poet before or since on love, but his second theme is death.

Hamlet considers what it means to die.

> To be, or not to be, that is the question:
> Whether 'tis nobler in the mind to suffer
> The slings and arrows of outrageous fortune,
> Or to take arms against a sea of troubles
> And by opposing end them. To die – to sleep,
> No more; and by a sleep to say we end
> The heartache and the thousand natural shocks
> That flesh is heir to: 'tis a consummation
> Devoutly to be wish'd. To die, to sleep;
> To sleep, perchance to dream – ay, there's the rub:
> For in that sleep of death what dreams may come,
> When we have shuffled off this mortal coil,
> Must give us pause – there's the respect
> That makes calamity of so long life.
> For who would bear the whips and scorns of time,
> Th'oppressor's wrong, the proud man's contumely,
> The pangs of dispriz'd love, the law's delay,
> The insolence of office, and the spurns
> That patient merit of th'unworthy takes,
> When he himself might his quietus make
> With a bare bodkin? Who would fardels bear,
> To grunt and sweat under a weary life,
> But that the dread of something after death,
> The undiscover'd country, from whose bourn
> No traveller returns, puzzles the will,
> And makes us rather bear those ills we have
> Than fly to others that we know not of?
> Thus conscience does make cowards of us all.
> (*Hamlet*, III.1)

Also from **Hamlet,** *Gertrude's description of finding Ophelia drowned has inspired many painters and poets. Shakespeare makes us almost fall in love with death.*

> There is a willow grows aslant a brook
> That shows his hoary leaves in the glassy stream;
> There with fantastic garlands did she make
> Of crow-flowers, nettles, daisies, and long purples
> That liberal shepherds give a grosser name,
> But our cold maids do dead men's fingers call them:
> There, on the pendent boughs her crownet weeds
> Clambering to hang, an envious sliver broke;
> When down the weedy trophies and herself
> Fell in the weeping brook. Her clothes spread wide;
> And, mermaid-like, awhile they bore her up:
> Which time she chanted snatches of old tunes;
> As one incapable of her own distress,
> Or like a creature native and endued
> Unto that element but long it could not be
> Till that her garments, heavy with their drink,
> Pull'd the poor wretch from her melodious lay
> To muddy death.
> (*Hamlet*, IV.7)

We should anticipate death, Isabella urges her brother. (It is possible to see why – so close to death – he cannot share her view of it.)

> ... The sense of death is most in apprehension,
> And the poor beetle that we tread upon
> In corporal sufferance finds a pang as great
> As when a giant dies.

Later, Claudio gives his perspective:

> Death is a fearful thing.
> …
> Ay, but to die, and go we know not where,
> To lie in cold obstruction and to rot,
> This sensible warm motion to become
> A kneaded clod, and the dilated spirit
> To bathe in fiery floods, or to reside
> In thrilling region of thick-ribbed ice;
> To be imprisoned in the viewless winds,
> And blown with restless violence round about
> The pendent world, or to be worse than worst
> Of those that lawless and incertain thought
> Imagine howling – 'tis too horrible!
> The weariest and most loathed worldly life
> That age, ache, penury, and imprisonment
> Can lay on nature is a paradise
> To what we fear of death.
> (*Measure for Measure*, III.1)

Julius Casesar, as a great soldier, perhaps has more right to echo Isabella.

> Cowards die many times before their deaths;
> The valiant never taste of death but once.
> Of all the wonders that I yet have heard,
> It seems to me most strange that men should fear,
> Seeing that death, a necessary end,
> Will come when it will come.
> (*Julius Caesar*, II.2)

Macbeth is told his wife is dead. He, too, is facing death and filled with bitterness at having no time to grieve.

> She should have died hereafter.
> There would have been a time for such a word.

Tomorrow, and tomorrow, and tomorrow
Creeps in this petty pace from day to day
To the last syllable of recorded time,
And all our yesterdays have lighted fools
The way to dusty death. Out, out, brief candle.
Life's but a walking shadow, a poor player
That struts and frets his hour upon the stage,
And then is heard no more. It is a tale
Told by an idiot, full of sound and fury,
Signifying nothing.
(*Macbeth*, V.5)

Macbeth had been made Thane of Cawdor after that
rebellious nobleman had been defeated in battle. However,
despite the Thane's treachery, his enemies recognized the
nobility of his death.

...
Nothing in his life
Became him like the leaving of it. He died
As one that had been studied in his death
To throw away the dearest thing he owed
As 'twere a careless trifle.
(*Macbeth*, I.4)

Falstaff does not appear in **Henry V**; *that would have changed*
the nature of the play, which is a hymn to patriotism. But
Shakespeare could not let the fat clown's death go unrecorded.
As a witness he chooses not the King or some other great man,
but one of the low people – the hostess of the inn where he lived.
She speaks of his passing with no high-flown phrases but with
the fellow feeling of one who loved the old man.

Nay, sure he's not in hell. He's in Arthur's bosom, if
ever man went to Arthur's bosom. A' made a finer
end, and went away an it had been any christom

child. A' parted ev'n just between twelve and one, ev'n at the turning o' th' tide – for after I saw him fumble with the sheets, and play with flowers, and smile upon his finger's end, I knew there was but one way. For his nose was as sharp as a pen, and a babbled of green fields. 'How now, Sir John?' quoth I. 'What, man! Be o' good cheer.' So I cried out, 'God, God, God', three or four times. Now I, to comfort him, bid him a' should not think of God; I hoped there was no need to trouble himself with any such thoughts yet. So I bade me lay more clothes on his feet. I put my hand into the bed and felt them, and they were as cold as any stone. Then I felt to his knees, and so up'ard and up'ard, and all was as cold as any stone.
(*Henry V*, II.3)

Othello, facing death, asks to be remembered fairly.

Soft you, a word or two before you go,
I have done the state some service and they know't:
No more of that I pray you in your letters,
When you shall these unlucky deeds relate,
Speak of me as I am. Nothing extenuate,
Nor set down aught in malice. Then must you speak
Of one that loved not wisely, but too well;
Of one not easily jealous, but being wrought,
Perplexed in the extreme; of one whose hand,
Like the base Indian, threw a pearl away
Richer than all his tribe.
(*Othello*, V.2)

Shakespeare wrote this heart-stopping epitaph, asserting the finality of death, in Cymbeline, *one of his enigmatic 'romances'.*

GUIDERIUS
Fear no more the heat o' th' sun,

Nor the furious winter's rages,
Thou thy worldly task has done,
Home art gone and ta'en thy wages.
Golden lads and girls all must,
As chimney-sweepers, come to dust.

ARVIRAGUS
The sceptre, learning, physic, must
All follow this and come to dust.
(*Cymbeline*, IV.2)

On Nature
Shakespeare was a countryman and he describes nature with unsentimental accuracy, particularly winter.

When icicles hang by the wall,
And Dick the shepherd blows his nail,
And Tom bears logs into the hall,
And milk comes frozen home in pail;
When blood is nipped, and ways be foul,
Then nightly sings the staring owl:
Tu-whit, tu-whoo! – a merry note,
While greasy Joan doth keel the pot.

When all aloud the wind doth blow,
And coughing drowns the parson's saw,
And birds sit brooding in the snow,
And Marian's nose looks red and raw;
When roasted crabs hiss in the bowl,
Then nightly sings the staring owl:
Tu-whit, tu-whoo! – a merry note,
While greasy Joan doth keel the pot.
(*Love's Labour's Lost*, V.2)

Another winter song, this time from **As You Like It.**

> Blow, blow, thou winter wind,
> Thou art not so unkind
> As man's ingratitude.
> Thy tooth is not so keen,
> Because thou art not seen,
> Although thy breath be rude.
> Heigh-ho! sing, heigh-ho! unto the green holly
> Most friendship is feigning, most loving mere folly.
> Then heigh-ho, the holly!
> This life is most jolly.
>
> Freeze, freeze, thou bitter sky,
> That dost not bite so nigh
> As benefits forgot.
> Though thou the waters warp,
> Thy sting is not so sharp,
> As friend remembered not.
> Heigh-ho, sing heigh-ho, unto the green holly
> Most friendship is feigning, most loving mere folly.
> Then heigh-ho the holly!
> This life is most jolly.
> (*As You Like It*, II.7)

In **A Midsummer Night's Dream,** *nature is gentler.*

> OBERON
> …
> I know a bank where the wild thyme blows,
> Where oxlips and the nodding violet grows;
> Quite overcanopied with luscious woodbine,
> With sweet musk roses, and with eglantine.
> There sleeps Titania sometime of the night,
> Lulled in these flowers with dances and delight.
> (*A Midsummer Night's Dream*, II.1)

In Richard II, *the Queen's gardener compares his garden to the King's court.*

GARDENER
Go, bind thou up yon dangling apricots,
Which, like unruly children, make their sire
Stoop with oppression of their prodigal weight.
Give some supportance to the bending twigs.
Go thou, and like an executioner,
Cut off the heads of too fast-growing sprays
That look too lofty in our commonwealth.
You thus employed, I will go root away
The noisome weeds which without profit suck
The soil's fertility from wholesome flowers.
...

QUEEN
...
Gardener, for telling me these news of woe,
Pray God the plants thou graft'st may never grow.

GARDENER
Poor Queen! So that thy state might be no worse,
I would my skill were subject to thy curse.
Here did she fall a tear; here in this place
I'll set a bank of rue, sour herb-of-grace.
Rue, even for ruth, here shortly shall be seen,
In the remembrance of a weeping queen.
(*Richard II*, III.4)

Rue is a herb of grace because rue means repent. Ruth means pity. We pity mad Ophelia. For her, herbs were 'a document in madness' as her brother Laertes says.

OPHELIA
There's fennel for you, and columbines. There's rue
for you, and here's some for me – we may call it

herb-of-grace o' Sundays. Oh, you must wear your
rue with a difference. There's a daisy. I would give
you some violets, but they withered all when my
father died.
(*Hamlet*, IV.5)

**Throughout Shakespeare's plays the weather reflects the
feelings of the characters, but nowhere more dramatically
than King Lear on his 'blasted heath'.**

Blow winds and crack your cheeks! Rage, blow!
You cataracts and hurricanoes, spout
Till you have drenched our steeples, drowned the
    cocks!
You sulphurous and thought-executing fires,
Vaunt-couriers of oak-cleaving thunderbolts,
Singe my white head! And thou, all-shaking
    thunder,
Strike flat the thick rotundity o' the world,
Crack nature's moulds, all germens spill at once
That makes ingrateful man!
(*King Lear*, III.2)

After storm comes sun and after winter, spring.

When daffodils begin to peer,
With heigh! the doxy over the dale,
Why then comes in the sweet o'the year,
For the red blood reigns in the winter's pale.
(*The Winter's Tale*, IV.3)

Spring is a time for lovers.

It was a lover and his lass,
With a hey and a ho and a hey-nonny-no,
That o'er the green cornfield did pass,

In spring-time, the only pretty ring-time,
When birds do sing, hey ding-a-ding, ding,
Sweet lovers love the spring

Between the acres of the rye,
With a hey and a ho and a hey-nonny-no
These pretty country-folks would lie,
In spring-time, the only pretty ring-time,
When birds do sing, hey ding-a-ding, ding,
Sweet lovers love the spring.
(*As You Like It*, V.3)

Also from As You Like It *comes this song of summer.*

Under the greenwood tree,
Who loves to lie with me,
And turn his merry note
Unto the sweet bird's throat,
Come hither, come hither, come hither.
Here shall he see
No enemy,
But winter and rough weather.

Who doth ambition shun
And loves to lie i' th' sun,
Seeking the food he eats,
And pleased with what he gets,
Come hither, come hither, come hither.
Here shall he see
No enemy,
But winter and rough weather.
(*As You Like It*, II.5)

On Drink

Drunkenness was one vice that united all the classes. A
'groundling' watching a play at the Globe in the open air –

standing, not sitting – would delight to see his betters guyed. Alcohol was everyone's escape from the pain of life but it deprived a man of his reason, making him ridiculous. Drink over a period of time painted a man's nose red – a public sign of his weakness.

Alcohol incapacitates in other ways, as the gatekeeper in **Macbeth** *explains.*

> PORTER
> ... drink, sir, is a great provoker of three things.
>
> MACDUFF
> What three things does drink especially provoke?
>
> PORTER
> Marry, sir, nose-painting, sleep and urine. Lechery, sir, it provokes, and unprovokes; it provokes the desire, but it takes away the performance.
> (*Macbeth*, II.3)

Cassio, in **Othello**, *knew he had a weak head: he only had to take a glass of wine and he was done for.*

> ... I have very poor and unhappy brains for drinking: I could well wish courtesy would invent some other custom of entertainment
> ...
> ... Do not think, gentlemen, I am drunk: this is my ensign; this is my right hand, and this is my left: I am not drunk now; I can stand well enough, and speak well enough
> ...
> ... you must not think then that I am drunk.
> ...

… Drunk? And speak parrot? And squabble? Swagger? Swear? And discourse fustian with one's own shadow? O thou invisible spirit of wine, if thou hast no name to be known by, let us call thee devil!
…
… O God, that men should put an enemy in their mouths to steal away their brains! That we should, with joy, pleasance revel and applause, transform ourselves into beasts!
(*Othello*, II.3)

In Twelfth Night, *Olivia asks her fool, Feste, what a drunk is like.*

Like a drowned man, a fool and a mad man: one draught above heat makes him a fool; the second mads him; and a third drowns him.
(T*welfth Night*, I.5)

Falstaff, *on the other hand, had a great respect for drink. This is what he had to say about sherry.*

… A good sherris sack hath a two-fold operation in it. It ascends me into the brain; dries me there all the foolish and dull and crudy vapours which environ it; makes it apprehensive, quick, forgetive, full of nimble fiery and delectable shapes, which, delivered o'er to the voice, the tongue, which is the birth, becomes excellent wit. The second property of your excellent sherris is, the warming of the blood; which, before cold and settled, left the liver white and pale, which is the badge of pusillanimity and cowardice; but the sherris warms it and makes it course from the inwards to the parts extreme: it illumineth the face, which as a beacon gives warning to all the rest of this little kingdom, man, to arm; and then the

vital commoners and inland petty spirits muster me
all to their captain, the heart, who, great and puffed
up with this retinue, doth any deed of courage; and
this valour comes of sherris.
(*Henry IV Part 2*, IV.2)

**This heartfelt cry has been echoed from century to century by
soldiers far from home.**

... I would give all my fame for a pot of ale, and
safety.
(*Henry V*, III.2)

Sir Toby Belch should have the last word on the subject.

... Dost thou think, because thou art virtuous, there
shall be no more cakes and ale?
(*Twelfth Night*, II.3)

On Curses and Insults
Aaron in Titus Andronicus *delivers a powerful curse.*

... Even now I curse the day – and yet I think
Few come within the compass of my curse –
Wherein I did not some notorious ill,
As kill a man, or else devise his death;
Ravish a maid, or plot the way to do it;
Accuse some innocent and forswear myself;
Set deadly enmity between two friends;
Make poor men's cattle break their necks;
Set fire on barns and haystacks in the night,
And bid the owners quench them with their tears.
Oft have I digged up dead men from their graves
And set them upright at their dear friends' door,
Even when their sorrows almost was forgot,
And on their skins, as on the bark of trees,

Have with my knife carved in Roman letters
'Let not your sorrow die though I am dead'.
But I have done a thousand dreadful things
As willingly as one would kill a fly,
And nothing grieves me heartily indeed
But that I cannot do ten thousand more.
(*Titus Andronicus*, V.1)

**King Lear also curses horribly and what makes it more
horrible is that he is cursing his own daughter.**

… Hear, nature; hear, dear goddess, hear:
Suspend thy purpose if thou didst intend
To make this creature fruitful.
Into her womb convey sterility.
Dry up in her the organs of increase,
And from her derogate body never spring
A babe to honour her. If she must teem,
Create her child of spleen, that it may live
And be a thwart disnatured torment to her.
Let it stamp wrinkles in her brow of youth,
With cadent tears fret channels in her cheeks,
Turn all her mother's pains and benefits
To laughter and contempt, that she may feel –
That she may feel
How sharper than a serpent's tooth it is
To have a thankless child.
(*King Lear*, I.4)

Caliban, being a monster and a slave, must also curse.

All the infections that the sun sucks up
From bogs, fens, flats, on Prospero fall, and make
   him
By inch-meal a disease!
[Thunder is heard]

His spirits hear me,
And yet I needs must curse. But they'll nor pinch,
Fright me with urchin-shows, pitch me i' th' mire,
Nor lead me like a fire-brand in the dark
Out of my way, unless he bid 'em. But
For every trifle are they set upon me;
Sometime like apes, that mow and chatter at me
And after bite me; then like hedgehogs, which
Lie tumbling in my barefoot way and mount
Their pricks at my footfall; Sometimes am I
All wound with adders, with cloven tongues
Do hiss me into madness.
(*The Tempest*, II.2)

Here are some more light-hearted curses and insults. Girls fighting over a man can be alarming.

HERMIA
Oh, me! You juggler! You canker blossom!
You thief of love! What, have you come by night
And stolen my love's heart from him?

HELENA
Fine, i' faith!
Have you no modesty, no maiden shame,
No touch of bashfulness? What, will you tear
Impatient answers from my gentle tongue?
Fie! Fie! You counterfeit, you puppet, you!

HERMIA
Puppet? Why so? Aye, that way goes the game.
Now I perceive she hath made compare
Between our statures, she hath urged her height.
And with her personage, her tall personage,
Her height, forsooth, she hath prevailed with him.
And are you grown so high in his esteem

Because I am so dwarfish and so low?
How low am I, thou painted maypole? Speak –
How low am I? I am not yet so low
But that my nails can reach unto thine eyes.
…

HELENA
Oh, when she is angry, she is keen and shrewd!
She was a vixen when she went to school,
And though she be but little, she is fierce.

HERMIA
Little again! Nothing but 'low' and 'little'!
Why will you suffer her to flout me thus?
Let me come to her.

LYSANDER
Get you gone, you dwarf,
You minimus, of hindering knotgrass made,
You bead, you acorn.
(*A Midsummer Night's Dream*, III.2)

When Richard Crookback, soon to be King Richard III, woos the widow of the man he killed he is at first rebuffed with a curse by Lady Anne.

Foul devil, for God's sake, hence, and trouble us
      not,
For thou hast made the happy earth thy Hell,
Filled it with cursing cries and deep exclaims.
If thou delight to view thy heinous deeds,
Behold this pattern of thy butcheries.
O gentlemen, see, see! Dead Henry's wounds
Open their congealed mouths and bleed afresh.
Blush, blush, thou lump of foul deformity,
For 'tis thy presence that exhales this blood

From cold and empty veins where no blood dwells;
Thy deed, inhuman and unnatural,
Provokes this deluge most unnatural.
O God, which this blood mad'st, revenge his death!
O earth, which this blood drink'st, revenge his
    death!
Either Heaven with lightning strike the murderer
    dead,
Or earth, gape open wide and eat him quick,
As thou dost swallow up this good King's blood,
Which his Hell-governed arm hath butchered!
(*Richard III*, I.2)

*Here is an exuberant description of a man making a fool of
himself – deliberately. Shakespeare gives Biondello
extravagant language to describe Petruchio's dress and it
hardly matters that we may not understand every word. The
sense is clear enough.*

Why, Petruchio is coming in a new hat and an old
jerkin; a pair of old breeches thrice turned; a pair of
boots that have been candle cases, one buckled,
another laced; an old rusty sword ta'en out of the
town armory, with a broken hilt, and chapeless,
with two broken points; his horse hipped with an
old mothy saddle and stirrups of no kindred,
besides, possessed with the glanders and like to
mose in the chine, troubled with the lampass,
infected with the fashions, full of windgalls, sped
with spavins, rayed with the yellows, past cure of
the fives, stark spoiled with the staggers, begnawn
with the bots, weighed in the back and shoulder-
shotten, near-legged before and with a half-cheeked
bit and a headstall of sheep's leather which, being
restrained to keep him from stumbling, hath been
often burst and now repaired with knots, one girth

six times pierced, and a woman's crupper of velure which hath two letters for her name fairly set down in studs and here and there pierced with pack-thread.
(*The Taming of the Shrew*, III.2)

Two final insults, both from **Henry IV Part 1.** *In the first, Prince Hal describes Falstaff and in the second, Falstaff abuses the Prince.*

PRINCE HENRY
... Why dost thou converse with that trunk of humours, that bolting-hutch of beastliness, that swollen parcel of dropsies, that huge bombard of sack, that stuffed cloakbag of guts, that roasted Manningtree ox with the pudding in his belly, that reverend Vice, that grey Iniquity, that father Ruffian, that Vanity in years?
...

FALSTAFF
You rogue, here's lime in this sack too. There is nothing but roguery to be found in a villainous man. Yet a coward is worse than a cup of sack with lime in it. A villainous coward! Go thy ways, old Jack, die when thou wilt. If manhood, good manhood, be not forgot upon the face of the earth, then am I a shotten herring. There live not three good men unhanged in England, and one of them is fat, and grows old ... A plague of all cowards, I say still.
(*Henry IV Part 1*, II.4)

All The World's a Stage

Shakespeare is fascinated by the brevity and fragility of life's journey and frequently compares it to performing on stage. This is his most famous meditation on life's transience.

JACQUES
All the world's a stage,
And all the men and women merely players.
They have their exits and their entrances,
And one man in his time plays many parts,
His acts being seven ages. At first the infant,
Mewling and puking in the nurse's arms.
Then, the whining schoolboy with his satchel
And shining morning face, creeping like a snail
Unwillingly to school. And then the lover,
Sighing like a furnace, with a woeful ballad
Made to his mistress' eyebrow. Then, a soldier,
Full of strange oaths, and bearded like the pard,
Jealous in honour, sudden, and quick in quarrel,
Seeking the bubble reputation
Even in the cannon's mouth. And then, the justice,
In fair round belly, with good capon lined,
With eyes severe, and beard of formal cut,
Full of wise saws, and modern instances,
And so he plays his part. The sixth age shifts
Into the lean and slippered pantaloon,
With spectacles on nose, and pouch on side,
His youthful hose well saved, a world too wide
For his shrunk shank, and his big manly voice,
Turning again towards childish treble, pipes
And whistles in his sound. Last scene of all,
That ends this strange eventful history,
Is second childishness and mere oblivion,
Sans teeth, sans eyes, sans taste, sans everything.
(*As You Like It*, II.7)

Cassius, at the moment of Caesar's killing, compares life to a theatrical performance.

BRUTUS
… Stoop, Romans, stoop,
And let us bathe our hands in Caesar's blood
Up to the elbows, and besmear our swords.
Then walk we forth, even to the marketplace,
And waving our red weapons o'er our heads,
Let's all cry 'peace, freedom, and liberty!'

CASSIUS
Stoop then, and wash. How many ages hence
Shall this our lofty scene be acted over
In states unborn and accents yet unknown!
(*Julius Caesar*, III.1)

Hamlet instructs the players how to act.

Speak the speech, I pray you, as I pronounced it to you, trippingly on the tongue. But if you mouth it, as many of your players do, I had as lief the town crier had spoke my lines. Nor do not saw the air too much with your hand, thus, but use all gently. For in the very torrent, tempest, and, as I may say, the whirlwind of your passion, you must acquire and beget a temperance that may give it smoothness. Oh, it offends me to the soul to hear a robustious periwig-pated fellow tear a passion to tatters, to very rags, to split the ears of the groundlings, who for the most part are capable of nothing but inexplicable dumb shows and noise. I would have such a fellow whipped for o'erdoing Termagant. It out-Herods Herod. Pray you, avoid it.

…

Be not too tame neither, but let your own discretion
be your tutor. Suit the action to the word, the word
to the action, with this special observance, that you
o'erstep not the modesty of nature. For anything so
overdone is from the purpose of playing, whose
end, both at the first and now, was and is to hold as
'twere the mirror up to nature – to show virtue her
own feature, scorn her own image, and the very age
and body of the time his form and pressure. Now
this overdone or come tardy off, though it makes
the unskillful laugh, cannot but make the judicious
grieve, the censure of the which one must in your
allowance o'er weigh a whole theatre of others.
(*Hamlet*, III.2)

Hamlet chides himself for not feeling the passion that the actor pretends to feel so convincingly.

… Oh, what a rogue and peasant slave am I!
Is it not monstrous that this player here
But in a fiction, in a dream of passion,
Could force his soul so to his own conceit
That from her working all his visage wanned,
Tears in his eyes, distraction in 's aspect,
A broken voice, and his whole function suiting
With forms to his conceit? And all for nothing!
For Hecuba!
What's Hecuba to him or he to Hecuba,
That he should weep for her? What would he do
Had he the motive and the cue for passion
That I have? He would drown the stage with tears
And cleave the general ear with horrid speech,
Make mad the guilty and appal the free,
Confound the ignorant, and amaze indeed
The very faculties of eyes and ears.
(*Hamlet*, II.2)

In **A Midsummer Night's Dream,** *honest labouring men gather in Peter Quince's house to discuss the play they will perform before the Duke. The play's director, Quince, has trouble with one talented but obstreperous member of the cast.*

QUINCE
Is all our company here?

BOTTOM
You were best to call them generally, man by man, according to the script.

QUINCE
Here is the scroll of every man's name which is thought fit, through all Athens, to play in our interlude before the Duke and Duchess on his wedding day at night.

BOTTOM
First, good Peter Quince, say what the play treats on. Then read the names of the actors, and so grow to a point.

QUINCE
Marry, our play is, 'The most lamentable comedy and most cruel death of Pyramus and Thisbe'.

BOTTOM
A very good piece of work, I assure you, and a merry. Now, good Peter Quince, call forth your actors by the scroll. Masters, spread yourselves.

QUINCE
Answer as I call you. Nick Bottom, the weaver.

BOTTOM
Ready. Name what part I am for, and proceed.

QUINCE
You, Nick Bottom, are set down for Pyramus.

BOTTOM
What is Pyramus? A lover or a tyrant?

QUINCE
A lover, that kills himself most gallant for love.

BOTTOM
That will ask some tears in the true performance of
it. If I do it, let the audience look to their eyes, I will
move stones, I will condole in some measure. To the
rest – yet my chief humour is for a tyrant. I could
play 'erc'les rarely, or a part to tear a cat in, to make
all split.
…

QUINCE
Francis Flute, the bellows-mender.

FLUTE
Here, Peter Quince.

QUINCE
Flute, you must take Thisbe on you.

FLUTE
What is Thisbe? A wandering knight?

QUINCE
It is the lady that Pyramus must love.

FLUTE
Nay, faith, let me not play a woman. I have a beard coming.

QUINCE
That's all one. You shall play it in a mask, and you may speak as small as you will.

BOTTOM
An I may hide my face, let me play Thisbe too. I'll speak in a monstrous little voice: 'Thisne, Thisne!' 'Ah, Pyramus, lover dear! thy Thisby dear, and lady dear!'
…

QUINCE
… Snug, the joiner, you, the lion's part. And, I hope, here is the play fitted.

SNUG
Have you the lion's part written? Pray you, if it be, give it me, for I am slow of study.

QUINCE
You may do it extempore, for it is nothing but roaring.

BOTTOM
Let me play the lion too. I will roar that I will do any man's heart good to hear me; I will roar that I will make the Duke say, 'Let him roar again, let him roar again.'

QUINCE

An you should do it too terribly, you would fright
the Duchess and the ladies, that they would shriek;
and that were enough to hang us all.
(*A Midsummer Night's Dream*, I.2)

INDEX

NB: Names in **bold type** are characters in Shakespeare's plays.